Drin

THIS BOOK was conceived some years ago by two untutored wine enthusiasts, both of them aspiring connoisseurs. Faced with a lifetime's hard drinking, and partly daunted by that prospect, they called in a Master of Wine and asked him to help them to realize their aspirations in the form of a book. *Drinking Wine*, the result, is offered to other enthusiasts – tutored or untutored – in exactly the same spirit.

Château de Juliénas
Dine with Deinhard
VINO FRASCATI
CANTINA SOCIALE DI MONTEPORZIO CATONE
(ROMA)
FATTORIA CASTELLINA
STRACCALI
CASTELLINA IN CHIANTI
3912
FATTORIA CASTELLINA
STRACCALI
CASTELLINA IN CHIANTI
MAISON
2.89
GLASS WITH CARE

David Peppercorn
MASTER OF WINE
Brian Cooper
Elwyn Blacker

Drinking WINE

A complete guide for the buyer & consumer

MACDONALD & CO
LONDON & SYDNEY

Written by David Peppercorn and Brian Cooper
Original concept by Brian Cooper and Elwyn Blacker
Designed by Elwyn Blacker
Edited by Richard Sachs

A MACDONALD BOOK

First published in Great Britain in 1979 by

MACDONALD GENERAL BOOKS
MACDONALD AND JANE'S PUBLISHING GROUP LTD

Revised edition published in Great Britain in 1982 by

MACDONALD & CO (PUBLISHERS) LTD

This edition published in Great Britain in 1984 by

MACDONALD & CO (PUBLISHERS) LTD
LONDON & SYDNEY

A member of BPCC plc

ISBN 0 356 10161 4

This book was designed and produced by
John Calmann and Cooper Ltd, London

Photocomposition by
Composing Operations Limited,
Tunbridge Wells,
Kent

Printed and bound in Great Britain by
Hazell Watson & Viney Limited,
Member of the BPCC Group,
Aylesbury, Bucks

Macdonald & Co (Publishers) Ltd
Maxwell House
74 Worship Street
London EC2A 2EN

Contents

Authors' preface

WINE, THE FERMENTED JUICE of the grape, is a variable beverage, unique in its complexity. It is made in one form or another in over fifty countries, and imported by at least as many others. It is sold under a range of labels and prices which leaves the ordinary mortal as thirsty for information as for refreshment – often more so.

Confronted with an unknown bottle, the potential purchaser needs to know three facts: where it comes from, how much it should cost and, above all, what it will taste like. He needs to know these facts not merely to impress his friends, or even to avoid being fobbed off by the unscrupulous, but so that he can appreciate the quality of the wine, and its subtleties, and enjoy them all to the full. An intelligent, questioning approach is the beginning of that process.

Too much information, it is true, can turn anybody into a wine bore. Worse, it can turn him into a wine snob – if that much over-used term means any more than a reasonable preference for good wines to bad ones. As joint authors of this book we are willing to take both those risks, for we are convinced that good wines may be enjoyed at a modest as well as a sophisticated level, and that the pleasures of drinking it need not be confined to the wealthy and the expert.

We have therefore searched out and identified wines of every style and origin, spread over the widest possible price range. We have endeavoured to offer some guidance as to their value, for we know that all too many wines are labelled with beguiling trade names which bear little enough reference to their provenance, let alone their quality. We know that sound regional wines may be obtained for a moderate outlay, and that fine wines need not cost the earth. This book, we hope, will help the reader to discover and enjoy them both.

Cabernet Sauvignon grapes growing at Château Lafite-Rothschild (G)

How to use this book

Drinking Wine has two purposes: to introduce the novice to the complexities of the subject, and to provide the initiated with additional information and a ready source of reference. The two purposes are complementary, and in time the second may perhaps supersede the first; but in either case the reader will derive best advantage from the book by carefully noting its structure.

The introductory chapter is concerned with wine in general – its historical and social significance; its chemistry and alcoholic content; the factors which contribute to its quality and its informed appraisal; and some of the ramifications of the international trade which it supports. The book then falls into three main sections:

Section 1

Detailed information, broken down where appropriate into regions, about the world's seven most important wine-producing countries: France, Germany, Italy, Spain, Portugal (including Madeira), Australia and the U.S.A. The chapters on each of these countries carry maps and national or regional gazetteers, listing and briefly describing some hundreds of individual wines or wineries. Separate glossaries translate the terms found on wine labels printed in each of the five European languages.

Section 2

Notes on the wines of seventeen other countries – their general character; the grapes from which they are made; regulations controlling their production and marketing; the meaning and significance of the words printed on their labels; and the overseas countries in which they are chiefly available.

Section 3

Guidance on the tasting, buying, storage and serving of wine, together with a chart of French and German vintages between 1961 and 1978. The chart indicates the quality of each vintage and its maturing characteristics.

A chapter on viticulture, a gazetteer of grape varieties and a wine-drinker's glossary appear at the end of the book, together with a bibliography and appendices naming some of the major producers and shippers of Bordeaux and Burgundy and reproducing the famous 1855 classification of the great wines of Bordeaux. Finally, there is an index carrying some 5,000 entries – a key feature of the book. If you do not already know which country or region a particular wine comes from, the index should be your first recourse; if the wine is listed in one of the national or regional gazetteers, the relevant page number will be printed in italic.

Peppercorn ratings ★ ★★ ★★★ ★★★★ ★★★★★

David Peppercorn, Master of Wine, has assessed the quality and value of several hundred individual wines and wineries from Bordeaux, California and Australia. He has specially rated each of them according to a number of red stars, ranging from one (modest but noteworthy) to five (the very finest).

Other major wine-producing areas do not lend themselves as readily, if at all, to this form of classification. In Burgundy and in Germany, for instance, the quality of individual wines is liable to vary so significantly from year to year – and, among the German growers, even from estate to estate – that any rating system must be open to infinite qualifications. In the former case, therefore, we have identified the most reliable *négociants* (see pages 65 and 236); in the German section we have indicated the estates and growers with the most consistent reputation for quality.

In Italy, where the range of wines is so enormous that it would clearly be impossible to list them all (let alone to classify them) in a volume of this size, we have concentrated on styles and characteristics; similar considerations apply in Spain and Portugal, and elsewhere in France and the United States. Peppercorn ratings have therefore been applied only to those areas where the number of wines and their consistency ensure a degree of accuracy and usefulness.

About wine

THE NATURE OF WINE MAY appear self-evident, but like those self-evident truths of the Declaration of Independence, a longer acquaintance raises as many questions as it answers. Wine is hailed as a product of Nature, yet it is as much a triumph of Man. For some it is the elixir of life, for others the Devil's work. Its place in life varies from those ordinary wines which are as much a part of man's staple diet as bread to those pinnacles of the vintner's art which mark the greatest moments of our lives and make them memorable.

What is wine? A classic definition insists that it is produced only from the juice of freshly gathered grapes fermented in the area in which they were grown and made according to local traditions. This form of words was carefully framed to exclude the so-called 'British Wines' which lost their right to be called wine at all when the U.K. entered the European Community. However, many local traditions insist that the grapes need not be pressed when freshly gathered. The practice of dehydrating grapes by various methods and for differing purposes is widespread. In Jerez the Pedro Ximénez grapes are dried in the sun to increase their sugar content; in Valpolicella they are dried in warehouses for about three months to

Old wine press at Chablis (G)

Testing the vintage in a Chablis wine cellar (G)

produce the famous Recioto; in Tuscany, at least by tradition, Vin Santo is made from grapes kept until Holy Week before being pressed.

For the chemist, wine consists of alcohol well diluted in water, perhaps with the addition of sugar, minerals, esters, acids, glycerine and traces of several other elements. For professional tasters, it is experienced and evaluated in relation to its colour, its bouquet or aroma, its flavour. Some of these various and complex elements are set out diagrammatically on the next page.

'Frankly, it is God's purpose to make vinegar.' This characteristically robust assertion from the doyen of Californian oenologists, Professor Maynard Amerine, states very clearly the modern answer to the belief that an unaided Nature is responsible for good or great wine. Of course it has to be a partnership between Man and Nature. Without the right weather to produce ripe and reasonably healthy grapes, even the most skilled oenologist can do very little. On the other hand, the most perfectly ripe and healthy grapes can soon be turned to vinegar by human incompetence.

The range of what can now be done to assist Nature is formidable. The soil can be disinfected against viruses, sprays can protect the vine and grapes from disease and pests. During the fermentation temperature control enhances the bouquet and protects the must from bacteriological infections; sulphur and fining can enhance the must's health. Up until the young wine is bottled finings and filtrations can preserve its health, and if necessary advance its maturity; similar techniques can ensure that it is bottled in a stable and healthy condition.

Elixir or primrose path?

The addictive as well as the health-giving properties of wine are more and more debated. Moderation is clearly the key-note, but just how much you can safely drink depends on many factors. Many of the traditional claims made for wine as a tonic and aid to digestion have a sound medical basis – recent work in California even suggests that it can be a positive aid to slimming! While alcoholism certainly exists in France and Italy, it is clear that this is chiefly due not to wine but to spirits. Indeed, in traditionally hard-liquor countries like the U.S.S.R. and the Scandinavian countries, the consumption of wine as a substitute for spirits is officially encouraged. The increasing use of the breathalyser to discourage drunken drivers has also focused attention on the wide variations in human tolerance of alcohol. It is becoming clearer that the symptoms which we loosely refer to as intoxication may be caused by the interaction of more complex chemical forces than mere degrees of alcohol. This could be why some people are able to drink several glasses of one wine without turning a hair while a single glass of another drink of very similar alcoholic strength rapidly incapacitates them.

Wine can be . . . .

SIMPLE
FRESH
CHARMING

COARSE
ROUGH
ASTRINGENT

DELICATE
SUBTLE
ELUSIVE
ELEGANT

BIG
FULL-BODIED
VINOUS
FRUITY

LIGHT
AROMATIC
SPICY
PIQUANT
SHARP

MELLOW
SWEET
HONEYED
LUSCIOUS
CLOYING

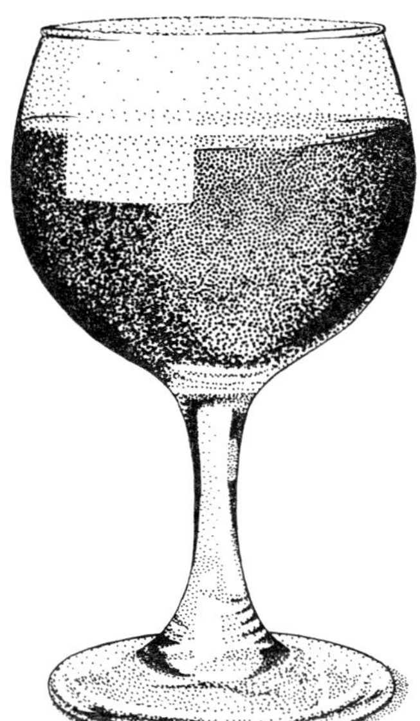

It has three main attributes . . . .

BOUQUET

The bouquet will reflect a wine's subtlety, or the lack of it, and can transmit a clear message about what is to come when the wine is tasted. In a young wine the grape aroma is likely to be predominant, giving an impression of freshness and fruitiness. In certain older wines with a capacity for ageing the fragrance of the grape tends to become submerged beneath the multi-faceted delicacy and subtlety of the wine's flavour, and it may not be possible to respond to all these elements at once. A tantalizing foretaste of the wine's physical content is conveyed to the nose by esters (a chemical term for alcohol compounds) contained in the volatile alcohol.

BODY

The taste of wine is a combination of its flavour (which may be simple or highly complex), its vinosity and its body. Together they contribute both to the initial impression conveyed – e.g. the wine's freshness, strength or fruitiness, the sense of fullness and roundness and weight in the mouth, or the lack of these qualities – and to the lingering sensations which the wine may (or may not) leave behind after it has been swallowed.

COLOUR

The colour of a wine is all-important, providing a clue both to its health and its nature. A healthy wine will have a clear, bright look, ranging from palest yellow to deep gold and from pale pink to a deep, intense red. Its likely nature – dry or sweet (in white wines), young or old, full-bodied or on the light side – may also be apparent from the depth of its colour.

In France, Italy, Spain and Portugal, wine is as much a part of any meal as bread: a meal without it seems unthinkable. But in the U.K. and the U.S.A., it remains a luxury and a minority interest. For this reason both these countries have traditionally consumed a high proportion of the best wines of France and Germany, but a relatively small amount of the more ordinary everyday wines of France, Italy and Spain – the exact reverse of the situation in the producing countries.

God's miracle or the work of Man?

What makes a wine fine rather than ordinary? Soil, climate and grape varieties are each enhanced by human skill. Contrary to what many people imagine, there has never been a time when so much good quality wine has been made. The climate and soil remain the same, some improvement in the selection of grape varieties has taken place, but the greatest change has been in the skill with which vines are tended, grape juice is converted to wine and wine is bottled: the fact that a Frascati can taste as good in New York as it does in Rome is no coincidence. Yet a wine made with the utmost care in the hills of Languedoc will not approach a wine made with similar care in Hermitage.

What criteria tell both the expert wine-taster and the average interested consumer that one wine is finer than another? When all the descriptions of sensation and technical explanations have been made, the short answer amounts to this: a fine wine has a complex aroma and a flavour that lingers in the mouth even after you have swallowed it. Ordinary wine has a simple grapey smell and a flavour which greets the taste-buds but leaves nothing to remember it by. One swallows and forgets.

Does alcoholic strength affect quality?

In the northerly climes of Germany the Riesling grape grown on the banks of the Moselle often produces wines of exquisite quality while only attaining between 8.5° and 9.5° of alcohol by volume. But in the mass production areas of the Midi of France, or in the northern Italian regions of the Veneto or Emilia-Romagna, 9° or 10° wines are a sign of inferior quality. Alcoholic strength is only significant in relation to the grape variety and where it is grown – i.e. in terms of its potential ripeness or otherwise in its particular environment. This is why in France *vin ordinaire* tends to be classified by alcoholic strength: a red one of 12° will be a lot better than one of 10°. *Appellation contrôlée* wines (see pages 24–5) must attain a minimum alcoholic degree before they can qualify, and for this reason the degree does not appear on the label. On the other hand, the Italians insist on having the alcoholic degree on all their wines, both DOC (see pages 115–16) and *vini da tavola*.

The lowest quality wines, assessed in purely alcoholic terms, are German. Those produced on the Moselle tend to be the lowest of these, and it is rare to get any German wine, even from further south, with more than 10.5° of alcohol. In France, red and white Burgundy tends to be between 12.5° and 13.5°, while the great red

Bordeaux from the Médoc are between 11° and 12°. Most wines from St Emilion and Pomerol are rather more powerful (between 12° and 13°); this is largely due to the influence of the Merlot grape, which is potentially richer in sugar than the Cabernet Sauvignon favoured in the Médoc. A delicate dry white wine from the Loire or from the Graves district of Bordeaux will usually be under 12° – indeed, exceptionally, the regulations for Muscadet stipulate this maximum. There has also been a distinct tendency in recent years to try to make certain wines – white Graves, for instance – at around 11° or 11.5°, in preference to more alcoholic wines which do not retain their freshness and crispness to the same extent. The most naturally powerful wines lie on either side of the Alps, at Châteauneuf on the Rhône and Barolo in Piedmont. Wines in both these areas have a minimum of 13° to 13.5°, frequently attaining 14° and even 15°; they deserve to be drunk with caution!

Château Berliquet, St Emilion (G)

Testing the wine, Châteauneuf du Pape (Zefa)

Wines which reach a high alcoholic degree naturally – i.e. by the conversion of sugar into alcohol – should not be confused with what are called fortified wines. These are wines where the alcoholic strength has been increased by the addition of spirit, either actually during the vinification of the wine, as with Port, or afterwards, as with Sherry. Vermouths also come into this category: they are in effect fortified wines, aromatized with herbs.

All the wines mentioned so far are what are called still wines as distinct from sparkling wines, but there are in fact different graduations of the sparkle. Of course the most famous sparkling wine is Champagne, a product which has been imitated all over the world. It is also possible to find wines with a much smaller sparkle; in France such wine is known as *pétillant*, in Italy as *frizzante* or (a further category) *frizzantino*. The classic method of introducing sparkle is by adding sugar and yeasts to a wine whose alcoholic fermentation has already finished, thus stimulating a secondary fermentation. This can be done either in bottle (known as the *méthode champenoise*; see pages 87–8) or in tank (*cuve close*); for the

Cellars at Johannisberg, one of the most famous villages of the Rheingau (G)

cheapest varieties it can also be done simply by introducing carbon dioxide under pressure, a method particularly favoured for certain sparkling Portuguese, Italian and German wines.

The colour problem

Colour, the very first aspect to be considered when appraising a wine, is sometimes forgotten. It has often been remarked that a great wine always has a beautiful colour; it is equally true that the colour of an unhealthy wine is usually suspect. The range, among reds alone, is immense. There is the deep purple of a young Rhône wine or a young Italian from Piedmont; there is the unique, usually lighter hue of the Gamay in Beaujolais; there are many, many gentle graduations, through brick-red and garnet to the deep scarlet of a mature Pinot from Burgundy or the different Cabernet Sauvignon/Merlot combinations from Bordeaux. Even the graduation from red to *rosé* is far from clear. Many of the German reds and those of the Trentino-Alto Adige in northern Italy could just as easily be classified as *rosé*, although they are normally described as red by those who produce them and drink them. Certainly the famous Tavel from the Rhône has a distinctly deep colour when compared with some of the pale *rosés* of the Loire.

Rosé wines, it can reasonably be said, fall into two distinct categories. There are those which have been vinified like red wines but removed from the skins after only a few hours' contact; such wines are, if you will, light reds which, because of their brief contact with the skins, are low in tannin and may thus be drunk chilled for summer drinking or drinking in warm climates. And there are wines made from red grapes which have been vinified more or less like white wines, with temperature control fermentations and emphasis on bouquet and freshness, which are of a much paler colour; these are substitute white wines, for they are made from different grape varieties and are influenced by the pigmentation of the skins. Their flavour is different, of course.

Even white wines provide an interesting variation of colours, from the practically colourless water-like appearance of many cheap German wines through the pale gold of a mature white Burgundy to the deep gold of mature Sauternes; the latter, when maderization has finally set in, with age, can eventually turn to an almost mahogany depth. Along the road there are some interesting variations: the Pinot Grigio in north-east Italy, for instance, is sometimes fermented partly on the skins, giving it a deep golden colour with almost a hint of orange. Many wines from Germany, and even some from northern France, have a distinctly green tinge when young.

The cellar of La Chaize, Beaujolais, at harvest time (G)

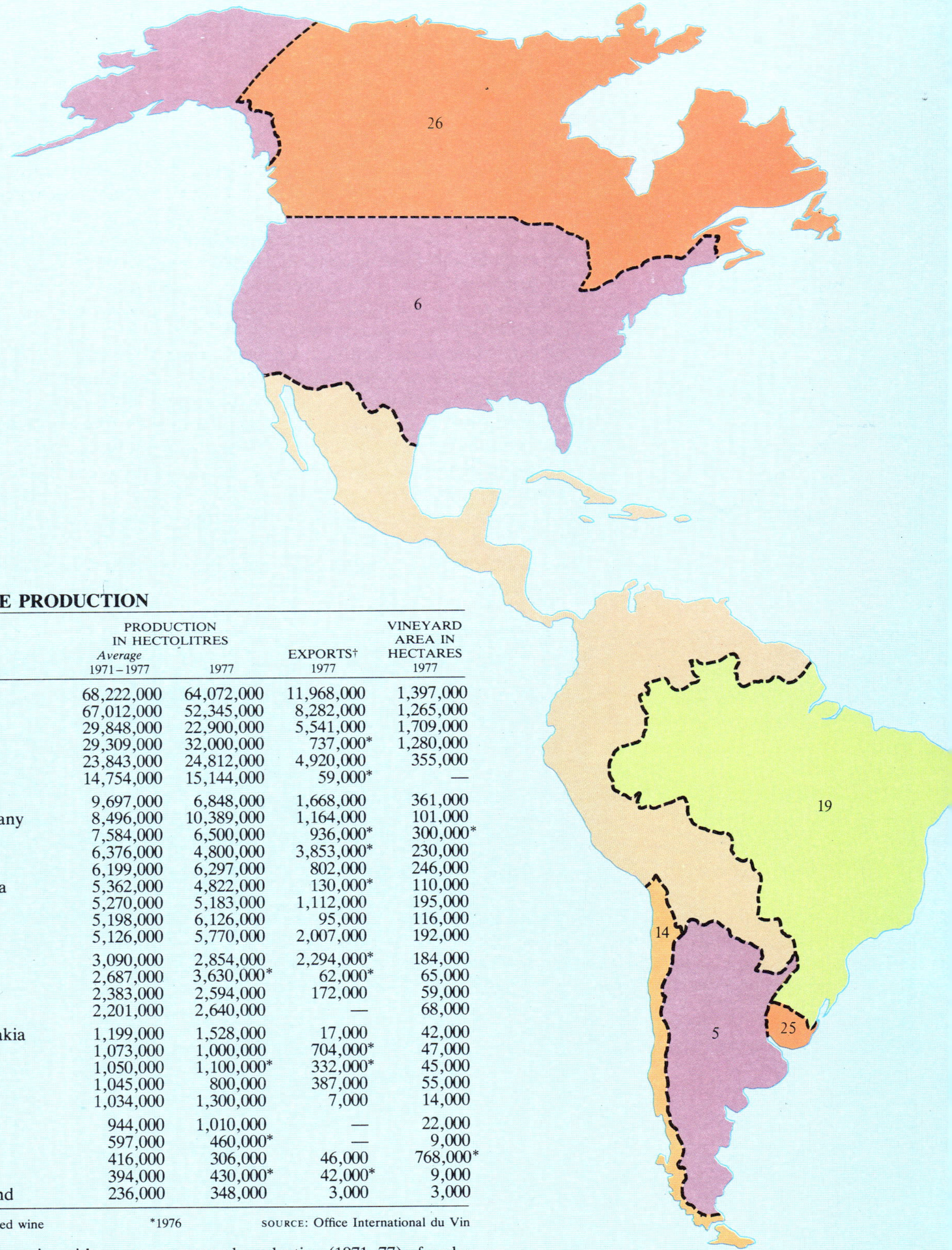

WORLD WINE PRODUCTION

	PRODUCTION IN HECTOLITRES *Average* 1971–1977	1977	EXPORTS† 1977	VINEYARD AREA IN HECTARES 1977
1. Italy	68,222,000	64,072,000	11,968,000	1,397,000
2. France	67,012,000	52,345,000	8,282,000	1,265,000
3. Spain	29,848,000	22,900,000	5,541,000	1,709,000
4. USSR	29,309,000	32,000,000	737,000*	1,280,000
5. Argentina	23,843,000	24,812,000	4,920,000	355,000
6. USA	14,754,000	15,144,000	59,000*	—
7. Portugal	9,697,000	6,848,000	1,668,000	361,000
8. West Germany	8,496,000	10,389,000	1,164,000	101,000
9. Romania	7,584,000	6,500,000	936,000*	300,000*
10. Algeria	6,376,000	4,800,000	3,853,000*	230,000
11. Jugoslavia	6,199,000	6,297,000	802,000	246,000
12. South Africa	5,362,000	4,822,000	130,000*	110,000
13. Greece	5,270,000	5,183,000	1,112,000	195,000
14. Chile	5,198,000	6,126,000	95,000	116,000
15. Hungary	5,126,000	5,770,000	2,007,000	192,000
16. Bulgaria	3,090,000	2,854,000	2,294,000*	184,000
17. Australia	2,687,000	3,630,000*	62,000*	65,000
18. Austria	2,383,000	2,594,000	172,000	59,000
19. Brazil	2,201,000	2,640,000	—	68,000
20. Czechoslovakia	1,199,000	1,528,000	17,000	42,000
21. Tunisia	1,073,000	1,000,000	704,000*	47,000
22. Cyprus	1,050,000	1,100,000*	332,000*	45,000
23. Morocco	1,045,000	800,000	387,000	55,000
24. Switzerland	1,034,000	1,300,000	7,000	14,000
25. Uruguay	944,000	1,010,000	—	22,000
26. Canada	597,000	460,000*	—	9,000
27. Turkey	416,000	306,000	46,000	768,000*
28. Israel	394,000	430,000*	42,000*	9,000
29. New Zealand	236,000	348,000	3,000	3,000

†may include imported wine *1976 SOURCE: Office International du Vin

Sixteen other countries with an average annual production (1971–77) of under 200,000 hectolitres are also listed by the O.I.V.: Japan (171,000hl), Mexico (148,000), Luxembourg (144,000), Albania (101,000), Venezuela (91,000), Peru (80,000), Egypt (63,000), Lebanon (39,000), Malta (24,000), Malagasy (19,000), Jordan (15,000), Bolivia (10,000), Holland (10,000), Syria (7,000), Belgium (6,000) and Iran (4,000). No figure is listed for the United Kingdom; current production is estimated by other sources at about 3,000 hectolitres.

WORLD WINE PRODUCERS

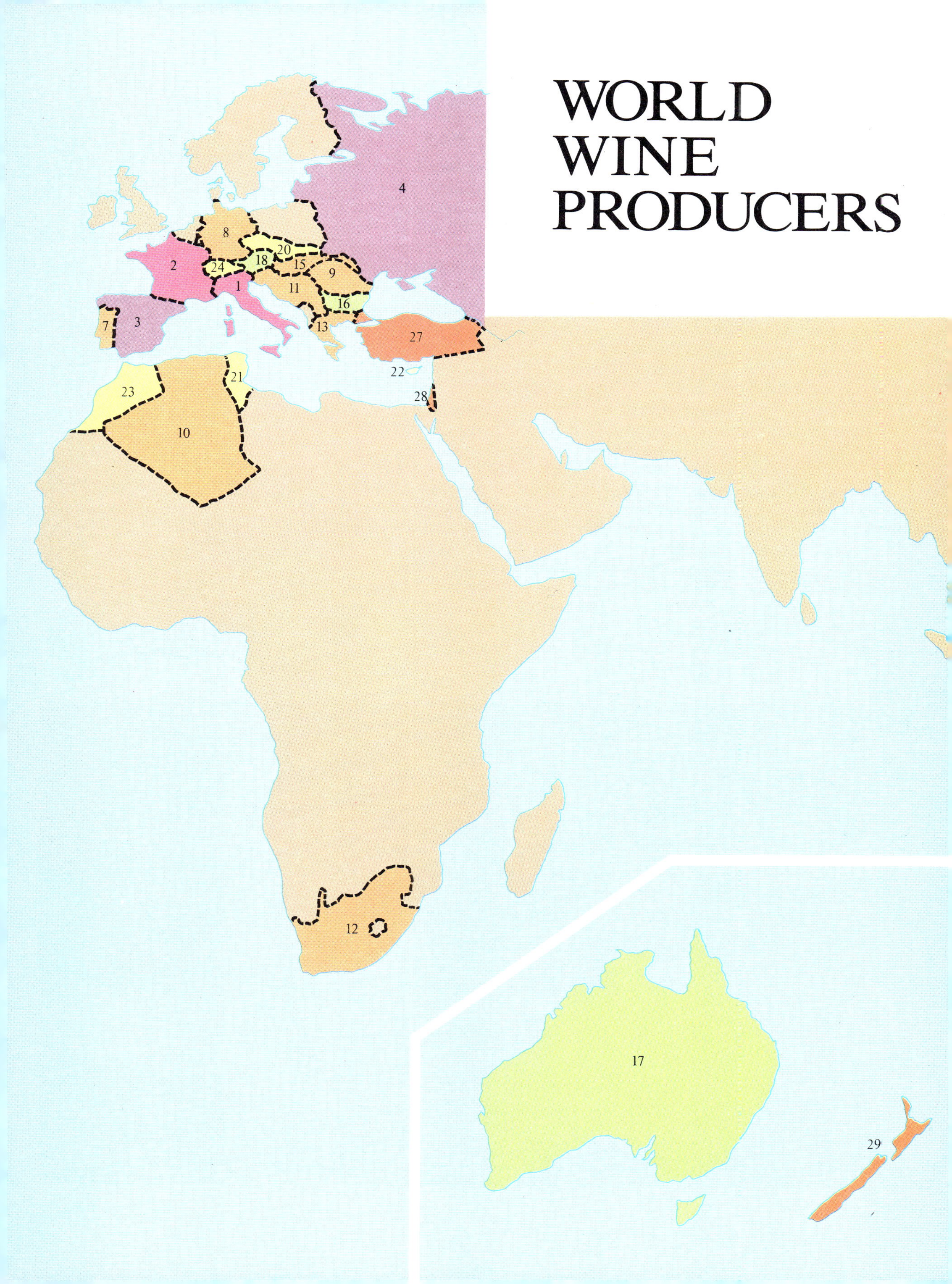

Who makes wine? Who sells it?

Wine production and consumption, although spread across the globe, is highly concentrated in a few areas. The European Economic Community, with the world's two largest wine-producing countries within its confines, accounts for nearly half of the world's wine production, and the French and the Italians also head the league of the world's greatest wine consumers. The greatest increase in the planting of vineyards and the production of wine is taking place in the Soviet Union, as part of its campaign to combat spirit drinking and perhaps to reduce its imports. Outside Europe, Argentina is the world's largest producer of wines. What the figures do not show is that it is in the United States, principally in California, and in Australia that the most interesting quality wines from outside Europe are now being produced – and in increasing quantities. At the other end of the spectrum, Algeria is producing only a fraction of its former output, and production is still in decline.

With the notable exception of the U.K., which has been one of the world's major importers since the Middle Ages, most countries have for most of their history drunk what they have produced, exporting little and importing little. Today the world's major importing countries are Germany, France, the U.K. and the U.S.A., while the major exporting countries are Italy, France and Spain. The major change in this picture over the last decade has been Italy. Until ten years ago Italy on the whole drank what it produced, exports were small and imports even smaller. Today the picture is completely changed due to the free market in wine created by the policies of the E.E.C.

Tilling the vineyards at Torgiano in Umbria (G)

SECTION 1

The big seven

WALES
ENGLAND
BELGIQUE
LUXEMBOURG
DEUTSCHLAND
Reims
Châlons sur Marne
Marne
Seine
Paris
CHAMPAGNE
Strasbourg
Rhin
VOSGES
ALSACE
Colmar
Orléans
Auxerre
CHABLIS
Loir
Loire
Tours
Nantes
LOIRE
Pouilly
sur Loire
CÔTE
D'OR
Dijon
Arbois
Nevers
Cher
Saône
JURA
SUISSE
BOURGOGNE
Mâcon
BEAUJOLAIS
Seyssel
SAVOIE
Clermont
Ferrand
Lyon
Rhône
Gironde
Libourne
Bordeaux
BERGERAC
Dordogne
Monbazillac
BORDEAUX
Garonne
Valence
Ardèche
COTES DU
RHONE
ITALIA
Avignon
GAILLAC
Albi
PROVENCE
Draguignan
LANGUEDOC
Montpellier
JURANCON
Madiran
Toulouse
Marseille
Toulon
Pau
Limoux
ROUSSILLON
Perpignan
ESPAÑA
Bordeaux
Bourgogne
Loire
Champagne
Alsace
Côtes du Rhône
0 km 50 100

FRANCE

WHY DOES FRANCE HOLD SUCH a special place in the tastes and loyalties of the wine-lover? Today she is no longer consistently the world's largest producer of wine (Italy challenges for that position) and we hear many complaints about the excessive price of French wine; we are even told that their quality is not what it was. Yet for many people, the world over, French wine is above all other.

The explanation is at least in good part historical; certainly it cannot be dismissed simply as an example of French chauvinism at work. Throughout Europe, wine-drinking has been a part of everyday life since at least Roman times. But it was only in the 18th century that a concept of quality was developed, and with it the idea that individual vineyards and vintages could be a matter for discussion and cultivated enjoyment. The first wine connoisseurs gathered in the salons of Paris and the drawing-rooms of London, in the age of the French Regency and the Whig ascendancy – and the wines they appreciated were for the most part French. This in its turn led to the 19th-century classifications of the great vineyards of Bordeaux and Burgundy. The wine drunk at the tables of the rich and cultivated ceased to be just a drink, like beer, and became an art.

Hence, all the deferential trappings surrounding wine – trappings which are sometimes today held responsible for suffocating our pleasure in it and for making us forget that wine is something to relax with and enjoy. We should see the whole process of the civilizing of wine in its historical context, and recognize what it has

Gipsy vendangeurs *at Château Lascombes, the property of Alexis Lichine (G)*

given us; all the generations of care and expertise which have resulted in the greatest Clarets, Sauternes, and Burgundies. Other countries now produce fine wines with regularity, but truly great wines take longer, and it is here that France still stands supreme.

The land

French viticulture is governed by three great river systems and a range of mountains. The Gironde and its tributaries, the Dordogne and Garonne, encompass not only Bordeaux, the largest quality wine region of France, but also the important secondary region of the Dordogne and a number of smaller wine-producing areas. The Rhône and its tributary, the Saône, account for two great regions, the Rhône itself, and the Beaujolais, Mâconnais and Côte d'Or districts of Burgundy. The Loire, the longest and greatest river in France, effectively marks the northern limit to French viticulture in the west, providing a great variety of wines all the way from Muscadet, near its Atlantic mouth to Pouilly Fumé and Sancerre in the very heart of France. And, finally, the Vosges mountains provide a special micro-climate for the western side of the Rhine valley, enabling the grapes of Alsace to ripen to a degree unusual in such latitudes.

These areas encompass all the great as well as some of the lesser wines of France. Champagne is in a different category. Here, as we shall see, it is the process of production rather than the quality of the raw materials which impart its special quality to the wine.

In exalting the great wines it would be a mistake to forget or belittle the many excellent and highly individual smaller *vins du pays* or country wines, using those terms in the large sense rather than according to the narrow connotations of the wine laws. Wines like Madiran and Jurançon in the south-west, Bandol and the *rosés* of Provence, Crépy and Seyssel in Savoy – all are part of the glories of that French provincial flavour which, when combined with their local *cuisine*, makes France what it is.

The wine laws

France has been a pioneer in the projection of wine names and the fight for authenticity and quality. The reason is not hard to seek. Since French wine names were the most famous in the world, and French wines the most widely exported, they were also the most vulnerable to imitation and fraud. After the First World War and during the period of the depression the crisis in many French wine-producing regions became acute, and growers demanded protection. It was clearly unfair and dishonest that producers from other districts, even other countries, should be allowed to sell their wines, nearly always produced in more favourable climatic conditions, under borrowed names, at far lower prices. The reason they did so was to sell their wines more readily and usually at a higher price than they might otherwise have obtained. In the process they made it difficult, and sometimes impossible, for the producers of the genuine article to make a living.

The result was the system of *appellations contrôlées*, which achieved its final form in 1935. It is important to understand not only what the AC system sets out to do, but also what it does not. First, it defines the area where vines may be planted if a wine is to bear a certain name. It also lays down the type or types of vine allowed, how many may be planted to the hectare, how they are to be pruned, how much they may produce, and the minimum alcoholic degree (there is a maximum for only one AC wine, Muscadet). Once the wine has been made, the yield obtained must be registered, and the wine may not leave the grower unless accompanied by a document recording all its relevant particulars. In its later stages the AC control system becomes a book-keeping operation, ensuring that the grower cannot sell more than he has declared, and that the merchant or *négociant* cannot sell more than he has bought.

What the system was *not* set up to control was quality. Only in quite recent years has the Institut National des Appellations d'Origine (I.N.A.O.), the body which controls and monitors the system nationally, become concerned with this factor. Although in certain areas there have been tastings for the *appellation* for some years, in many others, notably Burgundy, there have not. Now the aim is to ensure analysis and tasting of all wines – a system which Germany introduced in 1971.

In 1974 a major reform of French law took place, eliminating a serious defect in the original system. Until then there were certain rather inflexible limits to yield (*rendement*), but in years of high production growers were permitted to use the next *appellation* down for their surplus wine. Thus the objective of keeping yields down to protect quality was completely circumvented.

A village in Alsace, one of the six great wine-producing areas of France (G)

This has been replaced by a system which makes allowances for yearly variations, but then strictly enforces limits. Each *appellation* has a basic yield (*rendement de base*). Then, after each harvest, the *rendement* commissions of each wine-growing *syndicat* and the I.N.A.O. agree a *rendement annuel*; this can be above *or* below the *rendement de base*. Finally there is a fixed percentage which may be added to the *rendement annuel* by which growers can claim additional yield, but they must open their cellars for inspection and have samples submitted for tasting. Anything above this PLC (*plafond limité de classement*) must go for distillation. This extra allowance is usually 20 per cent so the grower has a fairly clear idea as to the limits within which he can profitably produce.

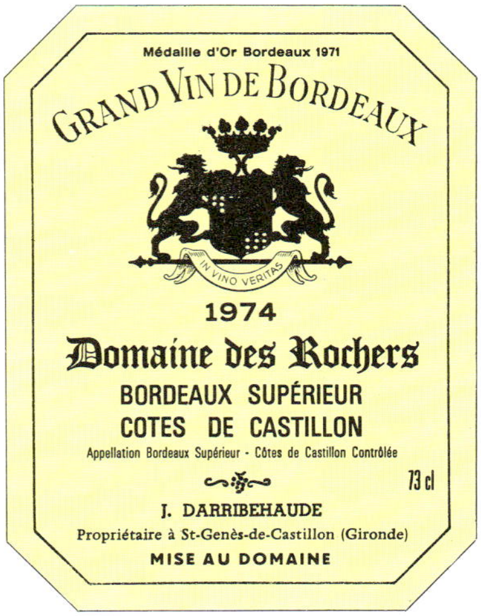

Must in fermentation at Château Cheval Blanc (G)

Old wine-making implements in a Chablis museum (G)

Since 1970 the French *appellation* system has been an integral part of the E.E.C. system, and thus ultimately subject to Brussels. In the European system wine is divided into two categories: VQPRD, that is to say quality wines from defined regions, and table wines – *vins de table*. This has placed France in the anomalous position of having a two-tier system of VQPRD wines, *appellation contrôlée* and *vin de qualité supérieur* (VDQS). In practice there has been a move to upgrade VDQS wines to AC status. But the VDQS regulations are stricter with regard to the control of quality than the existing AC regulations, since analyses and tasting are an integral part of the system. So today there are VDQS wines which are superior to certain AC wines. One disturbing feature of this evolution is a tendency for prices to rise sharply when a region moves from VDQS to AC, without any noticeable change in quality.

An important change to the French system brought about by Brussels affects *vins de table*. Previously *vin de table* could have no regional identity. Now a system of *vin du pays* has been introduced, thus encouraging the production of good local wines with some regional characteristics, rather than the dull industrial blends of *ordinaire* which existed before. These, of course, still exist, though more and more as E.E.C. blends – that is French base wines from the Midi improved with high degree wines from southern Italy. What the new system has done is to encourage the production of rather better quality wines outside the VQPRD category.

The labels

Although the information shown on French wine labels has long been strictly regulated, changes occur from time to time. The most recent was made in order to bring France into line with E.E.C. practice by showing the bottle content on the label: until then the French had used a confusing and misleading system by which the main bottle sizes shown (0.75cl and one litre) were merely nominal – i.e. the bottles could hold that amount only if filled to the brim. So when the new labelling started we had the curious experience of finding bottles labelled as containing 0.73cl. Now the system is changing again as the E.E.C. adopts 0.75cl contents as standard contents.

Another striking difference between French and, say, Italian labelling is that in France the alcoholic content appears only on *vins de table*. Part of the rationale for this lies in the fact that alcoholic degrees are a guide to the quality of a *vin de table*, but not to that of an AC or VDQS wine, where a minimum alcoholic degree is in any case part of the law. Other main points governing French labelling are as follows:

AC *and* VDQS *wines*

1. The AC or VDQS description must appear immediately beneath the name of the wine.
2. The design of the label must be consistent with the description – i.e. if the wine does not come from an individual property, there must be no illustration of a château or vineyard to suggest that it does.
3. If the wine is bottled by the grower, one of several different formulae may be used – e.g. *mise du château domaine* or *mise à la propriété*. Bottling at a co-operative counts as bottling by the proprietor: thus, *mise en bouteille par les producteurs réunis*.
4. If bottled by a *négociant*, his name and address must appear.

Vins de table

1. The alcoholic strength must be shown.
2. Property wines may not be called 'Château' but may be called 'Domaine'.
3. If a *vin de table* is sold by a *négociant* with an address in a commercial centre for AC wines, the names of neither *négociant* or town may appear – only a code. This is to avoid the impression that the wine comes from a famous region.

The bottle, hand-blown until the 19th century, has evolved down the centuries; but it is only in the last hundred years that the capacity to make reasonably tough glass bottles easily and cheaply has led to the development of the present variety of shapes.

Bordeaux. *This shape, which seems to have evolved by the early 19th century, is now a universally recognized standard-bearer, both for Bordeaux wines, red and white, and for Bordeaux-style wines*

Burgundy. *With its sloping shoulders and continuous line, the contrast with Bordeaux is clear.*

Champagne. *Basically a reinforced Burgundy bottle, but traditionally it contains 0.80cl. instead of 0.75cl. It is much heavier, since thicker and stronger glass is needed to resist internal pressure of around five atmospheres. Such bottles are also used for other sparkling wines all over France.*

Alsace. *A slightly taller version of the traditional German bottle, made from green glass (as for Moselle).*

Nantaise. *A specially designed bottle for Muscadet, but used only for a minority of its wines because of its higher cost.*

Véronique. *Similar to the Alsace flute, but with three rings round the top. Used for Gros Plant, other Loire wines and some white Dordogne wines.*

Occitane. *This dumpy bottle has been designed to give an identity to the better wines (*VDQS *and* AC*) of Languedoc.*

Basse Normande. *Another dumpy bottle, but the sides are almost straight; it is much used in the Rhône for domaine-bottled wines.*

Haute Normande. *A version of this shape, which is traditional to Calvados, is also used for Roussillon wines.*

Anjou. *A fatter, dumpier version of the flute, with the crest of Anjou on the shoulder.*

Châteauneuf du Pape. *A Burgundy bottle, with the Papal crossed keys embossed on the shoulder; reversed for domaine-bottled Châteauneufs.*

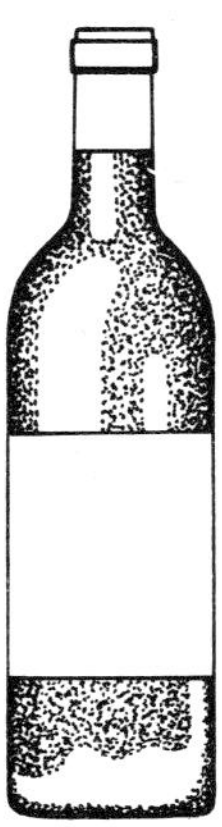

Bordeaux

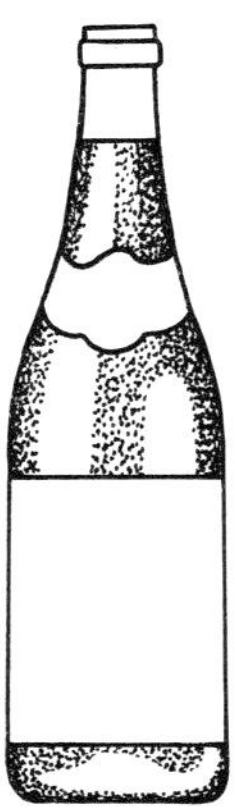

Burgundy

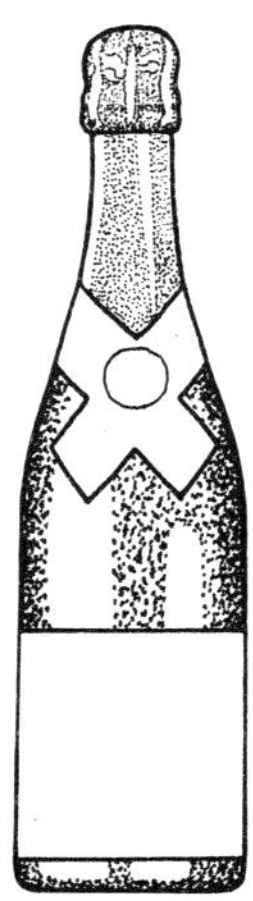

Champagne

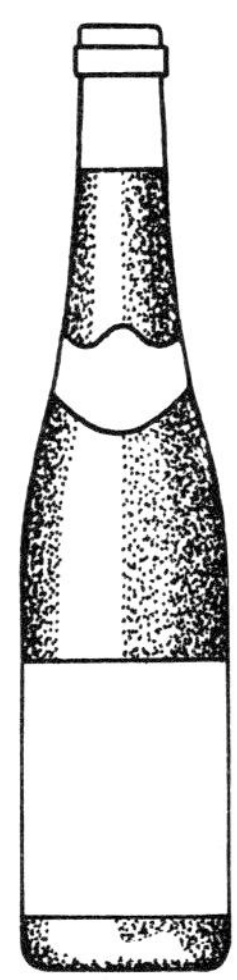

Alsace

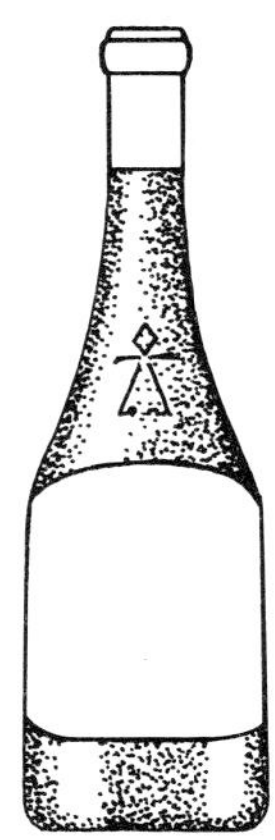

Nantaise

FRANCE

GLOSSARY

appellation contrôlée: the normally used shortened form of *appellation d'origine contrôlée* (abbreviated to AOC or AC); literally, a 'controlled name of origin'; it signifies a French wine of an agreed standard of quality and production from a named area, which complies with the requirements of the INAO (see below)

barrique: the wine cask of Bordeaux, holding 225 litres

bourgeois: a term rightly applied only in the Médoc to good unclassified wines – see *cru bourgeois*

cépage: the variety of vine or vines used to produce an individual wine

chai: warehouse in which wine is stored during maturation

chambrer: to bring red wine *gradually* up to room temperature for serving

château bottled: Bordeaux wines, bottled on the estate where they are grown

claret: the term originated from the anglicized form of *clairet*, light-coloured red Bordeaux wine; now customarily used for any form of red Bordeaux wine

classé/classified: used in this book to refer to the *cru classé* wines of Bordeaux

climat: a named vineyard in Burgundy where, by contrast with Bordeaux, it can be subdivided among a number of separate owners, and almost invariably is

clos: a vineyard which must be clearly enclosed, for example Clos de Vougeot in the Côte de Nuits

commune: the area embracing a small town or village and the surrounding land that lies within its boundaries

corsé: descriptive of wine that is robust and full of body

côte: a slope; used throughout France, sometimes in the singular (e.g. Côte de Nuits), more often in the plural (e.g. Côtes de Blaye), to identify a unified wine region

courtier: a wine broker; the middle-man between the grower and the merchant

cru: strictly, the locality in which vines are grown; transferred to mean the wines produced

cru bourgeois: a Médoc wine of good quality, but of lesser standing than the classified growths

cru classé: an expression used to apply to those wines of the Médoc, Graves, St Emilion and Sauternes which have been officially classified as leading growths

cru exceptionnel: a special category of seven outstanding bourgeois wines in the Médoc ranking immediately below the *crus classés*

cru grand bourgeois: the best of the *cru bourgeois* wines in the Médoc

cuvée: derived from *cuve* – a vat for fermenting or storing wine – the word is used in two quite different senses. In Burgundy it denotes wine from the best pressing; in Champagne it indicates a blend of different wines

demi-sec: literally half dry – in practice half sweet

domaine: the equivalent to *château*, mostly in Burgundy and the Rhône; it need not, however, be a single holding, and can be a collection of holdings in different vineyards belonging to the same person

doux: sweet

eau de vie de marc: spirit distilled from grape skins and pips

goût de terroir: a marked regional smell and flavour imparted by the soil to certain wines

grand cru: 'great growth' in Burgundy, better quality bourgeois wine in St Emilion

grand cru classé: a leading classified Médoc growth, or the wine made in that vineyard; in St Emilion, a wine just below the top rank

INAO: the Government-appointed Institut National des Appellations d'Origine des Vins et Eaux de Vie

liquoreux: white wine that is sweet and luscious

méthode champenoise: the method used, particularly in Champagne, to make sparkling wine by inducing a secondary fermentation when the wine is in the bottle

moelleux: white wine which is sweet, or appears so, with at the same time a certain richness

mousseux: sparkling

négociant: the merchant who buys the wine from the grower, usually for bottling, and then for shipping; in Burgundy, *négociants* may also be growers

nerveux: wine of vigour and vitality

parfum: grape fragrance or aroma

pétillant: slightly sparkling

pourriture noble: noble rot or *Botrytis* – a fungus which dehydrates the grape (in German, *Edelfaule*)

premier cru: translates as a 'first growth' but in fact refers to a leading wine of the second rank in Burgundy

premier grand cru classé: a wine of the first rank in St Emilion

primeur: this year's wine, fermented so that it can be drunk within a month or so of the vintage

récolte: the wine harvest

remuage: the process of shaking a bottle of Champagne in a particular manner, so that the sediment rests against the cork

rosé: a pink wine obtained through partial fermentation on red grape skins

sec: dry

sève: 'sap'; describes wine's youthfulness and vigour

tastevin: a saucer-like silver tasting vessel

tonneau: a standard wine measure in Bordeaux of 900 litres, which converts into 100 cases of wine

VDQS: *Vins Délimités de Qualité Supérieure* – regional wines of a quality level just below AC; their production is controlled by the INAO

velouté: describes wine of a supple, velvety texture

vendange: the grape harvest

vif: lively, fresh

vigneron: the wine grower

vignoble: a vineyard

vin de presse: red wine obtained from the pressings of the grapes after the first juices have been run off; it is used when an increase in colour and tannic effect is required

vin de marque: a wine made by a particular supplier whose name is its guarantee

vin de pays: a small regional wine produced locally, sold without a vineyard name

vin de table: under EEC regulations strictly a wine which has not been designated as *appellation contrôlée*

vin d'une nuit: cheap wine, fermented for 24 hours or less

Véronique

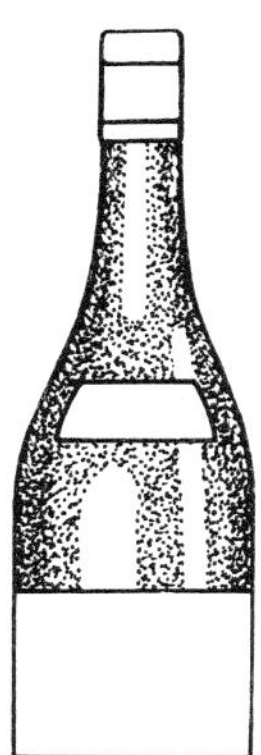

Occitane

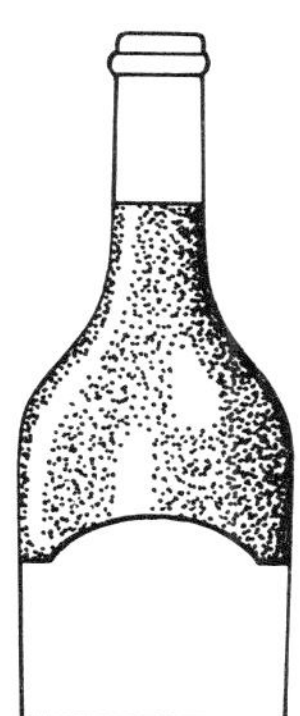

Basse Normande

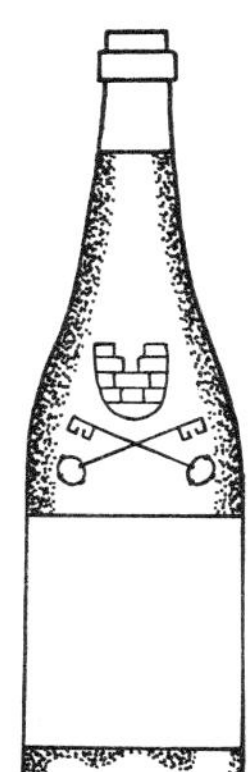

Châteauneuf du Pape

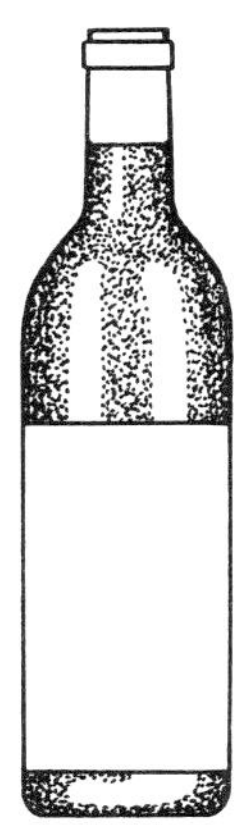

Haute Normande

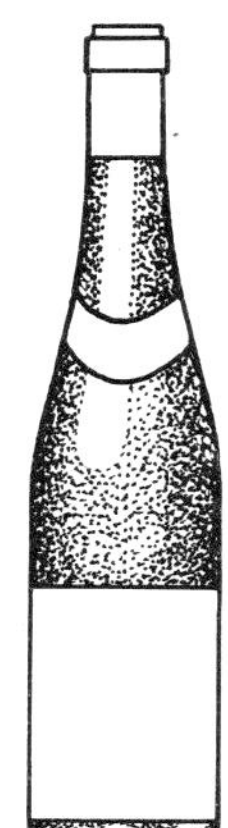

Anjou Rosé

Rivers and wine areas of Bordeaux

Bordeaux

MEDOC (pp. 34 to 41)
ST EMILION (pp. 42 to 47)
POMEROL (pp. 48 to 50)
GRAVES (pp. 51 to 53)
THE SWEET WHITE WINE AREAS (pp. 54 to 58)
BOURG/BLAYE/FRONSAC (pp. 59 to 61)

APPELLATIONS CONTROLEES

Barsac ○
Blaye/Blayais ● ○
Bordeaux ● ○
Bordeaux Clairet/Rosé ∅
Bordeaux Côtes de Castillon ●
Bordeaux Mousseux
Bordeaux Supérieur ● ○
Bordeaux Supérieur Côtes de Castillon ●
Bourg ● ○
Bourgeais ● ○
Cadillac ○
Cérons ○
Côtes de Blaye ○
Côtes de Bordeaux St Macaire ○
Côtes de Bourg ● ○
Côtes Canon Fronsac ●
Côtes de Fronsac ●
Entre Deux Mers ○
Entre Deux Mers Haut Benauge ○
Graves ● ○
Graves Supérieures ○
Graves de Vayres ● ○
Haut Médoc ●
Lalande de Pomerol ●
Listrac ●
Loupiac ○
Lussac St Emilion ●
Margaux ●
Médoc ●
Montagne St Emilion ●
Moulis ●
Parsac St Emilion ●
Pauillac ●
Pomerol ●
Premières Côtes de Blaye ● ○
Premières Côtes de Bordeaux ● ○
Puisseguin St Emilion ●
Sables St Emilion ●
St Emilion ●
St Estèphe ●
St Georges St Emilion ●
St Julien ●
Ste Croix du Mont ○
Ste Foy Bordeaux ● ○
Sauternes ○

● red ∅ rosé ○ white

CLARET, RED WINE FROM BORDEAUX, is a by-word for wine itself – at least to the Englishman, and probably the world over. Maurice Healy, in his 1940 classic, *Stay Me With Flagons*, stated quite simply 'Claret is wine. It is *the* wine'. Without doubt, red Bordeaux continues to provide the first and universal yardstick by which all other wines are compared and judged.

It must not be imagined, however, that one can therefore categorize the vineyards of Bordeaux in any simple or single way. There are over 3,000 reputable individual holdings, all of them marketing wines under their individual names; they represent an immense range of qualities and styles and are covered by at least 45 separate *appellations*. This diversity is their unique characteristic and their special attraction.

The vineyards of Bordeaux occupy 110,000 hectares (250,000 acres) – one-tenth of the Gironde which is itself the biggest *département* in France. Together, they form the largest single fine wine growing region in the world; their average annual yield of quality wines alone is some 500 million bottles – one-seventieth of the world total – and more than half of this output is white. The best of the Bordeaux reds, along with the sweet white Sauternes, are acknowledged by many as the finest wines in the world.

What to expect

It is characteristic of Bordeaux that the majority of its wines are marketed individually under the name of the château (which is often a mansion, but may only be a cottage) in which they were grown and produced. This personal attention to wine-making, reinforced and controlled by the very precise provision of the French wine laws, means that when purchasing a bottle of Bordeaux wine you are able to start out with a pretty good idea of what to expect.

The exceptional quality of Bordeaux wines stems from the nature and size of the vineyards in which they are produced. Elsewhere in France, particularly in Burgundy and the Loire, the effect of the French Revolution on land tenure was to fragment vineyard holdings; but in Bordeaux the bourgeoisie was already powerful before the Revolution and few properties were affected. From the wine lover's point of view this is advantageous, because many wines, even some of the very finest, come from comparatively big estates and tend to be widely available.

The geography

From a glance at the map it will immediately be seen that the region's principal wine-growing areas are carved out by the courses of the rivers Garonne and Dordogne, and like Caesar's Gaul divided into three parts. The left bank of the Garonne takes in the prime wine-growing areas of the Médoc, Graves and Sauternes; the right bank of the Dordogne, with its more cluttered assembly of smaller vineyards, includes the very important areas of St Emilion and Pomerol; these are not nearly as large as the Médoc in size but they are densely covered and highly cultivated, and their output is immense. The intervening area, the triangular slice between the two rivers, is known as Entre Deux Mers because both the Garonne and the Dordogne remain tidal for that part of their course.

At the commercial heart of the area, astride the Garonne, lies the city of Bordeaux, the greatest wine centre in the world. Here the region's routes converge, leading some 50 miles north into the Médoc, 30 miles south-east through Graves to Sauternes, and a similar distance eastwards across the Dordogne to Pomerol and St Emilion.

Grape varieties

All the quality red wines of Bordeaux are made from a judicious blend of the Cabernet Sauvignon grape and a varying proportion of Cabernet Franc and Merlot; the amounts differ with the tradition of the vineyard. The two Cabernet grapes complement each other, giving the wine its richness of colour and flavour, its distinctive and delicate bouquet and its firmness and ageing qualities. The Merlot is softer in character, lending the wine mellowness and suppleness; and outside the Médoc and Graves it is usually the most widely planted variety of red grape. Malbec is also used, but to a much lesser degree; Petit Verdot is planted on a small scale, and is regarded as a valuable component in some of the best Médoc vineyards, adding firmness and acidity in years when the Merlot can tend to be overripe. White wines are made from a combination of the Sauvignon (giving finesse and vigour and acidity), the Sémillon (softness and sweetness), and the Muscadelle, with its characteristic raisin flavour and smell.

Appellations d'origine contrôlées

The character of an honest wine is bound up with the place where it is produced, and the more restricted the *appellation* (or place name) the finer the quality of the wine.

Four generic *appellations – Bordeaux, Bordeaux Supérieur, Bordeaux Clairet* or *Rosé* and *Bordeaux Mousseux* – cover the whole of the Bordeaux wine country and embrace red, white, rosé and sparkling wines. They represent the lowest level of quality wines which the INAO will accept for its designation *appellation d'origine contrôlée*. Above this general level is the more restricted *appellation* for each of the districts into which Bordeaux is divided for wine purposes – that is to say Médoc, Graves, Entre Deux Mers and so on. A bottle of Bordeaux wine of regional quality may either be from a single vineyard, for example *Château Beau Rivage – Appellation Bordeaux Contrôlée*, or be a blend from anywhere in the region sold as *Bordeaux*. In the same way, at the district level, an *Appellation Graves Contrôlée* wine can be a blend of the products of several growers in the district, sold as Graves, or a named single vineyard wine. Exceptionally, within Médoc and adjacent to St Emilion, there are certain communes which are entitled to their own

PEPPERCORN ★ RATINGS

Bordeaux is riddled with classifications of one sort or another. In the Médoc there are the classified growths of 1855, divided into five categories, rather like the orders of nobility. In St Emilion there are two categories of *grands crus classés* and many of the unclassified wines are nevertheless referred to as *grands crus*; in Graves no distinctions are made within the tiny groups of classified wines, and in Pomerol there is no classification at all. To further confuse matters, a great number of Médoc wines not classified in 1855 are now officially designated as *crus bourgeois*; members of the Syndicat des Crus Bourgeois du Médoc have recently participated in a new three-tier classification of their own – *grand bourgeois exceptionnel, grand bourgeois* and *bourgeois*.

In order to avoid some of these complications, and to establish a reasonably consistent standard of comparison within each district, most of the wines listed in the Bordeaux gazetteers have been rated as follows:

★★★★★ The leading wines of the Gironde, including those classified as first growths and a small group which, although not obtaining such high prices, usually achieves a similar quality. At blind tastings these wines often do as well or better in particular vintages as the first growths; and, now that the latter can cost two or three times as much as other Bordeaux wines, some offer exceptional value for money.

★★★★ Classified growths of special merit – not quite up to ★★★★★ standard but usually no more expensive than the ★★★ wines.

★★★ The general run of classified growths of all regions, plus some unclassified wines of special merit which would certainly be recognized in any re-classification of the Bordeaux vineyards. Wines in this latter category are often cheaper than the classified growths, and offer correspondingly good value.

★★ In the Médoc, the best of the so-called *crus bourgeois*; in St Emilion, the best of the *grands crus*.

★ Good, sound wines of individuality, usually rated as *crus bourgeois* in Médoc or *grands crus* in St Emilion.

The fact that a wine is unstarred does not mean that it is not perfectly acceptable. Remember that there are several thousand growths sold under Château or Domaine names in the Bordeaux region, and to list them all would be impossible. Unstarred wines, therefore, have been listed chiefly because they are likely to be available outside France.

exclusive *appellations*; in the Médoc because of the outstanding character of the wines they produce, in St Emilion for other rather more commercial reasons.

Overlapping the AC regulations is the system of classification of leading growths which applies in Médoc, Graves, St Emilion and Sauternes. Many of these outstanding *château* wines, with appropriate designations such as *grand cru classé* (classified great growth) which the label will undoubtedly reveal, have a world-wide reputation, but the label still ought to (and within the EEC countries must) display the *appellation contrôlée* of the wine. The classic list of leading growths, still referred to today, is that of 1855 and is set out elsewhere in this book. There have been some important developments since, and official classifications of Graves and St Emilion wines were drawn up in the 1950s. Any similar listing today would have to include red wines of Pomerol and a number of white wines as well.

Experimentation and selection

Prices of the classified growths, *crus classés*, from Bordeaux are nowadays beyond the normal reach of all save the very rich, the very enthusiastic or the very fortunate. Even if you can afford them, there is little point in purchasing such wines unless you intend to take the trouble to appreciate their subtleties. 'It is no small matter getting to know the wines of Bordeaux', wrote Stendhal in 1838. 'It is an art which I love, for it leaves no room for hypocrisy.' Appreciation now, as then, demands application and financial outlay.

However, the enthusiast wishing to educate and indulge his palate does not need to spend extravagantly. A selective but wide-ranging experimentation will bring its own rewards. The first important step is to establish the regional differences between one Bordeaux wine and another; to see, for instance, in what way a straightforward red *appellation Bordeaux contrôlée* or a workaday Côtes de Bourg can differ from a Médoc or a Pomerol or a red Graves or a St Emilion. The second perspective is quality, which tends to be reflected in the price, and the third is timing: a fresh, fruity young Bordeaux or Bordeaux Supérieur can be thoroughly enjoyed when it is two or three years old, while a *grand cru classé* from the Médoc will often seem brusque and surly even at four or five years old, and at the peak of excellence at twenty. The vintage table at the end of the book is designed as a guide to the quality of the wine of a given year and when it may best be drunk.

Comparative tastings on the lines suggested here will enable you to establish whether you are really prepared to pay that extra money for the top wines. Taste is such a highly subjective matter: a fresh young Bordeaux or a fruity little St Emilion may well prove to be far more satisfying at a particular moment than a far more expensive big name. Your palate will undoubtedly become more sophisticated with experience, and this may lead on in due course to a desire to sample some of the leading growths.

BORDEAUX:
SAMPLE TASTINGS

Two kinds of tasting are proposed – one as a broad introduction to Bordeaux, the other (included in the notes on each of the separate areas) as a series of tastings in depth. The first might consist of:

(1) An ordinary red Bordeaux – each of the bigger Bordeaux shippers has one or more on his list and exports it under his own label.

(2) A Côtes de Bourg or a Côtes de Fronsac – choose an individual growth of four or five years old.

(3) A good St Emilion, but not a classified growth, such as Château Plaisance or Château Fombrauge, four to six years old.

(4) A good Pomerol of similar age to the St Emilion, but not one of the top growths – say Château Le Bon Pasteur or Château de Sales or Château Bourgneuf.

(5) A good bourgeois Médoc such as Château de Pez, Château Lanessan or Château Siran.

(6) A red Graves of similar standing (consult the Peppercorn rating in the gazetteer) could be added to this list for completeness.

Médoc

IN THE EYES of many wine drinkers Médoc wines are the archetype for Bordeaux itself. Alexis Lichine, the celebrated wine merchant and author of the classic *Encyclopaedia of Wines and Spirits*, describes a Médoc as a typical claret. Four communes principally contribute to this reputation – St Estèphe, Pauillac, St Julien and Margaux – and they set the standards for the rest of the Médoc, if not for the world. They all lie in the Haut Médoc.

The Médoc wine district comprises two distinct areas, and the name is used with several different connotations. Geographically, it applies to the whole of the peninsula, stretching some 60 miles from the border brook, the Jalle de Blanquefort, just north of the city of Bordeaux, to the Pointe de Grave at the mouth of the Gironde. As an *appellation contrôlée*, Médoc

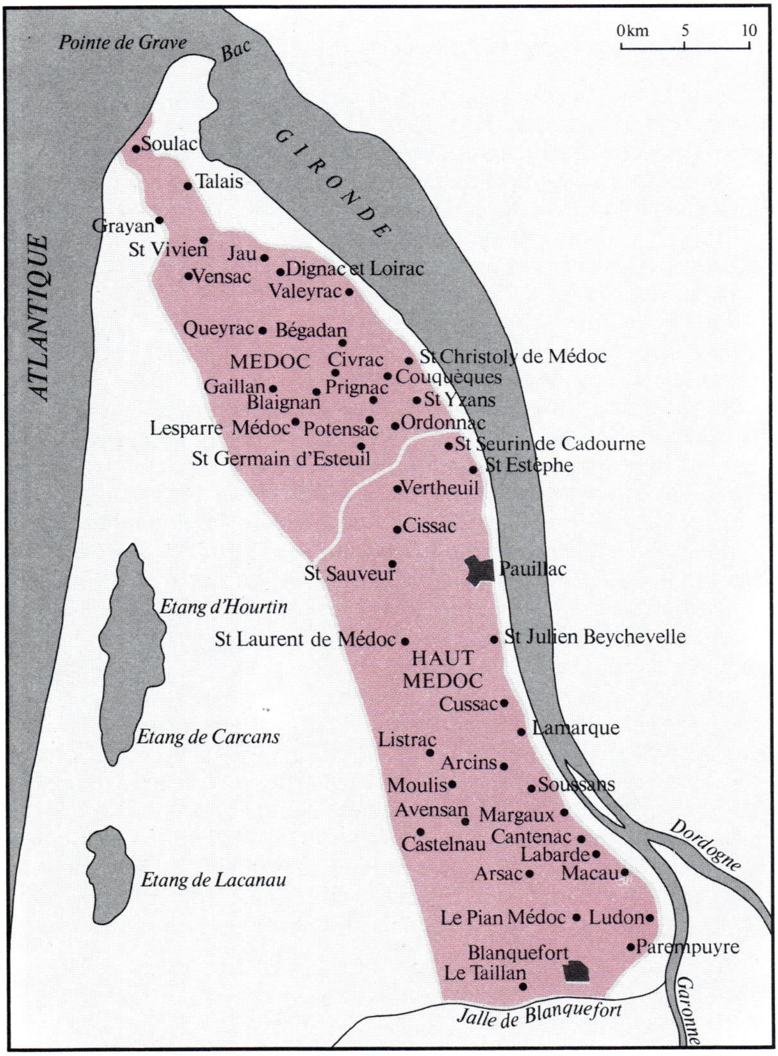

COMMUNES OF THE
HAUT MEDOC

Arcins
Arsac
Avensan
Blanquefort
Cantenac
Castelnau
Cissac
Cussac
Labarde
Lamarque
Listrac
Ludon
Macau
Margaux
Moulis
Parempuyre
Pauillac
Le Pian Médoc
St Estèphe
St Julien
St Laurent de Médoc
St Sauveur
St Seurin de Cadourne
Soussans
Le Taillan
Vertheuil

COMMUNES OF THE
MEDOC

Bégadan
Blaignan
Civrac
Couquèques
Dignac et Loirac
Gaillan
Jau
Lesparre
Ordonnac
Potensac
Prignac
Queyrac
St Christoly de Médoc
St Germain d'Esteuil
St Vivien
St Yzans
Valeyrac
Vensac

belongs properly to the northern area of the peninsula, known geographically as the Bas Médoc, which begins at St Germain d'Esteuil. The *appellation* and the geographical name for the southern section is Haut Médoc; this area is three times the size of the Bas Médoc, and its output of wine is in proportion and of superior quality. However, the name is often given loosely to the wines and the geography of both areas – a fact which can cause confusion both in the trade and to the consumer.

The best vineyards in the Haut Médoc lie on the slopes overlooking the Gironde Estuary, within a narrow strip of land no more than a mile or so wide and 30 miles long. The soil is of gravel and sand, with the larger pebbles thrusting through to the surface to hold the heat of the sun and reflect it back in the night hours onto the bunches of grapes on their low-cropped vines.

The micro-climate of the whole Médoc district is uniquely soft and damp, wedged as it is between the restless Atlantic and the more sedate estuary of the Gironde. The vineyards are protected from the rigours of the Atlantic by a broad band of pine forests which skirts the coastline southwards.

In the Médoc the grapes used for red wines are the *cépages fins*, the classic varieties of Bordeaux; these are the Cabernet Sauvignon, the Cabernet Franc and the Merlot. Malbec and Petit Verdot are also added, but in small quantities. Pride of place is accorded to the Cabernet Sauvignon. As a result, Médoc reds tend to be firmer and harder than others in Bordeaux; this is especially so when they are young and contain a lot of tannin and are purple in colour. The high tannin level, on the other hand, means that they have a strong capacity for ageing, and given time they mature with great elegance, developing in the process what for many is their most attractive feature, a lingering fragrant bouquet.

In a good year the total output of *appellation contrôlée* wine from the Médoc can be as much as 420,000 hectolitres, which represents some 50 million bottles of wine. Almost half of this comes from the four Haut Médoc communes already mentioned, assuring a ready availability of Médoc wines in overseas markets. It is the product of 50 big estates, some 450 smaller growers and fourteen or so cooperatives. The latter in their turn process the grapes from many hundreds of other small vineyards.

The quality of the wine is regulated by two regional *appellations – Haut Médoc* and *Médoc*, of which the latter signifies the wines from any of the 18 communes in the Bas Médoc. The former covers the wines of 26 communes from Blanquefort in the very south to St Seurin de Cadourne just to the north of St Estèphe. The pre-eminence of six of these – Margaux (including the communes of Arsac, Labarde, Cantenac and Soussand), Moulis, Listrac, St Julien, Pauillac and St Estèphe – entitles them to individual *appellations*.

The commune of Pauillac boasts the largest number of leading classified wines, and has three of the first growths – Château Lafite Rothschild, Château Latour and Château Mouton Rothschild. The finest Pauillacs have a full-bodied quality unsurpassed among Bordeaux wines; they boast a depth and concentration of colour, an elegant, powerful bouquet, and a rich, velvety texture quite free from any coarseness. They have a great capacity for keeping and development, and can be very long-lived.

St Julien wines are lighter in style, with more finesse and suppleness, but still more full-bodied than their southern neighbours in Margaux. They are described by Michael Broadbent, Christie's wine expert and author of *Wine Tasting*, as 'copybook claret'. Wines purporting to be generic St Juliens should be approached with caution.

Margaux wines tend not to be so powerful; they are characterized by their perfume and delicacy, great breed and elegance, and a soft velvety texture. They are often described as the most feminine of the clarets. Within an overall similarity they can however be variable in quality as the *appellation*

SAMPLE TASTING

(1) A good generic from one of the bigger shippers.

(2) A good bourgeois growth, say from St Estèphe: Château de Pez, perhaps, or Château Phelan Ségur.

(3) A leading growth from the Haut Médoc which has no distinctive regional connotation – e.g. Château La Lagune.

(4) A classified Margaux – Château Brane Cantenac, perhaps.

(5) A classified St Julien: for preference, Château Léoville Las Cases, Château Ducru Beaucaillou or Château Beychevelle.

(6) A classified Pauillac – Château Lynch Bages or Château Pichon Longueville Baron (the Lalande is often better, but is not so typical of Pauillac); Château Haut Batailley or Château Grand Puy Lacoste are alternatives.

extends to the neighbouring communes of Cantenac and Soussons on the north and Arsac and Labarde on the south.

Against the general tendency in the Médoc, which is for the wines to become fuller bodied, firmer and to an extent coarser as one goes north, the wines of St Estèphe, the most northerly of the four leading communes, are if anything less robust than the Pauillacs – but they are sturdy and powerful, and they are generally more fruity. The overall output of wine is large, and the commune is especially strong in good bourgeois growths.

The *bouquet* of a good Médoc is positive, that is to say well-projected, coming out of the glass to meet you, yet at the same time subtle and elusive, delicate yet definite, and fruity with firm undertones. In the mouth the flavour expands in response to the new-found warmth; firm and well-structured without coarseness, it fills the mouth but remains remarkably delicate. At the end, there is still something clean and fresh about the taste, whether it be a young and vigorous wine or a mature one at its zenith.

Even in poor years, Médoc wines do not tend to fall much below par. The best years are always slow in maturing: the wines are not really at their best in under ten years, and they will keep considerably longer. Lesser vintages are quicker to mature and ready to drink earlier.

MEDOC GAZETTEER

KEY TO SYMBOLS

● *grand cru classé*
○ *cru exceptionnel*
★ Peppercorn rating
■ average annual output of red wine, per case of 12 bottles
□ average annual output of white wine, per case of 12 bottles
Italic after the name indicates communes.

L'Abbé Gorsse *Margaux* ★ 4,000■ A bourgeois growth to be noted.
d'Agassac *Ludon* ★★ 10,000■ Now recognized as an outstanding *cru grand bourgeois*.
Andron Blanquet *St Estèphe* ★★ 6,000■ An outstanding *cru grand bourgeois* which has long enjoyed a reputation for quality.
Aney *Cussac* 1,000■ A small bourgeois growth.
○ **d'Angludet** *Cantenac* ★★★ 10,000 ■ An exceptionally fine unclassified wine; classed as a 4th growth up to the time of the French Revolution; placed just below the 5th growths in 1855; *appellation* Margaux.
d'Arche *Ludon* ★ 2,000■ *Cru grand bourgeois*; one of the better Ludon wines. Marketed exclusively by Dourthe Frères.
Ballac *St Laurent* 20,000■ A reconstituted vineyard, surrounding an 18th century château; the wine is at present categorized as *cru bourgeois*.
Barateau *St Laurent* 500■ A lesser known bourgeois growth.
● **Batailley** *Pauillac* ★★★ 20,000■ Classified as a 5th growth in 1855, a wine of quality which more than holds that position; has shown great consistency, though less full-bodied than some other classified Pauillacs except in best years; distributed by Borie-Manoux.
Beaumont *Cussac* ★ 10,000■ A wine of fine colour and delicacy of flavour; *cru grand bourgeois*.
Beau Rivage *Macau* 7,500■ An *appellation* Bordeaux Supérieur marketed by Borie-Manoux; full, fruity and well-balanced.
Beauséjour *St Estèphe* 6,000■ An attractive bourgeois growth with body and finesse.
Beau Site *St Estèphe* ★★ 13,000■ A rounded, elegant and outstanding *cru grand bourgeois*, neighbour of the illustrious Calon Ségur; owned by Borie-Manoux.
Beau Site Haut Vignoble *St Estèphe* ★ 6,000■ A bourgeois growth of good standing, unconnected neighbour of Beau Site.
Le Bécade *Listrac* ★ 5,000■ A mellow, bourgeois growth, some of it sold by Dourthe Frères under the name of Château La Fleur Bécade.
La Bégorce Zédé *Soussans* ★★ 6,000■ Notable bourgeois growth; *appellation* Margaux.
○ **Bel Air Marquis d'Aligre** *Soussans* ★★★ 5,000■ A consistent wine of finesse and breeding, regarded as of classified growth quality; *appellation* Margaux.
Bel Air La Grave *Moulis* 4,000■ A bourgeois growth situated on the Grand Poujeaux slopes.
● **Belgrave** *St Laurent* ★★ 12,000■ Classified as a *grand cru classé* 5th growth in 1855; can be quite attractive but is not up to its previous standing; on the edge of St Julien, and similar in character.
Bellegrave *Pauillac* ★ 2,000■ An excellent bourgeois wine; the vineyard is surrounded by *grands crus* Latour and Pichon Longueville.
Bellegrave *Listrac* 3,000■ Bourgeois growth; one of the better Listrac wines.
Bellerose *Pauillac* 3,500■ A bourgeois growth, sought after because situated in the midst of celebrated neighbours – notably Lafite and Pontet Canet.
des Belles Graves *Ordonnac et Potensac* 3,000■ A good but not outstanding Bas Médoc growth.
Bel Orme Tronquoy de Lalande *St Seurin de Cadourne* ★★ 12,000■ A vigorous, full-bodied wine, with the generosity of a St Estèphe but less finesse and bouquet, which ages well; marketed by Ginestet; Croizet Bages and Rauzan Gassies have same owner; *cru grand bourgeois*.
● **Beychevelle** *St Julien* ★★★★ 2,500■ A 4th growth in 1855, now regarded at its best as of 2nd growth quality; 'a good year for Bordeaux is a good year for Beychevelle'.
Bonneau *Avensan* 1,200■ A small vineyard, and a minor growth.
Le Bosq *St Estèphe* ★ 7,000■ A long-established vineyard, making a good bourgeois wine.
Le Bourdieu *Vertheuil* 15,000■ Full-bodied, bourgeois growth from the Haut Médoc.
● **Boyd Cantenac** *Margaux* ★★ 2,000■ Classified as a 3rd growth in 1855, but now thought to be of no more than 5th growth standing.
● **Branaire Ducru** *St Julien* ★★★ 12,000■ A big, full-bodied, robust wine that has improved in recent years; a 4th growth in 1855, but has been bought at 2nd and 3rd growth prices.
● **Brane Cantenac** *Cantenac* ★★★★ 20,000■ Typifies Margaux; one of the largest vineyards in the Médoc which retains its position as a 2nd growth; meticulously run; same owners as Durfort Vivens, Villegeorges and Climens.
de Breuilh *Cissac* ★ 10,000■ A bourgeois wine, not unlike a St Estèphe in character; one of the four best Cissac growths.
de la Bridane *St Julien* ★ 5,000■ Originally known as Moulin de la Bridane; bourgeois growth, made from Cabernet grapes only; exported to the UK and the US.
Brillette *Moulis* ★ 7,000■ A mellow, full-bodied *cru grand bourgeois*, worth looking out for.

Bouqueyran *Moulis* ★4,000■ Another bourgeois growth worth looking out for; also produces a full-bodied white.
de By *Bégadan* 2,000■ Among the better known Bégadan growths.
Le Caillou (see **Talbot**).
● **Calon Ségur** *St Estèphe* ★★★★15,000■ 3rd growth 1855, now rated as good as a 2nd; consistent, robust, supple, with character and breed.

● **Camensac** *St Laurent* ★★★15,000■ An 1855 5th growth of vigour, breed and attraction; it lacks its previous standing but has recently made significant progress under new management.
Canteloup *St Estèphe* ★8,000■ A good bourgeois wine; the estate is administered with that of La Commanderie.
● **Cantemerle** *Macau* ★★★★7,500■ The last in the list of classified growths in 1855, but now of outstanding quality and rated as good as a 2nd growth; exquisite, fine, strongly pronounced bouquet, and good keeping qualities; the vineyard has a high proportion of old vines and uses very traditional methods.
● **Cantenac Brown** *Cantenac* ★★★7,000■ A 3rd growth in 1855; it is not so well thought of now, but is still an elegant wine with an abundant bouquet; *appellation* Margaux.
Canuet *Margaux* 1,600■ A small vineyard producing a vigorous bourgeois wine.
Capbern Gasqueton *St Estèphe* ★★ 10,000■ An outstanding *cru grand bourgeois* with a noticeable softness; marketed by Dourthe Frères.
Cap Léon Veyrin *Listrac* 1,000■ One of several small bourgeois growths carrying the Veyrin name in the neighbourhood of La Bécade and Bellegrave.
Carcannieux les Graves *Queyrac* 1,000■ Light attractive wine; a long established *cru bourgeois* and the only wine of note from this northern commune, east of Bégadan.
La Cardonne *Blaignan* ★★20,000■ Large northern Médoc vineyard, producing a mellow, good quality *cru grand bourgeois*.
Caronne Ste Gemme *St Laurent* ★★ 15,000■ An exceptionally fine *cru grand bourgeois*; lasts well, has delicate bouquet and fine colour; worth looking out for.
Carruades Lafite *Pauillac* ★★★★ This was the 2nd growth from Château Lafite, from grapes grown on the Carruades plateau, until discontinued in 1967; a similar wine has recently been produced called Thoulin des Carruades.
du Cartillon *Lamarque* 9,000■ A bourgeois growth from the heart of the Médoc, between Margaux and St Julien.
Castelnau (see **Laujac**).
du Castera *St Germain d'Esteuil* ★15,000■ A good bourgeois growth, not far from St Estèphe; shipped by Alexis Lichine.
Chambert *St Estèphe* 3,000■ A lesser-known bourgeois growth.
○ **Chasse Spleen** *Moulis* ★★★18,000■ One of seven *crus exceptionnels* listed just below the 5th growths in 1855; now merits a more formal classification; has a subtle nose, combining richness and vinosity with finesse; marketed by Ginestet.
La Chesnaye Ste Gemme *Cussac* ★5,000■ A *cru bourgeois* with finesse and an attractive bouquet; from a vineyard close to the border with St Julien; same ownership as Lanessan.
Cissac *Cissac* ★★3,500■ One of the best growths from the commune, not unlike a St Estèphe; lies only 2km to the west of Château Lafite; a leading *cru grand bourgeois*.
Citran *Avensan* ★★10,000■ In effect two vineyards, one on gravel, the other on clay and limestone; *cru grand bourgeois*.
● **Clerc Milon Mondon** *Pauillac* ★★★5,000■ A classified 5th growth in 1955, now thought to be of average quality; belongs to Mouton.
Clos du Marquis *St Julien* ★★ The old part of the Léonville Las Cases vineyard; the *marque* usually occurs only in abundant years; high proportion of Merlot and young vines.
Clos du Moulin *St Christoly de Médoc* 2,500■ Small Médoc vineyard, grouped with a cluster of big producers, including St Christoly, Tour St Bonnet and La Tour Blanche.
La Closerie Grand Poujeaux *Moulis* ★ 3,800■ Good bourgeois growth worth looking for.
Colombier Monpelou *Pauillac* ★★500■ A tiny *cru grand bourgeois* of good repute.
La Commanderie *St Estèphe* ★5,000■ Originally a command-post of the Knights Templar; produces a full-bodied wine of the same standing as Canteloup.
Corconnac *St Laurent* 1,500■ Small vineyard producing a good bourgeois wine.
● **Cos d'Estournel** *St Estèphe* ★★★★ 20,000■ A wine with body, finesse, balance and a steady quality, even in off years; a 2nd great growth in 1855, it continues to display great elegance and generosity; at its best a very fine wine indeed and, after a lean patch in the 1960s, it is now in top form.
● **Cos Labory** *St Estèphe* ★★★6,000■ An 1855 5th growth which continues to hold that standing.
Coufran *St Seurin de Cadourne* ★★15,000■ One of the four good growths from this commune, the northernmost in the Haut Médoc; it has less bouquet and finesse, but is otherwise similar to a St Estèphe; *cru grand bourgeois*.
○ **La Couronne** *Pauillac* ★★★1,500■ An excellent bourgeois wine, remarkable for its balance and harmony; in same ownership as Ducru Beaucaillou and Haut Batailley, it is vinified and matured in the cellars of Ducru.
La Cour Pavillon *St Yzans* ★ A *vin de marque* marketed by Gilbey S.A. of Château Loudenne; maintains good standard.
Coutelin Merville *St Estèphe* ★6,000■ *Cru grand bourgeois*; neighbour of Mac-Carthy and Beau Site.
Le Crock *St Estèphe* ★★15,000■ *Cru grand bourgeois* of outstanding quality and big output.
La Croix Landon *Bégadan* 5,000■ Northern Médoc bourgeois growth, marketed by Dourthe Frères.
● **Croizet Bages** *Pauillac* ★★★6,000■ A big, generous fleshy wine, made almost entirely from Cabernet Sauvignon grapes; maintains the 5th growth position it was accorded in 1855; marketed by Ginestet; same owners as Rauzan Gassies and Bel Orme Tronquoy de Lalande.
La Dame Blanche *Blanquefort* 5,000□ One of the few Médoc white wines marketed in UK, US and elsewhere by Maison Cruse. The *appellation* is Bordeaux.
● **Dauzac** *Labarde* ★★★10,000■ 5th growth 1855 which takes the Margaux *appellation*; a full-bodied wine, harder than some and taking longer to develop.
Dillon *Blanquefort* ★★7,000■ Owned by the agricultural school of Bordeaux Blanquefort; one of the most important growths in the commune. Also makes a small quantity of white wine
Domeyne *St Estèphe* 1,000■ A small

White grapes are tipped into a Vaslin, the horizontal wine-press now widely used in Bordeaux for the vinification of dry white wine. The juice is then fermented separately; with red grapes, by contrast, it is left to ferment on the pips and skins of the fruit.

bourgeois growth, situated on the best hills of St Estèphe, made from old French vines.

● **Ducru Beaucaillou** *St Julien* ★★★★★ 20,000■ 2nd growth Médoc in 1855, situated on fine gravel slopes alongside the river; today often rivals Léoville Las Cases as the best of the St Julien wines; generous, full-bodied and of great elegance, its quality and reputation is steadily growing.

● **Duhart Milon Rothschild** *Pauillac* ★★★ 12,000■ Now has a better standing than its 4th growth 1855 classification; managed by the Rothschild family with Château Lafite; less body than some Pauillacs, but long-lasting, and on the up and up.

Duplessis Fabre *Moulis* 1,000■ A small bourgeois growth of note.

Duplessis Hauchecorne *Moulis* ★ 13,000■ *Cru grand bourgeois*, worth looking out for; marketed by Mestrezat Preller.

● **Durfort Vivens** *Margaux* ★★★★ 8,000■ One of the best 2nd growths in 1855, with an already established reputation; more recently has fallen away, but is now enjoying a new life with a change of ownership; the vineyard is in the best part of Margaux; the wine is delicate, with a fine bouquet, and is aged in underground cellars.

Dutruch Grand Poujeaux *Moulis* ★★★ 5,000■ An exceptional *cru grand bourgeois* which bids well to be a classified wine; combines a distinctive richness and vinosity with finesse.

L'Ermitage *Listrac* 1,800■ Supple, mellow wine, made from Merlot and Cabernet grapes, marketed by Ginestet.

● **Ferrière** *Margaux* ★★ 2,000■ Smallest *grand cru classé* of 1855, 3rd growth, which produces a fine wine, not always up to its class; managed with Château Lascombes.

La Fleur Milon *Pauillac* ★ 4,000■ A *cru grand bourgeois* which keeps well; neighbour of Lafite and Mouton Rothschild.

Fonbadet *Pauillac* ★ 10,000■ An excellent bourgeois wine; neighbour of Pontet Canet.

Fonpiqueyre *St Sauveur* ★ 6,000■ A reconstituted vineyard (see **Liversan**).

Fonréaud *Listrac* ★ 15,000■ A good bourgeois growth, one of the better of the Listrac wines.

Fontesteau *St Sauveur* ★ 5,000■ A fine full-bodied wine which has improved its standing to a *cru grand bourgeois*.

Fort Médoc *Cussac* 8,000■ Generous and fruity wine with a delicate nose; marketed by Ginestet.

Fort du Vauban *Cussac* ★ 2,000■ Bourgeois growth of great suppleness.

Les Forts de Latour *Pauillac* ★★★★ 5,000■ A selection from part of the Château Latour vineyard, with the characteristics of its illustrious namesake; matures more quickly.

Fourcas Dupré *Listrac* ★★ 5,000■ A robust *cru grand bourgeois*, less good than the best of Moulis, but among the best in Listrac.

Fourcas Hostein *Listrac* ★★★ 7,000■ An outstanding *cru grand bourgeois*; formerly made and matured with Gressier Grand Poujeaux; new management has greatly enhanced its standing.

La France *Blaignan* 1,500■ A small-holding in the northern Médoc with an improving reputation.

La Fuie St Bonnet *St Christoly de Médoc* 5,000■ A little-known St Christoly wine.

Gallais Bellevue *Ordonnac et Potensac* ★ 4,000■ A good bourgeois growth; part of a group from this northern commune which also includes Potensac and Lassalle, run by Château Léonville Las Cases with the same care and attention.

● **Giscours** *Labarde* ★★★★ 20,000■ From the commune of Labarde, but lapping over into three others, this large 3rd growth vineyard produces a wine that has not always been up to its class but has become very consistent in recent years; at its best light, graceful, perfumed and elegant, characteristic of its Margaux *appellation*.

du Glana *St Julien* ★★ 2,000■ An outstanding *cru grand bourgeois* with a big output, often seen abroad.

Gloria *St Julien* ★★★ 4,500■ Widely known and appreciated, this bourgeois wine has undoubted great growth standing – rich, fine and delicately bouqueted. The vineyard has been built up with parcels of vines from surrounding great growth St Julien estates; its second wine is Haut Beychevelle Gloria.

Gobinaud *Listrac* 3,000■ A small bourgeois growth set between Listrac and Grand Poujeaux.

Grand Clapeau Olivier *Blanquefort* 2,500■ A bourgeois wine, one of few from Blanquefort to be noted.

Grand Duroc Milon *Pauillac* ★ 1,500■ Like Bellerose, a small but excellent vineyard hemmed in by prestigious neighbours under the same ownership.

Grand Listrac *Listrac* ★ The Cave Co-opérative of the commune, with a reputation for quality.

● **Grand Puy Ducasse** *Pauillac* ★★★ 4,000■ Big, robust, very typical Pauillac wine; is now better considered than the 5th growth it was accorded in 1855; fuller, more vigorous than Grand Puy Lacoste; the vineyard was recently greatly extended.

● **Grand Puy Lacoste** *Pauillac* ★★★★ 10,000■ Also a 5th growth in 1855, now sells at 3rd and 4th growth prices; fairly full-bodied, elegant and with a fine bouquet; has a splendid reputation for consistency.

Grand St Julien *St Julien* ★ 3,000■ Used to be part of Léoville Las Cases, now a separate château. Marketed by Borie-Manoux.

Grand Village Capbern *St Estèphe* ★ 1,000■ Sold by Dourthe Frères; a bourgeois wine with breed and mellowness.

Gressier Grand Poujeaux *Moulis* ★★★ 4,000■ A distinctive wine, which combines richness and vinosity with finesse; one of several Moulis wines bidding to be classified.

Greysac *Bégadan* ★ 8,000■ A *cru grand bourgeois*, well-known in the United States.

● **Gruaud Larose** *St Julien* ★★★★★ 20,000■ 2nd growth 1855, maintaining its high standard; somewhat more body and less finesse than Ducru Beaucaillou, also a St Julien 2nd growth; marketed by Cordier.

La Gurgue Curton *Margaux* ★ 3,000■ A quality bourgeois wine with finesse, vigour and a delicate bouquet; in the centre of a group of Margaux great growths, part of the vineyard is made up of pieces from Rauzan Gassies, Lascombes and Malescot St Exupéry.

Hanteillan *Cissac* ★ 1,500■ A fairly big estate; one of the principal wines of Cissac; *cru grand bourgeois*.

Haut Bages Averous *Pauillac* ★★ 3,000■ Excellent bourgeois wine, enjoying a reputation at home and abroad; adjoins Lynch Bages and under the same management.

● **Haut Bages Libéral** *Pauillac* ★★ 9,000■ Smooth and delicate wine; 5th growth in 1855; owned by Cruse.

Haut Bages Monpelou *Pauillac* ★ 5,000■ Excellent bourgeois wine; originally part of the Duhart Milon vineyard.

● **Haut Batailley** *Pauillac* ★★★ 7,000■ Formerly part of Batailley, a 5th growth in 1855, it is now matured to produce an excellent wine which rivals Batailley in its own right.

Haut Marbuzet *St Estèphe* ★★ 20,000■ An exceptional *cru grand bourgeois*, fruity and full of charm.

Haut Pauillac *Pauillac* One of four adjoining properties in the same ownership, adjacent to Mouton Rothschild; the others are La Tour du Roc Milon, Padarnac and Montgrand Milon, all bourgeois growths.

Houissant *St Estèphe* ★ 10,000■ A good bourgeois wine, grown on pure gravel.

● **d'Issan** *Cantenac* ★★★ 8,000■ Attractive 3rd growth, typical of Margaux; belongs to a branch of the Cruse family who have restored the beautiful medieval château.

● **Kirwan** *Cantenac* ★★ 6,000■ Another 3rd growth from Cantenac but not quite so highly thought of as d'Issan; a delicate wine which develops bouquet and finesse with age.

de Labat *St Laurent* 2,500■ A smaller vineyard owned by the Nony-Borie family, who produce Caronne Ste Gemme; *cru bourgeois*.

de Labégorce *Margaux* ★★ 10,000■ Good bourgeois wine, marketed by Dourthe Frères; predominance of the Cabernet grape gives it ageing qualities.

Laffitte Carcasset *St Estèphe* ★ 6,000■ A good bourgeois wine of great finesse, made from old French vines.

Lafite Canteloup *Ludon* 2,000■ A good quality bourgeois wine, grown on sandy, gravelly soil; the vineyard was reconstituted in 1957.

● **Lafite Rothschild** *Pauillac* ★★★★★ 20,000■ 1st great growth 1855, with a very big output; at its best the greatest of the Bordeaux reds – a remarkable combination of power with grace, richness with finesse, and a bouquet of unforgettable distinction and beauty; attributed with 'the taste of almonds and the perfume of violets'; apart from classic vintages like 1953 and 1961 has not consistently lived up to its reputation.
Lafitte Laujac (see **Laujac**).
Lafon *Listrac* ★ 3,000■ A full-bodied wine of some finesse, grown on gravel from old vines; run together with La Bécade.
● **Lafon Rochet** *St Estèphe* ★★★ 15,000■ A 4th growth in 1855; the vines borrow qualities from distinguished neighbours to give the wine finesse and bouquet; has made great strides since the early 1960s under new ownership.
● **Lagrange** *St Julien* ★★★ 20,000■ A 3rd growth 1855 which has not maintained that high level, and is now of average but consistent St Julien quality.
● **La Lagune** *Ludon* ★★★★ 20,000■ A 3rd growth in 1855 and geographically the most southern of the great growths; a full-bodied, fruity wine with a marvellous bouquet. The vineyard has been extensively replanted and the wine has recently been on the light side – but its quality improves with almost every vintage.
Lamarque *Lamarque* ★★ 10,000■ A *cru grand bourgeois* from the heart of the Médoc; its splendid château is a medieval castle.
Lambert *Pauillac* An excellent bourgeois wine.
Lamorère *Moulis* 10,000■ Vineyard established in the late 19th century; the wine is a full-bodied, balanced and generous bourgeois; marketed by Dourthe Frères.
Lamothe *Cissac* ★ 16,500■ Reconstructed and improving vineyard; one of the four best bourgeois growths in the commune. Wine is not dissimilar to that of St Estèphe; *cru grand bourgeois*.
Lamothe de Bergeron *Cussac* ★ 6,000■ Wines of roundness and vigour of *cru grand bourgeois* quality.
Landon *Bégadan* ★ 4,000■ A good northern Médoc growth; neighbour of Château Greysac.
Lanessan *Cussac* ★★★ 10,000■ A fine, full-bodied wine from what is now regarded as an outstanding growth of classified quality; somewhat resembles a St Julien, but firmer; the château possesses an interesting collection of coaches and carriages, which can be viewed on request.
● **Langoa Barton** *St Julien* ★★★ 6,000■ A good consistent wine, which does not quite maintain its 1855 3rd growth rating; owned with Léoville Barton by the Barton family and distributed by Barton & Guestier.
Larose Trintandon *St Laurent* 80,000■ A large holding bordering on Pauillac and St Julien and incorporating five older estates; a *cru grand bourgeois*, not always consistent, but can be fine and full-bodied; the vineyard was entirely reconstituted in 1965–6.
● **Lascombes** *Margaux* ★★★ 20,000■ Flowery, full-flavoured, elegant wine; the vineyard has been reconstituted and is making steady progress; its high reputation generally preserves its 2nd growth status accorded in 1855; however, several recent vintages have been below standard.
Lassalle *Ordonnac et Potensac* ★ 3,000■ The vineyard is held and operated jointly with Potensac and Gallais Bellevue; *cru bourgeois*.
● **Latour** *Pauillac* ★★★★★ 25,000■ Unquestionably a 1st great growth in 1855, and still one of the world's great red wines; tremendous colour, full-bodied, slow to develop, becoming firm and rich with age: the quality is considerable even in years when other wines are poorer.
Laujac *Bégadan* ★ 5,000■ A good northern Médoc growth, held by Cruse since 1852; also produces Lafitte Laujac, La Tour Cordouan and Castelnau; *cru grand bourgeois*.
● **Léoville Barton** *St Julien* ★★★★ 10,000■ Has belonged to the same proprietors, the Barton family, longer than any other classed growth except possibly Las Cases, of which it was formerly a part; can make a wine which is sometimes richer and fuller than the other Léovilles.
● **Léoville Las Cases** *St Julien* ★★★★★ 20,000■ A wine of finesse and elegance, great richness and vigour, and a well-developed bouquet; the estate is large, stretching along the west bank of the Gironde from Beychevelle to Latour (in Pauillac); generally considered the best of the 2nd growths established in 1855 and of the three Léovilles; part of the output is sold as Clos du Marquis (*qv*).
● **Léoville Poyferré** *St Julien* ★★★★ 17,000■ Also an 1855 2nd growth and originally formed from the same vineyard as the Las Cases and Barton; a wine of great character and breed in the same mould; while Las Cases is usually the best of the three, Poyferré is sometimes better than Barton, and vice versa.
Lestage *Listrac* ★ 18,000■ A *cru grand bourgeois*, one of the best Listrac growths.
Lieujean *St Sauveur* Light, agreeable bourgeois wine from just north of St Laurent.
Liversan *St Sauveur* ★★ 7,000■ The most notable St Sauveur growth and similar to lesser Pauillac growths; the estate also produces Fonpiqueyre and des Moulinets, both wines of quality.
Livran *St Germain d'Esteuil* ★ 15,000■ A good, fruity, northern Médoc growth, with softness and body.
Loudenne *St Yzans* ★★ 10,000■ 1,000□ A good red wine from one of the largest of the northern Médoc vineyards, recently reclassified as a *cru grand bourgeois*; owned by W. A. Gilbey since 1875; the small output of white wine (AC Bordeaux Supérieur) is good and dry; château has an interesting exhibition of old vineyard and cellar implements.
● **Lynch Bages** *Pauillac* ★★★★ 20,000■ Lynch Bages was designated as a 5th growth in 1855, but has improved considerably since then; in recent years it has established a fine reputation for quality and consistency, worthy of a 2nd growth.
● **Lynch Moussas** *Pauillac* ★★★★ 5,000■ Small 5th growth 1855 which produces an attractive but not always outstanding full-bodied wine.
Mac Carthy *St Estèphe* ★★ 2,000■ Good quality growth, situated between Cos d'Estournel and Montrose; *cru grand bourgeois*.
● **Malescot St Exupéry** *Margaux* ★★★ 8,000■ Named after its 17th century owner, Simon Malescot, and his 19th century successor, the Comte de St Exupéry, 3rd growth 1855; a wine of finesse and distinction which has held its rating; a bit on the light side, but a characteristic Margaux with delicacy and a fine bouquet.
de Marbuzet *St Estèphe* ★★ 5,000■ Outstanding *cru grand bourgeois* – full-bodied, fruity with a vinosity in keeping with St Estèphe; owned by Ginestet with Cos d'Estournel.
● **Margaux** *Margaux* ★★★★★ 18,000■ 1st growth 1855, owned and marketed by Ginestet until recently, when it was bought by the owner of a large French supermarket chain. It is not the most consistent of the first growths, but at its best it is incomparable, for its nobility, refinement and flavour and for its distinctive bouquet and marvellous balance. There is also a dry white wine known as Pavillon Blanc du Château Margaux.
(N.B. Château Margaux should not be confused with the blended commune wine which is simply indicated by the word 'Margaux' on the label and is not at all of the same quality.)
● **Marquis d'Alesme Becker** *Margaux* ★★ 4,000■ A 3rd growth in the 1855 classification, this small vineyard occupies one of the finest positions in Margaux, but has not established itself as an outstanding wine.
Marquis de St Estèphe *St Estèphe* ★ This is a large and reputable co-operative selling the wine of a number of small bourgeois proprietors.
● **Marquis de Terme** *Margaux* ★★★ 15,000■ Although a 4th growth in 1855, this wine can sell at 2nd growth prices; it has great finesse and consistency.
Marsac Séguineaux *Soussans* ★ 4,000■ Makes claims to be one of the best Haut Médoc bourgeois growths; marketed exclusively by Mestrezat Preller; *appellation* Margaux.
Martinens *Cantenac* ★★ 5,000■ Noteworthy *cru grand bourgeois*, characteristic of Margaux in bouquet and elegance.
Maucaillou *Moulis* ★★ 4,000■ A newly reconstructed vineyard, exclusive to Dourthe Frères; an exceptionally good bourgeois growth which is worth looking out for.
Maucamps *Macau* 1,300■ Good bourgeois growth, well-balanced and full of flavour.
Meyney *St Estèphe* ★★ 20,000■ A big estate, close to the Gironde, which produces a *cru grand bourgeois* of exceptional quality; the same owner runs Talbot and Gruaud Larose, both St Julien 2nd growths; marketed by Cordier.
Montgrand Milon *Pauillac* (see **Haut Pauillac** and **Padarnac**).
du Monthil *Bégadan* 2 000■ Northern Médoc bourgeois growth, situated near Château Landon and Château Greysac.
● **Montrose** *St Estèphe* ★★★★ 24,000■ A big vineyard which slopes gently down to the river; 2nd growth in 1855; a full-bodied wine, tending to be stubborn at first, its reputation has grown considerably in recent years; many now think it the best wine in the district.

Morin *St Estèphe* ★ 5,000■ A sound, well-made wine; *cru grand bourgeois*.
Moulin de la Bridane *St Julien* 800■ A minor bourgeois growth; originally the name of Château de la Bridane and next door to it.
Moulin de Laborde *Listrac* 2,500■ A lesser Listrac bourgeois growth, near to Bellegrave.
du Moulin Rouge *Cussac* 4,000■ *Cru bourgeois*, owned by the same family for 200 years; the wine has finesse and quality.
Moulin de St Vincent *Moulis* 5,000■ Robust, full-bodied bourgeois growth, marketed by Ginestet.
Moulin à Vent *Moulis* ★ 5,000■ *Cru grand bourgeois*, worth looking out for.
des Moulinets *St Sauveur* (see **Liversan**).
Moulis *Moulis* 3,000■ A noteworthy bourgeois growth.
Mouton Baron Philippe *Pauillac* ★★★★ 15,000■ Took its name in 1956, being originally Mouton d'Armailhacq; the vineyard lies at the foot of the celebrated Mouton Rothschild and is in the same ownership; the wine enjoys a fine reputation in its own right.
Mouton Cadet The largest selling branded claret in the world. Blended to a consistent standard, it is a fruity wine with a fine bouquet; it is now made from quite separately grown grapes, although it started life as off-vintage Mouton Rothschild.
● **Mouton Rothschild** *Pauillac* ★★★★★ 25,000■ Was a 2nd growth in 1855, but has been classified as a 1st since 1973, alongside Lafite, Latour, Margaux and Haut Brion. Hard and slow to mature, it is full-bodied, elegant and rich – a wine of great vinosity and delicate bouquet, developing more quickly than Latour.
Nexon Lemogne *Ludon* ★ 2,000■ A bourgeois growth of quality.
Les Ormes de Pez *St Estèphe* ★★ 10,000■ *Cru grand bourgeois*, recognized as one of the best in the commune; a rich and mellow wine, in the same ownership as Lynch Bages.
Les Ormes de Sorbet *Couquèques* 4,000■ A solitary Couquèques representative, which has achieved *cru grand bourgeois* standing.
Padarnac *Pauillac* 1,000■ A small *cru bourgeois* in an ensemble of growths embracing Haut Pauillac, Montgrand Milon, and La Tour du Roc Milon.
● **Palmer** *Cantenac* ★★★★★ 12,000■ A 3rd growth 1855 which is considered today as of 2nd growth standard and among the best wines of the region; a rich, fairly full-bodied wine with a penetrating bouquet; *appellation* Margaux.

Panigon *Civrac* 5,000■ 2,000□ One of the four or five vineyards of any note in this northern commune.
Patache d'Aux *Bégadan* ★★ 1,500■ Good northern Médoc growth which shows finesse; *cru grand bourgeois*.
Paveil de Luze *Soussans* ★★ 3,500■ A *cru grand bourgeois* of note; *appellation* Margaux.
Pavillon Blanc (see **Margaux**).
● **Pédesclaux** *Pauillac* ★★ 6,000■ 5th growth 1855, but has lost its reputation and lacks consistency.
Peyrabon *St Sauveur* ★★ 20,000■ A *cru grand bourgeois* estate with a big output.
Peyredon la Gravette *Listrac* 900■ A supple bourgeois growth.
de Pez *St Estèphe* ★★★ 10,000■ A very consistent *cru grand bourgeois*, of 15th century origin, now reckoned to be of classified growth quality.
Phélan Ségur *St Estèphe* ★★★ 20,000■ Outstanding *cru grand bourgeois* with a big output, regarded as of classed growth quality; full-bodied with a rounded, fine bouquet.
Pibran *Pauillac* ★ 3,000■ Excellent bourgeois wine – well-balanced, fruity and keeps well.
● **Pichon Longueville Baron** *Pauillac* ★★★★ 9,000■ Situated on a high plateau, where Pauillac joins St Julien; a fine, robust wine with classic Pauillac characteristics; maintains its rank as an 1855 2nd growth; originally part of the same estate as Pichon Longueville Lalande.
● **Pichon Longueville Lalande** *Pauillac* ★★★★ 25,000■ The larger of the two vineyards to emerge from the original Pichon estate. One-third of it is in St Julien, and the resulting wine is quite distinct from Pichon Longueville Baron; Lalande, which is a 2nd growth of 1855 and continues to hold its own, has the greater finesse and is reckoned the better of the two Pichons. A second wine is sold as 'Réserve de la Comtesse'.
Plantey de la Croix *St Seurin de Cadourne* ★ 8,000■ In a single holding with Verdignan (*qv*).
Pomys *St Estèphe* ★ 2,500■ Full-bodied and fruity wine, made entirely from Cabernet Sauvignon grapes; a notable *cru grand bourgeois*.
Pontac Lynch *Cantenac* 1,500■ A small bourgeois growth, surrounded by Margaux, Palmer, Rauzan Gassies and d'Issan.
● **Pontet Canet** *Pauillac* ★★★★ 40,000■ Top of the list of 5th growths in 1855, often selling as well as good 2nd growths, and with a colossal output – nearly half a million bottles a year. Pontet Canet is a consistent wine, and until 1974, when it was sold by the Cruses to the Cognac family, Tesseron, it was one of the few Bordeaux wines never to be château-bottled. Lafon Rochet, 4th growth St Estèphe, is in the same ownership.
Pontet Caussan *Blaignan* 1,600■ A smaller *cru bourgeois* adjoining La Tour Haut Caussan.
Pontoise Cabarrus *St Seurin de Cadourne* 6,000■ A *cru grand bourgeois* made from old vines; fine, well-balanced wine with an attractive bouquet.
Potensac *Ordonnac et Potensac* ★★ 5,000■ A good northern Médoc growth, taking its name from the commune (see **Lassalle** and **Gallais Bellevue**); *cru grand bourgeois*.
● **Pouget** *Cantenac* ★★ 2,000■ An 1855 4th growth, now owned by and vinified with Boyd Cantenac; *appellation* Margaux.
○ **Poujeaux Theil** *Moulis* ★★★ 18,000■ Sometimes shown simply as Poujeaux, it is a common practice to tack on the existing owner's name; an exceptionally good Moulis growth – distinctive, combining richness and vinosity with finesse, it deserves to be classified.
Priban *Macau* ★ Good *cru bourgeois*, not to be confused with La Tour Priban from Pauillac.
● **Prieuré Lichine** *Cantenac* ★★★ 7,500■ 4th growth 1855, entitled to the Margaux *appellation*; a supple, fine-coloured wine, very fruity and elegant, and greatly improved of late.
La Providence *Ludon* 1,500■ A drinkable bourgeois wine, marketed by Dourthe Frères; AC Bordeaux.
Ramage la Batisse *St Sauveur* ★ 10,000■ A wine with a delicate bouquet; the vineyard was reconstituted by new owners in 1961.
● **Rausan Ségla** *Margaux* ★★★★ 7,000■ A 2nd growth of 1855, now belonging to Eschenauer; at its best a fine, perfumed wine, slightly fuller than other Margaux wines. Robust and stubborn to begin with, it is not always consistent and it has recently had a lean patch; a different, and better, wine than Rauzan Gassies, although once part of the same vineyard.
du Raux *Cussac* 2,000■ Handled by Ginestet; a full-bodied bourgeois growth lying close to the Gironde.
● **Rauzan Gassies** *Margaux* ★★★★ 6,000■ It has not maintained the 2nd growth standing which, like Rausan Ségla, it was accorded in 1855; its price has fallen with its reputation, but quality has recently improved.
Reysson *Vertheuil* ★ 10,000■ A *cru grand bourgeois*, supple and fruity, which acquires a delicate aroma with age.
Rolland *Pauillac* ★ 3,500■ An excellent bourgeois wine, full-bodied and lively.
La Roque *Margaux* – merits the commune *appellation*, but of no great distinction.
La Roque de By *Bégadan* 1,000■ A small, noteworthy *cru bourgeois*.
La Rose Pauillac *Pauillac* The co-operative for the commune and the largest in the Médoc; its wine has a good reputation.
St Ahon *Blanquefort* 5,000■ Bourgeois growth of some repute.
St Christoly *St Christoly de Médoc* 2,000■ Commune wine from the northern Médoc, of a good repute.
● **St Pierre** *St Julien* ★★★ 7,500■ 4th growth 1855, which has not entirely maintained its former standing.
St Roch *St Estèphe* 2,000■ A drinkable bourgeois growth, marketed by Ginestet.
Saransot Dupré *Listrac* 4,000■ One of the commune's better *crus bourgeois*; has a good colour, body and suppleness.
Ségur *Parempuyre* ★ 3,000■ A *cru grand bourgeois* from a lesser Haut Médoc commune; the wines are not unlike those of Ludon.
Ségur Fillon *Parempuyre* 1,000■ Another *cru grand bourgeois* from the Haut Médoc, much sought in Holland.
Sémeillan *Listrac* 4,500■ One of the better Listrac bourgeois wines.

In Bordeaux vineyards where the stocks have not been planted to allow for mechanical harvesting, picking the grapes is a hectic process which makes intensive demands on labour.

Sigognac *St Yzans* ★ 20,000■ *Cru grand bourgeois* with a reputation for finesse and vigour.
Siran *Labarde* ★★★ 12,000■ Forms a large estate together with Douzac; regularly included among the exceptional Médoc growths and now generally regarded as of classified quality; consistent in finesse and breed; *appellation* Margaux.
Sociando Mallet *St Seurin de Cadourne* ★ 3,500■ Carefully vinified *cru grand bourgeois*, made not far from St Estèphe.
du Taillan *Le Taillan* ★ 5,000■ The château is an historic monument, 12km out of Bordeaux; the wine is a *cru grand bourgeois*, supple with a good bouquet.
● **Talbot** *St Julien* ★★★★ 30,000■ Although 4th growth in 1855, Talbot is now held in higher regard; a good, consistent wine of character, richness and distinctive bouquet, though not quite in the first flight. Le Caillou, an elegant dry white wine, is also made; Gruaud Larose has the same proprietor.
Tayac *Soussans* ★ 10,000■ A bourgeois wine which merits its Margaux *appellation*.
● **du Tertre** *Arsac* ★★★ 10,000■ Lapsed 5th growth, it has recovered some of its breed and distinction since the middle 1960s, when it came under the same management as Calon Ségur.
du Testeron *Moulis* 500■ A small bourgeois growth, worth looking out for.
La Tour Blanche *Bégadan* ★ 10,000■ A pleasing, good quality bourgeois from the estuary hillside overlooking St Christoly; to be distinguished from the well-known Sauternes of the same name.
La Tour de By *Bégadan* ★★ 17,000■ Thought by some to be the best of the Bégadan bourgeois wines.
● **La Tour Carnet** *St Laurent* ★★ 8,000■ Can be attractive, lively and full-flavoured, with a subtle and flowery nose – but it is on the light side and at one time it was not up to its 4th growth 1855 standing.
La Tour Castillon *St Christoly de Médoc* 1,200■ A tiny estate, one of a bunch of bourgeois growths clustered around St Christoly.
La Tour Haut Caussan *Blaignan* ★ 2,500■ A small northern Médoc bourgeois estate of quality.
La Tour du Haut Moulin *Cussac* ★★ 5,000■ Grown from very old vines, and mostly exported to the UK and US; a powerful and concentrated *cru grand bourgeois*.
La Tour Marbuzet *St Estèphe* ★ 3,200■ A bourgeois wine of high quality.
La Tour du Mirail *Cissac* ★ 5,000■ Carefully tended bourgeois growth from old vines which impart a certain smoothness; the vineyard, which lies to the west of St Estèphe and is not dissimilar from it in character, is considered one of the four best in Cissac.
La Tour Milon *Pauillac* ★ 2,000■ A high quality bourgeois wine.
La Tour de Mons *Soussans* ★★★ 10,000■ The viticultural care taken by its owners has put it above its class of *cru grand bourgeois*; it is now generally regarded as of classified growth quality, consistent in its finish and breeding; *appellation* Margaux.
La Tour St Bonnet *St Christoly de Médoc* ★ 22,000■ A good northern Médoc growth from one of the larger of the St Christoly cluster of vineyards.
La Tour St Joseph *Cissac* 5,000■ Full-bodied bourgeois, distributed by Quancard Frères.
Tourteran *St Sauveur* 5,000■ Full-bodied bourgeois wine; neighbouring on Liversan and Peyrabon.
Tronquoy Lalande *St Estèphe* ★★ 7,500■ Cabernet Sauvignon grapes entirely produce this fine quality *cru grand bourgeois*.
Verdignan *St Seurin de Cadourne* ★ 8,000■ One of three or four good growths in the commune, with something of the generosity and body of its near neighbour, St Estèphe, but less finesse; incorporates Planey de la Croix.
Veyrin *Listrac* 2,000■ One of the better Listrac growths.
○ **de Villegeorge** *Avensan* ★★ 5,000■ The most important parts of this vineyard are in Moulis, and its exceptionally good, full-bodied wine is not far behind other Moulis wines vying for classification, such as Chasse Spleen.

St Emilion

THE ST EMILION WINE REGION is divided into two distinct areas. The first is the central part, which includes the small town and the commune of St Emilion, to which the *appellation St Emilion* applies. The second is a group of six associated communes which are entitled to add St Emilion to their own name to form their *appellation*; they are Montagne St Emilion, Lussac St Emilion, Puisseguin St Emilion, Parsac St Emilion, St Georges St Emilion and Sables St Emilion.

All the region's best wine is red, and although the area is smaller, its total output is higher than that of the Médoc. On the other hand, the average size of the classified vineyards, and thus of their production, is smaller than that of the leading vineyards in the Médoc. Almost all the important wines of the region in fact come from St Emilion itself; that is from the hills surrounding the town, called the Côtes St Emilion, and the plateau of the Graves St Emilion below, adjoining Pomerol. Between them these two areas account for 70 of the 73 classified growths.

It is the hilly area of the Côtes, an irregular series of slopes of silica, clay and chalk, which produces most of the classic St Emilions. The long list of its well-known *châteaux* is led by Ausone, followed by Belair, Beauséjour, Canon, Clos Fourtet, La Gaffelière, Pavie and Trottevieille.

The Graves, not to be confused with the well-known white wine region south of Bordeaux, was not recognized separately until just over a hundred years ago. The area has a gravelly, sandy soil, geologically similar to Pomerol, and its wines combine the velvety quality of its neighbour with the characteristic power of St Emilion. This formidable combination has contributed to the world-wide renown achieved by its leading vineyard, Château Cheval Blanc, and the handful of other classified growths which cluster around Cheval Blanc on the Pomerol border – Figeac, Corbin, Chauvin, Ripeau, La Dominique and Yon Figeac.

COMMUNES OF
ST EMILION

Lussac St Emilion
Montagne St Emilion
Parsac St Emilion
Puisseguin St Emilion
Sables St Emilion
St Christophe des Bardes
St Emilion
St Etienne de Lisse
St Georges St Emilion
St Hippolyte
St Laurent des Combes
St Pey d'Armens
St Sulpice de Faleyrens
Vignonet

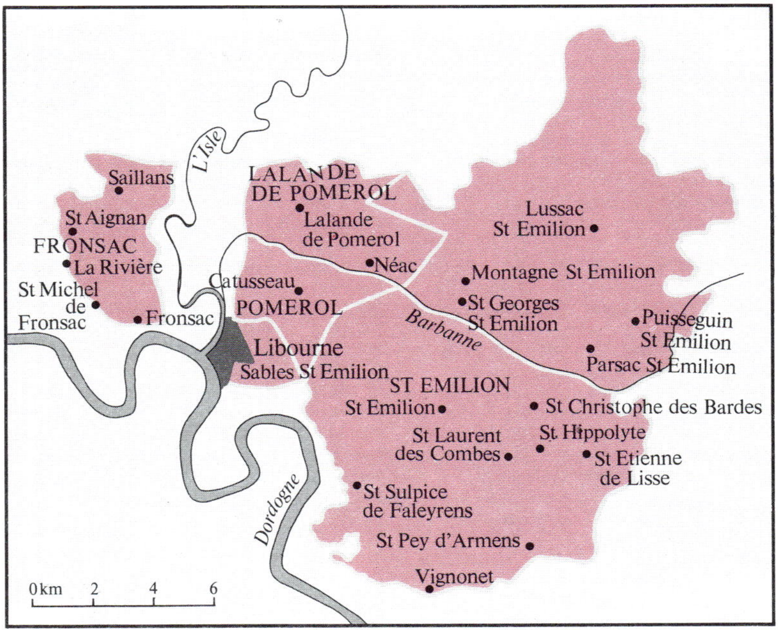

St Emilion, viewed from the ramparts. The spire belongs to l'Eglise Monolithe, a vast underground church carved out of the solid rock; the vineyards of the Côtes slope up almost to the walls of l'Eglise Collégiale, seen in the background (G)

Since 1936 the St Emilion *appellation* has embraced the wines from seven historically linked communes – St Christophe des Bardes, St Laurent des Combes, St Hippolyte, St Etienne de Lisse, St Sulpice de Faleyrens, St Pey d'Armens and Vignonet. With three classified exceptions – Larcis Ducasse from St Laurent and Le Couvent and Tertre Daugay, both from St Sulpice – the wines from these communes do not carry the same standing as other St Emilions.

Five of the associated communes – Montagne, Lussac, Puisseguin, Parsac and St Georges – lie to the north of St Emilion across the River Barbanne. Montagne produces two distinct sorts of wine, the one robust and purple in colour from the vineyards near the tops of the hills, the other light, more supple and delicate, from further down. Good, full-bodied wines emanate from the Lussac slopes. In Puisseguin they are, if anything, more robust and rather harder, whereas the few Parsac wines which may be encountered tend to be deep coloured and rich. Growers in Parsac may now opt to classify their wines as Puisseguin St Emilion, and most choose to do so. The wines of St Georges are comparable in style and quality to those of St Emilion itself; Sables, to the west of St Emilion, has little or no wine of note.

The wines of St Emilion were officially classified in 1954 by the INAO, to be updated every ten years, and the present position is as follows:

(1) *Premiers grands crus classés*
The twelve leading growths were accorded this title, with a distinction being drawn between the two finest (A) and the rest (B); they are Ausone (A), the two Beauséjours (B), Belair (B), Canon (B), Cheval Blanc (A), Clos Fourtet (B), Figeac (B), La Gaffelière (B), Magdelaine (B), Pavie (B) and Trottevieille (B).

(2) *Grands crus classés*
61 vineyards come into this category – see the gazetteer.

(3) *Grands crus*
Below the classified growths there continues to be the very confusing practice of describing many of the remaining wines, hopeful but untitled, as *grands crus* – and this term will often appear on the label. The title is awarded year by year to the better of the unclassified wines.

(4) *St Emilion*
The last group, some 900 wines in all, takes the plain *appellation St Emilion*, without any elaboration.

SAMPLE TASTING

(1) A generic St Emilion from any good shipper.

(2) An unclassified growth from Montagne St Emilion – e.g. Château Corbin or Château La Bastienne.

(3) A similar growth with an *appellation St Emilion* label – Château Fombrauge from St Christophe, perhaps, or Château Plaisance from St Sulpice.

(4) A classified growth from the Graves St Emilion, not quite in the top range – Château Ripeau or Château Chauvin are possibilities – complemented by . . .

(5) . . . a classified wine of similar standing from the Côtes St Emilion, such as Château L'Angélus or Château Canon La Gaffelière.

The best St Emilions are characterized by their richness, suppleness and fine colour. They are fruity and full-bodied and tend to be more powerful than the Médocs, with an alcoholic content of between 12° and 14° in fine years. St Emilion has been popularly regarded as 'the Burgundy of Bordeaux', but such a description helps only to indicate two particular facets – a greater richness in alcohol and a full, mellow flavour unmatched by any other red wine in the Bordeaux region. The bouquet of a St Emilion is more arresting and often more powerful than a Médoc; it has a more vivid fruitiness than that of a Pomerol, but at the same time it is less complex and subtle. Its flavour is rich and warm in the mouth; the great growths often have an almost unctious quality.

Even if the wines are big and powerful they can be drunk and enjoyed when very young – the lesser growths need to be three or four years old, great growths should be a year or two older; they can in any event be really ready for drinking in six to eight years, and reach perfection in ten to twenty. The readiness of St Emilion wines for drinking in those years when Médocs may display too much tannin to be agreeable may largely be accounted for by the use of the Merlot grape, which has long been the major variety in the district; it ripens earlier than the Cabernet Sauvignon and the Cabernet Franc, but presents a more serious rot problem in wet years. Although they have less tannin than Médocs, their fine balance and alcoholic content can enable them to flourish for as long as thirty or forty years.

ST EMILION GAZETTEER

KEY TO SYMBOLS

●A *premier grand cru classé* (top category)
●B *premier grand cru classé* (second category)
○ *grand cru classé*
Peppercorn rating
■ average annual output of red wine, per case of 12 bottles
□ average annual output of white wine, per case of 12 bottles
Italic after the name indicates the commune (e.g. *St Christophe des Bardes*) or the district of St Emilion (e.g. *Côtes*) in which the vineyard is located.
Côtes (or Côtes) = Côtes St Emilion, *Graves* (or Graves) = Graves St Emilion.

●A **Ausone** *Côtes* ★★★★★ 3,000■ For many years considered to be the best of the wines of St Emilion; at one stage it lost that reputation, but it appears now to be on the way to regaining it – the '75 and '76 vintages were outstanding. At its best, a wine of great distinction, less robust than many St Emilions. Belair and Chapelle Madeleine are in the same ownership.

Baleau *Côtes* ★★ 8,000■ A *grand cru* now regarded as of classified standing. In the same hands as Grandes Murailles.

○ **Balestard la Tonnelle** *Côtes* ★★★ 5,000■ A classified growth at the gates of the town, producing a generous and elegant wine.

Bardes Haut *St Christophe des Bardes* 10,000■ Robust, unclassified growth.

●B **Beauséjour** (Duffaut) *Côtes* ★★★ 2,500■ This holding is owned by the Société Civile Château Beauséjour; its wine is of similar character and standing to that of its namesake (below).

●B **Beauséjour** (Bécot) *Côtes* ★★★ 4,000■ The larger holding of an estate divided into two in 1869. Maintains its long-standing reputation for making a mellow, distinguished wine, vigorous and full-bodied, with the standing of a 4th growth Médoc.

Beauséjour *Montagne St Emilion* 6,000■ A notable unclassified growth, with plenty of body and a fine colour.

●B **Belair** *Côtes* ★★★★ 4,000■ A subtle elegant, full-flavoured wine, among the leading St Emilion growths. The Ausone vineyard adjoins it, using the same cellars and in the same ownership, but Belair is usually the lighter wine.

Bel Air *Lussac St Emilion* 4,000■ 3,000□ A small holding in the north-west of the commune producing both red and white wines.

Bellefont Bercier *St Laurent des Combes* ★★ 7,000■ One of the largest and most important growths in St Laurent after Larcis Ducasse.

Bellile Mondotte *St Hippolyte* 2,000■ A minor commune growth.

○ **Bellevue** *Côtes* ★★ 3,000■ A small *grand cru classé* of good standing.

Bellevue *Montagne St Emilion* ★ 5,000■ An unclassified growth worth looking out for.

○ **Bergat** *Côtes* ★★★ 1,500■ An excellent growth with a minute output; marketed by Borie-Manoux.

Harvest time at Château Ausone, Côtes St Emilion (G)

○ **Cadet Bon** *Côtes* ★★★ 2,500■ A warm and generous wine from a vineyard at the gates of the town.

○ **Cadet Piola** *Côtes* ★★★ 2,000■ A firm wine from an old-established, well-situated estate.

Calon *Montagne St Emilion* ★ 10,000■ Large, unclassified estate, co-owned with Corbin Michotte and Calon St Georges (*St Georges St Emilion*); generous wine from old vines.

●B **Canon** *Côtes* ★★★★ 7,500■ Well-known 1st growth, south-west of the town, producing a powerful, supple, generous wine of exceptional elegance; often rated immediately below Cheval Blanc and Ausone.

○ **Canon la Gaffelière** *Côtes* ★★★ 10,000■ Large property with an excellent reputation on the southern St Emilion slopes, developing under new direction. Very ripe, generous wine.

Cantenac or **L'Hermitage de Mazerat** *Côtes* 4,500■ Light, mellow, unclassified wine.

Capet Guillier *St Hippolyte* 5,000■ Mellow wine, agreeable bouquet; also sold as La Tour Capet.

○ **Cap de Mourlin** *Côtes* ★★★ 7,500■ Classified growth in the same family for five centuries; displays the qualities of the best St Emilions – generosity, finesse and a full bouquet.

Cardinal Villemaurine *Côtes* ★★★ 4,000■ Soft, light wines which can usually be recommended for quality.

○ **Chapelle Madeleine** *Côtes* ★★★ 3,000■ Reputable small growth run in consort with Ausone and Belair.

○ **Chauvin** *Graves* ★★★ 6,000■ A supple, rich wine from a commune bordering on Pomerol; fine bouquet.

●A **Cheval Blanc** *Graves* ★★★★★ 15,000■ One of the great wines of Bordeaux, and consistently the finest wine of St Emilion today. It combines great richness with elegance, suppleness and a superb bouquet; although it is a long-lived wine, it is often possible to drink it early. The estate is almost on the Pomerol border.

Cheval Noir *Côtes* 1,600■ Originally a single château unclassified wine; now a blend with other St Emilions, marketed by Mahler Besse; no connection with Cheval Blanc; attractive bouquet and smoothness.

Clos Castelot *Côtes* 2,200■ A little-known unclassified growth.

●B **Clos Fourtet** *Côtes* ★★★★ 6,000■ Uses more Cabernet grape than most St Emilions; it can therefore be hard at first, developing into a big, powerful wine – sometimes among the best in Bordeaux. Here, as at Ausone, the wine is cellared underground in old quarries; at Clos Fourtet these cellars are quite spectacular.

○ **Clos des Jacobins** *Côtes* ★★★ 4,000■ A middle-sized growth at the heart of the St Emilion vineyards, regarded as of 5th growth Médoc standing; sold by Cordier.

Clos La Figeac *Côtes* ★ Can usually be recommended.

Clos La Fleur Figeac *Graves* ★★ Owned by the Moueix family with La Tour du Pin Figeac, which it resembles.

Vineyards at Château Chapelle Madeleine, St Emilion (G)

○ **Clos La Madeleine** *Côtes* ★★★ 1,000■ A minute estate which has established a high reputation.

○ **Clos de l'Oratoire** *Côtes* ★★★ 2,500■ Small classified growth on well-exposed hill-side; elegant, supple, delicate wine, cellared at adjoining Feyreau. Off-year wines are sold as generic St Emilion.

Clos Pressac *St Etienne de Lisse* ★ 2,000■ An unclassified wine with attractive qualities, worth searching out.

Clos Rol de Fombrauge *St Christophe des Bardes* 2,000■ Unclassified growth; there is also a Château Rol de Fombrauge under quite separate ownership.

○ **Clos St Martin** *Côtes* ★★★ 2,000■ In the same ownership as Grandes Murailles; a fine and generous wine.

○ **Corbin (1)** *Graves* ★★★ 10,000■ One of the district's more outstanding wines, with a large output and a status equivalent to a 5th growth Médoc; combines the generosity of St Emilion with the vigour of a Pomerol.

Corbin (2) *Montagne St Emilion* ★ 10,000■ One of the largest and more important of the Montagne growths; unclassified.

○ **Corbin Michotte** *Graves* ★★★ 3,000■ A high proportion of Merlot mixed with Cabernet Sauvignon grapes makes this a powerful, deep coloured, fragrant wine; rated on a par with a 5th growth Médoc.

Cormey Figeac *Graves* ★★ 4,500■ Unclassified wine frequently found in the UK and US; full-bodied and fragrant.

○ **Coutet** *Côtes* ★★★ 5,000■ Mellow, fragrant, excellently balanced wines, from a well-placed estate overlooking the Dordogne valley; reckoned to be of 5th growth Médoc standing.

Couvent des Jacobins *Côtes* ★★★ 3,500■ An exceptional growth with the standing though not the formal accolade of a *grand cru classé*. The house is a 13th century foundation in the heart of St Emilion.

○ **Croque Michotte** *Graves* ★★★ 6,000■ Typical, full-bodied St Emilion made from old French vines; its reputation is comparable to a 4th growth Médoc.

○ **Curé Bon la Madeleine** *Côtes* ★★★ 2,500■ A classified growth producing a fine wine, distinctive in style; lying between Ausone, Belair and Canon; inclined to lack generosity.

○ **Dassault** *Côtes* ★★★ 10,000■ A big vineyard with modernised methods of vinification; yields a high quality wine.

Daugay *Côtes* ★★★ Unclassified, but produces a quality wine of *cru classé* standing. It is administered jointly with L'Angélus, a *grand cru classé*.

Faugères *St Etienne de Lisse* 5,000■ Medium-small, unclassified holding whose wines are sometimes exported.

de Ferrand *St Hippolyte* ★ 15,000/20,000■ Very good unclassified 'outer commune' wine.

●B **Figeac** *Graves* ★★★★ 10,000■ Rich, really fruity wine; enjoys a formidable reputation as one of the best after Cheval Blanc, whose property it adjoins and whose quality it often rivals.

Flouquet *Côtes* 1,100■ South of St Emilion, at the foot of the slope.

Fombrauge *St Christophe des Bardes* ★★ 15,000/20,000■ One of the oldest and best known of the St Emilion unclassified growths; a very full-bodied wine, with a distinct bouquet. Owns the adjoining Château Maurens.

○ **Fonplégade** *Côtes* ★★★ 5,000■ Full-bodied wine of breed and delicacy; acquires a firm bouquet with ageing; vineyard adjoins L'Angélus and is owned by A. Moueix.

Fonrazade *Côtes* 3,000■ An unclassified wine from the heart of St Emilion; full-bodied with finesse.

○ **Fonroque** *Côtes* ★★★ 8,000■ Big, full-bodied, robust wine which ages remarkably well; regarded as equivalent to a 5th growth Médoc.
○ **Franc Mayne** *Côtes* ★★★ 3,000■ Situated in the best part of the Côtes; a generous, full-bodied wine.
Franc Pourret *Côtes* 3,500■ Unclassified growth, centrally placed among a number of great growths on the edge of the village.
Franc Rosier *St Hippolyte* 1,000■ A small unclassified growth.
○ **Grand Barrail Lamarzelle Figeac** *Graves* ★★★ 12,000■ Rated on a par with a 5th growth Médoc; a generous wine, with charm, breed and a full bouquet.
○ **Grand Corbin Despagne** *Graves* ★★★ 10,000■ Planted with the classic Médoc vines on old French stocks; borders Pomerol, and combines a great finesse with a remarkable bouquet. Rated at the same level as a 5th growth Médoc.
○ **Grand Corbin Giraud** *Graves* ★★★ 5,000■ On a par with Grand Corbin Despagne; was spared the 1956 frosts; unites the finesse of St Emilion with the liveliness of Pomerol.
○ **Grand Mayne** *Côtes* ★★★ 6,000■ A full-bodied wine with finesse and a remarkable bouquet, from the edge of one of the best situated côtes; part of the output is sold as Château Cassevert.
○ **Grandes Murailles** *Côtes* ★★★ 1,000■ Classified growth with minute output, comparable to a 5th growth Médoc. Clos Martin is in the same ownership.
○ **Grand Pontet** *Côtes* ★★★ 5,000■ Powerful, supple, perfumed wine capable of holding up 50 years in bottle; the original French plantings escaped the frosts of 1956. Marketed by Barton & Guestier.
Gros Caillou *St Sulpice de Faleyrens* 4,000■ An unclassified growth worth looking for.
○ **Guadet St Julien** *Côtes* ★★★ 1,600■ Excellent wine, distinguished by its finesse and bouquet.
Guibeau Lafourvieille *Puisseguin St Emilion* ★ 10,000■ Commune wine, tougher and more robust than those of Montagne or Lussac.
Haut Cadet *Côtes* ★★ 2,500■ Grown just north of St Emilion; generous and full of flavour.
Haut Lavellade *St Christophe des Bardes* ★ 2,300■ Unclassified wine, well worth trying.
○ **Haut Sarpe** *Côtes* ★★★ 15,000■ Large estate east of St Emilion with a foot in the commune of St Christophe; generous, full-bodied, long-lasting wine, exported throughout the world.
Jacques Blanc *St Etienne de Lisse* 14,000■ Carefully made, unclassified wine; large output.
○ **Jean Faure** *Graves* ★★★ 8,000■ A Dourthe Frères holding with a long-standing reputation, adjoining Cheval Blanc; the wine is notable for its colour, body, generosity and bouquet.
○ **Jean du Mayne** *Côtes* ★★★ Contributes with others to the output of Château L'Angélus.
○ **L'Angélus** *Côtes* ★★★ 15,000■ Generous, full-bodied wine, consistent in quality and thought comparable with a 4th growth Médoc. In same ownership as Mazerat, Jean de Mayne and Daugay.

L'Hermitage du Mazerat (see **Cantenac**).
La Bastienne *Montagne St Emilion* ★ 8,000■ Noteworthy *grand cru* in a well-situated position; full-bodied, with good keeping qualities.
○ **La Carte et Le Châtelet** *Côtes* ★★★ 3,500■ Smallish growth centrally placed west of St Emilion.
○ **La Clotte** *Côtes* ★★★ 1,600■ At its best an elegant, generous, perfumed wine, which seems to have achieved a consistency and reputation worthy of a 5th growth Médoc; in great years it takes on an added dimension of colour and richness. There is also a Domaine de la Clotte (St Hippolyte), quite unconnected.
○ **La Clusière** *Côtes* ★★ 1,500■ Classified growth with a very small, good quality output.
○ **La Couspaude** *Côtes* ★★★ 3,000■ One of the district's better wines.
○ **La Dominique** *Graves* ★★★ 6,000■ A wine with the standing of a 5th growth Médoc and the same general qualities as its illustrious neighbour on the Pomerol border, Cheval Blanc; ages well.
La Fleur Pourret *Côtes* ★ 1,500■ A fairly full-bodied, fleshy wine from the heart of St Emilion which can usually be recommended; marketed by Ginestet.
●B **La Gaffelière** *Côtes* ★★★★ 10,000■ Generous, full-bodied, really fine wine, with a growing reputation; rated on a par with a 2nd growth Médoc; formerly La Gaffelière Naudes.
La Grace Dieu *Côtes* ★★ 3,800■ Subtle, delicate and well-bred.
La Grace Dieu les Menuits *Côtes* ★ 10,000■ Set between the Côtes and the Graves; unclassified wine with body and balance.
○ **La Marzelle** *Graves St Emilion* ★★★ 2,500■ A small *grand cru classé* with a growing reputation.
La Mondotte *St Laurent des Combes* ★ 15,000■ Mature, mellow, full-bodied wine, produced by the owners of Canon La Gaffelière from an estate adjoining Troplong Mondot.
La Rose Pourret *Côtes* ★★★ 3,500■ A *grand cru* wine grown 1 km from the centre of St Emilion, in the middle of more celebrated growths; velvety, delicate and attractive.
○ **La Serre** *Côtes* ★★★ 3,500■ Full-bodied, perfumed wine from the slopes east of St Emilion.
La Tour Blanche *Montagne St Emilion* Little-known unclassified growth, sold by Cruse.
La Tour Capet (see **Capet Guillier**).
La Tour des Combes *St Laurent des Combes* 4,000■ Unclassified growth; St Laurent vines are similar to, but less fine than St Emilions.
○ **La Tour Figeac** *Graves* ★★★ 8,000■ Part of Figeac until 1879; borders on Pomerol and reflects the qualities of other great growths there, like Cheval Blanc and Figeac; has been ranked with a 3rd or 4th growth Médoc.
La Tour Gilet *Montagne St Emilion* A noteworthy growth.
La Tour de Grenet *Lussac St Emilion* ★★ 12,500■ North of St Emilion on one of the highest points of the region; the planting is of the classic Médoc pattern, producing a full-bodied, supple wine, elegant and well-balanced, mostly from original French vine stocks.
○ **La Tour du Pin Figeac (Belivier)** *Graves*

★★★ 5,000■ Big, fruity wine, though not as good as that of the main Figeac estate; nonetheless one of the leading Graves growths.
○ **La Tour du Pin Figeac (Moueix)** *Graves* ★★★ 5,000■ Wine with plenty of body, breed and finesse; develops full bouquet with age.
La Tour de Pressac *St Etienne de Lisse* ★ 2,000■ Small unclassified growth marketed by Ginestet; an agreeable, firm wine with excellent keeping qualities. The truce ending the 100 years war was signed at the château.
La Tour Puyblanquet *St Etienne de Lisse* ★★ 2,000■ Unclassified growth, worth looking out for; the vineyard is on the edge of the Graves area, 5 km east of St Emilion.
La Tour St Pierre *Côtes* 4,000■ Situated north of St Emilion, between Trimoulet and Dassault; a well-balanced, supple *grand cru* that can be recommended.
Le Bon Pasteur *Côtes* An unclassified growth that can often be recommended.
○ **Le Châtelet** *Côtes* ★★★ 1,100■ A minute classified growth of 5th growth Médoc standing.
○ **Le Couvent** *Côtes* ★★ 500■ A toy-sized vineyard with *grand cru classé* standing, but not quite the reputation to sustain it at present; in the same ownership as Tertre Daugay.
○ **Le Prieuré** *Côtes* ★★★ 1,600■ An excellent wine with good keeping qualities. Neighbour of Trottevieille and Troplong Mondot.
Les Trois Moulins *Côtes* 1,500■ A *grand cru* on the main St Emilion plateau; produces wines with finesse and bouquet.
Lapelletrie *St Christophe des Bardes* 6,000■ Generous and fruity unclassed growth, aged in underground cellars.
Laplagnotte Bellevue *St Christophe des Bardes* 4,000■ Generous and well-finished wine, similar to Lapelletrie.
○ **Larcis Ducasse** *St Laurent des Combes* ★★★ 4,000■ One of only three *grands crus classés* outside St Emilion proper; a fine delicate wine with roundness and bouquet, on a par with a 4th growth Médoc.
○ **Larmande** *Côtes* ★★★ 4,500■ Very old grape stocks, planted on the northern slopes;

produces a fat, well-balanced wine of high quality. Marketed by Ginestet.
○ **Laroze** *Côtes* ★★★ 10,000■ A big estate at the foot of the St Emilion slopes, unscathed by the 19th-century phylloxera. Preserves the classic Médoc mixture of vines to provide a fairly full-bodied wine which develops slowly in the bottle, to great effect.
Lassegue *St Hippolyte* ★ 8,000■ Unclassified wine, vigorous with a fine bouquet.
des Laurets *Puisseguin St Emilion* ★ 20,000■ Large, unclassified growth, among the best in this commune; delicate and full-bodied.
Lyonnat *Lussac St Emilion* ★★★ 25,000■ Estate with a large output and a good reputation; a fine wine, full-bodied and rich in colour, with excellent keeping qualities.
●B **Magdelaine** *Côtes* ★★★★ 2,000■ Wine of exceptional breed, suppleness, and bouquet, with a full, ripe, flavour, ranked with a 2nd or 3rd growth Médoc; produced on the same slopes as Ausone.
Maison Blanche *Montagne St Emilion* ★ 13,000■ Large output; unpretentious but good.
Martinet *Sables St Emilion* 10,000■ A light, agreeable wine.
○ **Matras** *Côtes* ★★★ 4,000■ Not of the top quality, but a consistent classed growth – mellow, fleshy and mature. Neighbour to L'Angélus and Tertre Daugay.
Maurens *St Hippolyte* 10,000■ Full-bodied wine, lively and perfumed, made by the owners of Fombrauge.
○ **Mauvezin** *Côtes* ★★★ 2,000■ A classified wine of good standing.
Milon *Côtes* ★★ 7,000■ A Dourthe Frères holding; regularly merits *grand cru* status.
des Moines *St Christophe des Bardes* 2,000■ Unclassified growth with a good colour.
Monbousquet *St Sulpice des Faleyrens* ★★ 15,000■ Fine, rich, supple wine; one of the most popular of the lesser St Emilions, it is widely exported.
Monlot Capet *St Hippolyte* 4,000■ Unclassified growth; close neighbour of Maurens and Lassegue.
Moulin Bellegrave *Vignonet* 2,500■ An unclassified wine worth seeking out.
○ **Moulin du Cadet** *Côtes* ★★★ 2,000■ One of the smaller classified growths of good standing; neighbour of Tertre Daugay and Petit Faurie de Souchard.
Naude *St Sulpice des Faleyrens* Supple, attractive wine produced by the owners of La Croix Fourney.
du Paradis *Vignonet* 5,000■ Unclassified wine, but widely exported.
Patris *Côtes* ★★ 4,500■ On the south-facing slopes adjoining L'Angélus; a wine of delicacy and subtlety.
●B **Pavie** *Côtes* ★★★★ 15,000/20,000■ The largest vineyard among the St Emilion great growths has improved of late; rich, generous, supple rounded wine, comparable to 3rd growth Médoc. Also owns Pavie Decesse and La Clusière.
○ **Pavie Decesse** *Côtes* ★★★ 4,000■ Generous, lively, fleshy wines, mostly château-bottled (see **Pavie**).
○ **Pavie Macquin** *Côtes* ★★★ 6,000■ Larger estate than Pavie Decesse; both were split off from Pavie and placed in a slightly lower category.
○ **Pavillon du Cadet** *Côtes* ★★★ 2,500■ Not a widely known classified growth which maintains a good standing.
Pelletan *St Christophe des Bardes* 2,000■ Little regarded unclassified growth.
○ **Petit Faurie de Souchard** *Côtes* ★★★ 8,000■ Generous, supple wine growth with a fragrant individuality, grown on a well-exposed site north of St Emilion.
○ **Petit Faurie de Soutard** *Côtes* ★★★ 5,500■ Split off from the main Soutard estate in 1850; stands at the gates of the town on the north-east; fine, supple wine with a distinct bouquet which has always found a place among the great growths of St Emilion.
Peyreau *Côtes* ★ 6,000■ Supple, full-bodied *grand cru*; wines of poor vintages are sold as generic St Emilions.
Plaisance (1) *St Sulpice de Faleyrens* ★ 5,000■ A small unclassified growth on the edge of the Graves, worth seeking out; can be consumed young.
Plaisance (2) *Montagne St Emilion* 8,000■ Larger estate just outside the Graves area; fruity wine with attractive bouquet; develops well in bottle.
Puyblanquet (1) *St Christophe des Bardes* ★★ 2,500■ Vigorous and long-lasting *grand cru*.
Puyblanquet (2) *St Etienne de Lisse* 15,000■ Large estate, unclassified; St Etienne wines are fine and firm without being coarse.
Puy Razac *Côtes* 2,000■ *Grand cru* made from a high proportion of Cabernet grapes; marketed widely by Maison Querre; straightforward, generous wine.
○ **Ripeau** *Graves* ★★★ 5,000■ A very attractive wine, supple and rich, produced from original French vine stocks and rated by some as equal to 4th growth Médoc.
du Roc de Boissac *Puisseguin St Emilion* 10,000■ Robust, unclassified wine; Puisseguin wines are firmer and tougher than many.
Rocher Corbin *Montagne St Emilion* ★ 4,000■ Full-bodied wine with a delicate flavour from the western flank of Château Calon; in demand in Belgium and Holland. The estate was originally part of St André Corbin.
Roudier *Montagne St Emilion* 12,500■ Fruity, supple, agreeable wine from the southern slopes of Montagne and St Georges, north of St Emilion.

St André de Corbin *St Georges St Emilion* ★ 5,000■ Comparable in style and quality to a St Emilion proper – i.e. a wine from the Côtes or Graves districts.
St Emilion Royale 60,000■ The wine of the St Emilion co-operative; an enormous total from many small growers.
St Georges *St Georges St Emilion* ★★ 25,000■ Big producer of fine, well-balanced wine, generous and full-flavoured; comparable in style and quality to wines of St Emilion proper; the principal growth of the commune.
○ **St Georges Côte Pavie** *Côtes* ★★★ 2,500■ Small select, classified growth, not to be confused with the one above; near neighbour of Laroze and Trimoulet; regarded as of equivalent standing to a 5th growth Médoc.
de St Pey *St Pey d'Armens* 10,000■ A reconstituted vineyard giving wine of a consistent quality.
○ **Sansonnet** *Côtes* ★★★ 3,500■ A smaller classified growth of good standing.
○ **Soutard** *Côtes* ★★★ 9,000■ Though comparable to a 5th growth Médoc, the wine has a fine bouquet; it is fleshy but elegant at the same time and it lasts well.
Tauzinat L'Hermitage *St Christophe des Bardes* ★ 5,000■ A wine to be recommended from the edge of the Côtes; the reconstituted vineyard is owned by A. Moueix.
○ **Tertre Daugay** *Côtes* 3,000■ Set on the edge of the Côtes, flanked by Ausone, Belair and Magdelaine; the wine is full-bodied, and has great elegance and bouquet; in the same ownership as Le Couvent.
Teyssier *Vignonet* ★ 1,000■ An attractive, robust wine.
des Tours *Montagne St Emilion* 3,000■ Very big producer, though none of the wine is in the classified category; the vineyard surrounds a magnificent 14th-century castle.
Trianon *Côtes* 2,000■ A fruity, mellow *grand cru* from old French vine stocks; sited west of St Emilion.
○ **Trimoulet** *Côtes* ★★★ 6,000■ Middle-sized classified growth; generous, lively, full-bodied wines, widely exported.
○ **Troplong Mondot** *Côtes* ★★★ 12,500■ Borders Pavie and faces onto the old village of St Emilion; the wine has been inclined of late to be light, but it has finesse and considerable charm and is of equivalent standing to a 5th growth Médoc.
●B **Trottevieille** *Côtes* ★★★★ 5,000■ A smallish vineyard on a splendidly exposed site, east of the town; the wine is full-bodied and powerful, and develops great charm with ageing; has been compared in standing with a 4th growth Médoc; marketed by Borie-Manoux.
Vieux Castel Robin *St Christophe des Bardes* 1,500■ Unclassified wine, worth looking for.
○ **Villemaurine** *Côtes* ★★★ 7,000■ Classified growth beside the ramparts of St Emilion, one of the most renowned sites in the area; the vines are a mixture of original French stock and new plantings; a fine, attractive wine thought to be of Trottevieille quality.
○ **Yon Figeac** *Graves* ★★★ 9,000■ Well-known classified growth from a reconstituted vineyard; attracts by its finesse, mellowness and vinosity.

Pomerol

POMEROL IS THE SMALLEST of the great red wine districts of Bordeaux. In some respects it is also the least known, even though its vineyards existed in Roman times; until the late 19th century it was regarded as no more than an extension to St Emilion, a role which obscured the distinction and originality of its wines. It has now come into its own and its leading growth, Pétrus, stands in quality and reputation alongside the first growths of the Médoc.

Despite its small size – some 1,500 acres contained within the single commune of Pomerol and a small area within the neighbouring commune of Libourne – it is so intensely cultivated that it can produce about a quarter of a million cases of red wine each year. Few estates are large by Médoc standards. Pétrus makes 2,000 cases in a good year; Lafite produces about ten times as much.

Pomerol's vineyards have never been formally classified, and after naming Pétrus and a dozen or so other growths whose standing would be universally recognized, the pecking order is open to opinion. The list given here comprises all the wines that naturally fall into the former category, together with a number of others which deserve similar consideration, having regard to their Peppercorn ratings in the gazetteer.

Pomerol at its best is a full, velvety, generous wine, instantly attractive to both nose and palate, with a brilliant, deep ruby colour, and at one and the same time both a vigour and a softness. It is quicker maturing and less capricious than a Médoc, and less alcoholic than a St Emilion: in a curious way it combines some of the qualities of each. It is rich and powerful, like St Emilion, but the bouquet develops more hesitantly; and the very best Pomerols often have a Médoc-like hardness at the beginning, which however disappears quickly. Its bouquet is elusive, in keeping with the subtlety of a Médoc; but while it lacks the projection and immediacy of St Emilion, underneath it has the same richness and robustness. In the

Château Pétrus, the most celebrated of the Pomerol vineyards (G)

PEPPERCORN ★ RATINGS

The principles are those described on page 32. When assessing Pomerols in terms of their cost, and the value which they offer, remember that they tend to maintain higher prices than St Emilions or Médocs. There are three main reasons for this: the estates are small, their reputation has remained steady over many years and their markets are traditionally concentrated in rich countries, such as Belgium and France itself.

LEADING GROWTHS

★★★★★ PEPPERCORN RATING

Pétrus

★★★★ PEPPERCORN RATING

Conseillante
Gazin
L'Evangile
La Fleur Pétrus
Lafleur
Latour Pomerol
Trotanoy
Vieux Château Certan

★★★ PEPPERCORN RATING

Beauregard
Bourgneuf Vayron
Certan de May
Certan Giraud
Certan Marzelle
Clos de l'Eglise
Clos René
Domaine de l'Eglise
L'Enclos
La Croix
La Croix du Casse
La Croix de Gay
La Pointe
Lagrange
Le Gay
Mazeyres
Moulinet
Nenin
Petit Village
Rouget

SAMPLE TASTING

(1) A generic Pomerol from a reputable supplier
(2) A good bourgeois growth, say Le Bon Pasteur or de Sales
(3) One of the bigger, better estates like La Pointe, or Nenin
(4) A more select, expensive growth – while still not quite the best! – Trotanoy, for example, or La Fleur Pétrus

The lifespan and readiness of a Pomerol closely resembles that of a St Emilion; samples ought to be three or four years old and ideally should be of the same vintage.

mouth Pomerol is big and strong, the body and tannin clothed in a warm vinosity; its initial toughness gives way to reveal a flavour of many facets.

In part, these characteristics stem from the use of a greater proportion of Merlot grapes as against the other great Bordeaux varieties, Cabernet Sauvignon (known here as Bouchet) and Cabernet Franc. Malbec (or Noir de Pressac here) is also occasionally used in small quantities. Exceptional frosts in 1956 caused widespread damage in Pomerol, but they provided the opportunity for extensive replanting. As a result, Merlot has become established as the most widely used vinestock.

The nature of individual wines is also affected by variations in soil conditions. The Pomerol terrain consists of a slightly undulating, gravelly plateau, overlooking the Dordogne and the town of Libourne. The highest ridges are only 130ft above sea level. Pebbles, gravel, sand and clay combine in varying proportions over an iron-bearing subsoil; and to the latter is attributed the characteristic taste of Pomerol wines – a fruity, earthy flavour, which the French call *goût de truffes* (taste of truffles).

Immediately to the north of Pomerol, incorporating the commune and former *appellation* of Néac, lies Lalande de Pomerol. Its wines are similar to those of its neighbour, but not so fine: Bel Air (Lalande de Pomerol) and Siaurac (Néac) are the two best. Belles Graves, Bourseau, de la Commanderie, Domaine du Grand Ormeau, Château Grand Ormeau, Moulin à Vent, Sergant, de Teysson, Tournefeuille and de Viaud are among the more notable growths.

POMEROL GAZETTEER

★ Peppercorn rating
■ average annual output of red wine, per case of 12 bottles

Beauregard ★★★ 6,500■ A rich, powerful wine of quality, with charm, finesse and a delicate bouquet. The estate is on the southern face of the Pomerol plateau, near the St Emilion border. A replica of the picturesque, moated château stands on Long Island, USA.
Bel Air ★★ 6,000■ A wine of some note, supple and soft, reflecting the qualities of the best Pomerol growths. The estate is in Libourne but carries the Pomerol *appellation*.
Bellegrave ★ 3,000■ A Libourne growth, warm, attractive and generous. Like Bel Air, a balance of Cabernet and Merlot grapes, with a little Malbec.
Bellevue On the outskirts of the area, in the commune of Libourne; a soft, supple wine made predominantly from Merlot grapes.
Bourgneuf Vayron (or **Bourgneuf**) ★★★ 4,500■ Fine wine with a well-developed bouquet, plenty of body and a deep colour. The estate lies to the south-west of the village of Pomerol and has belonged to the Vayron family for 150 years.
Certan de May ★★★ 1,800■ A fine quality wine from an estate originally part of the better-known Vieux Château Certan.
Certan Giraud ★★★ 2,000■ A full-bodied and generous wine, the less renowned neighbour of Vieux Château Certan.
Certan Marzelle ★★★ 2,000■ A wine of similar quality to Certan Giraud; the estate is run by the same company.
Clinet ★★ 3,000■ Robust, full-bodied wine from a central Pomerol estate which takes longer to mature than some; it then acquires a pronounced perfume.
Clos Beauregard (see **Taillefer**).
Clos de l'Eglise ★★★ 2,500■ A central Pomerol estate taking its name from the 12th century church built by the Knights Templar. Among the better Pomerol wines, although lighter than some.
Clos René ★★★ 5,000■ A wine to be noted; among the better Pomerols.
Clos Toulifaut (see **Taillefer**) 1,000■
Côte l'Eglise ★ 3,000■ A wine of more humble standing among the estates clustered around the central church of Pomerol.
Domaine de l'Eglise ★★★ 2,000■ A distinguished and elegant wine, from a central Pomerol estate reputed to be the oldest in the commune; also uses the name Couvent de l'Eglise on labels.
Ferrand ★★ 7,500■ A large estate on the south-western slopes of the Pomerol uplands; fine bouquet, great finesse. 'Château Ferrand' is the second quality wine; the first quality is sold as Vieux Château Ferrand or Château Haut Ferrand.
Feytit Clinet ★★ 2,500■ An old-established central Pomerol vineyard; quite well thought of.
Franc Maillet ★★ 3,000■ A noteworthy wine from the St Emilion border.
Gazin ★★★★ 8,000■ Once a holding of the Knights Templar, situated in the middle of a group of great vineyards, including Pétrus, Vieux Certan and La Conseillante; a fine, robust, full-bodied wine that is delicious when mature.
Gombaude Guillot 2,500■ A good, medium quality growth.
Grate Cap 3,000■ Full-bodied wine with a firm bouquet.
L'Eglise Clinet ★★ 2,000■ One of the better growths clustered around the church of Pomerol; a generous, balanced wine.
L'Enclos ★★★ 4,000■ An estate on the north-western outskirts of the region which produces good quality, noteworthy wines.
L'Evangile ★★★★ 4,500■ A fine, full wine with a great reputation. Full-bodied; often very stubborn and firm at first, it matures to a remarkable finesse, elegance and bouquet. A close neighbour of La Conseillante.
La Cabanne ★ 6,000■ Situated a stone's throw from the church in the centre of Pomerol village; Bouchet, Merlot and Pressac grapes give body, delicacy and a firm bouquet.
La Commanderie ★★ 2,000■ Delicately bouqueted wine of good medium standing.

73d

Latour Pomerol: its wines have a four-star Peppercorn rating (G)

In the 13th century the estate formed the command post for the Knights of St John of Jerusalem.
La Conseillante ★★★★ 4,000■ Adjoins Cheval Blanc in St Emilion, but not quite in the same league; full-bodied, hard at first, consistent in quality and delicately perfumed; bottled entirely at the château, it is a widely appreciated and long-lived wine.
La Croix ★★★ 6,000■ Among the better Pomerol growths; a mellow wine which has finesse and an attractive bouquet, and a relatively big output. Geographically situated between Nenin, Petit Village and Beauregard.
La Croix du Casse ★★★ 4,000■ Delicately bouqueted and full-bodied wine, made with a high proportion of Merlot grapes.
La Croix de Gay ★★★ 2,000■ A good class Pomerol, sited on the summit of the plateau, with a soft, full bouquet.
La Croix St Georges ★★ 2,000■ Good quality, well-considered Pomerol of bourgeois growth standard; near neighbour of the Certans and Petit Village.
La Fleur Pétrus ★★★★ 3,500■ A rich, generous, characteristically fine Pomerol; a neighbour of the great Château Pétrus.
La Grave Trigant de Boisset ★★ 2,500■ A fine, smooth, generous wine, with a reputation abroad.
La Pointe ★★★ 7,000■ One of the bigger estates, whose merits are well recognized, but not in the best part of Pomerol. The wine is fairly light, with great charm and finesse.
Lafleur ★★★★ 1,600■ A much sought after smaller vineyard, producing a wine of great charm and distinction.
Lafleur du Roy 2,500■ The high proportion of Merlot grapes used gives it delicacy and a highly developed bouquet; neighbour of Plince and La Croix.
Lagrange ★★★ 2,000■ Generous wine of great finesse and vitality, from the southern edge of Pomerol village.
Latour Pomerol ★★★★ 4,000■ Combines richness, charm and breeding with a lovely bouquet; one of several outstandingly good growths clustered around the church at Pomerol.
Le Bon Pasteur ★ 3,000■ Fleshy and full-flavoured; a good example of a Pomerol bourgeois growth.
Le Caillou ★★ 3,000■ Made from a predominance of Merlot grapes, giving a fine flavour, bouquet and mellowness: a neighbour of Nenin and Plince.
Le Gay ★★★ 2,500■ An ancient growth with a long established reputation, maintaining a high standard of quality; a generous wine with a good deep colour.
Mazeyres ★★★ 5,000■ A wine from west of Pomerol, in Libourne, which has established a reputation for quality and is widely exported.
Monregard Lacroix 2,000■ In the same ownership as Clos du Clocher and of similar medium quality.
Moulinet ★★★ 4,000■ A larger holding, whose wine is well regarded for its colour, finesse, and excellent bouquet.
Nenin ★★★ 10,000■ A mellow wine with an established reputation, full of aroma and fruit; it has a firm, strong character, and the estate's output is high, but it is not in the best part of Pomerol.
de la Nouvelle Eglise 1,000■ A small estate next door to the church at Pomerol and built on some of its land; a medium quality growth.
Petit Village ★★★ 6,000■ A wine with a good reputation, marketed by Maison Ginestet; less generous than some, but with great finesse, full-bodied with a delicate fragrance. Part of the vintage is mixed with others and sold as 'Sélection du Maître de Chai'.
Pétrus ★★★★★ 2,000■ Acknowledged as the finest of the Pomerol wines; of great individuality and vinosity, rich, generous and complex in flavour, it ages superbly. The vineyard, which lies south-east of the village, dominates the commune by virtue of its geographical position and its prestige.
Plince ★★ 4,000■ Often ranked among the better Pomerols; mellow, generous, with a fine bouquet.
Rêve d'Or 2,500■ The estate, which lies on the north-western side of the route N89, is a near neighbour of Moulinet and Latour Pomerol.
Rouget ★★★ 7,500■ Balanced, full-bodied wine, with a fine colour; it had a very high reputation in the last century, and is still regarded among the more notable growths of Pomerol.
de Sales ★★ 18,000■ Combines delicacy and a fine bouquet; an unusually large vineyard for Pomerol, and the northernmost of any note, it has been in the same ownership for four centuries.
du Tailhas ★ 4,500■ The southernmost Pomerol vineyard of any note; has established a reputation abroad.
Taillefer ★★ 5,000■ Taking its name from the iron-bearing sub-soil of its vineyard, the wine acquires delicacy and an attractive bouquet with age. Clos Beauregard (not to be confused with the nearby Château Beauregard) and Clos Toulifaut adjoin and are in the same ownership.
Thibaud Maillet 1,500■ Similar in quality to nearby Franc Maillet, on the eastern fringe of the commune.
Tristant 2,000■ Subtle, full-bodied wine displaying the general characteristics of Pomerol.
Trotanoy ★★★★ 3,000■ An outstanding wine, close in style to Pétrus; it is generous, delicate and elegant, and has a pronounced bouquet. The vineyard escaped the bad frosts of 1956 and retained its older vines.
Vieux Château Bourgneuf ★★ 2,000■ A good medium quality growth; in different ownership from Bourgneuf.
Vieux Château Certan ★★★★ 5,000■ Adjoining Pétrus, this is indisputably one of the great growths of Pomerol; remarkable for its finesse and bouquet, and for its great vinosity and ripeness, it ages well.

Graves

APPELLATIONS CONTROLEES

Graves ● ○
Graves Supérieures ○

COMMUNES

Arbanats
Ayguemorte
Beautiran
Bègles
Budos
Cadaujac
Castres
Gradignan
Illats
La Brède (or Labrède)
Landiras
Langon
Léognan
Martillac
Mazères
Mérignac
Pessac
Podensac
Portets
Pujols
Roaillan
St Médard d'Eyrans
St Morillon
St Pierre de Mons
St Selve
Talence
Toulenne
Villenave d'Ornon
Virelade

CLASSIFIED GROWTHS

Bouscaut ● ○
Carbonnieux ● ○
Couhins ○
Domaine de Chevalier ● ○
de Fieuzal ●
Haut Bailly ●
Haut Brion ● ○
La Mission Haut Brion ●
La Tour Haut Brion ●
Latour Martillac ● ○
Laville Haut Brion ○
Malartic Lagravière ● ○
Olivier ● ○
Pape Clément ●
Smith Haut Lafitte ●

● red ○ white

UP TO NINE MILES wide in places, and almost 40 miles long, the Graves wine district runs from the northern outskirts of Bordeaux (the city itself lies actually within the district), wraps itself around Sauternes and Barsac and ends up at St Pierre de Mons. Its 29 wine communes are flanked on one side by the river Garonne, and on the other by a forest, Les Landes, which constantly intrudes further inland into the wine-growing areas and tends to separate the vineyards one from another.

It has achieved a popular reputation as a white wine producer, but in fact it produces both reds and whites, and has done so since ancient times; the quantity of its fine quality red wines exceeds that of the dry whites from the leading growths. These individual wines are eclipsed, however, by the large output of blended generic whites, sold as *Graves* or *Graves Supérieures*, which are dry in the north of the district and traverse the range of sweetness from *moelleux* to *liquoreux* as they approach the classic sweet white wine districts of Sauternes and Barsac. Cérons, really part of Graves but having its own *appellation*, produces sweet white wine like Barsac with a *Cérons* AC, and dry white wine with a *Graves* AC.

The individual wines included in the following gazetteer are almost without exception dry. With generic whites, dry or sweet, one has to buy the merchant rather than the wine to ensure both character and quality. The finest white Graves is truly dry, with a firm bouquet and a distinctly fruity and individual flavour – fine, powerful and long-lasting. A good red Graves is a powerful, vigorous, elegant wine; the leading growths have a very marked bouquet, as clean and fresh as a Médoc, but with an extra touch of vividness which is entirely their own. In the mouth they have a striking individuality: Pape Clément, recommended in the sample tasting, is a case in point.

Gateway to the vineyard of Château Carbonnieux, Graves (G)

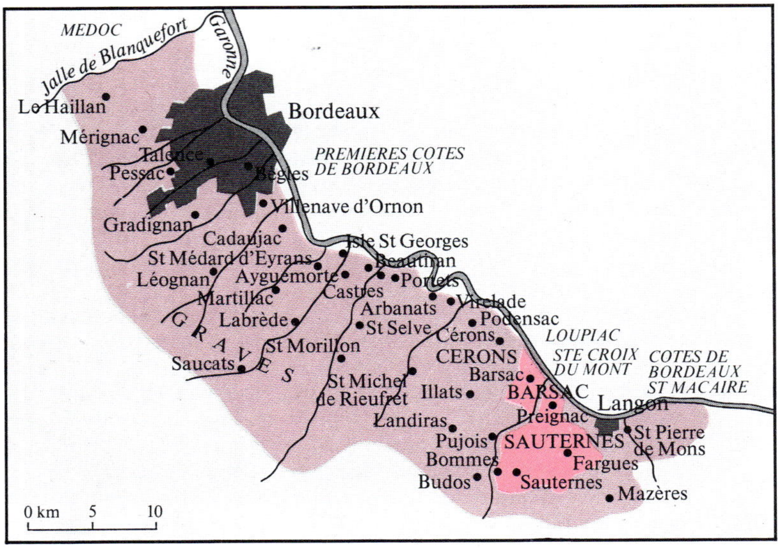

The very best red Graves, led by Haut Brion, rank with the best in Bordeaux. Haut Brion itself was singled out as a first growth – and the only Graves wine – in the 1855 classification. It appealed to the palate of Samuel Pepys in the 17th century, and took its rightful place at the head of the leading Graves vineyards when they were officially classified in 1953.

Geologically Graves is a southern continuation of the Médoc, and all the outstanding growths, both red and white, are in the northern part, principally in the communes of Pessac and Léognan. The district takes its name directly from the gravelly character of the soil. It is light, sandy, thin and dry, and it is covered with quartz pebbles of different colours and sizes. This gravel layer can go very deep – at Haut Brion it is thought to be as much as 60ft; below it is a stratum of iron-bearing sandstone which gives the wine its special character.

As in the Médoc, the red wine grapes are predominantly Cabernet Sauvignon, Cabernet Franc and Merlot, with a little Petit Verdot and Malbec. The proportions vary, the Cabernets normally being preponderant. Sauvignon, Sémillon and a minimum of Muscadelle, as in Sauternes, are used for the white wines. Better vineyards dispense with Muscadelle.

SAMPLE TASTING

Graves is the one district in Bordeaux which truly comprises both red and white wines, and any introductory tasting must embrace both. The whites selected for comparison can be tasted against a run-of-the-mill generic which is AC *Graves*, likely to be sweetish and of indifferent character. Because there is no generic red equivalent (any declassified red is sold as AC *Bordeaux*), the choice is restricted to a lesser and a bigger *château* wine.

Red wines

(1) A small *château* wine, such as des Graves (from Portets, which produces a number of good bourgeois class wines), or de Roquetaillade (from Mazères)
(2) A leading growth of character and individuality, say Pape Clément or Haut Bailly

White wines

(1) A run-of-the-mill AC *Graves*
(2) A good generic *Graves Supérieur* from one of the Bordeaux shippers listed at the end of the book
(3) A quality classified white, e.g. Château Carbonnieux

GRAVES GAZETTEER

● *premier grand cru classé*
○ *grand cru classé*
★ Peppercorn rating
■ average annual output of red wine, per case of 12 bottles
□ average annual output of white wine, per case of 12 bottles

Italic indicates name of commune.

Baret *Villenave d'Ornon* ★★★ 1,800■ 2,000□ Reds and whites are both excellent; the estate borders on Léognan.

○ **Bouscaut** *Cadaujac* ★★★ 10,000■ 2,000□ An important classified growth; supple red wines, and fine, dry, long-lasting whites; Valoux adjoins and is in the same ownership.

Cantebeau Couhins *Villenave d'Ornon* ★★★ 1,000□ Originally part of Château Couhins. These are white wines of delicacy and character; includes a small planting of red wine vines.

○ **Carbonnieux** *Léognan* ★★★★ (red) ★★★ (white) 8,000■ 8,000□ Big estate; red and white growths are both classified. Reds are on the light side, but well considered. Whites had a good reputation for elegance and breeding, marred by inconsistency; but since the 1975 vintage, under a new proprietor and with changed vinification, they have acquired real distinction.

Châteauneuf *Léognan* 2,000■ 2,000□ Both reds and whites are of characteristic Graves quality; robust with pronounced bouquet and some finesse.

Clos Louloumet *Toulenne* 800■ 3,000□ A lesser growth, developed by Ed. Coste et Fils; the white is full-bodied and sweetish, the red is a good *vin ordinaire*.

Clos de Monastère (see **Doms**).

Clos d'Uza *St Pierre de Mons* 1,000■ 8,000□ A neighbour of Queyrats; its wines are similar in character.

○ **Couhins** *Villenave d'Ornon* ★★★ 3,000□ A classified white wine with real finesse and distinction; the estate is owned by the Ministry of Agriculture for the use of its Research Institute.

○ **Domaine de Chevalier** *Léognan* ★★★★ 3,000■ 1,500□ One of the leading Graves growths for both reds and whites. Reds are of 2nd growth Médoc standing, lighter and more delicate than many red Graves; the whites, perhaps the finest of all white Graves, are light and dry, with a very fine flavour and great finesse.

Domaine de la Courrège *Illats* A completely renovated vineyard, producing red wine from Cabernet, Sauvignon and Merlot grapes and a range of sweet and dry white wines.

Domaine de Gaillat *Langon* 3,500■ 500□ From the very south of Graves; marketed by Ed. Coste et Fils.
Doms *Portets* ★ 3,000■ 3,500□ Generous red and white wines, some sold as Clos de Monastère or Moulins de Doms.
Ferran *Martillac* 1,200■ 1,200□ Dry white wines, and reds of a good flavour; marketed exclusively by Dourthe Frères.
Ferrande *Castres* 5,000■ 5,000□ Smooth, full-bodied reds; little known 20 years ago, but with a growing reputation now; good quality whites, with a distinctive bouquet.
○ **de Fieuzal** *Léognan* ★★★ 4,000■ 2,000□ Among the best of the classified Léognan growths, the reds are perfumed and elegant and are winning an increasing reputation abroad; the whites are also very attractive.
de France *Léognan* 9,000■ A big producer, situated on one of the highest slopes of the commune, adjoining de Fieuzal; a good medium-quality red, with a delicate bouquet.
Gazin *Léognan* 1,200■ A small vineyard producing red wine with body and a developed bouquet; not to be confused with the great Pomerol vineyard of the same name.
des Graves *Portets* ★ 1,000■ 1,000□ The reds are supple and long-lasting, the whites are fruity; marketed by Ginestet.
des Gravettes *St Morillon* 400■ 5,000□ Whites have a certain finesse and a generous character.
○ **Haut Bailly** *Léognan* ★★★★ 6,000■ A rich, distinctive wine of 2nd growth Médoc equivalence, increasingly re-establishing its reputation year by year.
● **Haut Brion** *Pessac* ★★★★★ 15,000■ 1,000□ One of the greatest and oldest of the red wines of Bordeaux; a 1st growth in the 1855 classification and still in that top rank; a very powerful wine, inclined to be hard at first, it has a heady bouquet and a big, powerful flavour when mature. Sold in bottles of a unique shape.
de Hilde *Bègles* 7,000■ The only major holding in the northern commune of Bègles; the wines have body and colour, and are particularly well thought of in Holland.
des Jaubertes *St Pierre de Mons* 5,000■ 4,000□ White wines, and – exceptionally – a largish output of red wine, from the extreme south-east of the district.
Jean Gervais *Portets* 6,000■ 4,000□ Supple, fruity red; dry, sappy white.
Kressman La Tour (see **Latour Martillac**).
La Blancherie *La Brède* ★★ 1,000■ 5,000□ One of the finest wines of this commune.
La Garde *Martillac* ★★ Good bourgeois growth, with a large output of supple and drinkable red wine; whites are dry, lively and elegant.
La Louvière *Léognan* ★★★ 8,000■ 12,000□ Reds are powerful and full-bodied, improving with age, and under new management there is also a large output of good quality white – dry, elegant and fruity. The estate is flanked by Carbonnieux and Haut Bailly and the best wines are sold as Château La Louvière; lesser bottles carry the names of associated vineyards incorporated in the estate: Le Vieux Moulin, Clos du Roy, La Haute Marnière, La Tourette, Le Pin Franc, La Haute Gravière, Coucheroy, Les Agunelles and Les Lions.
○ **La Mission Haut Brion** *Talence* ★★★★★ 8,000■ Red wine of marvellous finesse and a fine colour. Well ahead of other Graves reds except Haut Brion, and inclined in lesser years to be more consistent and finer than its illustrious neighbour.
○ **La Tour Haut Brion** *Talence* ★★★ 1,800■ Racy and flavoursome, full-bodied red wine; one of the trio of classified growths of Talence, along with La Mission Haut Brion and Laville Haut Brion which adjoin it.
La Vieille France *Portets* 1,000■ 2,000□ Produces reds of two standards, and a dry white; from Ginestet.
Larrivet Haut Brion *Léognan* ★★ 3,000■ 500□ A good growth of bourgeois standing, despite the implications of its name. Reds are delicate and mellow; white are very dry, fruity and distinctive.
○ **Latour Martillac** *Léognan* ★★★ 4,000■ 1,500□ Both reds and whites are classified. The reds have breeding, suppleness and flavour; like Smith Haut Lafitte, they have the reputation and standing of 5th growth Médoc. The whites are dry, vigorous and fruity; they can also be bought under the name Kressman La Tour in the UK and the US.
○ **Laville Haut Brion** *Talence* ★★★★★ 2,200□ An outstandingly fine quality dry, white wine; at its best after as many as a dozen years in the bottle.
Le Pape *Léognan* ★★ 1,500■ 1,000□ A good red growth known for its bouquet, finesse and long lasting quality. Whites are also good.
Lehoult *Langon* 500■ 1,500□ A small lesser growth from the south of the district; marketed by Ed. Coste et Fils.
Les Carmes Haut Brion *Pessac* ★★ 1,500■ A wine of passing good quality which finds its way abroad; the vineyard is a less illustrious neighbour of Haut Brion and La Mission Haut Brion.
Magence *St Pierre de Mons* ★★ 5,000■ 5,000□ Unusually, this estate concentrates on Cabernet grapes for red wines and Sauvignon for the whites, producing a very untypical wine.
○ **Malartic Lagravière** *Léognan* ★★★ (red) ★★★★ (white) 6,000■ 1,000□ Big, powerful red wine, with long keeping qualities, hard at first and not always well-balanced; has an equivalent standing to a 4th or 5th growth Médoc. The white is fine and very distinctive – a good example of a dry white Bordeaux.
Millet *Portets* 25,000■ 25,000□ Describes itself as a *grand cru exceptionnel*, and certainly has a massive output. Both reds and whites have flavour, delicacy and keeping qualities, and a growing reputation abroad.
du Mirail *Portets* ★★ 5,000■ 2,500□ The red wine is light and distinctive.
Moulins de Doms (see **Doms**).
○ **Olivier** *Léognan* ★★★ (white) 2,000■ 10,000□ One of the leading Graves estates, well-known for both its red and white wines.
○ **Pape Clément** *Pessac* ★★★ 10,000■ A generous and fine wine, with more delicacy than most of its neighbours; just below the very top rank of Bordeaux reds. The vineyard is ancient and famous; it once belonged to the Archbishops of Bordeaux.
Picque Caillou *Mérignac* 5,000■ Survivor of an older, larger estate which was used for the airfield outside Bordeaux, the vineyard is a near neighbour of Haut Brion and Pape Clément, but is not in the same commune, or league. The wine has suppleness and delicacy.
Piron *St Morillon* 1,000■ 5,000□ Whites are light, dry and fruity.
Port du Roy (see **de Portets**).
de Portets *Portets* ★★ 6,000■ 6,000□ Reds have body and bouquet; whites are dry and fruity. Port du Roy (AC *Bordeaux Supérieur*) is in the same ownership.
Poumey *Gradignan* ★ 2,000■ The only notable growth in the Gradignan commune; strong, characterful red wine.
Queyrats *St Pierre de Mons* 5,000□ Light, dry white wines made principally from Sauvignon grapes. Reds from the same vineyard are marketed as Ch. St Pierre.
de Roquetaillade *Mazères* ★ 1,200■ 700□ A smaller, lesser growth, named after a magnificent medieval fortress, five miles south of Langon.
○ **Smith Haut Lafitte** *Martillac* ★★★ (red) 20,000■ 2,000□ A big estate with a good reputation; among the better reds of Graves, the wine has a fine colour and a distinctive bouquet; but it is very variable and is often not up to its classification. The white wine is not classified.
de Terrefort de Fortissan *Villenave d'Ornon* 4,000■ 1,000□ Full-bodied, sappy reds.
des Tuilleries *Virelade* 1,500■ 1,000□ Good coloured reds; whites are mellow and can be perfumed.
Valoux *Cadaujac* 1,800■ (see **Bouscaut**).
de Virelade *Virelade* 2,000■ 1,000□ Whites may be sweet or semi-sweet; reds have finesse and colour.

Sauternes, Barsac and other sweet white wine areas of Bordeaux

To OBTAIN A COMPREHENSIVE PICTURE of the sweet white wines from Bordeaux one needs to look not only at the well-known districts in the south-east corner of Graves – notably Sauternes and Barsac – but also at the much larger but less distinguished area which lies across the Garonne, south of the Dordogne. Physically dominated by Entre Deux Mers, this region has always been famed for the sweetness of its white wines. Today, however, in order to cater for changing tastes, it also produces an increasing number of dry wines; and in certain areas, notably in the Premières Côtes de Bordeaux, there is now a considerable output of reds.

Sauternes and Barsac produce the most luscious, sweet white dessert wines in the world, and the leading growth in Sauternes, Château d'Yquem, is hailed as the greatest of them all. To say that these wines are sweet is only to state the obvious, and their deep, golden colour declares the fact immediately. Their bouquet gives the instant impression of ripe grapes: it holds a tremendous sweetness and fruitiness – the type of aroma one gets from a ripe peach – and with age it often acquires a hint of raisins. The flavour, while immensely unctious and rich, is harmonious and not at all cloying. It is like tasting the essence of ripe fruit, with a strong, alcoholic undertone which sets it apart from the lighter, more delicate German wines.

APPELLATIONS CONTROLEES

Barsac ○
Cadillac ○
Cérons ○
Côtes de Bordeaux St Macaire ○
Graves de Vayres ● ○
Loupiac ○
Entre Deux Mers ○
Entre Deux Mers Haut Benauge ○
Premières Côtes de Bordeaux ● ○
Ste Croix du Mont ○
Ste Foy Bordeaux ● ○
Sauternes ○

● red ○ white

ANNUAL PRODUCTION
(no. of cases)

Entre Deux Mers	875,000
Sauternes	200,000
Cadillac	170,000
Barsac	150,000
Cérons	135,000
Loupiac	130,000

Sauternes and Barsac

After four or five years in the bottle Sauternes achieves a balance of youthful fruitiness and vigour, richness and strength. It also acquires the distinctive aftertaste typical of botrytized wine (see below); nuances of flavour among the finest reveal an unexpected range of individual personality. It is its balance that determines the longevity of a Sauternes: very rich wines, like d'Yquem and others in big vintages such as 1945 or 1961, are often at their best at ten years old and past it after 25 years. Others can live for 50 years and still be fresh, sweet and delicious.

Sémillon and Sauvignon Blanc grapes are chiefly used, with the occasional addition of Muscadelles. Picked individually and progressively as

View of the Dordogne valley, near St Jean de Blaignac (G)

Ste Croix du Mont, overlooking the valley of the Garonne (G)

they ripen, they become shrivelled under the dual effect of the sun's rays and *pourriture noble* – a fungus (*Botrytis cinerea*) which feeds on and diminishes the water content of the fruit, causing a concentration of sugar, glycerine and aromatic elements. At Château d'Yquem the individual grapes are selected so meticulously that only one glass of wine is likely to emanate from each vine stock.

Twenty-four vineyards from the district's five communes – Barsac, Bommes, Fargues, Preignac and Sauternes – were classified in 1855. These are identified by the symbols 01 and 02 in the following gazetteer; at least 300 minor individual growths will usually be sold simply as AC *Sauternes*. The wine's minimum alcoholic content is 13°.

Barsac wines, which have the same alcoholic content and a full bouquet, are generally lighter and a little less sweet than Sauternes. Since 1936 they have been entitled to call themselves AC *Sauternes*, and sometimes both names appear on the label. Climens and Coutet are the commune's two finest, and both appear in the list of Sauternes 1st growths. Seven others are classified among the 2nds.

Cérons, Ste Croix du Mont, Loupiac, Cadillac

Slightly less sweet than the Barsacs, and with a slightly lower minimum alcoholic content (12.5°), are the wines from the three Cérons communes – Illats, Podensac and Cérons. These are popular wines in France, but not so far abroad. When vinified dry they are sold as AC *Graves*, as is the area's small output of reds.

The much higher and more steeply sloping vineyards of Ste Croix du Mont and Loupiac look down across the Garonne to those of Sauternes and Barsac. Their wines, though not well-known abroad, have a stature and quality next to those of Sauternes and Barsac; they are produced from the

SAMPLE TASTING

(1) A Premières Côtes de Bordeaux (which could be dry, sweet or semi-sweet) or a Cadillac
(2) A Ste Croix du Mont or a Loupiac
(3) A generic Sauternes
(4) A *cru classé* Sauternes of ★★★ or ★★★★ rating

same three grape varieties and have the same alcoholic minimum. Outstanding vineyards in Ste Croix du Mont are Loubens and de Tastes; those in Loupiac include du Cros, Loupiac Gaudiet and de Ricaud.

Wines from the neighbouring area of Cadillac, which only acquired their own *appellation* in 1969, are not dissimilar and are produced in comparatively large quantities. Those from St Macaire, a short way upstream from Ste Croix du Mont, are of less distinction and have an alcoholic minimum of only 11.5°.

Premières Côtes de Bordeaux, Entre Deux Mers, Ste Foy Bordeaux, Graves de Vayres

In the Premières Côtes de Bordeaux especially, the need has been recognized to escape from a traditional dependency on sweet white wines. The customary smooth and sweet whites from Sauternes, with their high alcoholic minimum of 13°, have had to give way to dry and semi-sweet wines. The better examples come from the communes of Gabarnac and Langoiran, both of which require a 12° minimum. North of Cambes most wines are made red from the Médoc grapes – Cabernet, Merlot, Malbec and Petit Verdot.

Some 875,000 cases of everyday white wines are produced each year as AC *Entre Deux Mers*. Their commercial presentation as *moelleux* (semi-sweet) has not done them justice: a good Entre Deux Mers is pleasingly fruity and dry, and the best examples are comparable in quality to a good Muscadet, serving the same purpose as everyday wines which need to be drunk young. Any red wine of sufficient standard is sold 'incognito' as AC *Bordeaux* or *Bordeaux Supérieur*.

Nine communes in the region of Haut Benauge are entitled to the distinguishing AC *Entre Deux Mers Haut Benauge* (or *Bordeaux Haut Benauge*), but their wines do not otherwise seem to differ from those of their neighbours. In the far north-east corner of the *département* of Gironde, just within the limits of Entre Deux Mers, lie the 19 communes of Ste Foy Bordeaux. These too are entitled to their own *appellation*; they share a gravel soil outcrop producing sweet and dry white wines and a minimal quantity of reds. A similar small enclave, also bearing its own *appellation*, is Graves de Vayres; it lies at the opposite end of Entre Deux Mers, a mile or two south-west of Libourne.

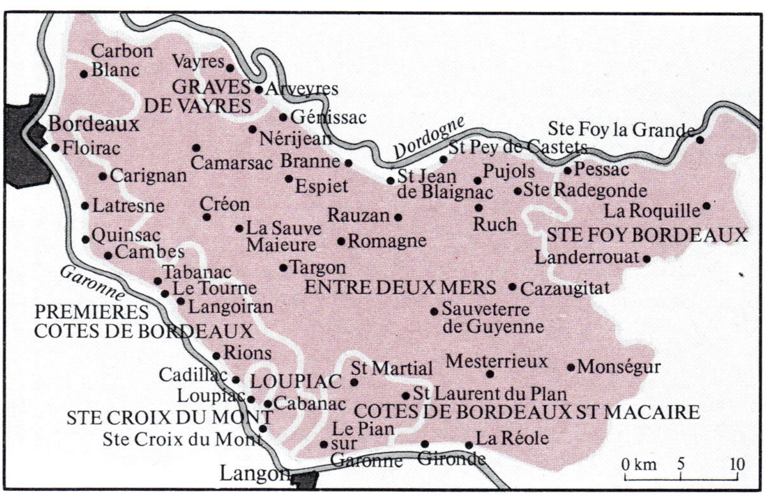

SAUTERNES and BARSAC

GAZETTEER

● *premier grand cru*
○1 *premier cru*
○2 *deuxième cru*
★ Peppercorn rating
□ average annual output of white wine, per case of 12 bottles

Italic indicates name of commune.

○2 **d'Arche** *Sauternes* ★★★ 7,200□ A well-balanced wine with a good reputation.
○2 **d'Arche Lafaurie** *Sauternes* ★★ 4,800□ Fairly rich wine of good quality; the vineyard belongs to the same owner as d'Arche and the two were originally run as one estate.
d'Arche Pugneau *Preignac* ★ 3,200□ An unclassified growth of very high quality, offering excellent value.
Bastor Lamontagne *Preignac* ★★ 9,000□ Also an unclassified growth of exceptional value, considered on a par with a number of 2nd growths.
○2 **Broustet** *Sauternes* ★★★ 3,000□ A typical sweet, quality Sauternes.

○2 **Caillou** *Barsac* ★★★ 4,000□ The sweet is a very fine wine, deserving to be better known; there is also some dry white.
○1 **Climens** *Barsac* ★★★★ 6,500□ With Coutet, the best in Barsac; lighter than d'Yquem but still rich and luscious, and running d'Yquem close in quality.
Coustet *Barsac* 2,000□ Not to be confused with the great Coutet, but still a wine of note.
○1 **Coutet** *Barsac* ★★★★ 7,500□ The other great wine of Barsac, sweet, luscious, of decided fragrance and elegance; scarcely distinguishable from Climens.
○2 **Doisy Daëne** *Barsac* ★★★ 2,000□ An outstanding wine, one of the best in the region : elegant, delicate, rich without any heaviness; deserves 1st growth status. A dry Sauternes of distinctive flavour is also made from Riesling grapes, and sold as AC *Bordeaux Supérieur*.
○2 **Doisy Dubroca** *Barsac* 5,000□ Rich and fine.
○2 **Doisy Védrines** *Barsac* 6,000□ A rich, full wine. Some red is sold as AC *Bordeaux*.
Dudon Barsac ★ 2,000□ An unclassified growth of fine quality.
de Fargues *Fargues* 1,600□ A good unclassified growth.
○2 **Filhot** *Sauternes* ★★★ 10,000□ A fine quality wine on a par with the 1st growths, not always as luscious as some, but of great breed. A dry Sauternes is sold as AC *Bordeaux Supérieur*.
Gilette *Preignac* 3,000□ A good unclassified growth.
○1 **Guiraud** *Sauternes* ★★★ 12,000□ The other 1st growth in Sauternes, though without quite the breed of d'Yquem, lighter in body, less luscious, but of great elegance. There is also a dry white and some red.
Haut Bommes *Bommes* ★ 1,400□ A fine quality, unclassified growth.
○1 **Haut Peyraguey** *Bommes* ★★★ 2,000□ A sweet, rich wine of distinction and breed, different in character from Lafaurie Peyraguey below.
○1 **La Tour Blanche** *Bommes* ★★ 5,000□ Rich wine of breed and finesse, typical of Bommes; originally, but no longer, second only to d'Yquem, it is lighter, less powerful and less sweet.
○1 **Lafaurie Peyraguey** *Bommes* ★★★ 6,000□ A fine, reputable wine, not as rich as some. Also makes a truly dry, light white AC *Bordeaux Supérieur*.
Lafon *Sauternes* ★ 1,500□ An attractive unclassified wine of good standing.
○2 **Lamothe** *Sauternes* ★★ 2,500□ Not the best of the 2nd growths, and not so well known outside France.
Liot *Barsac* ★★ 2,900□ An outstandingly good quality unclassified growth.
○2 **de Malle** *Preignac* ★★★ 4,000□ Light, fresh, distinguished wine; some red is sold as AC *Graves*.
de Ménota *Barsac* ★★ 5,000□
○2 **Myrat** Barsac ★★ 5,000□ Heavier and sweeter than most Barsacs.
○2 **Nairac** *Barsac* ★★ 2,500□ A typical Barsac, up to its class.
Piada *Barsac* ★★ 2,900□ An outstandingly good unclassified vineyard, approaching 2nd growth standards.
○1 **Rabaud Promis** *Bommes* ★★★ 7,500□ A really sweet wine; not one of the best 1st growths, but attractive in good years.
Raymond Lafon *Sauternes* ★ 400□ An unclassified growth of minute output.
○2 **de Rayne Vigneau** *Bommes* ★★★ 11,000□ A dryish 1st growth which once produced some of the finest Sauternes; not quite so outstanding now.
○1 **Rieussec** *Fargues* ★★★★ 9,000□ A very rich, distinctive wine of outstanding character.
○2 **Romer** *Fargues* ★★ 1,500□ A heavy, sweet wine, little known but of fine quality.
Roumieu Bernadet *Barsac* 1,400□ Not quite as good as Goyaud or Lacoste.
Roumieu Goyaud Barsac ★ 4,000□ An unclassified growth of good quality.
Roumieu Lacoste *Barsac* ★★ 1,400□ Unclassified, like its two namesakes, but deserves 2nd growth status.
○1 **Sigalas Rabaud** *Bommes* ★★★★ 3,500□ A wine of marked breed; in good years one of the best and most attractive of the Sauternes.
○2 **Suau** *Barsac* ★★ 1,300□ A good 2nd growth with a small output.
○1 **de Suduiraut** *Preignac* ★★★★ 11,000□ A full and rich, well-balanced and long-lasting wine; one of the great wines of Sauternes.
● **d'Yquem** *Sauternes* ★★★★ 8,000□ Château d'Yquem has long enjoyed the reputation of being the supreme sweet white wine of France. It usually achieves a high degree of alcohol (14° to 17°) and a high sugar content, giving it great power and strength. The meticulous care with which individual berries are picked and the skill exercised in making the wine, coupled with a limited output which can be sharply reduced by poor weather, makes it extremely expensive. Wine which does not reach the vineyard's exacting standards is sold as AC *Sauternes*. A totally dry white wine, called Ygrec, is also made.

The road to Château d'Yquem (G)

Bourg, Blaye, Fronsac

THE RIGHT BANKS of the Gironde and the Dordogne, north-west of Pomerol and St Emilion, take in three of Bordeaux's lesser known wine-growing areas, the Côtes de Bourg, the Côtes de Blaye and Fronsac. They produce large quantities of average to good wine from hundreds of individual holdings; each has three *appellations* of its own, or the wine is sold as *Bordeaux* or *Bordeaux Supérieur*.

In true Bordelais style the better reds are made from Cabernet, Merlot and Malbec grapes, and the better whites from Sauvignon, Sémillon and Muscadelle. Petit Verdot and one or two more local grape varieties – Prolongeau and Cahors (red) and Colombard (white) – are also used.

Bourg

Côtes de Bourg châteaux

★★ de Barbe
Guerry

★ Croûte Charlus
Eyquem
Guionne
Hautes Combes
Mendoce
Plaisance
Rousselle
Rousset
de Samonac
Sauman
Tayac
Verger

Stars indicate Peppercorn ratings. These are graded according to the principles explained on page 32.

The ancient town of Bourg overlooks the Gironde at Bec d'Etampes, where the Dordogne and the Garonne meet. It is the centre of a very small wine area, almost completely surrounded by its neighbouring area of Blaye. There is nonetheless a considerable output: over 1,000,000 cases of red wine and about half as much white. The district has, confusingly, three *appellations – Bourg, Bourgeais* and *Côtes de Bourg*. For practical purposes they can be regarded as the same.

A bottle of red Bourg wine is always at the cheaper end of the price range and can represent excellent value; it has a deep colour, is noted for its keeping qualities, and at its best is rich, fruity and soft. In style it is nearest to St Emilion, 'the most Burgundian of Bordeaux'. In recent years more reds have begun to be exported, and those most likely to appear in a catalogue or on the shelves of a retailer are listed here; the whites, which are usually dry, are less important.

The Black Prince's Tower at Château Tayac in the Bourgeais (Hughes-Gilbey)

A small but interesting area nearby, along the road from Bourg to Libourne, is Cubzac. It too produces some good AC *Bordeaux* and *Bordeaux Supérieur*, as well as some pleasant red and white *château* wines; de Terrefort is a name to seek out.

Blaye

The large area surrounding the little town of Blaye (pop. 4,300) has three *appellations – Blaye* (or *Blayais*), *Côtes de Blaye* and *Premières Côtes de Blaye*. The first two apply to the commoner wines, some red but mostly white. *Côtes de Blaye* is entirely white, while the better whites and reds are sold as *Premières Côtes de Blaye*. Although the area produces only 55,000 hectolitres (600,000 cases) of red, as against 280,000 hectolitres (3,000,000 cases) of white, it is the best of the reds that are of real interest. They are similar in style to those of Bourg, combining a fine colour with body and suppleness; at the same time they are lighter in character than Bourg and they mature faster. The whites can be *moelleux*, but are more usually dry. Those listed here consist mostly of Premières Côtes reds.

Côtes de Blaye châteaux

★ Barbé
Bourdieu
Chante Alouette
Grand Barrail
Haut Sociondo
L'Escadre
Le Menaudat
Videau

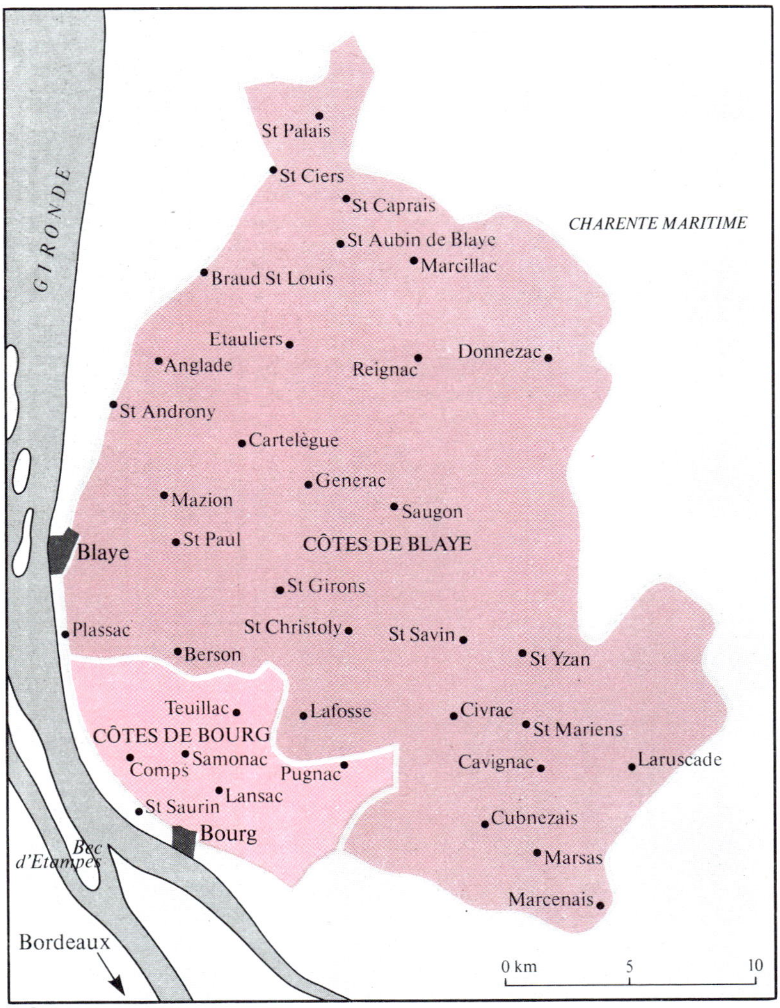

The wine areas of Bourg and Blaye; Fronsac is shown on page 42

Château Pérenne in the Blayais (Hughes-Gilbey)

SAMPLE TASTING

(1) A Premières Côtes de Blaye (red) of starred quality
(2) A Bourg red of starred quality
(3) A Côtes de Fronsac or Canon Fronsac of starred quality
(4) For comparison, a Côtes de Castillon from one of eight communes adjoining St Emilion to the south-east (AC *Bordeaux Côtes de Castillon* and *Bordeaux Supérieur Côtes de Castillon*)
(5) A good (say ★★) bourgeois St Emilion, also for comparison

Look for wines of at least three years old.

Fronsac

Fronsac and six adjoining communes (Galgan, La Rivière, Saillans, St Aignan, St Germain la Rivière and St Michel de Fronsac) lie clustered in a corner between the river Dordogne and the Isle. They produce red wines of sufficient individuality and quality to merit their own *appellations*: either *Côtes de Fronsac* (425,000 cases, mostly from the northern part) or *Côtes Canon Fronsac* or simply *Canon Fronsac* (145,000 cases from the two southern communes of Fronsac and St Michel de Fronsac).

Wines from these communes are robust and deep purple coloured; they are heavier than Médocs, with the 11° minimum alcoholic strength of Pomerol and St Emilion. Often hard at first, they can develop excellently after sufficient ageing (not more than four or five years) into soft, rich and velvety wines, sometimes with a very marked individuality both in their bouquet and their lightly spiced flavour. The Canon Fronsac slopes are considered generally to produce the better, fuller wines. White wine is made in the area, but does not carry the *appellation*.

Côtes de Fronsac châteaux

★ de Carles
du Gazin
Jeandeman
La Dauphine
La Rivière
La Valade
Mayne Vieil
Tasta
des Tonnelles
Villars
Vincent

Canon Fronsac châteaux

★★ Canon
Canon de Brem
Junayme
Vrai Canon Bouché
Vray Canon Boyer

★ Belloy
Coustelle
Gaby
Haut Mazeris
La Marche
Mausse
Mazeris
Mazeris Belle Vue
Moulin Pey Labrie

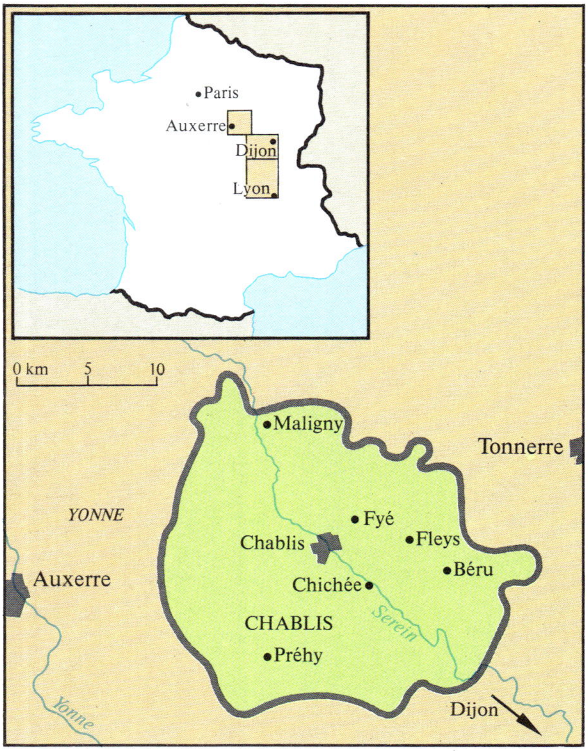
Paris
Auxerre
Dijon
Lyon
0 km 5 10
Maligny
Tonnerre
YONNE
Fyé
Chablis
Fleys
Auxerre
Béru
Chichée
CHABLIS
Serein
Préhy
Yonne
Dijon

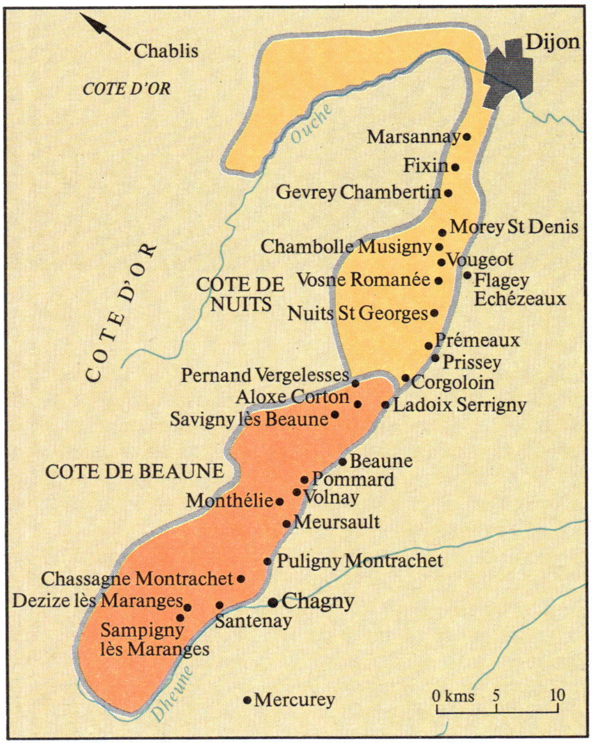
Chablis
Dijon
COTE D'OR
Ouche
Marsannay
Fixin
Gevrey Chambertin
Morey St Denis
Chambolle Musigny
Vougeot
COTE D'OR
COTE DE NUITS
Vosne Romanée
Flagey Echézeaux
Nuits St Georges
Prémeaux
Prissey
Pernand Vergelesses
Corgoloin
Aloxe Corton
Ladoix Serrigny
Savigny lès Beaune
Beaune
COTE DE BEAUNE
Pommard
Monthélie
Volnay
Meursault
Puligny Montrachet
Chassagne Montrachet
Dezize lès Maranges
Chagny
Santenay
Sampigny lès Maranges
Dheune
Mercurey
0 kms 5 10

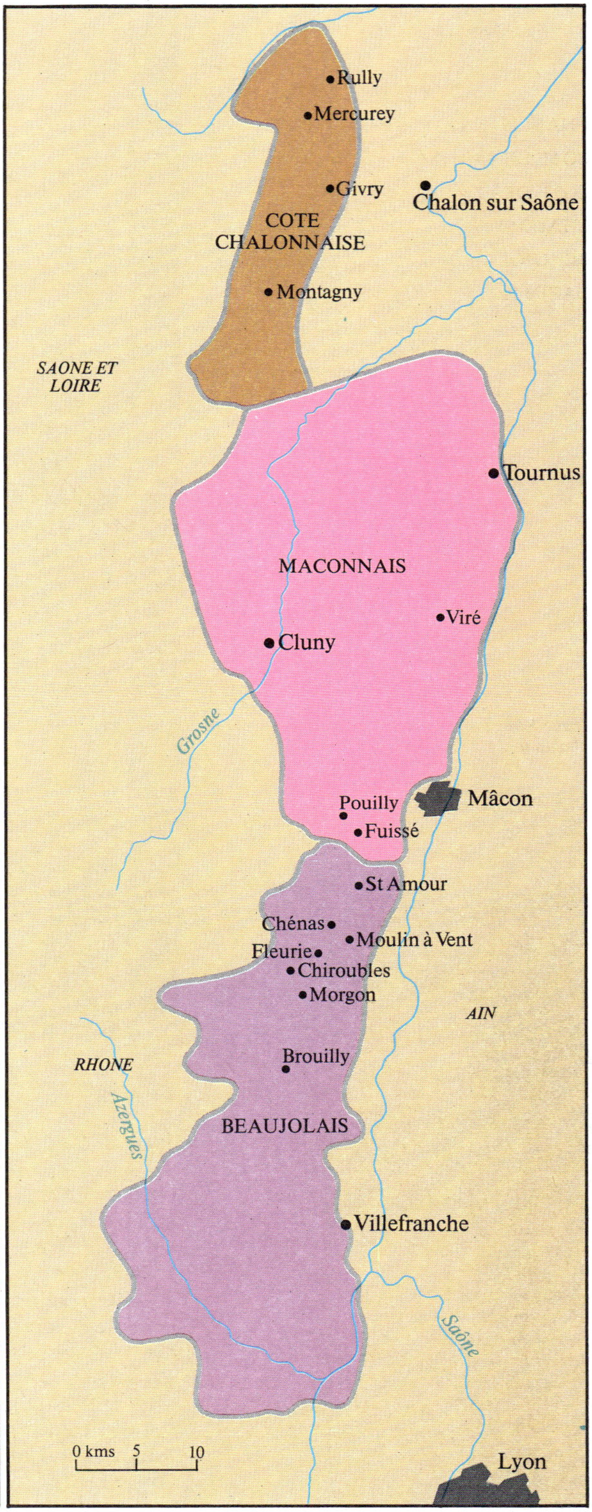
Rully
Mercurey
Givry
Chalon sur Saône
COTE CHALONNAISE
Montagny
SAONE ET LOIRE
Tournus
MACONNAIS
Viré
Cluny
Grosne
Pouilly
Mâcon
Fuissé
St Amour
Chénas
Moulin à Vent
Fleurie
Chiroubles
Morgon
AIN
RHONE
Brouilly
Azergues
BEAUJOLAIS
Villefranche
Saône
0 kms 5 10
Lyon

Burgundy

THE BURGUNDY WINE REGION (i.e. Bourgogne) embraces six separately identifiable wine-growing districts whose names are known the world over – from north to south Chablis, the Côte de Nuits and Côte de Beaune, together forming the Côte d'Or, the Côte Chalonnaise, Mâconnais and Beaujolais; all were formerly part of the Duchy of Burgundy. The province was split up at the time of the French Revolution and even individual vineyards were fragmented. Burgundy now extends across four *départements* – Yonne, Côte d'Or, Saone et Loire and the Villefranche district of the Rhône. It is not a consolidated area like Bordeaux, but a straggle of vineyards along a narrow series of hills ranging south-eastwards for 120 miles from Dijon to a point just north of Lyon. Separate, and away to the north-west, halfway to Paris, is Chablis.

The soil and climatic changes to which this geographical spread gives rise produce a great variety of wines, both white and red, dry and sparkling, and even an occasional rosé. All *appellation Chablis* wines are white, although there are some reds in Yonne; south from Dijon both red and white wines of quality are to be found, the reds tending to become progressively lighter in colour and style the further south one goes. Nuits St Georges, Beaune and Mâcon are the important wine centres.

The region splits clearly into a northern and a southern half, the Côte Chalonnaise linking with the Côte d'Or in the north, and

Vosne Romanée, one of the most renowned villages in the Côte de Nuits (G)

Mâconnais and Beaujolais forming the southern group. The two sub-districts of the Côte d'Or produce in small quantity some of the most celebrated red wines in the world, and also in the Côte de Beaune the greatest dry, white table wines.

Appellations

Of the 114 individual *appellations d'origine contrôlées* most occur in the Côte de Nuits and Côte de Beaune, where each commune, as well as every *grand cru*, is entitled to use its own name as an *appellation*. The *premiers crus*, next below in standing, are permitted to add their own name in letters of the same size to that of the commune to form the *appellation contrôlée* – e.g. GEVREY CHAMBERTIN, LE CLOS ST JACQUES. Alternatively, the label can read Gevrey Chambertin Premier Cru. The blended commercial wines carry a commune *appellation*.

Further south wines take the district name, except for a handful of outstanding wines in Beaujolais which can use their own. AC wine of lesser standing than any of these is sold either as *Bourgogne*, *Bourgogne Ordinaire* or *Bourgogne Grand Ordinaire*. A fairly ordinary generic red wine made from a mixture of Pinot Noir (minimum one third) and Gamay grapes can be sold as *Bourgogne Passe Tout Grains*. The hills to the west of the Côte d'Or produce wines under the *appellations* of *Bourgogne Hautes Côtes de Nuits* and *Bourgogne Hautes Côtes de Beaune*.

Grape varieties

Burgundy is pre-eminently a region where by dint of long experience and careful selection single grape varieties have been married to a matching climate and soil. Red wines of quality in the Côte d'Or are all made from the Pinot Noir, a small, dark blue grape with a fine aroma. The vine that bears it is a delicate plant with a low yield, and demands the best situated vineyards in south-facing, sheltered pockets, halfway up the slopes where the soil is neither too thin nor too acid. The output of great red Burgundies in a good year is not much more than 140,000 cases, the equivalent of any one of a dozen middle-sized Californian wineries.

The Gamay on the other hand, rejected in the Côte d'Or, has found its natural habitat in Beaujolais. It is a hardy plant with large black grapes, three times more prolific than the Pinot. Something like 1,000,000 cases of Beaujolais are produced in a year, which is more than the whole of the rest of the region.

The classic white wines of the Côte de Beaune – Meursault, Puligny Montrachet, Chassagne Montrachet, Corton Charlemagne and Montrachet itself – all come from the small, shiny, golden Chardonnay grape; so do the dry, crisp, steely wines from Chablis, and Pouilly Fuissé in Mâconnais. Like the Pinot Noir, the Chardonnay has its less fine but more prolific counterpart in the Aligoté grape, from which nearly 80,000 cases of white wine are made in the Côte d'Or and elsewhere. The wine is sold under a generic *appellation*, *Bourgogne Aligoté*, since it is not a 'noble' variety and is not permitted to use the more prestigious localized geographic names.

TYPOGRAPHY ON THE LABEL

Complex legislation requires that the status of a Burgundy vineyard is indicated either by the words that appear on a label or by the typography. The simplest indication is by the use of the words '*Premier Cru*'. When these words do not appear, it is important to note whether there is any typographical distinction between the name of the commune and that of the vineyard. If both are printed in the same weight of face of type – e.g. 'ALOXE CORTON LES BRESSANDES' – this indicates that the vineyard (Les Bressandes) is rated as a *premier cru*; a lesser weight or type-face – e.g. 'BEAUNE Lulunne' – indicates that it is not so classified. In the latter case it is obligatory that the name of the district is printed between the words '*appellation*' and '*contrôlée*' – e.g. '*Appellation Beaune contrôlée*'.

Role of the shipper

When buying Burgundy the shipper's name is all-important. The early fragmentation of the vineyards has if anything increased with time, and as a result most proprietors make too little wine to market it themselves. They therefore sell it to a *négociant*, or dealer, who will blend it with the wine of other growers and ship it under his own label. Most commune wines and many single vineyard wines are blended in this way.

Clos de Vougeot is often cited as an example; with its 50 hectares it is the largest vineyard in the Côte de Nuits, but it is divided up between over 70 small proprietors. Two bottles of Clos de Vougeot of the same year can be quite different in quality and character because they are from different parts of the vineyard and have been blended by a different *négociant*; his integrity and discrimination are critical, and it is a prime necessity to identify his name on the label. Leading shippers are listed at the end of the book.

Burgundy or Claret?

Distinguishing Burgundy from Claret presents an amusing challenge to the novice wine drinker; comparing the two is the subject of continuing debate among wine writers and connoisseurs. Each acquires its character from the grapes employed, and one is therefore comparing the Cabernet and Merlot wines of Bordeaux with the Pinot Noir reds of northern Burgundy. South of the Côte de Beaune, red wines become lighter in colour and style; Pinot Noir wines from the Côte Chalonnaise are medium light; in Mâconnais the reds begin to be a mixture of Pinot and Gamay grapes; and in the very south the much vaunted Beaujolais Nouveau – clear ruby, fresh, fruity and ready for immediate drinking – is made solely from the Gamay grape.

The red wines of the Côte de Nuits and the Côte de Beaune are rich, warm, generous, fragrant and made for keeping. A good Burgundy has less tannin and is sweeter and fuller than a Claret, the flavour not so much astringent as full and alcoholic; the colour can be intense, but is garnet rather than purple. It is drinkable within three to four years. The greater tannin and acidity of a fine Bordeaux endows it with its deep purplish colour, and that astringent, inky sensation on the nose and the palate when young; as it matures, which can take five to eight years or more, the astringency and acidity mellow into a complex and well-balanced flavour and bouquet.

Chablis

Although the district is geographically separate, the better wines of Yonne, from 19 communes around the little town of Chablis, rank as fine white Burgundies. Chablis is made, like Meursault and Montrachet, from the Chardonnay grape (locally known as Beaunois). Once a synonym for cheap white wine, very little real Chablis is in fact available, even in a good year. Only selected vineyards were replanted after the phylloxera devastation in 1890. Of its present 1,000 hectares not all are fully productive. As a result Chablis is relatively expensive, but it travels well and much of what is available is exported to the US and Britain.

The best individual wines come from the seven *grands crus* clustered on a single hill north-east of the town. They occupy a tenth of the total acreage and account for some 40,000 cases of wine in years when the frosts permit. 22 *climats* are entitled to *Chablis premier cru* as their *appellation*; among the best are Châtain, Fourchaume, Côte de Léchet, Les Lys, Mont de Milieu, Montée de Tonnerre, Montmain, Vaillon, Vaucoupin and Vosgros. The absence of a single vineyard name on the label is likely to indicate a blend of several. Since, as elsewhere in Burgundy, vineyards are divided, the wine should always be selected from a producer of repute.

AC *Chablis* covers the bulk of the district's output, either single vineyard or blended wine; a small quantity from outlying areas still qualifies as *Petit Chablis*, and can occasionally be better than some *Chablis*. In descending order the minimum alcoholic strengths are 11°, 10.5°, 10° and 9.5°. Chaptalization is permitted and is commonly necessary.

Thin, pebbly top soil, and underlying white marly limestone, in combination with late frosts, give Chablis wines a greener and more acid character than the classic wines of the Côte de Beaune. In the *grands crus* this is more than compensated for by a great richness and fruitiness, producing a dry or very dry finely balanced wine. The *premiers crus* have a firmness and delicacy which makes them very typical of Chablis. At its best the wine has a clear golden colour with a hint of green, a light, subtle bouquet, and a firmness and freshness on the palate from the blend of acidity and fruit which creates a steely, crisp impression. *Grands crus* need from five to ten years to come to maturity; *premiers crus* from three to eight; ordinary Chablis should be ready to drink within two years and is not likely to improve beyond four.

APPELLATIONS CONTROLEES

Chablis grand cru
Chablis premier cru
Chablis
Petit Chablis

GRANDS CRUS

Blanchots
Bougros
Les Clos
Grenouilles
Les Preuses
Valmur
Vaudésir (to which is attached Moutonne)

LEADING CHABLIS WINE PRODUCERS

J. Moreau*
A. Regnard*
Domaine de l'Eglantière
Simonnet-Febvres*
Albert Pic*
Robert Vocoret
Testut
Lamblin et Fils
Domaine de la Maladière of William Fevre
Louis Michel
Domaine Laroche

*also *négociant*

Côte d'Or: Côte de Nuits

APPELLATIONS CONTROLEES

Communes

Bourgogne Hautes Côtes de Nuits ● ○
Bourgogne Marsannay la Côte ●
Chambolle Musigny ● ○
Côtes de Nuits Villages ●
Fixin ●
Gevrey Chambertin ●
Morey St Denis ● ○
Nuits St Georges ● ○
Vosne Romanée ●
Vougeot ● ○

Grands crus

Bonnes Mares ●
Chambertin ●
Chambertin Clos de Bèze ●
Chapelle Chambertin ●
Charmes Chambertin ●
Clos de la Roche ●
Clos St Denis ●
Clos de Tart ●
Clos de Vougeot ●
Echézeaux ●
Grands Echézeaux ●
Griotte Chambertin ●
La Tâche ●
Latricières Chambertin ●
Mazis Chambertin ●
Mazoyères Chambertin ●
Musigny ● ○
Richebourg ●
La Romanée ●
Romanée Conti ●
Romanée St Vivant ●
Ruchottes Chambertin ●

● red ○ white

THE COTE DE NUITS forms the northern and smaller part of the Côte d'Or, with some 1,500 hectares of vineyard, out of a total of 4,400 hectares. Nuits St Georges, its principal township, is second only to Beaune in commercial importance. Almost all the wines are red and for Burgundy lovers they number among them the finest in the world – Chambertin, Clos de Vougeot, La Tâche, Richebourg and a dozen others from the 22 *grands crus*. A narrow range of hills runs twelve miles southwards from Dijon to the little village of Corgoloin, and the Pinot Noir grows on its lower slopes. The reddish, clay soil contains small slabs of chalk ploughed up from the iron-bearing clay and chalk subsoil. The area is split up into countless small *climats*, as vineyards are called in Burgundy, situated wherever the soil will allow vines to grow facing south-east, to catch the sun.

The *grands crus* provide on average 100,000 cases of fine red wine a year, Clos de Vougeot, Echézeaux and Charmes Chambertin being the big contributors. Gevrey Chambertin and Nuits St Georges have the biggest output of commune and *premier cru* wines, and are the most likely to figure on wine lists. A group of lesser communes south of Nuits St Georges together with Fixin are entitled to sell their wines as *Côtes de Nuits Villages*. In the hilly area to the west local wines can take the name *Bourgogne Hautes Côtes de Nuits*.

Celebration at Clos de Vougeot, pride of the Côte de Nuits (G)

Côte d'Or: Côte de Beaune

THE PICTURESQUE WALLED TOWN of Beaune is the wine capital of the Côte d'Or. From the 3,000 hectares along a fifteen-mile stretch from Ladoix to Santenay, nearly twice as much red wine is made as in the Côte de Nuits – on average some 1,250,000 cases. Somewhat surprisingly, only 36,000 cases of this wine is of *grand cru* quality, all Corton. The rest is *premier cru* and blended commune wine, mostly from Beaune, Pommard, Savigny lès Beaune and Santenay, in that order. Sixteen communes, specifically excluding Aloxe Corton, Pommard, Volnay and Beaune itself, can blend and sell their wines as *Côte de Beaune Villages*. Wine from the hills to the west takes *Bourgogne Hautes Côtes de Beaune* as its *appellation*.

The prime contribution of the Côte de Beaune is the very small quantity of superb white wines, some 30,000 cases a year, which emanate from a small patch of hilly country around the village of Meursault. The Chardonnay grape is the progenitor of Montrachet (pronounced 'mon-rashay') – the finest dry white table wine in the world – as well as a handful of wines from a clutch of associated vineyards in Puligny and Chassagne Montrachet. These are complemented by Corton Charlemagne from Aloxe Corton. A further 350,000 cases of white Burgundy a year, of similar character if less prestigious standing, is produced under the *premier cru* and commune *appellations*.

Wines from vineyards donated to the Hospices de Beaune, an almshouse founded in 1443 by Nicholas Rollin, are auctioned for the benefit of the Hospices every November – an event which has become a world-wide attraction. Among the finest of the wines from the Côte d'Or, they are usually known by the name of the donor – e.g. Beaune Cuvée Nicholas Rollin or Meursault Genevrières Cuvée Baudot; they are bottled by the purchaser, whose name appears on the label and whose reputation is thus of great importance in buying Hospices wine.

APPELLATIONS CONTROLEES

Communes

Aloxe Corton ● ○
Auxey Duresses ● ○
Beaune ● ○
Blagny ●
Bourgogne Hautes Côtes de Beaune ● ○
Chassagne Montrachet ● ○
Cheilly lès Maranges ● ○
Chorey lès Beaune ● ○
Côte de Beaune ● ○
Côte de Beaune Villages ●
Dezize lès Maranges ● ○
Ladoix ● ○
Meursault ● ○
Monthélie ● ○
Pernand Vergelesses ● ○
Pommard ●
Puligny Montrachet ● ○
St Aubin ● ○
St Romain ● ○
Sampigny lès Maranges ● ○
Santenay ● ○
Savigny ● ○
Volnay ●

Grands crus

Bâtard Montrachet ○
Bienvenue Bâtard Montrachet ○
Chevalier Montrachet ○
Corton ● ○
Corton Charlemagne ○
Croits Bâtard Montrachet ○
Montrachet ○

● red ○ white

The medieval Hôtel-Dieu at Beaune (G)

Chalonnais, Mâconnais

COTE CHALONNAISE:
APPELLATIONS CONTROLEES

Givry ● ○
Mercurey ● ○
Montagny ○
Rully ● ○

● red ○ white

COTE MACONNAISE:
APPELLATIONS CONTROLEES

Mâcon ● ○
Mâcon Supérieur ● ○
Mâcon Villages ○
Pinot Chardonnay Mâcon ○
Pouilly Fuissé ○
Pouilly Loché ○
Pouilly Vinzelles ○
St Véran ○

● red ○ white

THE COTE CHALONNAISE is often referred to as the Mercurey region after one of the four communes which it comprises and which give their names to its generic wines. The district is in effect an extension of its northern neighbour, the Côte de Beaune, making red wines from the Pinot Noir grape and whites from the Chardonnay. The reds are powerful and generous, purplish in colour, not too dry, but lighter than those of the Côte de Beaune. The whites are firm and dry, fruity wines with a light bouquet, a good proportion of them sparkling.

In the Mâconnais one is truly in southern Burgundy. Its principal output, about 1,500,000 cases a year, consists of agreeable, light white wine made from the Chardonnay grape. A smaller output of Mâcon Rouge (about 75,000 cases) is produced from Pinot and Gamay grapes, it has less charm than the more northern reds and a tendency to coarseness.

Over 1,000,000 cases of the white are sold as Mâcon Villages; better whites and reds are also bottled as Mâcon Supérieur, or as Mâcon followed by the name of one of the better communes – e.g. Mâcon Viré, Prissé or Lugny. There is little to choose between them, except that Mâcon Villages is never used for red wines. At the lowest quality and alcoholic level are small quantities of Mâcon Blanc and Mâcon Rouge.

The jewel of the Mâconnais, when it is well made, is Pouilly Fuissé (550,000 cases); however, there are marked variations in quality, and also differences in character according to which of the five communes – Pouilly, Fuissé, Solutré, Vergisson and Chaintré – the wine comes from. At its best it is a pale golden colour, with a light, attractive bouquet, vigorous, high in alcohol (11° or 12°), dry, rich and altogether refreshing. The adjoining communes of Pouilly Loché and Pouilly Vinzelles have small outputs, similar to Pouilly Fuissé but not so fine, and a tendency to oxidize prematurely.

St Véran (18,000 cases) is a more recently established *appellation* for white Chardonnay grape wines from eight other communes in the area. White wines from Pinot Blanc or Chardonnay grapes may take *Pinot Chardonnay Mâcon* as their *appellation*.

Beaujolais

THE BEAUJOLAIS REGION is the largest and most productive in Burgundy, and produces the most pleasurable quick-maturing red wine in the world, when it is genuine. The popularity of the wine, however, has left it open to abuse, despite the fact that the region's 16,000 hectares of vineyards yield between ten and eleven million cases of wine a year. Beaujolais has been described as a wine 'whose name is soft on the ear and gay on the palate'. A bottle of such wine will not necessarily be cheap, and one needs to be discriminating in buying it. As usual with Burgundy, a reliable shipper or producer is the best insurance.

Wines made from the Gamay Noir à Jus Blanc, to give its full title, are quite different from those of northern Burgundy. The Gamay is a more prolific and coarser grape than the Pinot Noir, and it thrives on the granitic soil of the south. The resulting wine is lighter in both colour and style; it is almost always fresh and fruity, it is not nearly so rich in bouquet, and is intended to be drunk – or rather guzzled – young. Beaujolais Primeur or Nouveau is made to be sold within a month of the vintage and bottled before 15 December; it is rushed frenetically to Paris and points west and north, to be consumed on the first permissible day, 15 November. Depending on the vintage it can well be kept beyond the first twelve months, but the general rule is 'Don't'.

Out of a group of communes in the better, more granitic, northern end of Beaujolais, nine particular growths merit special attention – Brouilly, Chenas, Chiroubles, Côte de Brouilly, Fleurie, Juliénas, Morgon, Moulin à Vent and St Amour. Each carries its own *appellation*, the commune name, except for Moulin à Vent which lies partly in Chenas and partly in Romanèche Thorins, and they range in style from the fullness and fatness of Morgon or Moulin à Vent, perhaps the most celebrated, to the elegance and lightness of Chiroubles. All retain the characteristic Beaujolais fruitiness.

BEAUJOLAIS VILLAGES:
APPELLATIONS CONTROLEES

Arbuissonas
Beaujeu
Blacé
Cercié
Chânes
La Chapelle de Guinchay
Charentay
Durette
Emeringes
Jullié
Lancié
Lantigné
Leynes
Montmélas St Sorlin
Odenas
Le Perréon
Pruzilly
Quincié
Régnié
Rivolet
Romanèche Thorins
St Etienne des Ouillières
St Etienne la Varenne
St Julien en Montmélas
St Lager
St Symphorien d'Ancelles
St Vérand
Salles
Vaux en Beaujolais
Villié Morgon

Picking grapes in the Maconnais (G)

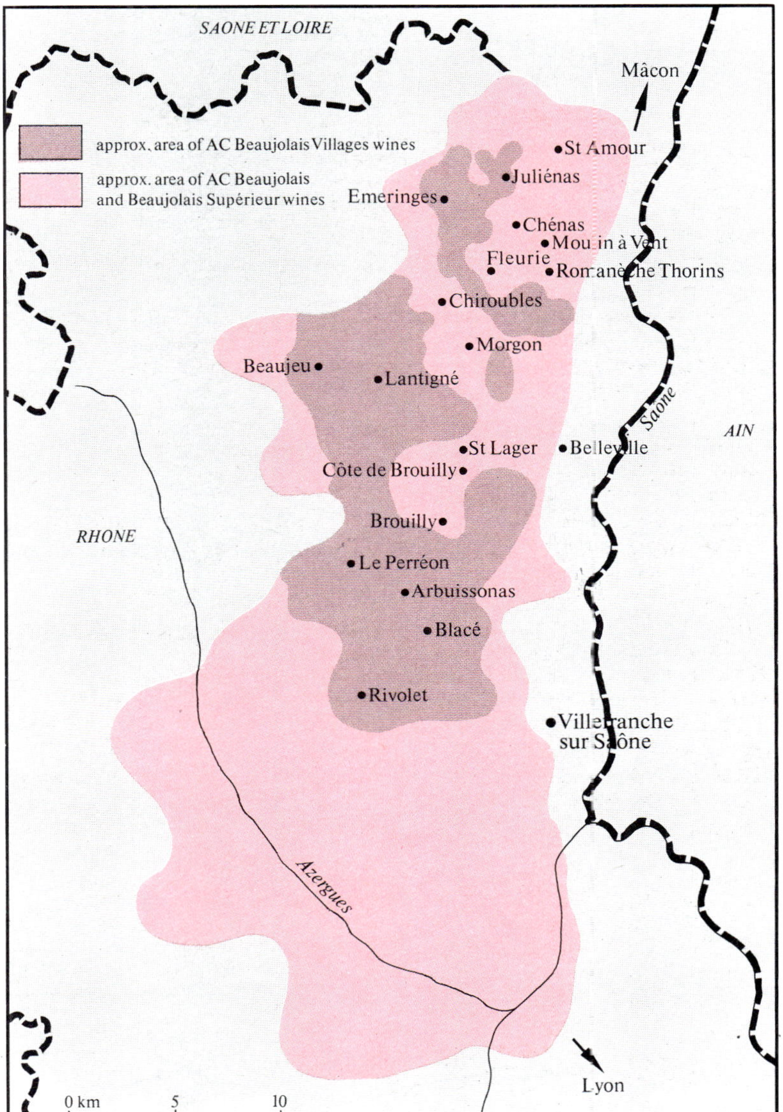

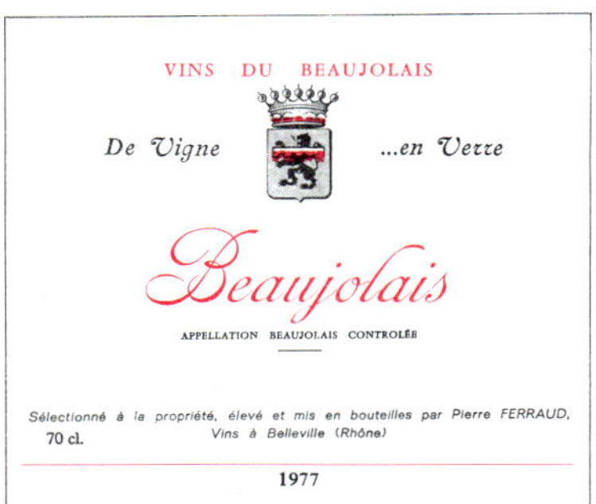

The district starts just south of the white wine Mâconnais vineyards of Pouilly Fuissé, and one or two properties in Mâconnais lie within areas which carry Beaujolais *appellations.* Some part of the small quantity of white wine in Beaujolais, from Chardonnay and Aligoté grapes, is sold as Mâconnais Blanc. Beaujolais mainly lies within the *département* of the Rhône, stretching 45 miles southwards to the approaches of Lyons. From the southern half come copious supplies of *Beaujolais* and *Beaujolais Supérieur* (the latter being simply Beaujolais with a higher degree of alcohol; the one below and the other above 10°). Somewhere between these and the nine northern growths, in terms of quality, come the Beaujolais Villages wines. These are produced in 27 northern communes adjoining the nine, and they possess some of their neighbours' finer characteristics; but they are meant to be drunk young, and they rarely gain from ageing.

BURGUNDY GAZETTEER

■ average annual output of red wine, per case of 12 bottles
□ average annual output of white wine, per case of 12 bottles
▲ commune *appellations*
● *grands crus*
∅ noteworthy *premiers crus*; a figure in brackets at the end of the list indicates total number of *premiers crus*
△ leading growers or producers
Ch. = Château, Cl. = Clos, D. = Domaine

Names in italic immediately following the name of the wine refer to the districts which the wine comes from.

Aloxe Corton *Beaune* 100,000■ 950□ Firm red wines, the finest in the Côte de Beaune, slower to mature than others; they have the intensity and flavour of the immediately adjoining Côte de Nuits reds, without quite their body and richness. A third of the output is of Corton, a wine for keeping. The tiny production of whites includes the famous Corton Charlemagne. 'Aloxe' is pronounced 'Alosse'. ▲ *Aloxe Corton*. ● Corton (red and some white), Corton Charlemagne (white only). ∅ Les Bressandes, Le Cl. du Roi, Les Maréchaudes, Les Perrières, Les Pougets. (37). △ D. Bonneau du Martray, D. Bouchard Père et Fils, D. Chandon des Brailles, D. Pierre Dubreuil Fontaine, D. Louis Jadot, D. Louis Latour, D. Daniel Sénard, D. Baron Thénard, D. Michel Voarick.
Auxey Duresses *Beaune* 36,500■ 14,000□ Little known commune, whose wines have a similar delicacy and charm to those of Volnay but not their fine quality. ▲ *Auxey Duresses* or *Auxey Duresses Côte de Beaune*. ∅ Les Bas des Duresses, Les Bretterins, Climat du Val (or Cl. du Val), Les Duresses, Les Ecusseaux, Les Grands Champs, Reugne. △ D. Duc de Magenta, D. du Moulin aux Moines (Roland Thévenin).
Bâtard Montrachet (see **Chassagne Montrachet** and **Puligny Montrachet**).
Beaune *Beaune* 170,000■ 8,000□ Most wines of Beaune are red, soft, full-bodied, frank and four-square; they have a fruity aroma when young, which ages into a most attractive spicey bouquet, and they keep well. ▲ *Beaune* and *Côte de Beaune* (rarely used). ∅ Les Aigrots, Les Avaux, Les Bressandes, Les Cents Vignes, Champimonts, Les Cl. des Mouches, Cl. de la Mousse, Cl. du Roi, Les Cras, Les Fèves, Les Grèves, Les Marconnets, Les Teurons, Les Vignes Franches. (36). △ D. Besancenot, D. Bouchard Père et Fils, D. Chanson Père et Fils, D. Joseph Drouhin, D. Jaboulet Verchère, D. Louis Jadot, D. Albert Morey, D. Albert Morot.
Blagny *Beaune* 2,500□ Small hamlet wedged between Meursault and Puligny Montrachet, with six first growth vineyards. It has its own *appellation* for red wines, but little or no output; the whites take *Meursault* or *Meursault Blagny*. ▲ *Blagny* or *Blagny Côte de Beaune*. ∅ Meursault, Meursault Blagny, La Pièce sous le Bois.
Bienvenue Bâtard Montrachet (see **Puligny Montrachet**).
Bonnes Mares (see **Chambolle Musigny** and **Morey St Denis**).
Brouilly *Beaujolais* 500,000■ Southernmost and largest of the nine Beaujolais fine growths. Wines from the centre of the area, on the slopes of the Montagne de Brouilly, are the better and have a separate *appellation* as *Côte de Brouilly* (q.v.): the two names are not interchangeable. The wine is soft, extremely fruity and very light, similar in style to a Beaujolais Villages, and should be drunk young. ▲ *Brouilly*. △ Ch. de la Chaise, Ch. de Pierreux, Ch. des Tours.
Chablis (see page 66).
Chambertin (see **Gevrey Chambertin**).
Chambolle Musigny *Nuits* 66,000■ Of high vinosity, with a highly scented and penetrating bouquet, these wines are thought by some to be the finest and most elegant in the whole of Burgundy. Chambolle has two *grands crus*, Bonnes Mares and Musigny. Most of the Bonnes Mares vineyard lies within Chambolle, the rest is in Morey St Denis; each has its place among the great red Burgundies, full of flavour and interest, rich in tannin and long-lived. Musigny, which has overshadowed its companion, is a wine of supreme delicacy – silky, feminine and ethereal. ▲ *Chambolle Musigny*. ● Bonnes Mares, Les Musigny. ∅ Les Amoureuses, Les Charmes. (25). △ D. Joseph Drouhin, D. Drouhin Laroze, D. Dujac, D. Joseph Faiveley, D. Jacques Prieur, D. Roumier, D. Comte Georges de Vogüé.
Chapelle Chambertin, Charmes Chambertin (see **Gevrey Chambertin**).
Chassagne Montrachet *Beaune* 67,000■ 48,000□ Often thought of as solely producing white Burgundy, since Chassagne shares the famous Montrachet and Bâtard Montrachet vineyards with its neighbour Puligny; in fact, it makes more red than white wine, of good rather than exceptional quality, combining body and flavour with softness and readiness for drinking. The outstanding whites from vineyards shared with Puligny are the incomparable Montrachet (2,500□), Bâtard Montrachet (3,500□) and Criot Bâtard Montrachet (400□). White wines of the *premiers crus* and the commune are dry and fruity, and are often characterized by the Chardonnay bouquet. ▲ *Chassagne Montrachet* or *Chassagne Montrachet Côte de Beaune*. ● Montrachet, Bâtard Montrachet, Criot Bâtard Montrachet. ∅ La Boudriotte, Cl. St Jean, Morgeot, Les Ruchottes. △ D. Delagrange Bachelet, D. Duc de Magenta, Ch. de la Maltroye (Marcel Picard), D. Albert Morey, D. Ramonet Prudhon.
Cheilly les Maranges, Dezizes les Maranges, Sampigny les Maranges *Beaune* 5,500■ Three linked communes in the very south of the Côte de Beaune. The wines from each can carry the commune *appellations*, with or without the addition of *Côte de Beaune*, but are more likely to be sold as *Côte de Beaune Villages* or *Bourgogne*.

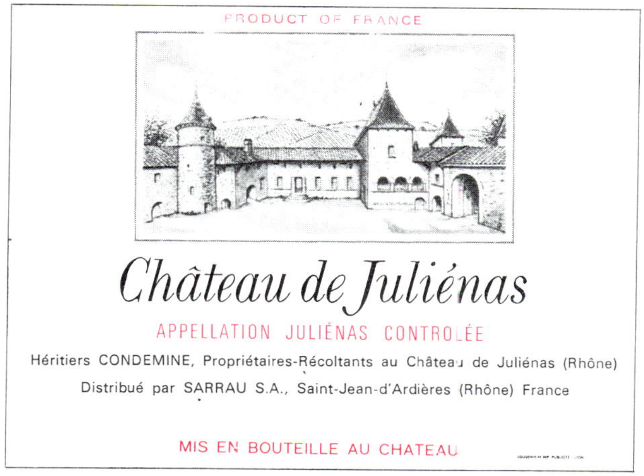

Chénas *Beaujolais* 130,000■ Small commune adjoining Moulin à Vent; fruity and generous wine, without quite the standing of its celebrated neighbour. ▲ *Chénas.* △ D. des Journets, Les Rougemonts.
Chevalier Montrachet (see **Puligny Montrachet**).
Chiroubles *Beaujolais* 130,000■ One of the lightest of the fine growth Beaujolais with a small output; fresh, fruity and generous wine, worth seeking out; very popular in France. Should be drunk as young as possible. ▲ *Chiroubles.* △ de Raousset.
Chorey lès Beaune *Beaune* 10,000■ Can be a most attractive wine; *appellation* may be *Chorey lès Beaune* or *Chorey lès Beaune Côte de Beaune*, but more often sold as *Côte de Beaune Villages.*
Cl. de Bèze (see **Gevrey Chambertin**).
Cl. de la Roche, Cl. St Denis, Cl. de Tart (see **Morey St Denis**).
Cl. de Vougeot (see **Vougeot**).
Corton, Corton Charlemagne (see **Aloxe Corton**).
Côte de Beaune (see **Beaune**).
Côte de Brouilly *Beaujolais* 110,000■ Central section of Brouilly (q.v.) on slopes of the Montagne de Brouilly. The wines are richer and more full-bodied than those from surrounding vineyards, with better keeping qualities; fruity and well flavoured, inclined to be hard when very young. ▲ *Côte de Brouilly.* △ de Pierreux, Thivin.
Croit Bâtard Montrachet (see **Chassagne Montrachet** and **Puligny Montrachet**).
Dezizes les Maranges (see **Cheilly les Maranges**).
Echézeaux (see **Vosne Romanée**).
Fixin *Nuits* 14,000■ The northernmost and least known of the Côte de Nuits communes. Its wines are similar in character to those of its neighbour, Gevrey Chambertin, but are not so fine and are likely to be sold as *Côte de Nuits Villages.* First growths are often labelled *Fixin Premier Cru. Fixin.* ∅ Cl. du Châpitre, Les Hervelets, Cl. Napoléon, Cl. de la Perrière. (6). △ D. Pierre Gelin.
Flagey Echézeaux (see **Vosne Romanée**).
Fleurie *Beaujolais* 320,000■ The finest, most feminine of the Beaujolais *crus*, lighter than its northern neighbour, Moulin à Vent. A large output has helped to establish its wide reputation as a perfumed, fairly powerful and extremely fruity wine, fresh and delicious drunk young. For many it is the epitome of what Beaujolais should be. Good vintages keep for about five years. ▲ *Fleurie.* △ Cave Co-opérative des Grands Vins, La Chapelle des Bois, Cl. de la Roilette, La Fierté, Les Labouronnes, Les Moriers, Le Point du Jour, Quatre Vents.
Gevrey Chambertin *Nuits* 175,000■ This tiny village, eight miles south of Dijon, possesses nine *grands crus*, of which Chambertin and Chambertin Clos de Bèze are the most celebrated. Chambertin, it has been said, 'combines grace with vigour; firmness and strength with finesse and delicacy. All these contradictory qualities make an admirable synthesis of unique generosity and complete virtue. The best that Burgundy can offer.' Clos de Bèze stands on a par with Chambertin – occasionally, some would say, above it. The other great wines of the commune are entitled to add the name of Chambertin without the communal prefix Gevrey. Both the generic wines and the *premiers crus* reflect the characteristics of the top growths – firm, powerful and deep coloured, with an enveloping bouquet; they are slower to develop than most Côte de Nuits wines. Three of the first growths – Clos St Jacques, Combe aux Moines and Varoilles – are outstanding. Many *premiers crus* are seldom seen individually; they are more likely to be blended and sold as *Gevrey Chambertin Premier Cru.* ▲ *Gevrey Chambertin.* ● Chambertin, Chambertin Cl. de Bèze, Chapelle Chambertin, Charmes Chambertin, Griotte Chambertin, Latricières Chambertin, Mazis Chambertin, Mazoyères Chambertin, Ruchottes Chambertin. ∅ Champeaux, Cl. St Jacques, Combe aux Moines, Varoilles. △ D. Camus Père et Fils, D. Pierre Damoy, D. Clair Däu, D. Drouhin Laroze, D. Dujac, D. Henri Rebourseau, Louis Latour, D. Louis Rémy, D. Armand Rousseau, D. Tortochot, D. Trapet Père et Fils, D. des Varoilles.
Givry *Chalonnais* 40,000■ 5,400□ Straightforward, dry and moderately rich, Givry is somewhat lighter in style than Mercurey; it can be rather firm at first and should be drunk between 3 and 5 years of age. Reds from the Pinot Noir, whites from the Chardonnay. ▲ *Givry.* △ Cl. St Pierre, Cl. St Paul, Cellier aux Moines, Cl. Salomon, D. Baron Thénard.
Grands Echézeaux (see **Vosne Romanée**).
Griotte Chambertin (see **Gevrey Chambertin**).
Juliénas *Beaujolais* 250,000■ Juliénas wines are among the more distinguished in the region: they have a superb, silky texture when they are at their best and well matured. Rather fuller than some of the other leading Beaujolais growths, they can be drunk when very young, but may be hard. ▲ *Juliénas.* △ Les Capitans, d'Envaux, Cl. des Poulettes, de Juliénas, Les Mouilles.
Ladoix Serrigny *Beaune* 4,000■ Commune *appellation* is *Ladoix* or *Ladoix Côte de Beaune*, but wine is more likely to be blended and sold as *Côte de Beaune Villages.*
La Romanée (see **Vosne Romanée**).
La Tâche (see **Vosne Romanée**).
Latricières Chambertin (see **Gevrey Chambertin**).
Mazis Chambertin (see **Gevrey Chambertin**).
Mazoyères Chambertin (see **Gevrey Chambertin**).
Meursault *Beaune* 8,500■ 160,000□ By far the largest producer of white wine in the Côte de Beaune, Meursault rests its reputation on a number of outstanding *premiers crus* grown on large *climats*. The wines are usually yellowish, with a subtle captivating bouquet, a soft texture and a lasting after-taste: dry, but not so dry as Chablis. The finest are Clos des Perrières, Les Perrieres and Les Charmes, closely followed by Genevrières (each of which may either be termed *dessus* or *dessous*), Blagny, Goutte d'Or and Le Poruzot. ▲ *Meursault* or *Meursault Côte de Beaune.* ∅ Blagny, Les Bouchères, Les Caillerets, Les Charmes, Cl. de la Barre, Cl. des Perrières, Les Cras, Les Genevrières, La Goutte d'Or, Les Perrières, Les Petures, La Pièce sous le Bois, Le Poruzot, Les Santenots (red, sold as Volnay). △ D. Robert Ampeau, D. du Ch. de Meursault, D. des Comtes Lafon, D. Raymond Javillier, D. Joseph Matrot, D. Bernard Michelot, D. Jacques Prieur, D. Ropiteau Mignon.

Mâcon, Mâcon Supérieur, Mâcon Villages (see page 69).

Mercurey *Chalonnais* 240,000■ 12,500□ By far the largest output in the Chalonnaise – most of it red wine from the Pinot Noir, perfumed and fairly light in colour and body; it resembles a Côte de Beaune but it lacks its depth. Amounts of well balanced, dry, white wine from the Chardonnay grape are small and difficult to find. ▲ *Mercurey.* ∅ Cl. des Fourneaux, Cl. Marcilly, Cl. des Montaigus, Cl. du Roi, Cl. Voyen or Les Voyens. △ Bouchard Ainé, Ch. de Chamirey, D. Joseph Faiveley, Michel Juillot, D. Protheau, D. de Suremain, D. Voarick.

Montagny *Chalonnaise* 41,500□ Attractive and straightforward white Burgundy, made from the Chardonnay grape; little of it is of top quality, despite a long list of *premiers crus* which are rarely seen. The area also produces a large quantity of generic red *Bourgogne* and white *Bourgogne Aligoté.* ▲ *Montagny.*

Monthélie *Beaune* 35,000■ 750□ A little known Côte d'Or commune which produces red wines almost entirely. Similar in character to those of its famous neighbour, Volnay, these represent good value if they can be found. Also sold as *Côte de Beaune Villages.* ▲ *Monthélie* or *Monthélie Côte de Beaune.* ∅ Monthélie Les Champs Fulliot. (11). △ Ch. de Monthélie, D. Ropiteau Mignon, D. de Suremain.

Montrachet (see **Chassagne Montrachet** and **Puligny Montrachet**).

Morey St Denis *Nuits* 31,500■ Less well known than their distinguished neighbours from Gevrey Chambertin on the north and Chambolle Musigny on the south, Morey wines are sturdy and can be very long-lived; they have been described as 'powerful nectars', and they can display either the austerity and robustness of Gevrey (Cl. de Tart and the admirable Cl. de la Roche) or the elegance and delicacy of Chambolle (Cl. St Denis and Bonnes Mares). Cl. de Tart is remarkable among important Burgundian vineyards for being in the ownership of a single proprietor, the Mâcon firm of Mommesin. ▲ *Morey St Denis.* ● Cl. de la Bussière, Cl. des Lambrays. ∅ Bonnes Mares, Cl. de la Roche, Cl. de St Denis, Cl. de Tart. (19). △ Pierre Amiot, D. Clair Däu, D. Dujac, Cl. des Lambrays, D. Ponsot, Louis Rémy, Armand Rousseau, Cl. de Tart.

Morgon *Beaujolais* 410,000■ A robust and full-bodied wine, Morgon – unlike most Beaujolais – is still powerful and hard when young. Six to ten years are needed before it matures into a pleasing wine, full of flavour, beefy rather than elegant. ▲ *Morgon.* △ de Bellevue, Le Pez, Pizay.

Moulin à Vent *Beaujolais* 450,000■ Regarded as the noblest of the Beaujolais growths, Moulin à Vent produces wines of great breed – robust, strongly flavoured and of considerable power. They can be delicious when young, yet they age splendidly: the Gamay grape seems to take on a quite different character here, and a mature Moulin à Vent often tastes more like a Côte d'Or than a Beaujolais. However, not all wines sold under the name stand up to its reputation. ▲ *Moulin à Vent.* △ Les Bresses, des Gimarets, des Jacques, Montperay, Ch. du Moulin à Vent, Cl. du Moulin à Vent, Hospices du Moulin à Vent.

Musigny (see **Chambolle Musigny**).

Nuits St Georges *Nuits* 129,000■ Ironically, the commune that gives its name to the Côte does not possess any of the *grand cru* wines. It does, however, produce more red wine than any other Nuits commune except Gevrey Chambertin – to which its 38 *premiers crus* contribute. Nuits wines are robust and full-flavoured, with less of the initial harshness (and also less majesty) than those of Gevrey, and they mature more rapidly; they have more body and colour than Chambolle, and are wines for laying down. The similar wines of the commune of Prémeaux are sold as Nuits St Georges, including one or two excellent *premiers crus.* ▲ *Nuits St Georges.* ∅ Aux Boudots, Les Cailles, Aux Cras, Les Porets, Les Pruliers, La Richemone, Les St Georges, Aux Thorey, Les Vaucrains. At Prémeaux: Cl. des Arlots, Les Corvées Pagets, Les Didiers, Cl. des Forêts, Cl. de la Maréchale, Les Perdrix. (38). △ D. Joseph Faiveley, D. Henri Gouges, Ch. Gris (D. Lupe Cholet).

Pernand Vergelesses *Beaune* 30,000■ 6,000□ Minor, quick-maturing reds – light, though firmer than those of Savigny just to the south. Whites are of comparable standing, but cannot vie with Corton Charlemagne, although a portion of the latter vineyard, and of the equally famous red Corton, both lie within the commune. ▲ *Pernand Vergelesses* or *Pernand Vergelesses Côte de Beaune.* ∅ Pernand Vergelesses Ile de Vergelesses. (5).

Pommard *Beaune* 150,000■ Pommard is a well-known name, and its wines are in great demand (except, strangely, in the US). The commune has a large output, but no *grands crus*, and its reputation largely rests on the distinguished flavour, the fine bouquet and the delicacy of its best *premiers crus.* The commune wines are strong, firm and well-coloured, with a deep, spicy aroma; full-bodied, but less so than the Côte de Nuits. ▲ *Pommard.* ∅ Les Argillières, Les Arvelets, Cl. de la Commaraine, Les Epenots (Petits and Grands), Les Fremiers, Les Pezerolles, La Platière, Les Rugiens (Bas and Haut). (26). △ D. Count Armand, D. de Courcel, Michel Gaunoux, D. Parent, Ch. de Pommard, D. de la Pousse d'Or.

Pinot Chardonnay Mâcon (see page 69).

Pouilly Fuissé, Pouilly Loché, Pouilly Vinzelles (see page 69).

Puligny Montrachet *Beaune* 3,600■ 88,000□ This is *par excellence* the white wine commune. There is in fact some good red wine, which has plenty of body and finesse; this develops well with age, but is not the equal of its neighbour, Chassagne. The whites have a greeny-gold colour; they are dry, lively and rounded, though they are not quite so mellow as Meursault, and they are rich with a positive, flowery bouquet. Their firmness gives way to delicacy in the *grands crus*, and they are crisp and refreshing to drink. The character of the *premiers crus* varies according to their propinquity to Meursault or Montrachet. The list of distinguished white wines is headed by Montrachet (pronounced 'mon-rash-ay'), hailed at its best as the greatest dry white table wine in the world; fresh and velvety, with a superb, elegant bouquet, it is full-bodied and rich, without being truly sweet. Montrachet is closely rivalled by Chevalier Montrachet and Bâtard Montrachet, both of which display similar qualities; the Bâtard vineyards are divided by *appellation* into three parts, the other two being Bienvenue Bâtard Montrachet and Criots Bâtard Montrachet. Wines from the two latter do not always live up to their price and reputation. ▲ *Puligny*

Montrachet or *Puligny Montrachet Côte de Beaune.* ● Bâtard Montrachet (partly in Chassagne), Bienvenue Bâtard Montrachet, Chevalier Montrachet, Criots Bâtard Montrachet (wholly in Chassagne), Montrachet (partly in Chassagne). ∅ Le Cailleret, Le Champ Canet, Clavoillons, Les Combettes, Les Folatières, Les Pucelles, Les Referts. (11). △ D. Bouchard Père et Fils, D. Delagrange Bachelet, D. René Fleurot, D. du Marquis de la Guiche, D. Louis Jadot, D. Louis Latour, D. Leflaive, D. Duc de Magenta, D. Albert Morey, D. Jacques Prieur, D. du Ch. de Puligny Montrachet (Roland Thévenin), D. Ramonet Prudhon, D. de la Romanée Conti, D. Etienne Sauzet, D. Baron Thénard.
Richebourg (see **Vosne Romanée**).
Romanée Conti, Romanée St Vivant (see **Vosne Romanée**).
Ruchottes Chambertin (see **Gevrey Chambertin**).
Rully *Chalonnais* 22,000■ 25,500□ The commune produces both red and white wines, a large part of the latter making remarkably good sparkling wine. Rully has been a centre for the sparkling wine business since the early 19th century; some of the red is also turned into sparkling Burgundy by the *méthode champenoise* (see page 87). The still white is light and fruity, with a pronounced bouquet and vinosity, often reminiscent of a small Meursault. ▲ *Rully.* ∅ La Bressande, Meix Caillet, Mont Palais, Les Pierres, La Renarde, Vauvry. (19). △ D. de la Folie, D. de la Renarde (Jean François Delorme).
St Amour *Beaujolais* 185,000■ The most northerly of the leading Beaujolais fine growths; very light and fruity, with a certain richness. Delightful wines which should be drunk young and fresh. ▲ *St Amour.* ∅ de Billards, Ch. de St Amour.
Sampigny les Maranges (see **Cheilly les Maranges**).
Santenay *Beaune* 125,000■ 2,500□ The most southerly important commune of the Côte de Beaune, where the Côte d'Or is reputed to die 'a beautiful death'. The wines are relatively minor, pleasant and not as widely appreciated as they deserve. The reds are light in colour and body, *moelleux* rather than dry, and velvety in texture. They mature in about four years, but their firmness means that they keep well. ▲ *Santenay* or *Santenay Côte de Beaune.* ∅ La Comme, Les Gravières, La Madelière, Le Passe Temps, Cl. de Tavannes. (7). △ D. de la Pousse d'Or.
Savigny lès Beaune *Beaune* 128,000■ 4,800□ Savigny reds are light, supple and pleasantly perfumed, but rather overshadowed by Beaune to the south-east; within their limitations they can be excellent value. They can also be blended and sold as *Côte de Beaune Villages.* ▲ *Savigny* or *Savigny Côte de Beaune.* ∅ La Dominode, Les Gravains, Les Jarrons, Les Lavières, Les Marconnets, Aux Vergelesses. (18). △ D. Bouchard Père et Fils, Champ Gevrey, D. Chanson Père et Fils, D. Clair Däu.
St Aubin *Beaune* 22,500■ 12,000□ A little known Côte de Beaune commune, in the hills to the west of Puligny and Chassagne Montrachet. Both reds and whites are lighter and less fine than those of its celebrated neighbours, but a few first growths can be good value, particularly among the whites. The reds can also be blended as *Côte de Beaune Villages.* ▲ *St Aubin* or *St Aubin Côte de Beaune.* ∅ St Aubin les Frionnes. (8). △ Castets.
St Romain *Beaune* 8,500■ 15,000□ Small quantities of ordinary, straightforward wines, with no *premiers* or *grands crus* among them, but they may well represent good value. Whites are dry, lively, light and fruity; reds are usually blended as *Côte de Beaune Villages.* ▲ *St Romain* or *St Romain Côte de Beaune.*
St Véran (see page 69).
Volnay *Beaune* 100,000■ Volnay is a highly agreeable, light-bodied red wine, rounded and well balanced; it is quick to mature – within three years, but it will keep for 15 – and it has a pronounced bouquet of great charm. As Burgundies go it is rather delicate, with less depth of colour than a Beaune or a Pommard; nearest in style, perhaps, to a Chambolle Musigny. Whites are sold as *Meursault.* ▲ *Volnay.* ∅ Les Angles, Les Caillerets, Les Champans, Les Chevrets, Le Cl. des Chênes, Cl. des Ducs, Fremiets, Santenots. (36). △ Robert Ampeau, Bouchard Père et Fils, D. Jean Clerget, D. du Marquis de D'Angerville, D. des Comtes Lafon, Monthélie, Ch. de Monthélie, D. de la Pousse d'Or, D. A. Ropiteau Mignon, D. de Suremain.
Vosne Romanée *Nuits* 104,000■ It has been said that there are no ordinary wines in Vosne Romanée, and as a group they have held their place at the head of the wines of Burgundy for centuries. Of the 31 *grands crus* in the whole region Vosne lays claim to seven – five in its own right, two which the *appellation* laws admit from the commune of Flagey Echézeaux. Pride of place belongs to Romanée Conti, less than 4½ acres in size, hailed as a wine capable of perfection; it is closely followed by La Tâche and Richebourg, and then by Romanée St Vivant and La Romanée, all made in very small quantities. These *grands crus* account for little more than 25,000 cases, of which Echézeaux (10,000) and Grands Echézeaux (3,500) provide the lion's share; La Romanée produces a mere 300 cases and Romanee Conti only twice that figure. The wines are characterized by a superb bouquet, lightness, delicacy and balance, velvety softness, and tremendous flavour; all the lesser wines of the commune possess these qualities to some degree. They should be kept for at least five years. ▲ *Vosne Romanée.* ● Richebourg, La Romanée, Romanée Conti, Romanée St Vivant, La Tâche, Echézeaux, Grands Echézeaux. ∅ Les Beaux Monts, Aux Brûlées, La Grande Rue, Les Malconsorts, Les Suchots. (10). △ D. du Cl. Frantin (Albert Bichot), D. Henry Lamarche, D. Louis Latour, D. Charles Noellat, D. de la Romanée Conti.
Vougeot *Nuits* 27,500■ 1,250□ The commune is dominated by its most famous name, Clos de Vougeot, both in reputation and in output. In an average year, three-quarters of all its reds come from the great walled vineyard of just over 124 acres. At its best, Clos de Vougeot provides one of the great wines of Burgundy – velvety, rich and perfumed; but it is worked by over 70 proprietors, and this fact (coupled with variations in the sloping terrain) can mean that two bottles of the same year can be quite different in quality and style; those from higher up the hill are likely to be better. Elsewhere in the commune there are a number of first growth wines; one of them, unusually for the Côte de Nuits, is a white (Le Clos Blanc). ▲ *Vougeot.* ∅ Le Cl. Blanc, Les Cras, Cl. de la Perrière, Les Petits Vougeots. △ D. Drouhin Laroze, D. René Engel, D. Jean Grivot, D. Henry Lamarche, D. Charles Noellat, D. Jacques Prieur, Ch. de la Tour.

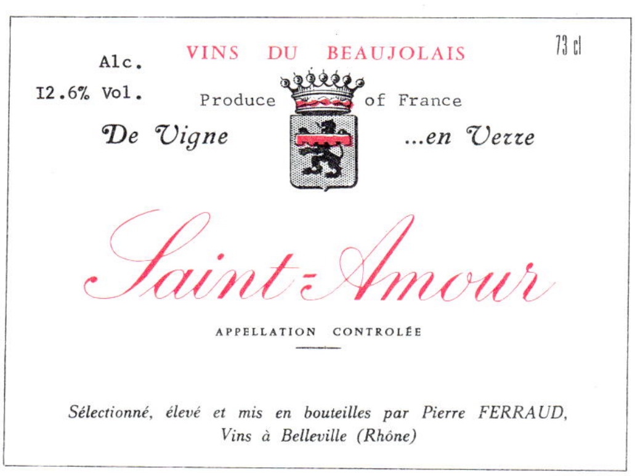

Loire

THE VALLEY OF THE LOIRE provides a fascinating field of discovery for the wine drinker. Everything is offered. Primarily it is a great white wine district, with a variety ranging from the light, dry wines of Muscadet to the rich, *liquoreux* wines of the Coteaux du Layon. Reds and *rosés* are produced in abundance, but they are outnumbered by two-to-one by the whites. All three can be found in sparkling form.

The different wine areas seem to tumble over each other as the Loire sweeps majestically down from its origins in the Massif Central, until it reaches its first major vineyards around Sancerre; it then follows a northern sweep towards Orléans and on to Touraine, Anjou and the Muscadet country, eventually to pass beyond Nantes to the ocean. The three biggest districts, Touraine, Anjou and Muscadet – or rather the Pays Nantais, for Muscadet is not a geographical area but the local name for the grape used, the Melon of Burgundy – are each full of sub-divisions and distinct *appellations*; many of these derive their names from the river or its tributaries – *Anjou Coteaux de la Loire*, for example, or *Muscadet de Sèvre et Maine*. There are six other major districts – Coteaux du Loir, Jasnières, Pouilly sur Loire, Quincy, Reuilly and Sancerre.

The most important varieties of white grape are the Chenin Blanc, known locally as the Pineau de la Loire, and the Muscadet. For reds and *rosés*, there are the Cabernet – i.e. mostly the Cabernet Franc – and the Gamay. Other grapes, among them local varieties, include the Sauvignon, Gros Plant (the Folle Blanche of Cognac), Cot, Groslot and Pineau d'Aunis.

APPELLATIONS CONTROLEES

Anjou ● ⦶ ○ (A) *†
Anjou Coteaux de la Loire ○ (A)
Bonnezeaux ○ (A)
Bourgeuil ● (T)
Cabernet d'Anjou ⦶ (A)
Cabernet de Saumur ⦶ (A)
Chinon ● ⦶ ○ (T)
Coteaux de l'Aubance ○ (A)
Coteaux du Layon ○ (A)
Coteaux du Layon Chaume ○ (A)
Coteaux du Loir ● ⦶ ○
Jasnières ○
Menetou Salon ● ○ (S)
Montlouis ○ (T) *†
Muscadet ○ (M)
Muscadet des Coteaux de la Loire ○ (M)
Muscadet de Sèvre et Maine ○ (M)
Pouilly Fumé ○ (P)
Pouilly sur Loire ○ (P)
Quarts de Chaume ○ (A)
Quincy ○
Reuilly ● ○
Rosé d'Anjou ⦶ (A) †
St Nicolas de Bourgeuil ● (T)
Sancerre ● ⦶ ○ (S)
Saumur ● ⦶ ○ (A) *†
Saumur Champigny ● (A)
Savennières ○ (A)
Touraine ● ⦶ ○ (T) *†
Touraine Amboise ● ⦶ ○ (T)
Touraine Azay le Rideau ○ (T)
Touraine Mesland ● ⦶ ○ (T)
Vouvray ○ (T) *†

● red ⦶ *rosé* ○ white

Districts: (A) Anjou, (M) Muscadet, (P) Pouilly sur Loire, (S) Sancerre, (T) Touraine

*The word '*Mousseux*' may be added to the *appell*
†The word '*Pétillant*' may be added to the *appellation*

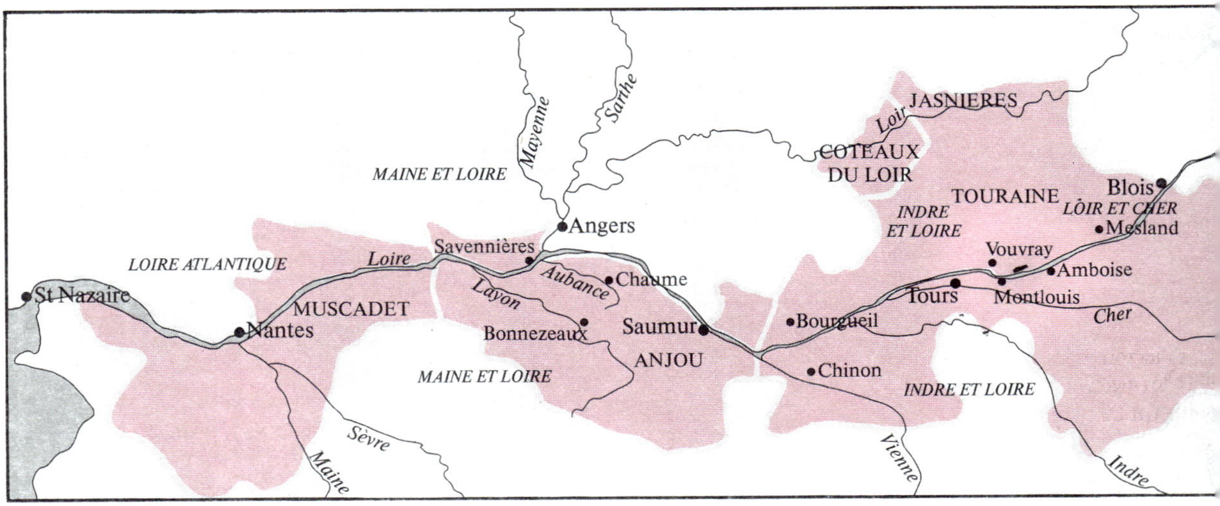

LOIRE GAZETTEER

KEY TO SYMBOLS

- ■ average annual output of red wine, per case of 12 bottles
- ⧄ average annual output of *rosé* wine, per case of 12 bottles
- ■⧄ average annual output of red and *rosé* wines combined, per case of 12 bottles
- □ average annual output of white wine, per case of 12 bottles

Anjou 220,000■⧄ 1,150,000□ *Anjou* is one of two regional *appellations* (*Saumur* is the other) for red, white (still and sparkling) and *rosé* wines; for the most part, however, the *rosé* wines for which the district is best known have separate *appellations*. White Anjou, of which there is a vast quantity, is a pleasant, every-day wine, semi-sweet, fresh and lively; unlike the finer whites in the district, e.g. Savennières or Coteaux du Layon, which must be made entirely from the Chenin Blanc grape, it is a mixture of Chenin Blanc, Chardonnay and Sauvignon. Sparkling and semi-sparkling wines are produced under the *appellations Anjou Mousseux* and *Anjou Pétillant*. Red Anjou is a fruity, soft wine made from Cabernet Franc and Cabernet Sauvignon grapes, with an admixture of Pineau d'Aunis, a local variety.

There is a separate *appellation Anjou Gamay*, for red wines, made from the white-juiced black Gamay grape used in Beaujolais. Lighter, lesser red wines tend to be labelled *Anjou*, the better quality reds being sold as *Saumur*.

Anjou Coteaux de la Loire 40,000□ A small, specialized area of Anjou, straddling the north and south banks of the Loire west of Angers (not to be confused with Coteaux du Loir). White wines from the Chenin Blanc grape, which have remarkable quality and finesse; lively, firm, both dry and semi-sweet; they take a number of years to mature. The best are from Savennières which has its own *appellation*.

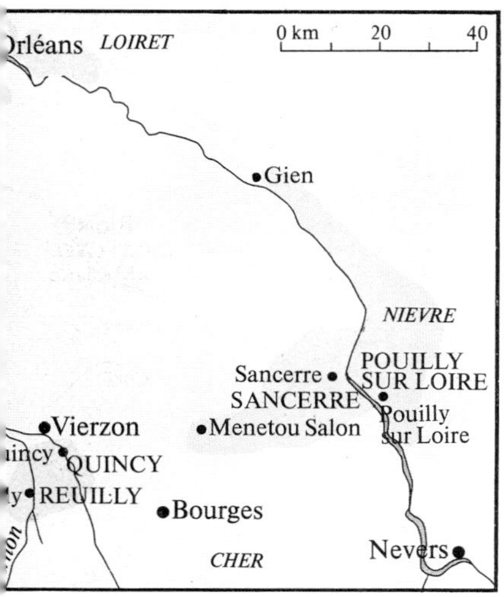

Bonnezeaux 10,000□ One of the two outstanding growths of the Coteaux du Layon (Quarts de Chaume is the other); these sweet, scented wines, made from Chenin Blanc grapes which have developed *pourriture noble*, bear some resemblance to Sauternes.

Bourgeuil 400,000■⧄ Bourgeuil and Chinon, facing each other across the Loire, together form a large wine area which accounts for the best, though by no means all, of the red wines of Touraine and the Loire Valley. Bourgeuil is a purplish wine, deeper in colour and tending to be firmer than Chinon when young; with maturity it becomes softer and more supple, developing a fine, raspberry-scented bouquet. Both Chinon and Bourgeuil are also made to be drunk young and fresh by some producers. Some *rosé* is also sold as Bourgeuil.

Cabernet d'Anjou 1,500,000⧄ Finer, fruitier wines than the Rosé d'Anjou, made exclusively from Cabernet grapes, with a 10° minimum alcoholic strength. Like Rosé d'Anjou, it is best drunk young.

Cheverny (see **Touraine**).

Chinon 390,000■⧄ 1,200□ The red wines of Chinon, like those of Bourgeuil, are made from the Cabernet Franc grape; light and bright red in colour, they are less hard and faster maturing than Bourgeuil. At their best, which means at infrequent vintage years, they can be the most elegant of the Loire red wines; a soft, flowery aroma develops strongly in the more mature wines. At the same time the bouquet can be especially grapey and marked in young wines when produced for early drinking. There is a small output of white Chinon from Chenin Blanc grapes.

Coteaux d'Ancenis (see **Muscadet**).

Coteaux de l'Aubance 27,000□ A small area immediately south of Angers on the south bank of the Loire, taking its name from its situation on the banks of the tributary, the Aubance; medium-dry, white wines which are light and agreeable but less well known and not as fine as those of its Coteaux du Layon neighbour. Its best commune, Brissac, also produces a small quantity of good *rosé*.

Coteaux du Layon 630,000□ This is the largest of the individual areas in the Anjou district, incorporating 25 communes on both banks of the River Layon. All made from the Chenin grape, the wines are among the most celebrated in Anjou; sometimes dry, more often sweet and rich, they are fresher and less luscious than a sweet Bordeaux, and they vary in character from one commune to another; but they share a golden yellow colour and a fullness of body, and they last well. In the better vineyards, the grapes are only picked after the *pourriture noble* has set in.

Bonnezeaux and Quarts de Chaume are the two outstanding growths, and have their own *appellations*. Six other leading communes – Beaulieu, Faye, Rablay, Rochefort, St Aubin and St Lambert – are entitled to add their names to the *appellation*.

Coteaux du Loir 1,500■⧄ 1,000□ Small quantities of white, red and *rosé* wines from an area 40km north of Tours; the white is better than the red, the *rosé* is the best. There is also a similar and rare, very pale *rosé* VDQS wine, Coteaux du Vendômois, made from Pineau d'Aunis grapes.

Coteaux de Saumur [illegible],000□ A small part of the harvest in the *appellation* area of Saumur is used to produce a better quality, very dry wine with an attractive bouquet, not unlike Vouvray, under this *appellation*.

Coteaux du Vendômois (see **Coteaux du Loir**).

Gros Plant du Pays Nantais (see **Muscadet**).

Jasnières 3,000□ The output of this corner of the Coteaux du Loir is dwindling, and is significant only after fine summers. The wines are white, very acidic and hard when young, and need some years in bottle to mellow.

Menetou Salon 5,000■ 15,000□ Excellent little wines, mainly white from the Sauvignon grape (the red from Pinot Noir), similar to Sancerre but not as good; light, fruity, refreshing.

Montlouis 130,000□ On the southern bank of the Loire, opposite Vouvray, Montlouis produces wines of the same style and range of taste – dry, semi-sweet, sweet and sparkling – but less full-bodied than those of its illustrious and larger neighbour (until 1938 they were sold as Vouvray); best known for its sparkling wines.

Muscadet 525,000□ The Muscadet vineyards lie north and south of Nantes, almost at the mouth of the Loire, and take their celebrated name from the local word for the Melon of Burgundy grape. Of the three *appellations*, two attach to the finer wine areas of *Muscadet Coteaux de la Loire* and *Muscadet de Sèvre et Maine*; the third, *Muscadet*, is the generic for the rest of the district. Muscadet is pale coloured, fresh, fruity and light, and has a slight bouquet. It is meant to be drunk young and is sometimes seen as the white counterpart of Beaujolais

(the alcoholic strength of both is carefully regulated between 9° and 12°).
The practice of harvesting early and fermenting the wine on its lees (*sur lies*) gives it a characteristic liveliness and a slight prickle on the tongue; it also preserves the fruitiness and guards against oxidization. Adjoining the district is the VDQS area of Coteaux d'Ancenis (white from the Chenin Blanc, red from the Gamay). Another up-and-coming VDQS is Gros Plant du Pays Nantais, a 'little Muscadet' made from the Folle Blanche grape of Cognac.

Muscadet Coteaux de la Loire 225,000□ Characteristic Muscadets, with the same fresh aroma and flavour; but they are drier, fuller bodied and fruitier, and they have a higher acidity.

Muscadet de Sèvre et Maine 4,500,000□ At its best a fine, light, supple and fruity white, sometimes with a slight saltiness at the finish; it demands to be drunk very young, when it is the best of the Muscadets. The prodigious output comes from a group of communes lying to the south-east of Nantes, along the line of the two little rivers that give it their name. With so many producers, the standard varies: the best is probably from the communes of St Fiacre, Gorges, La Haie Fouassière, Monnières, Mouzillon, Le Pallet, Vallet and Verton.

Pouilly Fumé 200,000□ The Sauvignon grape from which the wine is made is known locally as Blanc Fumé (smokey white): thus its name. It is the finer and more select of the two Pouilly wines, but has the larger output. Commonly described as having a flinty, aromatic bouquet and flavour, it is light, crisp and dry; lively and refreshing at all times, fine and delicate in good years, it closely resembles Sancerre.

Pouilly sur Loire 59,000□ This, the generic and lesser white wine from Pouilly, is made from the Chasselas grape. It is dry, with no great pretensions.

Quincy 48,000□ The Sauvignon grape, used with great success in Sancerre, is also employed in Quincy, which with Reuilly lies just to the west of Bourges. The wine is lighter and tends to be more acid than Sancerre; it is somewhat low in alcohol (10.5° min.).

Reuilly 4,000■▨ 14,000□ Only the dry, white wine made from the Sauvignon grape is of AC standing. It is small in quantity – dry and crisp, in the style of Sancerre, but not so good. The reds are made from Pinot Noir, and *rosés* from Pinot Gris.

Rosé d'Anjou 2,550,000▨ Anjou produces more *rosé* wines than anything else, and a good half of that output is AC *Rosé d'Anjou*. It is – or should be – a pleasant, light, medium-dry wine, fresh and thirst-quenching; of a fine, pale red colour it is best served cool and drunk very young. Sweeter versions are also made. The grapes used are a mixture of Cabernet Franc and Sauvignon, with Gamay, Pineau d'Aunis, Cot (the Malbec of Bordeaux) and Groslot. It does not boast quite the breed of the single-grape *rosé*, Cabernet d'Anjou.

St Nicolas de Bourgeuil 200,000■▨ Among wines from the eight communes of Bourgeuil, the best come from St Nicolas, just to the west of the village. They are lightish reds, with a great fruitiness and a fine bouquet, and they repay keeping; made from the Cabernet Franc.

Sancerre 47,000■▨ 107,000□ The 700 acres of vineyards in Sancerre produce a straw-yellow wine, slightly greenish tinged, very dry and fruity. It is wine to be drunk young, and does not improve with age. At its best, the acidity is balanced by an adequate alcoholic content; but in wet summers it can be too fiercely acid for many palates. A dry, elegant *rosé* is also made, unusually, from the Pinot Noir, and a small quantity is now vinified as red.
The soil and climatic conditions in Sancerre develop the aromatic characteristics of the Sauvignon grape to a degree not found elsewhere. There is little serious difference between the wines of Sancerre and Pouilly Fumé: variations between producers are often more significant. Wines from Sancerre, however, are not quite as consistent in quality as those from Pouilly.

Saumur 36,000■▨ 795,000□ *Saumur* is the other regional *appellation* of the Anjou district. The bulk of its wine is white; three-quarters of it is sparkling, with the *appellations Saumur Pétillant* or *Saumur Mousseux*. The little French military town (pop. 34,000) is the capital of the Loire's sparkling wine industry, for the local wines from Chenin Blanc, Cabernet Franc and Groslot grapes lend themselves well to the *méthode champenoise*. The still whites tend to be dry and fresh. A few reds are made from Cabernet and Pineau d'Aunis; the only one of any note comes from Champigny and is sold under a separate *appellation*.

Saumur Champigny 195,000■ Cabernet Franc grapes alone are used to produce a better than ordinary quality red wine in the hamlet of Champigny to the east of Saumur, sold under its own *appellation*. It is reminiscent of Chinon but lighter, with less distinction.

Savennières 13,250□ The outstanding growth of the Coteaux de la Loire. It is a dry, lively, full-bodied white wine from the Chenin Blanc, high in alcohol, slow to mature, with a powerful fragrance. There are five particularly well-known individual vineyards: the Châteaux de la Bizolière, d'Epiré and de Savennières, the Clos de la Coulée de Serrant and the Clos de Papillon. Also worthy of mention are the Château de Chamboureau and the Domaine de Closel.
Style varies, some wines being fuller and fruitier than others. All have the ability to age, and some have been drinkable for up to 50 years. Until 20 years ago most were vinified *demi-sec*, now nearly all are dry. If drunk too young they seem rather ordinary; one should wait for three to five years for their complexity to develop in the bottle.

Touraine 970,000■▨ 1,180,000□ *Touraine* is the district *appellation* for a large quantity of white, red and *rosé* wine, some of it sold as *Touraine Mousseux* or *Pétillant*. Under the generic name can be found mention of individual grape varieties – Cabernet, Gamay, Chenin and Sauvignon. The reds are characteristic and charming; those from the Cabernet can improve for two or three years, while the Sauvignons soon lose their freshness and should be drunk within the year. The *rosés* are light and fruity.
Three communes have individual *appellations*: Amboise (55,000 cases of red and *rosé*, 10,000 of white), Azay Le Rideau (35,000 white), and Mesland (137,000 red and *rosé*; 25,000 white). Two smaller wine areas fringe Touraine, both VDQS: Cheverny, round the lovely town of Blois, and Valençay further south in Indre.

Vouvray 680,000□ Vouvray produces an extraordinary range of fine white wines – or more accurately different shades of yellow – ranging from dry to quite sweet. Much of its output is sparkling or semi-sparkling, sold under the separate *appellations* of *Vouvray Mousseux* and *Vouvray Pétillant*; both are made by the *méthode champenoise*.
Non-sparkling Vouvray is a fruity, flowery wine with a touch of acidity and a tendency towards sweetness, especially in the better vintages and the more expensive examples. Drier, more ordinary wines are selected for treatment by the *méthode champenoise*, the better ones are bottled still. Vouvray is arguably the finest white wine of the Loire, with great richness and aroma. Examples of the 1947 and 1921 vintages are still well preserved.

SAMPLE TASTING

The following selection will serve to highlight the rich variety of Loire wines – red, *rosé* and white. The grape from which each wine is made is indicated in brackets.

(1) A light everyday white – e.g. Muscadet de Sèvre et Maine (Muscadet)
(2) A supple white, dry and fruity with a touch of acidity – a Sancerre, perhaps, or a Pouilly Fumé (both Sauvignon)
(3) A full-bodied dry white needing some maturity – e.g. Savennières (Chenin Blanc)
(4) A sweeter, richer white, such as Coteaux du Layon (Chenin Blanc)
(5) One of the better *rosés* – e.g. Cabernet d'Anjou (Cabernet)
(6) A red – a Bourgeuil, perhaps, or the lighter Chinon (Cabernet Franc)
(7) A sparkling wine from Saumur or Vouvray

Côtes du Rhône

APPELLATIONS CONTROLEES

Château Grillet ○
Châteauneuf du Pape ● ○
Chatillon en Diois ● ⦶ ○
Clairette de Die ○ *
Condrieu ○
Cornas ●
Coteaux du Tricastin ● ⦶ ○
Côtes du Rhône ● ⦶ ○
Côtes du Rhône Villages ● ⦶
Côte Rôtie ●
Côtes du Ventoux ● ⦶ ○
Crozes Hermitage ● ○
Gigondas ● ⦶
Hermitage ● ○
Lirac ● ⦶ ○
St Joseph ● ○
St Péray ○ *
Tavel ⦶

● red ⦶ *rosé* ○ white

*The word '*Mousseux*' may be added to the *appellation*

THE RHONE VINEYARDS ARE STRUNG out sparsely along 125 miles of steep-sided river valley between Lyon (or more accurately Vienne, just south of Lyon) and Avignon. In spite of this lack of concentration the output of ordinary Côtes du Rhône is enormous, as much as 15,000,000 cases a year. White and *rosé* wines are also made under this generic *appellation*. The reds, which come mainly from the Vaucluse *département*, can be a mixture of any of 16 permitted grapes: accordingly, they can vary considerably in quality and style – from a light-coloured fruitiness for everyday drinking to a robust wine, full of tannin, which requires some maturing before it is ready to consume.

Better quality reds and *rosés*, and a small proportion of whites, from 14 communes in the southern *départements* of Vaucluse, Drôme and Gard, have since 1967 been sold under the more restricted *appellation* of *Côtes du Rhône Villages*.

The reputation of the Rhône wines has been built up on a small number of leading growths, in particular Châteauneuf du Pape, Hermitage and Côte Rôtie (reds) and Tavel (*rosé*). In all there are at least 18 area *appellations*; two of them, Coteaux du Tricastin and Côtes du Ventoux, are very recent; the others are all outstanding wines, four predominantly white, ten predominantly red and two – Tavel and Lirac – *rosé*, although the latter is increasingly vinified as a red.

The Rhône vineyards split geographically into three groups, the two in the northern half sharing hard, granitic hillside terraces. First, a few miles south of Vienne, comes the celebrated Côte Rôtie (red) and Condrieu and Château Grillet (both white). 30 miles further down river, Hermitage and the larger area of Crozes Hermitage on the left bank look across the river to Cornas, St Joseph

Planting the vines at Châteauneuf du Pape (G)

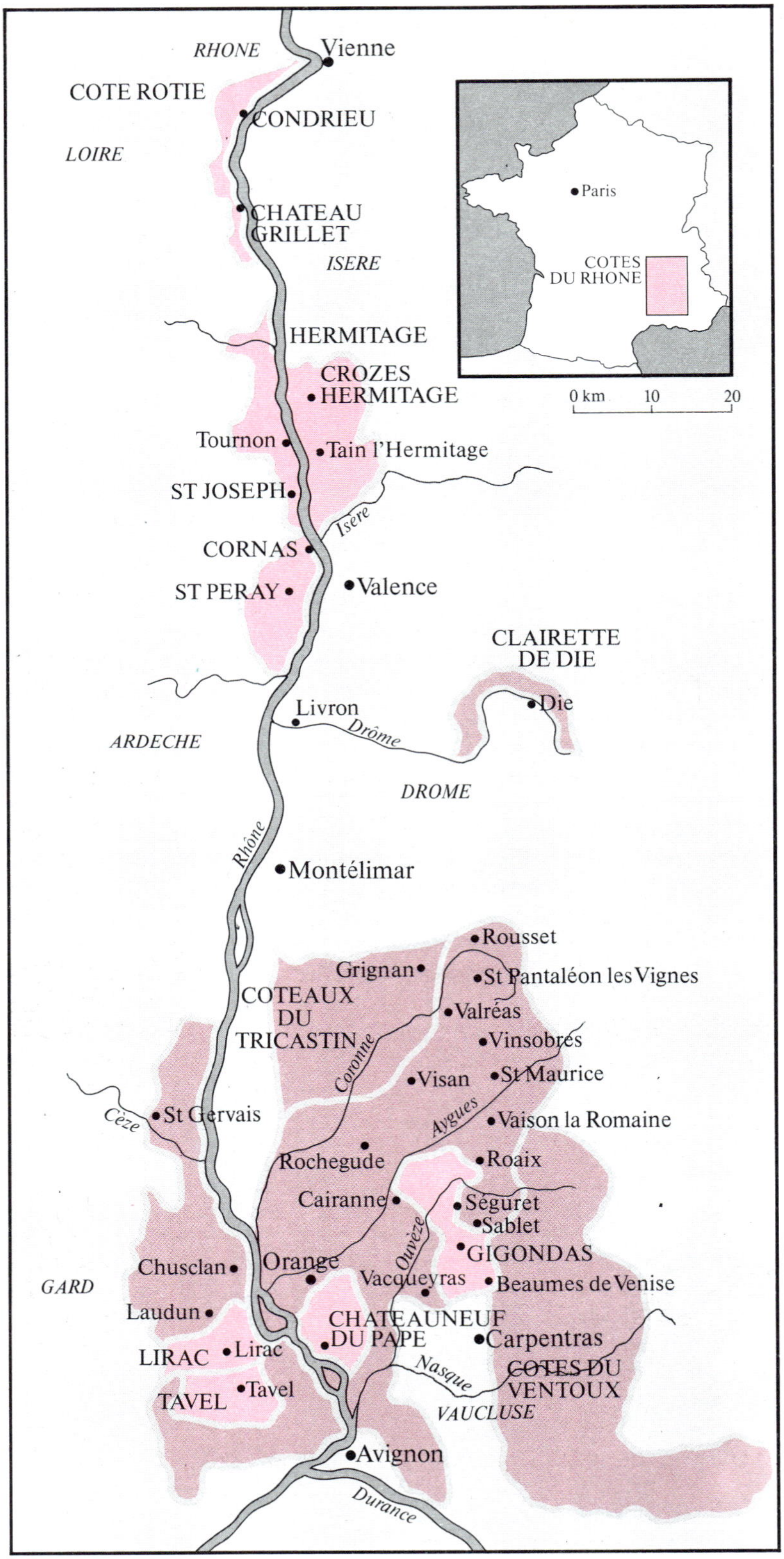

COTES DU RHONE VILLAGES

Cairanne (V)
Chusclan (G)
Laudun (G)
Rasteau (V)
Roaix (V)
Rochegude (D)
Rousset (D)
St Maurice (D)
St Pantaléon (D)
Séguret (V)
Vacqueyras (V)
Valréas (V)
Vinsobres (D)
Visan (V)

Départements: (D) Drôme, (G) Gard, (V) Vaucluse.

Ruins of the castle of Châteauneuf du Pape, in the little town that bears its name (G)

and St Péray. Then, south of the plain surrounding the famous nougat centre of Montélimar, are the shallower, sandier, pebbled slopes of Drôme, Gard, and Vaucluse, which produce the bulk of the Rhône's output, embracing Châteauneuf du Pape, Lirac, Tavel and the communes of the Côtes du Rhône Villages.

The great northern reds are predominantly from the Syrah grape; the southern ones are from mixed varieties but are centred firmly on Grenache. If one is used to the idea of single grape wines in Burgundy and a small number of *cépages fins* in Bordeaux, it may come as a surprise to discover that 13 different varieties are employed to make Châteauneuf du Pape. The total volume of white Rhône wine is relatively small; the special situations needed to ensure lightness and freshness are available in the north, but not in the south. Whites are normally made for immediate drinking; and both whites and *rosés* from the Rhône should be consumed within a period of between six months and two years. Reds require from one to four years, or up to five in the case of Villages wines. Leading growths have longer maturation periods.

SAMPLE TASTING

(1) An ordinary Côtes du Rhône: this may be light (11.5° min.) or heavy (13.5° min.)
(2) A Gigondas ('the poor man's Châteauneuf du Pape')
(3) Either a Crozes Hermitage or a St Joseph (as representing a lesser *appellation*, typical of the Syrah grape in character)
(4) An Hermitage or a Côte Rôtie, the two great Syrah wines
(5) A Châteauneuf du Pape

COTES DU RHONE GAZETTEER

KEY TO SYMBOLS

- ■ average annual output of red wine, per case of 12 bottles
- ◪ average annual output of *rosé* wine, per case of 12 bottles
- ■◪ average annual output of red and *rosé* wines combined, per case of 12 bottles
- □ average annual output of white wine, per case of 12 bottles

Names in italic, immediately following the name of the wine, refer to the *départements* which the wine comes from.

Beaumes de Venise *Vaucluse* 30,000□ One of the two natural sweet golden wines in the Rhône Valley, the other being from nearby Rasteau; light and balanced, it is made from the Muscat grape, which gives it a delicious, flowery perfume and a luscious, raisiny flavour. Excellent as an aperitif or to accompany a dessert. Attains 14° of alcohol. For drinking young and fresh.
Château Grillet *Rhône* 900□ Château Grillet is one of the rarest and most expensive of Rhône wines, and one of the great white wines of France; it has the distinction of being a single property with its own *appellation*. The 1½ hectares lie in the communes of Vérin and St Michel sous Condrieu. The minute output comes from the Voignier grape, grown on small walled terraces of granite. It has been compared to a Chablis *grand cru* or a Montrachet with overtones of the Rheingau. Normally dry, it has great vigour as well as finesse and a marked flowery bouquet of violets and almonds; it has richness and strength (11° min.); but with all this it is a wine which can be drunk young.
Châteauneuf du Pape *Vaucluse* 1,000,000■ 15,500□ The most famous of the Rhône vineyards – or rather *appellations*, for the name embraces wines from five communes: Châteauneuf, Courthézon, Bédarrides, Orange and Sorgues. 13 grapes – Cinsault, Grenache, Clairette, Syrah, Mourvèdre, Picpoule, Terret Noir, Counoise, Muscardin, Vaccarèse, Picardin, Roussanne and Bourboulenc – are traditionally blended to produce the wine; but there is beginning to be a move away from this and Château Fortia, one of the leading growths, uses half this number. Plots are split, and quality can vary among producers.
At best, Châteauneuf du Pape is a rich, heady wine, high in fruitiness and alcohol, big, dark coloured, with tremendous flavour. It has the highest minimum alcohol content of any French wine, 12.5°, but levels of 13.5° to 14.5° are common. Quicker to mature than Côte Rôtie, it can reach its best in two to five years, but will last well for 15. A small quantity of white wine finds its way abroad; it has a fruity aroma, and should be drunk young. Among leading vineyards are Domaine des Fines Roches, Château Fortia and Domaine de la Nerthe.
Chatillon en Diois *Drôme* Recently elevated, AC red and *rosé* wines, made from Gamay grapes; whites from Aligoté and Chardonnay.
Clairette de Die *Drôme* 450,000□ Small, agreeable whites from Clairette and Muscat grapes; light and very fruity, dry or medium sweet; more commonly produced sparkling, by the local *Dioise* method or the *méthode champenoise*.
Condrieu *Rhône* 1,900□ A delicately perfumed white wine, dry or medium dry, from seven hectares of vineyards distributed through seven communes on the right bank of the Rhône, south of Vienne: Chavanay, Condrieu, Limony, St Michel, St Pierre de Boeuf, Malleval and Vérin. The character of Condrieu is one of great originality, quite unlike any other. The little terraced vineyards are hacked out of the steep granite hillsides. The total production is small, and the wine is expensive. Made from the Voignier grape.
Cornas *Ardèche* 20,000■ The vineyards surrounding the village of Cornas in the middle Rhône group, on the right bank facing Valence, have been established since the Roman period. A dark, rich-hued garnet wine is made from the Syrah grape. Slow to mature, its initial harshness turns to a velvety smoothness after four or five years' maturation, when a flowery, raspberry-like bouquet emerges, reminiscent of Hermitage. Cornas will improve for 15 to 20 years in the bottle.
Côte Rôtie *Rhône* 22,000■ One of the three great red wines of the Rhône, delicate and elegant. The aromatic richness of the Syrah grape (80 per cent) combines with the softer Voignier to produce a scented wine with a required minimum alcoholic content of only 10°. The granite slopes with their terraced vineyards are in the communes of Tupin Semons and Ampuis, the best being in Ampuis on the Côte Brune (firmer, full-bodied wines) and the Côte Blonde (softer, lighter, fruitier and faster maturing). Most Côte Rôtie wine is a blend of the two, and the term '*Brune et Blonde*' is sometimes added on the label. Six to seven years in bottle are normally required, and the wine can go on maturing for up to 20 years.
Coteaux du Tricastin *Drôme* 550,000■◪ Red, *rosé* and white wines of average standing from a large area of production, embracing 22 communes; until recently rated as VDQS. Most of the output is red from Grenache, Mourvèdre and Cinsault grapes.
Côtes du Rhône *Loire, Rhône, Ardèche, Drôme, Gard, Vaucluse* 1,490,000■◪ 85,000□ Red, white and *rosé* wines from six *départements* bordering the valley of the Rhône. Due to the enormous output of reds in particular, and to the wide range of permissible grapes, standards and style vary enormously. The greatest production or reds is centred on Vaucluse, Drôme and Gard; some are full-bodied, fruity wines requiring years of ageing, others are soft and easy to drink, moderately light, with a full and fruity taste; in recent years there has been a move to produce a Côtes du Rhône *primeur*. Grenache, Cinsault, Mourvèdre, Carignan and Syrah grapes are principally used, but as many as 16 varieties may be employed; white grapes are used in vinifying red wines.
Côtes du Rhône Villages *Vaucluse, Drôme, Gard* 1,600,000■◪ 27,500□ The *appellation Côtes du Rhône Villages* was introduced in 1967 for the red, white and *rosé* wines from 14 communes or villages in the three southern *départements*. As with *Côtes du Rhône*, there is a choice between young, fresh, fruity wines, ready for the table, and more full-bodied, tannined wines that require longer keeping. The five villages in Drôme produce reds predominantly;
Chusclan and Laudun in Gard, among the first to benefit from the new *appellation*, have excellent *rosés*; the seven Vaucluse villages contribute mainly strong reds. Grenache and Syrah are the grapes most used, along with Cinsault, Clairette and Mourvèdre.
Côtes du Ventoux *Vaucluse* 1,000,000■◪ A vast area of 10,000 hectares on the Vaucluse plateau producing mostly red but

Hilly terrain in the south of the Côtes du Rhône (G)

also some *rosé* and white wines; recently elevated from VDQS to AC status. Grenache, Mourvèdre, Cinsault, Syrah and Carignan grapes.

Crozes Hermitage *Drôme* 285,000■ 18,500□ Light but distinctive reds, and a smaller output of dry whites – fresh, but somewhat austere; the reds are from the Syrah grape and the whites from a combination of Marsanne and Roussanne. 11 communes have the right to the *appellation*, Chanos Curson, Beaumont Monteux, Crozes, Erôme, Gervans, Larnage, Mercurol, Pont de l'Isère, La Roche de Glun, Serves and Tain. Reds need three to five years to mature, but the whites should be drunk while they are fresh and young. Crozes Hermitage is a less powerful wine than Hermitage, with less character, but it is well balanced and fruity, and has an attractive bouquet. The many small owners combine to blend their wines, producing a stable product, slow to mature and having a distinct *goût de terroir.*

Gigondas *Vaucluse* 330,000■⊠ Mostly red wines, but some *rosé*, from the Grenache grape, with the occasional addition of Cinsault, Mourvèdre or Syrah. The 2,000-year-old vineyards, in sandy, pebbly soil, are in the communes of Sablet, Séguret, Beaume de Venise and Vacqueyras. The red wine of Gigondas is nearest in character to Châteauneuf du Pape, and in the bad old days was sold as such. It is hard when young, yet powerful and consistently good; it can be drunk after ageing for three years in the barrel, but will continue to mature for seven years or more.

Haut Comtat *Drôme* Red and *rosé* VDQS wines, similar to but lesser in quality than AC *Côtes du Rhône*, from six communes in Drôme.

Hermitage *Drôme* 33,500■ 11,500□ The vineyards of Hermitage – Les Bessards, Chante Alouette, La Chapelle, Les Diognières, Les Greffieux, L'Hermitage, La Pierelle, Le Méal and La Varogne among others – cling to the south face of the hill with the Crozes Hermitage vineyards below and around them, looking down onto the village of Tain. The granitic soil and the robustness of the Syrah grape combine to produce one of the three great red wines of the Rhône, rich ruby, full of tannin, taking a good five years to mellow. When it does so Hermitage emerges as a lighter wine than Châteauneuf du Pape, with style and elegance and generosity, and a marked flowery bouquet. The outstanding producer is Paul Jaboulet, the Tain *négociant*, with his Hermitage La Chapelle; another very good grower is Chave. White Hermitage is a superb, fruity, dry wine, made from Marsanne and Roussanne grapes; Jaboulet's Chevalier de Sterimberg is among the finest, and ages remarkably; Chapoutier's Chante Alouette is another leading white.

Lirac *Gard* 250,000■⊠ 5,000□ Lirac has sandier soil than its celebrated neighbour, Tavel, and its *rosés*, dry, fruity and scented, and made to be drunk young and fresh, do not quite match Tavel's fullness and distinction. The reds, light and fruity and very dry, are now gaining in importance at the expense of the *rosés*. Grenache and Cinsault grapes are used, with the addition of Mourvèdre and Syrah for the reds, and Clairette for the whites.

Rasteau *Vaucluse* 30,000■⊠ Like Beaumes de Venise, Rasteau is celebrated for its natural sweet wines, both red and golden; they are admirably suited for drinking as aperitifs or to accompany dessert. Made exclusively from the Grenache grape, they can easily attain 15° of alcohol; they should be well aged – three to eight years for the white and ten years or more for the red.

St Joseph *Ardèche* 48,000■ 5,250□ The red and white wines of St Joseph were previously *Côtes du Rhône*, but acquired their own *appellation* in 1955. As with the other northern Rhône reds, Côte Rôtie and Hermitage, the Syrah grape is used. The wine is of a ruby colour, with finesse and unfailing elegance; it has subtlety and a soft, vivid, raspberry scent. Its style is reminiscent of Cornas and Hermitage, livelier than the former and less robust than the latter without quite its nobility. White St Joseph is not so well known; it is a fresh and light, dry, fruity wine, made from Marsanne and Roussanne grapes. The *appellation* covers also vineyards in the adjoining communes of Glun, Lemps, Maures, St Jean de Mazols, Tournon and Vion.

St Péray *Ardèche* 15,500□ Most of the output is sparkling wine, fruity and heavier than most. The still white is dry and lively, of a golden yellow colour and pleasant aroma, and strong. The wines are made from Marsanne (80 per cent) and Roussanne grapes. The sparkling wine has its own *appellation* of St Péray Mousseux; its *réclame* is more local than international.

Tavel *Gard* 305,000⊠ Tavel lays claim to be the best dry *rosé* in France, and the winemakers of the Loire are not likely to dispute that since the best Rosé d'Anjou is *demi-sec*. Its most notable features are a fine, deep colour, dryness, body and strength – the alcoholic minimum is 11° but it is usually 12° or more. It is vinified principally from Grenache and Clairette, with some Cinsault, Picpoule and Bourboulenc. While it can be drunk young and fresh, it also ages well up to about five years. Great variations in style and quality occur because of the number of growers and the different combinations of grapes permitted. The largest output comes from a good co-operative.

Alsace

ALSACE, PART OF GERMANY FROM 1870 to 1918, has recently come into its own as a French wine region, striving very successfully to raise its standards and to establish its own individuality. The tall, slender, characteristic bottles are now protected by law. Almost all the wines they contain are white, and mostly dry. They take both their style and their *appellations*, not from place names, but from seven grape varieties known as 'noble' (*edel* in German) – Riesling, Muscat d'Alsace, Gewürztraminer, Tokay d'Alsace (Pinot Gris), Silvaner, Pinot Blanc and Pinot Noir. Each produces a distinctive and agreeable wine, recognized by the INAO in 1962 as *appellation Alsace* or *Vin d'Alsace* followed by the name of the grape.

SOME LEADING COMMUNES	*Leading vineyards*
Ammerschwihr	Kaefferkopf
Barr	
Bergheim	Kanzlerberg
Eguisheim	Pfersigberg
Guebwiller	Wannen
Kaysersberg	
Mittelbergheim	Schlossberg, Zotzenberg
Mittelwihr	
Ribeauvillé	
Riquewihr	Sporen, Schoenenberg
Thann	Rangen
Turckheim	Brand

LEADING PRODUCERS AND SHIPPERS

Leon Beyer
Emile Boekel
Cave Coopérative de Cleebourg
Dopff 'Au Moulin'
Dopff et Irion
Hugel et Fils
Klipfel
Kuentz Bas
Gustave Lorentz
Jos Meyer
Preiss Zimmer
Schlumberger
A. Seltz et Fils
Sparr et Fils
Trimbach
Adolphe et Emile Wilm
Zindt Humbrecht

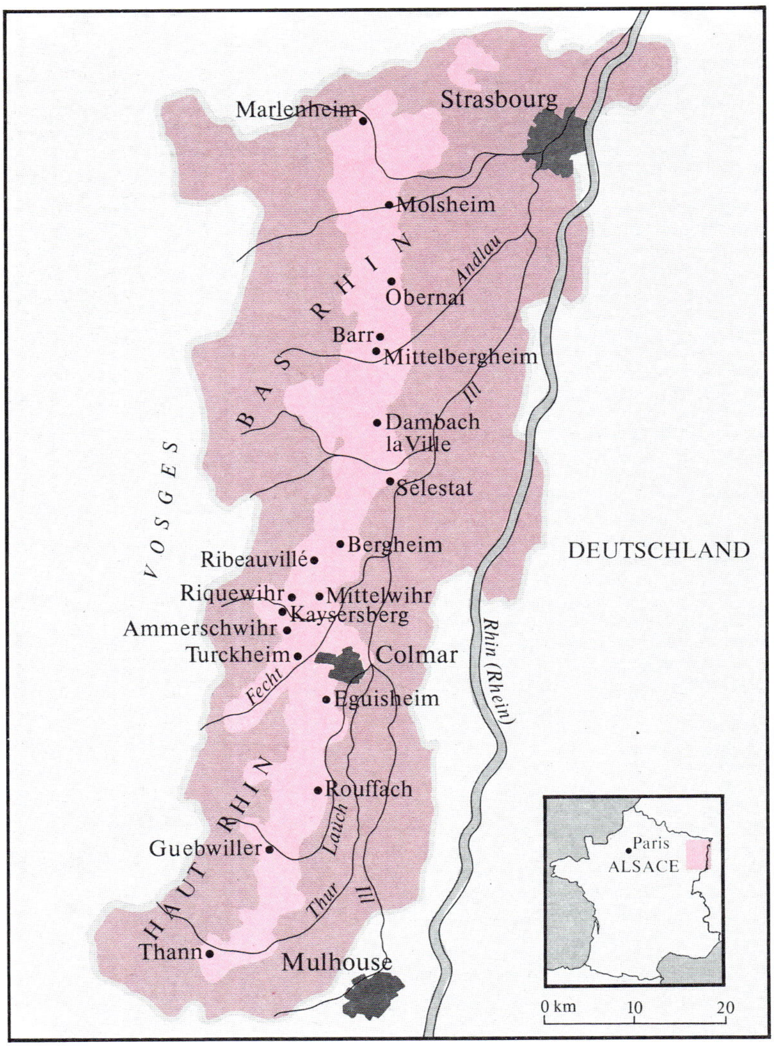

Riquewihr, one of the best-known wine-producing villages of Alsace (G)

The 'noble' varieties, when blended, are sold as *appellation Edelzwicker*. In the case of the finest wines the *appellation* can be followed by the expression *grand cru* or the name of the vineyard (so far only Schlossberg near Kaysersberg is so privileged). The terms *grand vin* or *grand réserve*, often applied to the finer wines, simply indicate an 11° minimum alcoholic strength. *Zwicker* is a mixture of ordinary grape varieties, and is not an *appellation contrôlée* wine.

10,000,000 cases of white wine can be vinified in a good year in the 109 communes stretching 75 miles from Thann (the southernmost commune, near Mulhouse) to Marlenheim (the northernmost, to the west of Strasbourg). There is also a small but increasing quantity (about 200,000 cases) of *rosés* or deep *rosé* reds made from the Pinot Noir. The lesser quality *rosé*, known as *vin gris*, is not an AC wine. There are no VDQS wines in Alsace.

The vineyards lie in a narrow, mile-wide strip at the foot of the Vosges mountains, west of the rivers Rhine and Ill, from the latter of which Alsace derives its name. Alsatian wines can originate in any part of the region, but the better vineyards are grouped in the central section immediately north and south of Colmar.

Alsatian wines begin to show their qualities after six months to one year in the bottle. Better vintages need three to eight years to reach their best; they do not really improve after that, but they *will* keep.

SAMPLE TASTING

(1) A Silvaner, which should be young (when it can be slightly *pétillant*)
(2) A Tokay d'Alsace, again light and young
(3) A Riesling, to display increasing flavour and balance
(4) A Muscat d'Alsace, fruity and dry, a nice comparison with the Riesling
(5) A Gewürztraminer, which could be as much as five years old
(6) A *grand réserve* or late-harvested Riesling might also be tried for comparison (available in the better vintages; 1976 is thought to be the best of the century).

ALSACE GAZETTEER

Edelzwicker Wine of a recognized AC standard, strictly speaking a blend of two or more 'noble' grape varieties.
Gewürztraminer A 'noble' version of the Traminer grape of the Tyrol, which, although grown as well in Germany and Eastern Europe, is held to achieve its finest results in Alsace; distinctly aromatic (*Gewürz* is the German for spice), yielding a full-bodied wine with a richly perfumed bouquet and a distinctly musky flavour. High in alcohol, and not always completely dry, it is excellent as an aperitif. Good vintages age well.
Muscat d'Alsace A noble variety, producing a delicious – and it should be noted dry – white wine, with a flowery bouquet and fresh, grapey flavour (not the raisiny flavour usual in other types of Muscat wines). It comes into its own as an aperitif.
Pinot Blanc Otherwise known as Klevner or Clevner, this grape produces a small and lively dry wine for everyday drinking.
Pinot Noir A 'noble' grape in both Burgundy and Champagne, but not especially outstanding here. However, it produces Alsace's only non-white wine, a deep rosy red known as Rosé d'Alsace. An increasing quantity is being made, but it is very rarely exported.
Riesling A 'noble' variety, producing the leading wine of Alsace – dry and firm, with a lovely fruitiness and a fine bouquet. The best comes from Riquewihr and Ribeauvillé; Kellenberg and Dambach are also worth looking out for. Rieslings of good vintages – exceptionally for Alsace wines – may be expected to last as long as 20 years; they achieve both a higher quality and *grand réserve* (higher alcohol) standing on such occasions. The 1976 vintage was outstanding.
Silvaner Although named as a 'noble' variety with the others in 1945, the Silvaner can produce a rather dull wine; it remains, however, the most widely cultivated grape, especially in the Bas Rhin, and accounts for a quarter of all Alsatian wines. Generally they are light and refreshing, with a slight acidity; they become excellent in good vintages and certain vineyards when well exposed to the sun, especially in Barr, Ronflach and Mittelbergheim (where the Zotzenberg vineyard is outstanding).
Tokay d'Alsace The Tokay d'Alsace or Pinot Gris is the same grape as the Rülander in Germany, and is a 'noble' variety here. It produces a dry, or slightly sweet, white wine – no relation to the Hungarian Tokay, which is made from the Furmint grape – and has plenty of bouquet. It is full-bodied and keeps well. The best comes from Riquewihr.
Zwicker A blend of 'noble' and common varieties (Chasselas and Auxerrois, often mixed with Silvaner).

A street in Riquewihr (G)

Champagne

SUCCESS STORY

The growth of Champagne sales since the Second World War has been one of the success stories of the wine trade. In 1950, sales of 33,000,000 bottles were exactly the same as those for 1935. However, by 1960 they had risen to 49,000,000, and from then on Champagne never looked back, except during the world-wide wine slump of 1974; by 1977 sales had reached 170,000,000 bottles.

This has naturally led to marketing problems. In 1950, only 10,500 out of the authorized 35,000 hectares of vineyards were in production; by the end of 1978, in an effort to keep pace with the soaring demand, over 24,000 hectares had been planted. This figure is expected to rise to 28,500 hectares by 1983.

Nature is capricious, however, and every now and then she withholds her favours. The summer of 1978 was cold and wet, and after an average of 690,000 hectolitres over the previous five years, production fell to 290,000 hectolitres. A serious supply problem was the result, and prices rose to a new record.

It is a perhaps surprising fact that Champagne shares any attribute in common with Port, Sherry and Madeira: yet all four, however different in taste and origin, are fortified wines. Not, of course, that Champagne is fortified with spirit; but in the centuries before Pasteur brought science to wine, men were always looking for ways of preserving it, so that it could travel without spoilage, and the wines of Champagne were no exception. In most other areas preservation was achieved by the addition of brandy; in Champagne it was effected by more natural means, requiring a much more difficult process – the retention in the bottle of carbon dioxide. This instantly overcame the problem of oxidization, to which white wines are especially prone.

It is important to realise that Champagne is an industrial product, and that the *méthode champenoise* is an industrial process, transforming a really very moderate white wine into one of the most delectable drinks in the world. Indeed, it is highly probable that had the process not been discovered at the end of the 17th century, and perfected in the 18th, little or no wine would be produced in the region today.

The *méthode champenoise*

In its initial stages Champagne is made like any other white wine. However, special care is needed in the vinification of the red grapes, so that the wines do not take on a pinkish hue. Of those that do, some are allowed to remain that way, to make pink Champagne; the rest have the colour removed by fining.

In January the wines are finished, racked and ready to be tasted. This is when the crucial tastings occur to determine the composition of the *cuvées* (blends – see glossary). All houses make at least two *cuvées* in a good year – their habitual non-vintage, and their vintage; to the latter can be added the *de luxe* vintage wines of some of the top *marques*, of which Moët et Chandon's Dom Pérignon was the forerunner. Some houses also have a *Blanc de Blancs* and perhaps a *Crémant* – i.e. a wine which 'creams' rather than fizzes, because it has been subjected to less pressure.

The blends are now made and allowed to marry, before bottling begins in April. This is done in the normal way except that a *liqueur de tirage* is added, consisting of a solution of cane sugar in wine and some cultured yeasts. If the wine is to be a *Crémant*, less sugar is added.

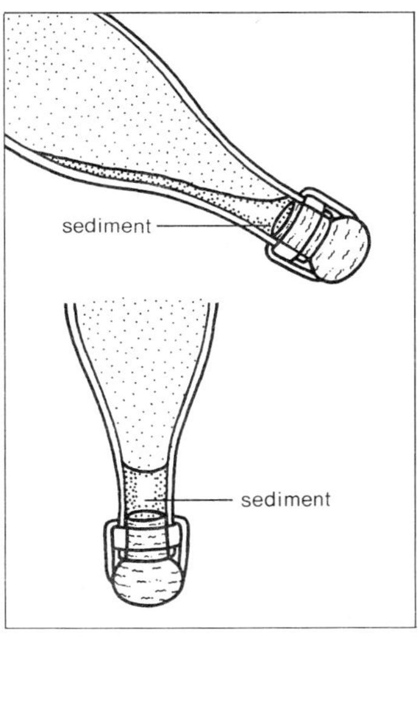

The bottles are then stored in the cool, dark cellars hewn out of chalk which riddle the hillsides of the region. Many of those in Rheims itself are old quarries going back to Roman times. The long, slow fermentation takes about three months. Then the bottles are transferred to special racks (*pupitres*) for the *remuage* (see diagram A) – an elaborate process by which sediment left behind by the fermentation is carefully shaken down the bottle until it rests neatly on the cork. Alternatives are being sought to this costly and exacting process, but so far the skill of the human hand cannot be matched.

The bottles, which are now upside down (*sur pointe*), are stored in this position until disgorgement – a process which may take either months or years (diagram B). The laws governing the sale of Champagne lay down a minimum of one year between the end of the second fermentation and the moment when a wine can be put on sale. Most good firms store their non-vintage wines for between two and two and a half years – but the longer the better; a modest non-vintage (NV) Champagne kept in good storage conditions for a year can be greatly improved.

There is an interesting variant to this sequence. If a wine is kept some years *sur pointe* it retains its youth better than if it had been disgorged earlier. Hence the success of Bollinger's late-disgorged vintage wines.

Until recently much of the disgorgement was still done by hand; now all is mechanical. The bottles pass through a tank where a saline solution is maintained at a temperature of about −16°C, so that the wine in the neck of the bottles is frozen, encapsulating the sediment. They are then put into a bottling line which removes the crown cork. The pressure blows out the small piece of ice, but being very cold the carbon dioxide in the bottle does not cause much further loss. The deficit is made up by adding some wine; this includes a liquid known as *liqueur d'expédition*, the composition of which will depend on whether the Champagne is to be *brut* (the dryest), extra-dry, dry, semi-dry or sweet. The mushroom cork is then inserted and held in place by its wire, and the bottle is finished by the splendid gold foil which is the hallmark of Champagne. The wine is now ready to meet its public.

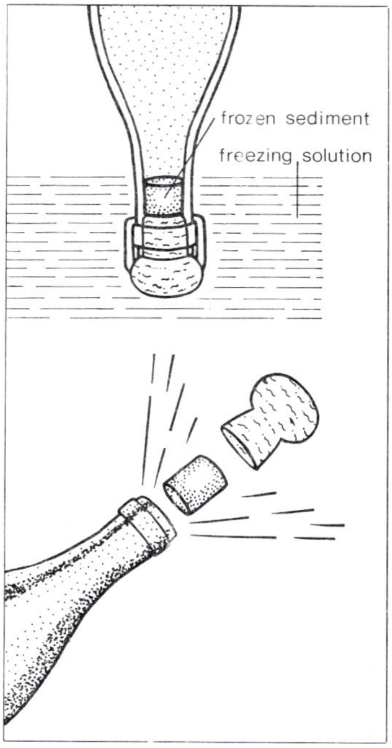

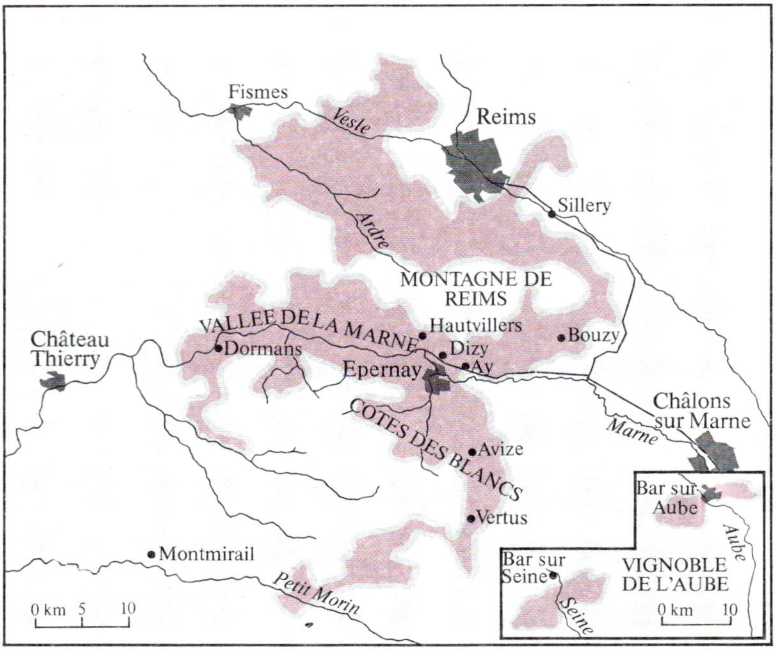

The vineyards of Champagne are concentrated in four areas:

(1) The Montagne de Reims, a low wooded hill to the north and east of Epernay, separating the rivers Ardre and Vesle.

(2) The Vallée de la Marne, running from Epernay west to Dormans.

(3) The Côte des Blancs, south of Epernay, on either side of a small rivulet called the Cubry.

(4) The quite separate Vignoble de l'Aube, some 60 miles south-east of Epernay, lying between the rivers Seine and Aube.

STILL CHAMPAGNES

Still wines are also made in Champagne. The red is called Bouzy; the more plentiful white, once known as Champagne Nature, is now called Coteaux Champenois. Such wines sell more often by virtue of their famous pedigree than on their own merits.

The land and the grapes

The wine takes its name from the old province of France in which the vineyards are situated – a province which once stretched from Luxembourg in the north to Burgundy in the south, and from the Isle de France in the west to Lorraine in the east: its capital was the cathedral city of Rheims, where the kings of France from Pépin to Charles X went to be crowned. The rolling countryside is dominated by a series of escarpments, often wooded, overlooking intensively planted slopes that fall away towards the valley of the Marne. It is a spacious landscape, redolent with memories of the First World War, in which the little villages, with their solid stone houses and massive churches, are often hidden away around a corner in the road.

Some of the most important vineyards can be seen by driving the 17 miles from Rheims south to Epernay, but in the last 25 years, in a vain effort to keep abreast of demand, there has been a spectacular increase in the area under vine.

Two main grape varieties are used, the black Pinot and the white Chardonnay, just as in Burgundy. The classic blend is usually said to be one-third Chardonnay and two-thirds Pinot. A wine made only from the Chardonnay is called a *Blanc de Blancs*. Only a few growers' wines are made entirely from the Pinot, and many would claim, with some justification, that such a wine was not a true Champagne.

For Champagne is essentially centred round the art of blending. The great Champagne houses, many of which have become household names, have created and maintained the reputation of their wines by blending them from different areas, and from different vineyards within those areas – thus creating and maintaining the particular style of Champagne for which their house is known. That is why there is such 'brand-loyalty' among seasoned Champagne drinkers.

CHAMPAGNE HOUSES

The greatest firms in terms of consistent quality of all their wines:

Bollinger
Krug
Louis Roederer
Ruinart
Veuve Clicquot Ponsardin.

Fine houses, some of which produce some exceptional wines:

Abel Lepitre
Canard Duchene
Charles Heidsieck
Deutz Champagne
George Goulet
Heidsieck
Lanson
Laurent Perrier
Mercier
Moët et Chandon
G. H. Mumm
Perrier Jouët
Piper Heidsieck
Pol Roger
Pommery & Greno
Taittinger.

Small, good quality houses worth looking for:

Alfred Gratien
Joseph Perrier
St Marceaux
De Venoge.

Several co-operatives market excellent Champagnes under brand names – e.g. St Gall and St Simon.

View of a Champagne vineyard; the town of Epernay is in the background (Fotofass)

The other wines of France

MANY HUNDREDS OF FRENCH WINES are produced in areas outside the six great regions covered in the preceding pages. Most of them are accounted for by the mass-production of the Midi, from the *départements* of Pyrénées Orientales, Aude, Hérault and Gard; these are *vins ordinaires*, and they fall outside the scope of this book. But the Midi and Provence also produce a number of VDQS and AC wines which are worth noting, and there are also a number of wines, smaller in quantity but higher in quality, in the south-west, outside the Gironde. In eastern France there are the wines of the Jura, Savoie and the foothills of the Massif Central, west of Lyon.

Once outside the classic wine areas of France, AC and VDQS designations have to be interpreted with a degree of caution. Some, like the wines of the Jura or the Tarn, are little more than good *vin du pays*, with a local tradition and a lot of recent hard work behind them. On the other hand, the vineyards of the Dordogne and the Lot et Garonne are really a continuation of those of Bordeaux; most of their wines are excellent, suffering only from comparison with the great wines of their neighbours, and the best Dordogne wines are better than many lesser Bordeaux.

There are also the old vineyard areas, such as Côtes de Buzet in Aquitaine and Haut Poitou, which are being replanted, and where good co-operatives are transforming the quality of the wines; and, finally, there are the historic vineyard areas whose reputation and production were once much greater than they are today, such as Cahors in Lot and Jurançon in the Pyrenees, near Pau. How much the wines have changed and how much tastes have changed is often hard to say.

THE SOUTH-WEST: Dordogne, Hautes Pyrénées, Lot, Lot et Garonne, Pyrénées Atlantiques, Tarn, Vienne.

THE MIDI: Alpes Maritimes, Aude, Bouches du Rhône, Gard, Hérault, Pyrénées Orientales, Var.

EASTERN FRANCE: Ain, Haute Savoie, Isère, Jura, Loire, Savoie.

THE SOUTH-EAST, THE MIDI, EASTERN FRANCE

GAZETTEER

● red
⦶ rosé
○ white
Italic indicates name of *département(s)*

Arbois ●⦶○ *Jura.* The most important of the Jura *appellations.* Reds are the least interesting, the local grape varieties producing wines that lack charm. Whites are like full-blown, old-fashioned Burgundy; the Chardonnay gives some style to the local Savagnin grape, but the wine tends to oxidize quickly. The *rosés* are full-bodied, like Tavel, and have a deserved reputation.
Vin jaune – a white wine made exclusively from the Savagnin grape and aged for a minimum of six years in cask – is one of the area's two great specialities: a film of yeast cells, similar to the *flor* found in Jerez, grows on the surface of the wine which tastes like a light, unfortified sherry. The other speciality, *vin de paille*, is made from fully-ripe grapes which are then dried for at least two months; it is high in alcohol (15° to 16°) and deep in colour.

Bandol ●⦶○ *Var.* The best-known of the Provence *appellations.* Reds, with a little ageing, are full-bodied and individual, like good Rhône wines. *Rosés* are more fruity than ordinary Côtes de Provence. Whites are full-flavoured, but are not in the same class as the other two.

Bergerac ●⦶○ *Dordogne.* The major *appellation* of this region, which immediately adjoins the Bordeaux vineyards of the Gironde. Red wines resemble lesser Bordeaux; whites, formerly *demi-sec*, are now dry and distinctly fruity, with the Sauvignon grape becoming more predominant; *rosés* are light and attractive. Co-operatives are important, but there are also some good *château* wines.

Blanquette de Limoux ○ *Aude.* This AC wine, made by the *méthode champenoise*, comes from the mountainous region south of Carcassonne. Very dry and crisp, with a refreshing tang at the finish, it is the outstanding white wine of the whole Languedoc and one of the best sparkling wines in France. The still version is relatively ordinary. The co-operative is the major producer.
Cahors ● *Lot.* A dark-coloured, rather coarse wine made from Malbec grapes, with some Merlot and Jurançon. The area is famous historically for its 'black' wines, which were once used to add colour and body to clarets. Today's wines are less tannic and alcoholic, but they still need ageing in cask and bottle.
Château Chalon ○ *Jura.* The *appellation* is applied entirely to *vin jaune* (see **Arbois**) produced in four communes to the south-west of Arbois. Misleadingly, this is *not* a property wine: Château Chalon is the name of the town. The wine, which is the finest example of *vin jaune*, is bottled in special, dumpy-shaped *clavelins*.
Clairette de Languedoc ○ *Hérault.* The best-known white wine of the Midi; has a propensity for rapid oxidization.
Corbières ● *Aude.* The mountainous interior of a mass-production *département* produces this well-known red. There are great variations of quality, from full-bodied wines, strong flavoured if coarse, to austere, hard ones with the bitter after-taste typical of the Midi.

Costières du Gard ●⊘ *Gard*. Lighter in colour and softer than other Midi wines, with a pleasing perfume; they are closer in character to the Rhône than the Midi.
Coteaux d'Aix en Provence ●⊘○ *Bouches du Rhône*. VDQS wines, slightly lighter in alcohol but often more perfumed and interesting than the AC Côtes de Provence. Interest has been aroused in the area by the success of Château Vignelaure, a property where Cabernet Sauvignon grapes have been planted, producing a wine well above the normal quality for Provence.
Coteaux de Languedoc ●○ *Hérault*. The best of these light, rather austere wines are usually sold under their commune names, such as St Saturnin and Faugères.
Côtes de Buzet ● *Lot et Garonne*. Recently up-graded from VDQS to AC. Excellent red wines of Bordeaux character are all produced by one co-operative. Grape varieties are as for Bordeaux.
Côtes de Duras ●○ *Lot et Garonne*. Mostly dry white wines, very similar to those of Bergerac to the north; increasing quantities are being produced from Sauvignon grapes.
Côtes de Forez ●⊘ *Loire*. A VDQS wine, made from the Gamay and produced in the hills west of Lyon. In good years it is fruity and typical of Gamay wines; in other vintages the colour is a greyish *rosé*, more akin to the *vin gris* of old.
Côtes de Jura ●⊘○ *Jura*. An AC which covers all the types of wine found under the Arbois *appellation*, including *mousseux*. Normally of lower quality than Arbois.
Côtes de Marmandais ●○ *Lot et Garonne*. Two co-operatives have produced much improved wines, especially red, in the last decade, as Bordeaux grape varieties replace more rustic ones. The red is soft, fruity and quick-maturing; the white has more character than one would expect.
Côtes de Provence ●⊘○ *Bouches du Rhône, Var, Alpes Maritimes*. Recently up-graded from VDQS to AC, these wines owe much of their popularity to the attractions of Provence as a holiday area. Reds are full-bodied with a dry finish and rather dull. *Rosés*, when at their best, are fruity and easy to drink, but they can also be hard and dry. Whites are often more pleasing than the reds, but tend to be rather ordinary.

Côtes Roannaises ● *Loire*. A Gamay VDQS from vineyards just north of the Côtes de Forez; very similar wines, but not quite so good.
Côtes de Roussillon ● *Pyrénées Orientales*. This mountainous region produces AC wines, probably the best reds of the Midi; they have a richness of flavour and bouquet not found further north. Note that *Grand Roussillon* is an *appellation* for *vins doux naturels*, the sweet dessert wines of the Midi which bear some resemblance to Port. The best, Banyuls, has its own AC.
Côtes de Saussignac ○ *Dordogne*. A decent dry Bergerac from a small area just south of the river and west of the town.
Fitou ● *Aude*. An AC area, close to the Spanish border, where the wines are aged longer than nearby Corbières but are only marginally better.
Gaillac ●⊘○ *Tarn*. A decent *vin du pays*, dignified with an AC. The sweet whites, which are traditional to the region, have a pungent nose and are rather ordinary; so are the reds and *rosés* and the sparkling wines.
Haut Poitou ●○ *Vienne*. These wines, from an area bordering on the Loire, only gained VDQS status in 1970; however, the co-operative is already producing whites which rival many AC wines. Sauvignon is the most widely planted vine, producing an excellent, full-bodied wine which can easily be mistaken for Sancerre; Pinot Chardonnay wines are also excellent, resembling a small Mâcon Blanc, while those from the Chenin tend to be rather acid. Gamay, Cabernet and Pinot Noir are surprisingly blended to produce fruity, vivid reds for early drinking; but these are not of the same quality as the whites.
Jurançon ○ *Pyrénées Atlantiques*. The famous dessert wine of the Pyrenees, much reduced in quantity since the phylloxera. The grapes, which are peculiar to the region, are left until over-ripe and affected by *pourriture noble*. The wine is high in alcohol (14° to 15°); it is moderately sweet, very perfumed and has a most individual and attractive flavour.

Madiran ● *Hautes Pyrénées*. In the old province of Béarn and adjoining the famous Armagnac district, a local grape variety called Tannat (50 per cent to 70 per cent) mixed with some Cabernet Sauvignon produces an excellent, full-flavoured and scented red wine, at its best between five and ten years old.
Minervois ● *Aude, Hérault*. Nicely balanced VDQS wines, lighter in degree and body than Corbières and closer to Bordeaux in character.
Monbazillac ○ *Dordogne*. Sweet white wines from the hills south of Bergerac, made by the same method and with the same grape varieties as sweet Bordeaux. In quality they range from something near to an ordinary Premières Côtes de Bordeaux to a good Ste Croix du Mont.
Montravel ○ *Dordogne*. Adjoins Castillon on the west side and Ste Foy across the Dordogne. Mostly light dry white wines, well vinified by four co-operatives. The AC *Côtes de Montravel* is used for sweet wines, *Haut Montravel* for the higher degree wines whether dry or *demi-sec*. Same grape varieties as Bordeaux.
Pécharmant ● *Dordogne*. A small AC for the best red wines of the Bergerac region, produced on hillsides just to the north-east of the town. Grape varieties as for Bordeaux. Quality depends on the producer: some are excellent, others are inferior to the better Bergeracs.
St Chinian ● *Hérault*. A good VDQS, with more fruit and plumpness than most Midi wines.
Sauvignon de St Bris ○ *Yonne*. These excellent wines, which come from an area south-west of Chablis, were awarded VDQS status in 1974. Quality resembles that of a good Sauvignon de Touraine, but prices are usually higher.
Vin de Savoie ○ *Savoie, Haute Savoie, Ain, Isère*. Light, fresh wines from the alpine valleys south of Lake Geneva; the best bear the separate *appellations* of *Crépy*, *Seyssel* and *Seyssel Mousseux*. The sparkling wines are some of the most attractive in France, but production is small.

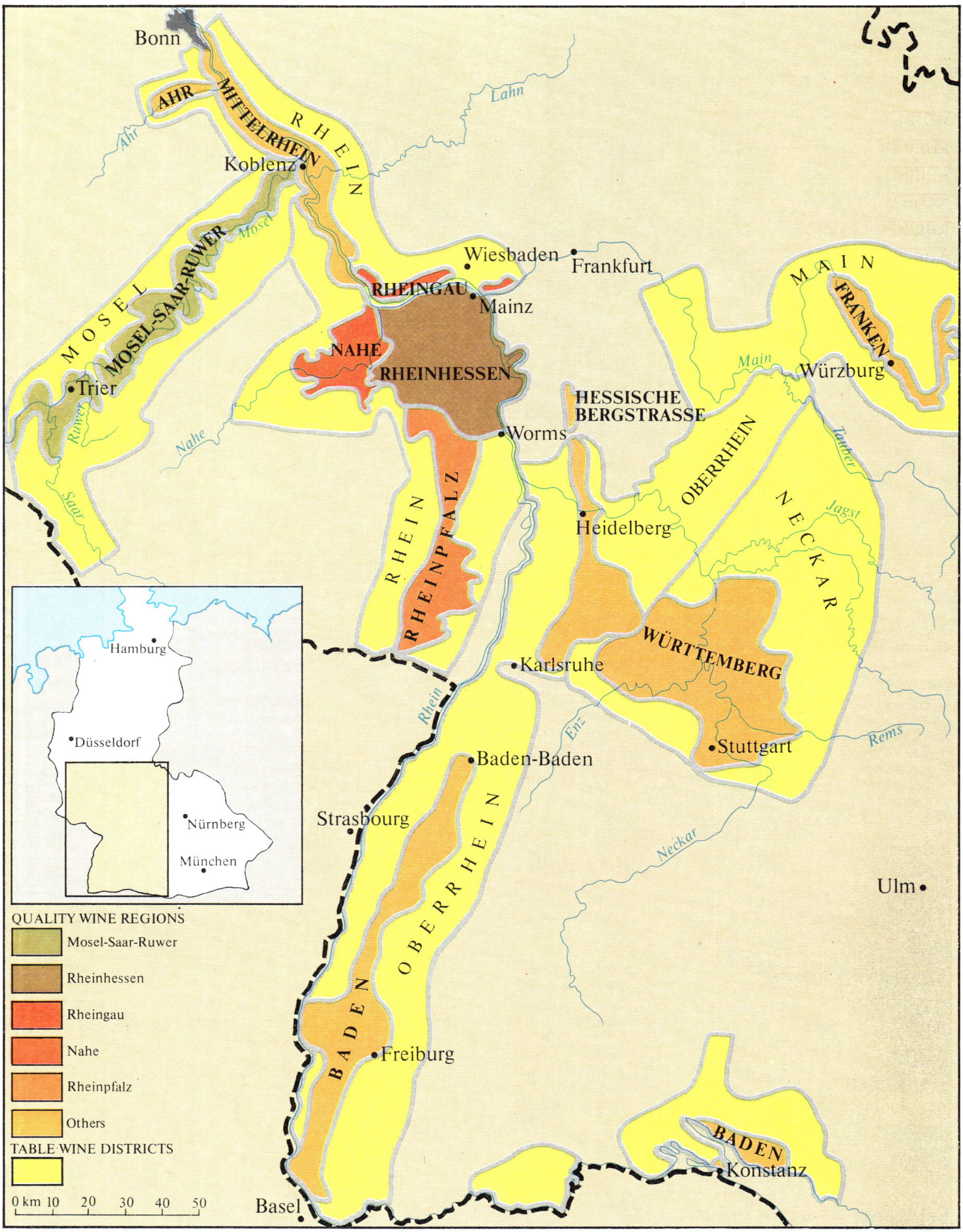
Bonn
AHR
MITTELRHEIN
RHEIN
Koblenz
Lahn
Ahr
Mosel
MOSEL
MOSEL-SAAR-RUWER
Trier
Ruwer
Saar
Wiesbaden
Frankfurt
RHEINGAU
Mainz
NAHE
RHEINHESSEN
Nahe
Worms
HESSISCHE BERGSTRASSE
MAIN
FRANKEN
Main
Würzburg
OBERRHEIN
Tauber
NECKAR
Jagst
Heidelberg
RHEIN
RHEINPFALZ
WÜRTTEMBERG
Karlsruhe
Rhein
Enz
Stuttgart
Rems
Baden-Baden
Strasbourg
OBERRHEIN
Neckar
Ulm
BADEN
Freiburg
BADEN
Konstanz
Basel
Hamburg
Düsseldorf
Nürnberg
München
QUALITY WINE REGIONS
Mosel-Saar-Ruwer
Rheinhessen
Rheingau
Nahe
Rheinpfalz
Others
TABLE WINE DISTRICTS
0 km 10 20 30 40 50

GERMANY

GERMANY HOLDS A SPECIAL PLACE among European wine producers. Nowhere else in such northern latitudes are quality wines produced in such quantity. The problems created by cold continental winters and irregular, sometimes capricious summers, explain most of the characteristics which differentiate German wines from other European wines.

Climate is thus the over-riding consideration in the siting of a vineyard, in deciding what grape varieties to plant, and in determining the eventual quality of the wine. Because of the relative unpredictability of summers, good ripening conditions for the traditional grape varieties – especially the classic Riesling – occur on average only every three or four years in the most northerly regions. Ideal conditions producing great years are far rarer.

It is not surprising, therefore, that the main thrust of research at the world-famous Wine Institute of Geisenheim has been toward developing new early-ripening grape varieties. Such research is a long-term venture of its very nature. It may take thousands of crosses to produce a satisfactory new variety which can then be tested in vineyards, and it will take many years of wine-producing experience to discover whether it will prove to be a commercial proposition.

A number of questions needs to be asked. Does the wine have a character acceptable on its own? If not, does it blend in well with other existing varieties? Is its character such that the wine still

The church at Wiltingen, in the Saar-Ruwer Bereich *(G)*

resembles others of whichever district it is planted in? Does the wood ripen and resist disease? When does the vine flower? Does the fruit set well? How great is the yield? Is the vine capable of a long and productive life? It is not hard to see why viticultural research is the work of a life-time!

It is only after long practical experience that a new variety is eventually approved for general use. When a new cross has reached the stage when it is believed that its potential is interesting enough to justify more prolonged field tests, it is licensed to be tried out on a limited and controlled basis, and a number of growers will plant small quantities in agreed locations. After the results of such plantings have been monitored over a number of years, and the results found to be satisfactory, permission will be given for the general release of the new vine.

From the vine to the cellar

In 'difficult' years one hears the sage comment 'this is a year when the wines will be made in cellar'. Not quite so sinister as it sounds, this means that it will be the skill in vinification which will produce quality, rather than the intrinsic characteristics of the grapes. Other countries may produce magnificent grapes, ripe and healthy, but they somehow continue to produce dull, flat and even faulty wines. It is in Germany that the wine-maker's skill has been developed to its apogee. Green, soggy grapes, sprinkled with the first snow, may enter the press-house in November – but clean, crisp refreshing wines will shortly emerge.

German wine cellars are cold and damp, an ideal setting for what the wine-maker wishes to achieve: cold induces the long slow fermentation that ensures the bouquet for which his wines are famous. These same conditions also begin to inhibit the activities of the yeasts which turn the sugar into alcohol, thus making it possible for wines of which the alcoholic content remains relatively low (around 10° by volume) but which still contain some unfermented sugar to stop fermenting. In normal circumstances, the fermenting would begin again when warmer conditions prevailed. But the German cellar-master will often filter the wine into a clean sterile cask to remove the inert but still living yeasts, so that it can then be sterile-bottled. This will produce a wine low in alcohol; but it will have that engaging touch of sweetness which, in concert with a naturally high acidity, creates the balanced fruitiness so prized in German wines.

Not all German wines have the inherent qualities necessary to produce residual sugar by these natural means. In the 1950s a very simple method was perfected, capable of routine use in large commercial or co-operative cellars, known as *Süss-reserve*. When the wine is about to be bottled, unfermented grape-juice – usually concentrated, and naturally kept in strictly sterile conditions (otherwise it would start fermenting) – is added in a carefully calculated dose; the quantity varies according to the constitution of the wine, and in particular to the level of acidity. This, of course, makes the sterility of the bottling operation vital: if any yeasts were to get into the bottle, fermentation would begin again.

SPARKLING WINES

Wine producers in Germany long ago escaped from the trap into which so many imitators of Champagne have fallen; instead of trying to usurp the French name, now protected in most parts of the world, they adopted their own – Sekt.

Because of the great demand in Germany for sparkling wines, much Sekt is made from imported wines, but since the new German Wine Law the situation has changed somewhat. Sekt itself is now a *Qualitätswein* and must be made from a German wine. Blends of German and imported wine, or sparkling wine made purely from imported wine, are now known as Schaumwein.

Nearly all German sparkling wine is made by the *cuvée close* method, but there are a few high quality wines for which a compromise system has been devised between this and the *méthode champenoise*. This wine is first bottle-fermented and is then disgorged into a tank for final bottling.

All this may sound very strange and unnatural. But the German cellar-master's problem is to try to simulate the wine made in good years in other years when grapes are far from ripe, and when their high acidity would render them almost undrinkable. It is most instructive to taste a base wine – without any residual sugar – and then the same wine with different degrees of added sweetness, and see how the rasping acidity can be transformed into a refreshing fruitiness. But the degree of sweetening is all-important: in many of the cheaper German wines it is excessive, and they are insipid and characterless as a result.

Location of vineyards

The German vineyards are divided into eleven designated regions. Four of these produce most of the wines for which the nation is famous in its export markets – namely Mosel-Saar-Ruwer, Rheingau, Rheinhessen and Rheinpfalz (known in the English-speaking world as the Palatinate). The smaller regions of Nahe and Franconia (famous for its bag-shaped *Bocksbeutel* flask) make a much smaller but nevertheless interesting contribution. Baden is large and growing in importance, but its wines are still mostly drunk within Germany; no doubt more will be heard of them in due course. Württemberg is best known for its red wines, which are hardly drunk abroad. Ahr, Mittelrhein and Hessische Bergstrasse are of purely local significance.

The regions producing *Tafelwein* are of little practical interest for the non-German drinker. Very light and fresh, but generally rather sweetened, *Tafelwein* should be regarded as a local tipple rather than as representative of German wines abroad. You can find much more enjoyable everyday wines from elsewhere.

Classification

The crucial difference between German wines and all others lies in the criteria by which Germans judge quality, and in their basic intentions in making their wines. These differences are now enshrined in the new German Wine Law which became operative with the 1971 vintage.

In another section of this book you can see how, over the course of many years, the French have classified their vineyards in the greatest districts. Thus, normally speaking, a Château Latour will be better than a Château Batailley, and a Chambertin will be better than a Gevrey Chambertin *1er cru*. But in Germany every wine is classified only at the time of its birth. The concentration of sugar in the grape juice is measured by the Oechsle system and will determine how the wine is to be classified[1].

This classification is most clearly illustrated by the accompanying diagram, which shows that all wines must fall initially into one of two categories: *Tafelwein* (table wine) or *Qualitätswein* (quality wine). There are two distinct categories of the latter:

1. *QbA* wines (*Qualitätswein bestimmter Anbaugebiete*) which are improved in terms of their alcoholic strength by chaptalization.

[1]OECHSLE DEGREES

The specific gravity of grape must is measured in Oechsle degrees. These indicate how many grammes of sugar a litre of must contains. 100° Oechsle means that 100 litres of must contains some 25kg of sugar. Then, if the measurement is below a certain figure (these figures differ according to the region) the must can be chaptalized – its alcoholic strength is increased by adding sugar. Classification of the resulting wine, either as a *Tafelwein* or as a *Qualitätswein*, will vary according to the standing of the vineyard and the amount of improvement required. Once the Oechsle degree rises over the threshold where chaptalization is no longer automatic it becomes a *Prädikat* wine.

A German label may contain information about . . . .

the quality of the wine	its origin	and . . .
This may be either:		
1. TABLE WINE: either *Deutscher Tafelwein* or *DTW* (100 per cent German wine) or *Tafelwein* (German wine blended with other wine of EEC origin).	The label on a *DTW* wine may name one of the five authorized areas of production (*Weinbaugebiete*) – i.e. Mosel, Rhein, Main, Neckar or Oberrhein.	**The grape variety** used to make the wine. Some of the most common are Riesling, Sylvaner (or Silvaner), Ruländer and Gewürztraminer. **The vintage:** the year shown must be that in which at least 75 per cent of the wine was produced. **The producer or shipper** **The bottler** (*Abfüller*). **The control number** (*QmP* and *QbA* wines only).
2. QUALITY WINE FROM A DESIGNATED REGION (*Qualitätswein bestimmter Anbaugebiete* or *QbA*). 3. QUALITY WINE OF PARTICULAR DISTINCTION (*Qualitätswein mit Prädikat* or *QmP*) – either: ***Trockenbeerenauslese:*** the finest German wine, made from individually selected single grapes, dried on the vine. ***Beerenauslese:*** wines of exceptional quality made from individually selected single grapes. ***Auslese:*** wines made from selected bunches of late-harvested, fully ripe grapes. ***Spätlese:*** wines made from late-harvested, fully ripe grapes. ***Kabinett:*** lightest of the *QmP* wines, usually drier than the others.	All quality wines must carry the name of one of the eleven designated regions (*Anbaugebiete*). The names of a *Bereich*, *Grosslage* or single vineyard may also be added.	

The Mosel-Saar-Ruwer region consists of four Bereiche *and nineteen* Grosslagen. *This* QbA *wine comes from Bernkastel, best-known of the* Bereiche

Hock (brown)
Moselle (green)

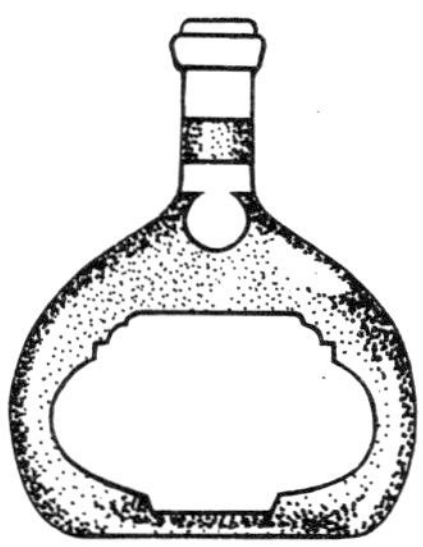
Steinwein

The control number

*The official control number (*Amtliche Prüfungsnummer, *usually abbreviated on the label to* AP Nummer*) is made up of five units. A typical example from Mosel-Saar-Ruwer could read 4.382.263 35/72, indicating:*
The examination area (4 = Alzey)
The bottler's village code (382 = Nierstein)
The bottler's own code (263 = Seip)
The bottler's application number (i.e. Seip's 35th application)
The year of application (1972)

2. *QmP* wines (*Qualitätswein mit Prädikat*) which are never permitted to be chaptalized. These in turn fall into five categories – *Kabinett, Spätlese, Auslese, Beerenauslese, Trockenbeerenauslese* – according to the original Oechsle degree of their musts.

None of this means, of course, that German vineyard names do not matter. Indeed they do: but they have to be judged alongside these basic classifications of quality. In practice, the best positioned vineyards tend to produce *Prädikat* wines more often than others. Such a system has two outstanding advantages. It means that however famous the village or vineyard name, if the grower harvests a wine with a low Oechsle degree he will only be awarded a *QbA* designation for it, while in a fine year if a producer on a third rate site leaves his grapes longer to achieve maximum ripeness, and is successful, he can produce a *Beerenauslese*.

Understanding the label

Behind these classifications there lies the important assumption, unique to Germany, that the greater the sugar content of the grapes, the greater can be the resulting wine. Thus a *Trockenbeerenauslese* is *per se* the greatest wine a grower can produce (equally, viewed through German eyes, a great Sauternes must be better than the best dry white Graves). As a result, the consumer can find considerable guidance on a German wine label as to what he may expect to find inside the bottle: his problem is to grasp the key to that information.

The first essential to understand is the somewhat perplexing classification of *Grosslagen*, or collective sites. The progression from the designated wine region (*Anbaugebiet*) to the sub-region (*Bereich*) is logical enough; but it is important to note that the name of a *Grosslage* attaches to a vineyard which has been allowed to stray far from its original boundaries, and so it is usually applicable to several villages.[1] This system was devised in order to reduce vineyard names and help the consumer, but some of the results have tended to muddy the waters rather than to clarify them. However, it is important to note that the finest wines are nearly always sold under the name of a particular vineyard rather than of a collective *Grosslage*.

[1]In Nierstein, however, the contrary is true. This one village in the Rheinhessen enjoys four different *Grosslage* names (see page 103).

GLOSSARY

Amtliche Prüfungsnummer (abbreviated as AP Nummer): number shown on labels of all *Qualitätsweine* since 1971, indicating that the wine has been officially checked by analysis and tasting
Auslese: wine made from selected bunches of fully ripe grapes; third rating in the *QmP* category. Minimum 95° Oechsle
Beerenauslese: wine made from selected individual grapes, subjected to *Edelfaule* (*qv*); second rating in the *QmP* category. Minimum 125° Oechsle
Bereich: an area of Germany's 11 regions producing quality wine; there are 32 altogether.
Bocksbeutel: flat, bag-shaped flask in which most Franconian wines are bottled
Deutsche Weinsiegel Trocken: yellow seal applied to wine with less than 4gm per litre of residual sugar – a useful means of identifying a truly dry wine
DLG (Deutsche Landwirtschafts-Gesellschaft): German Agricultural Association. These initials are printed on strip labels carrying wine awards – thus: *Grosser Preis der DLG* (highest award)
Diabetiker Weinsiegel: seal given by the DLG (*qv*) to wines selected as suitable for diabetics – i.e. with a maximum of 4gm per litre of residual sugar and 12 per cent alcohol
Edelfaule: noble rot or *Botrytis* – a fungus which dehydrates the grape (in French, *pourriture noble*)
Einzellage: single, individual vineyard
Eiswein: literally 'ice wine', made when water content of grapes is frozen, thus increasing the concentration of sugar. The word is appended to the *QmP* designation – thus, *Auslese Eiswein, Beerenauslese Eiswein* etc.
Erzeugerabfüllung: wine bottled by the producer rather than a merchant
Grosslage: a collection of vineyards, not necessarily adjacent, all entitled to use the same name
Hybride: cross between a European and an American vine; permitted in France, other than for AC wines, but not in Germany
Jungfernwein: literally 'virgin wine': term applied to the first wine made from a new vineyard, usually in its third year.
Kabinett: lowest (fifth) rating in the *QmP* category of wine. Minimum 73° Oechsle
Lage: vineyard or site
Naturrein: 'pure' – i.e. unchaptalized – wine, a term made obsolete under the 1971 Wine Law
Oechsle: degree rating used for measuring the strength of grape must
Originalabfüllung: estate bottling (obsolete term and process since 1971)
Prädikat: literally, 'mark' (see *QmP*)
QbA (Qualitätswein bestimmter Anbaugebiete): quality wine from a designated region
QmP (Qualitätswein mit Prädikat): quality wine of particular distinction
Qualitätswein: quality wine
Rotling: a light red wine made by blending red and white grapes
Schillerwein: name for Rotling (see above) made in Württemberg
Spätlese: wine made from late-harvested, fully ripened grapes; fourth rating in the *QmP* category. Minimum 85° Oechsle
Tafelwein: table wine
Trockenbeerenauslese: wine made from selected individual grapes, dried or shrivelled from exposure to *Edelfaule* (*qv*); top rating in the *QmP* category. Minimum 150° Oechsle
Weissherbst: light *rosé* wine, the product of only one grape variety
Winzergenossenschaft or ***Winzerverein:*** wine co-operative

VARIETIES OF GRAPE

*crossing.

***Ehrenfelser** (Riesling × Silvaner): high sugar content, producing wines of marked Riesling character in the Rheingau.
***Faber** (Weissburgunder × Müller-Thurgau): high sugar content, producing full-bodied, flowery wines.
Gewürztraminer: produces very aromatic, spicy wine. Found mainly in Rheinpfalz and Baden.
***Huxelrebe** (Gutedel × Courtillier Musque): produces a delicate, fruity wine with a pleasing flavour.
***Kanzler** (Müller-Thurgau × Silvaner): a small-yielding vine. Grapes have high sugar content; wines are full-bodied and fruity.
***Kerner** (Trollinger × Riesling): one of the most successful and pleasing new varieties. The Trollinger is a red grape, but the resulting wine is white.
***Mario-Muskat** (Weissburgunder × Silvaner): mainly found in Rheinhessen and Rheinpfalz. The wine is very aromatic and highly spiced.
***Müller-Thurgau** (Riesling × Riesling): an early-ripening grape, traditionally but mistakenly believed to be Riesling × Silvaner; accounts for 30 per cent of white wine plantings.
***Optima** (Silvaner × Riesling × Müller-Thurgau): some very interesting *Beerenauslesen* and *Trockenbeerenauslesen* have resulted from this complex new crossing.
Portugieser: red wine grape grown mainly in Rheinhessen, Württemberg and Ahr; 42 per cent of red wine plantings.
***Rieslander** (Riesling × Silvaner): ripens two weeks earlier than the Riesling and shows all the Riesling characteristics. Considered to have a bright future.
Riesling: the most famous German grape variety, grown in all regions but especially in Rheingau and Mosel; accounts for 26 per cent of white wine plantings.
Rülander: German name for the Pinot Gris in France and the Pinot Grigio in Italy. Grown mainly in Baden, Rheinpfalz and Rheinhessen.
***Scheurebe** (Riesling × Silvaner): produces wine with a marked aromatic character. Mainly planted in Rheinhessen and Rheinpfalz.
***Siegerrebe** (Madeleine Angevine × Gewürztraminer): very fruity, grapey bouquet with high sugar content. Used either for blending or on its own to make *Beerenauslesen*.
Spätburgunder: German name for the Pinot Noir. Grown mainly in Baden, Württemberg and Ahr.
Silvaner (or **Sylvaner**): grown mainly in Rheinhessen, Rheinpfalz and Franconia.
Trollinger: the principal red grape variety of Württemberg. Produces pleasantly full-flavoured soft wines.
Weissburgunder: German name for the Pinot Blanc. Produces mild, slightly spicy wines in Rheinpfalz and Baden which have little resemblance to their French counterparts.

Mosel-Saar-Ruwer

THIS IS THE OFFICIAL NAME for the district formed by the river Mosel (or Moselle to give the French spelling which is frequently employed outside Germany) and its two tributaries, the Saar and the Ruwer. As will be seen by studying the illustrated labels, it is usual to use the full name Mosel-Saar-Ruwer, irrespective of which of the three rivers a wine comes from. But in general parlance these wines are referred to simply as Mosel or Moselle.

The river of this name rises in France, passing through Luxembourg on its way to Germany, and then flows north-east until it joins the Rhine at Koblenz. The Saar tributary joins it just to the west of Trier and the much smaller Ruwer flows in immediately to the city's east. In terms of wine production the region is the third most important in Germany, producing on average some 900,000 hectolitres. Considering the unfriendly terrain, the yield is also surprisingly high, at around 74 hectolitres per hectare.

The characteristics of Mosel wines are determined by three main factors: the Riesling grape, which accounts for nearly three-quarters of the vines planted, the river's steep slopes which ensure rapid drainage and maximum exposure to the sun, and the slate and shale which reflect the sun's rays. The result is a wine low in alcohol, seldom more than 9° by volume, with an outstanding bouquet and a crisp acidity which truly refreshes. Nowhere are the breed and elegance of the Riesling grape more in evidence. It is only in less favoured sites, where the Riesling has a poor ripening record, that the Müller-Thurgau grape is now established, accounting for 13 per cent of the area under vine. These wines are perfumed and elegant, but they lack the characteristic fruit-acidity of the Riesling.

Canalization of the river, which began in 1951, is now complete and has had a significant influence on the micro-climate. The wider areas of water created by the new locks on the stretch between Trier and Koblenz have improved the climate and thus the wines.

The region is divided into four *Bereiche* and nineteen *Grosslagen*. The names of only two *Bereiche*, Bernkastel and Zell, are significant for the buyer, for in Obermosel and Saar-Ruwer all the most interesting wines are sold under village names. Of the *Grosslagen*, eight are of particular interest.

Bereich	*Grosslage*	*Villages*
Saar-Ruwer	Scharzberg	Ockfen, Wiltingen, Kanzem, Oberemmel, Filzen, Ayl, Saarberg, Serrig
Bernkastel	Michelsberg	Piesport, Trittenheim, Dhron
Bernkastel	Kurfürstlay	Brauneberg, Bernkastel Kues, Lieser
Bernkastel	Badstube	Bernkastel
Bernkastel	Münzlay	Wehlen, Graach, Zeltingen
Bernkastel	Schwarzlay	Traben Trarbach, Uerzig, Enkirch, Kinheim
Bernkastel	Kröver Nacktarsch	Kröv
Zell	Schwarze Katz	Zell

Guidelines for selecting a Mosel should now begin to emerge. A Bereich Bernkastel or Zell will normally be a *QbA* wine, a good commercial blend,

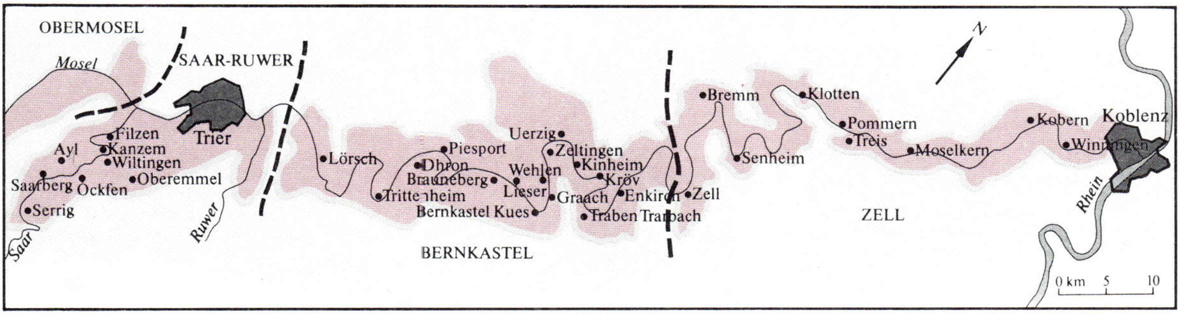

reasonably priced, perhaps a shade over-sweetened and thus inclined to blandness rather than the crisp acidity typical of the best Mosels. Here also the vintage will not matter greatly. At this level there is less variation between one vintage and another than among the higher quality wines.

The next wine up the quality ladder might be a Wehlener Münzlay or a Wiltingener Schwarzlay, *QbA* or *Kabinett*. The first is a typical Mittel-Mosel – that is to say it comes from the central section of the river which lies in the Bernkastel *Bereich*. These wines have more vinosity and body than other Mosels, and produce especially fine *Spätlese* and *Auslese* wines. The Wiltingener, being a Saar wine, would be lighter and crisper with a more noticeable acidity. Here a note of caution must be sounded. In theory the *Kabinett* should be better than the *QbA*. But Mosels are naturally low in alcohol, and can be classified as *QmP* at a lower Oechsle reading than is the case for Rhine wines. If a wine is only just within the Oechsle limit for *Kabinett*, the producer still has the option to chaptalize if he thinks he can make a better wine that way; but of course the wine is then a *QbA*, not a *Kabinett*, so some *QbA* wines can be better than some *Kabinett*. All wines in this category will be essentially dry.

Because of their basic acidity *Spätlese* and even *Auslese* wines on the Mosel are normally much drier than similar categories on the Rhine. But if you want to experience really fine quality Mosels then vintages and estates become important. Because of their magnificent Riesling stocks and their superb and traditionally based techniques one should look for examples from among the following top estates.

The *Kabinett* and *Spätlese* qualities will show these estates at their most typical in terms of Mosel, but the *Auslesen* too should be sampled to taste the intense fruitiness with balancing acidity that can be achieved in great years, such as 1971 and 1976.

SAMPLE TASTINGS

A. To show differences within the region:
(1) A Saar *QbA* or *Kabinett*
(2) A Ruwer *QbA* or *Kabinett*
(3) A Bernkasteler *QbA* or *Kabinett*
(4) A Zeltinger or Wehlener *QbA* or *Kabinett*

B. To show differences of quality:
(1) A Saar or Ruwer *Kabinett*
(2) A Saar or Ruwer *Spätlese*
(3) A Bernkasteler or Zeltinger *Spätlese*
(4) A Saar or Ruwer *Auslese*
(5) A Bernkasteler or Zeltinger *Auslese*

A Graacher, Piesporter or Wehlener may be substituted for the Bernkastelers or Zeltingers. Wines from recommended estates or from co-operatives will provide the most reliable examples.

MOSEL-SAAR-RUWER ESTATES

R percentage of Riesling vines planted

Bischöflichen Weingüter (R90) Since 1966 three great church estates in Trier have been joined together under this name: Bischöfliches Priesterseminar, Bischöfliches Konvict and Hohe Domkirche. The names and coats of arms of each are retained on the labels. This is the largest estate on the Mosel and its wines are a by-word for classically made dry Rieslings; they are very long lasting, and in great years the *Auslesen* are especially fine. The estate is particularly strong on the Saar and Ruwer.

Deinhard (R98) A small estate, but it includes the famous Bernkasteler Doctor vineyard as well as others in Bernkastel and Graach. Fine typical wines are made, including *Beeren-* and *Trockenbeerenauslese* wines in great years.

Dr Thanisch (R93) The other principal owner of the Doctor vineyard at Bernkastel (see Deinhard). The estate also owns vineyards in Brauneberger, Wehlen (the famous Sonnenuhr) and Graach. Elegant, classical Mosel wines are made.

Friedrich-Wilhelm Gymnasium (R88) An independent school foundation, based in Trier, producing fine Mosels, many of them typically *spritzig* in character. Vineyards are on the Saar and Mittel-Mosel.

Reichsgraf von Kesselstatt (R98) The family has resided on the Mosel since the 13th century. Fine dry wines and *Auslesen* and *Beerenauslesen* are made in the great years. Vineyards are centred on Graach, Piesport and on the Ruwer and Saar.

Staatlichen Weinbaudomänen (R85) An important Trier estate producing classic dry *Kabinett* and *Spätlese* wines, as well as *Eiswein* and *Auslesen* in great years. Vineyards are on the Saar, at Avelsbach, Ockfen and Serrig.

Vereinigte Hospitien (R95) This Trier estate – it means 'United Hospitals' – was founded in medieval times; today its revenues are used to provide for about 600 patients. The cellars are probably the oldest in Germany, with Roman origins. Most of the vineyards are on the Saar, but important holdings in Piesport include the famous Goldtropfchen vineyard. Very fine classic wines are made.

Rheinhessen

THIS SECOND MOST IMPORTANT wine-growing region of Germany, bounded by the Rhine to the north and to the east, produces on average some 1,500,000 hectolitres of wine. Silvaner and the Müller-Thurgau vines vie for supremacy; the present ratio is 39 per cent to 36 per cent. This mixture – Silvaner, giving body and softness; Müller-Thurgau contributing elegance to the bouquet and extra fruitiness to the flavour – combines to make the typical Rheinhessen wine at the *QbA* or *Kabinett* levels. Although the Riesling only has 6 per cent this is concentrated in the famous Rheinfront vineyards of Nierstein and Oppenheim.

Rheinhessen has two distinct sides. The east-facing slopes of the Rheinfront, running from Nackenheim through Nierstein and on to Oppenheim, produce wines of real quality; they are steep and spectacular, with deep red soil and intensively planted slopes, and the names of the vineyards are prominently marked. The hinterland is a high, undulating plateau producing high yields of mild, inoffensive wines which are the largest source for the medium and better quality Liebfraumilchs with their typical, slightly oversweet flavour.

LIEBFRAUMILCH

The brand-name Liebfraumilch originated from vineyards in Worms, surrounding the famous Liebfrauen Kirche, and there was formerly a supposition – for which there was no legal basis whatever – that a Liebfraumilch was a Rheinhessen wine. Since the 1971 German Wine Law, however, Liebfraumilch has acquired an established quality and geographical designation. It must be a *Qualitätswein*, not a *Tafelwein*, and can only come from Rheinpfalz, Rheinhessen, Nahe or Rheingau. The major proportion of the blend must be produced from Riesling, Silvaner or Müller-Thurgau grapes and must possess the characteristics of one of these types; the grape variety may not be named on the label, however.

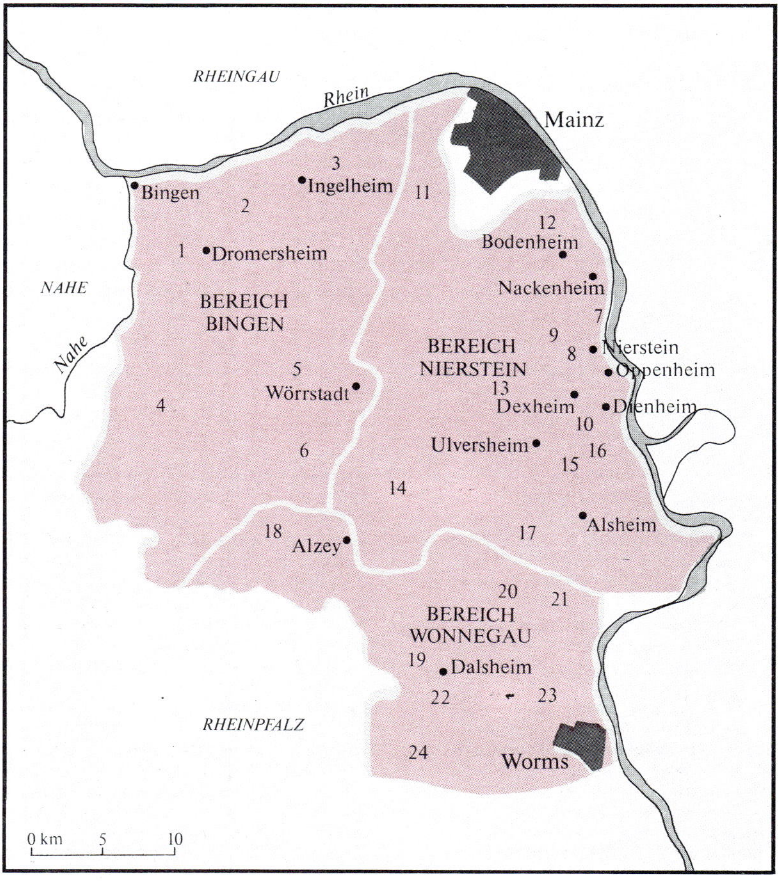

GROSSLAGEN OF RHEINHESSEN

Bereich Bingen

1 St Rochuskapelle
2 Abtei
3 Kaiserpfalz
4 Rheingrafenstein
5 Kurfürstenstück
6 Adelberg

Bereich Nierstein

7 Rehbach
8 Auflangen
9 Spiegelberg
10 Güldenmorgen
11 Domherr
12 St Alban
13 Gutes Domtal
14 Petersberg
15 Krötenbrunnen
16 Vogelsgärten
17 Rheinblick

Bereich Wonnegau

18 Sybillenstein
19 Bergkloster
20 Pilgerpfad
21 Gotteshilfe
22 Burg Rodenstein
23 Liebfrauenmorgen
24 Domblick

Inflatable nylon storage shed at Bornheim in the Rheinhessen (G)

The region is divided up into three *Bereiche* and no fewer than 24 *Grosslagen*. The most important names are:

Bereich	*Grosslage*	*Towns/Villages*
Bingen	Sankt Rochuskapelle	Bingen
Nierstein	Auflangen	Nierstein
Nierstein	Güldenmorgen	Dienheim, Oppenheim
Nierstein	Gutes Domtal	Dexheim, Nackenheim, Nierstein
Nierstein	Krötenbrunnen	Alsheim, Dienheim, Guntersblum, Oppenheim
Nierstein	Rehbach	Nackenheim, Nierstein
Nierstein	Rheinblick	Alsheim
Nierstein	Sankt Alban	Bodenheim, Mainz
Nierstein	Spiegelberg	Nackenheim, Nierstein
Wonnegau	Liebfrauenmorgen	Worms

Rheinhessen wines will normally come from one of the famous commercial houses or from one of the big co-operatives which dominate the region. For the better quality wines which are produced on the Rheinfront it is again worth looking for the best estates.

SAMPLE TASTING

(1) A Niersteiner *QbA* or *Kabinett*
(2) A Binger *QbA* or *Kabinett*
(3) A Niersteiner *Spätlese* (estate); Riesling if possible
(4) An Oppenheimer *Auslese* (estate); Riesling if possible

This tasting is designed to show the differences between the main Rheinfront wines, and the lighter wines to the west.

RHEINHESSEN ESTATES

R percentage of Riesling vines planted
S percentage of Silvaner vines planted
☆ location of main estate offices

Anton Balbach (R70) One of the most famous Rheinhessen estates with vineyards entirely in Nierstein.
Franz Karl Schmitt (S50, R25) Perhaps the most famous of all the Nierstein estates, particularly for its *Trockenbeerenauslesen*. Other vineyards are in Oppenheim and Dienheim.
H. A. Sturb Medium-sized estate of high quality; vineyards are in Nierstein (☆) and Dienheim.
Karl Sittmann (S37, R18) The largest private estate in Rheinhessen. Vineyards are in Nierstein, Oppenheim (☆), Dienheim and Alsheim.
Louis Guntrum (R30, S25) This is one of the most important estates in Rheinhessen and belongs to wine merchants of the same name. Vineyards are in Nierstein, Oppenheim and Dienheim; many new grape varieties are grown, including Kerner, Bacchus and Rieslaner.
Schuch (R35, S25) A relatively small estate, making typical high quality Rheinhessen wines. Vineyards are in Nierstein, Oppenheim and Dienheim.
Staatlichen Weinbaudomänen This estate, which has a most distinctive diamond-shaped label, has produced excellent wines; in recent years, however, results have been disappointing, and serious efforts are now being made to improve quality. The best vineyards are in Bingen, Bodenheim, Nackenheim, Oppenheim and Dienheim.
Winzermeister Heinrich Seip An interesting estate in Nierstein, particularly well known for its numerous plantings of experimental grape varieties. Most vineyards are in Nierstein; Oppenheim, Dienheim and Nackenheim are also represented.

Rheingau

THIS REGION has an importance out of all proportion to its actual size. It yields on average only 210,000 hectolitres, which is not only smaller than any of the other famous regions, including the Nahe, but also produces less than even Baden or Württemberg – but then quality has nothing to do with size.

The geographical situation of the Rheingau is remarkably favoured. Between Wiesbaden and Rüdesheim the Rhine flows from east to west instead of pursuing its habitual course which is north-north-west. On its northern perimeter the region is sheltered by the Taunus mountains which form a protective barrier against northern and easterly winds. From the Taunus down to the Rhine the range descends, forming a number of valleys but mostly providing a remarkable series of southern sloping sites. This combination of geographical features results in a micro-climate which gives more concentrated heat from the sun during the brief and vital summer months than in any other part of Germany, including the more southerly Rheinpfalz. The soil is also more favourable to viticulture than the Mosel with much loam and clay mixed with gravel, schist and marl.

In this setting the traditional vine is the Riesling, as on the Mosel; but here, due to the more favourable climatic circumstances, the Riesling has retained its ascendancy even more strongly. At the present time some 78 per cent of the plantings are Riesling, with 11 per cent Müller-Thurgau and 6 per cent Silvaner. On these favoured slopes the Riesling produces a wine noted for its flowery bouquet and depth of flavour. The great *Auslesen*, *Beerenauslesen* and *Trockenbeerenauslesen* are wines which develop an unrivalled honeyed bouquet with extraordinary vinosity, breed and finesse. These are fascinating wines to compare with those of the Mosel, for they show what the Riesling can do in more favourable conditions when greater ripeness is achieved. There is a gain in the depth of flavour and in body, without any loss of finesse or breed, but of course they lack the extra delicacy of the best Mosels.

It seems appropriate that many of these most aristocratic of German wines should still be produced on large, noble estates. Nowhere else in Germany are the estates so important, and when seeking a great Rheingau one should certainly search for one produced from one of them.

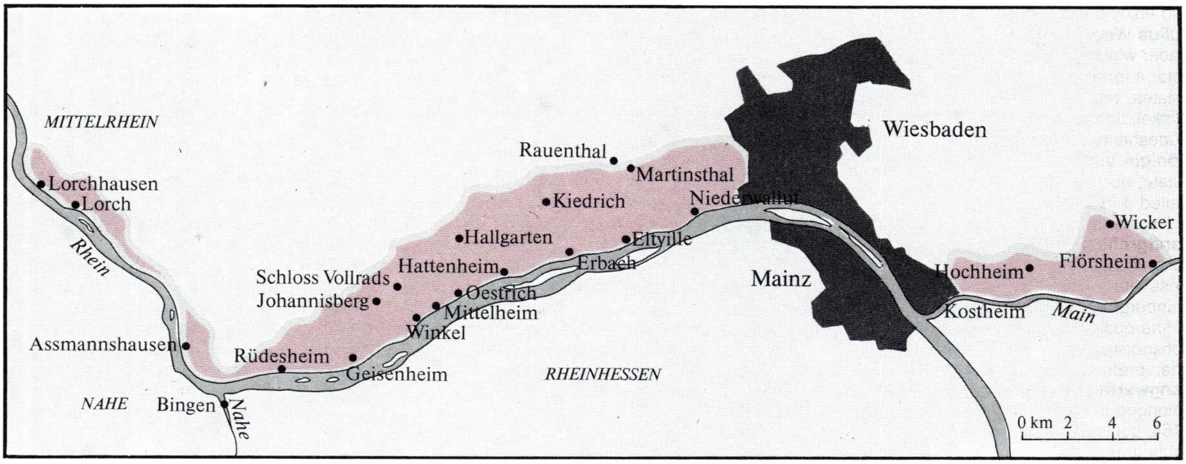

The region of the Rheingau is unusual in having only one *Bereich*, which uses the name of its most famous village, Johannisberg. There are then ten *Grosslagen*, listed here with their most important village names:

Bereich	*Grosslage*	*Villages*
Johannisberg	Burgweg	Assmannshausen, Geisenheim, Rüdesheim
Johannisberg	Daubhaus	Hochheim
Johannisberg	Deutelsberg	Erbach, Hattenheim
Johannisberg	Erntebringer	Geisenheim, Johannisberg, Mittelheim, Winkel
Johannisberg	Gottesthal	Oestrich
Johannisberg	Heiligenstock	Eltville, Kiedrich
Johannisberg	Honigberg	Mittelheim, Winkel
Johannisberg	Mehrhölzchen	Hallgarten, Oestrich
Johannisberg	Steil	Assmannshausen
Johannisberg	Steinmächer	Eltville, Martinsthal, Niederwalluf, Rauenthal

It will be clear from all this that our principles in buying Rheingau wines will be slightly different to those applicable in other districts. If you aim to buy a wine of better quality than the basic Bereich Johannisberg, it is well worth looking for an example from one of the above mentioned estates, even if you are only buying a *QbA* or *Kabinett* wine; this is all the more the case when you move up the quality scale in order to select *Spätlesen* or *Auslesen*. There are also small but excellent co-operatives (*Winzergenossenschäfte*) at Erbach and Hattenheim, producing wines which often match those of good estates.

SAMPLE TASTING

Look for a *QbA*, *Kabinett*, *Spätlese* and *Auslese* example from each of the estates on the recommended list. A co-operative could also be included.

RHEINGAU ESTATES

☆ location of main estate offices

Dr Weil Vineyards are restricted to Kiedrich and enjoy a high reputation.

Julius Wegeler Erben This is the name under which Deinhard's Rheingau wines are sold; it forms an important collection of estates, with its finest vineyards in Oestrich, Winkel, Johannisberg, Geisenheim and Rüdesheim.

Königin Viktoria-Berg A relatively small estate, named after Queen Victoria who visited it in 1850. The wines are very typical of Hochheim and traditional in style.

Landgräflich Hessisches Weingut This Johannisberg estate has only belonged to the Hess family (close relatives of the Duke of Edinburgh) since 1956, but produces wines of fine quality from vineyards in Johannisberg and Winkel. The latter are often preferable.

Langwerth von Simmern The estate has belonged to the Von Simmern family since 1464, but their famous Schloss at Hattenheim dates from 1118. The wines have a fine reputation. The vineyards are in Eltville (☆), Rauenthal, Erbacher, Hattenheim and Hochheim.

Schloss Eltz Wines here are less traditional, with an emphasis on light elegance. The vineyards are in Eltville (☆), Kiedrich, Rauenthal and Rüdesheim and are especially famous for their *Beerenauslesen* and *Trockenbeerenauslesen*.

Schloss Groenesteyn Proprietors are the Reichsfreiherrn von Ritter zu Groenesteyn. Very fine and typical Riesling wines are made from vineyards in Kiedrich and Rüdesheim.

Schloss Johannisberg This property is certainly one of the most famous vineyards in Germany, partly because it was granted after the death of Napoleon to the famous Austrian statesman Prince Metternich. At one time the property of the famous Champagne firm, G. H. von Mumm, the estate has belonged to the German industrialist Rudolph Oetker since 1957.

Schloss Rheinhartshausen The property of the last Crown Prince of Germany, Prince Frederick of Prussia, the estate is still owned by his heirs. Vineyards are in different villages and sold under those names – Erbach, Hattenheim, Kiedrich, Rauenthal and Rüdesheim.

Schloss Schönborn Unlike Schloss Vollrads and Schloss Johannisberg, the vineyards are spread over a number of different villages and are therefore sold under various names. Particularly famous for producing classic Rieslings, its most important holdings are in Hattenheim, Erbacher Marcobrunn, Hallgarten, Oestrich, Johannisberg, Winkel, Geisenheim, Rüdesheim and Hochheim.

Schloss Vollrads The magnificent Schloss itself was built about 1300, and the estate has been owned by the same family for almost 900 years. All the vineyards are in Winkel, but the wine is always sold under the name of the Schloss without mentioning the vineyard name.

Staatsweingüter Composed of seven separate wine estates, this group is the largest wine producer in Germany. Six are important: Assmannshausen, which produces the famous red wines made from the Spätburgunder grape (Pinot Noir); Rüdesheim, Schloss Hochheim and Hattenheim, which includes the famous Erbacher Marcobrunn; Steinberg, the famous walled vineyard of Kloster Eberbach; and Rauenthal, which includes vineyards in Kiedrich and Eltville (☆).

Nahe

THIS MOST PICTURESQUE WINE REGION takes its name from the small river which eventually flows into the Rhine at Bingen, at a right-angled bend almost opposite Rüdesheim. On its eastern limits it borders on Rheinhessen, but its wines are quite distinct and very different from those of its neighbour. The centre of the region is the charming spa town of Bad Kreuznach.

This is a region of precipitous slopes which rival those of the Mosel for their density of cultivation – one sometimes wonders how they came to be fashioned out of such inhospitable mountain-sides. Indeed, one of the

The old town of Bad Kreuznach, on the Nahe (Popperfoto)

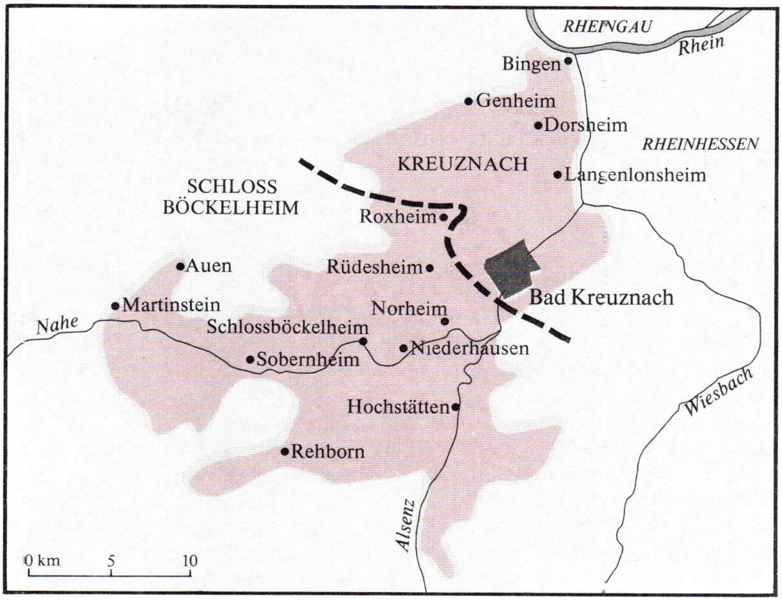

most famous of the domains now belonging to the State was constructed, with the use of convict labour, at the end of the last century when it belonged to the Prussian State.

Of nearly 400,000 hectolitres of wine produced, 32 per cent comes from the Silvaner grape, 30 per cent from the Müller-Thurgau and 25 per cent from the Riesling. The wines which result are often said to represent the half-way house between those of the Mosel and the Rhine. Certainly they are lighter and more delicate than most Rhine wines and have something of the flair and steely finesse of Mosels; but they are more full-bodied, and they have a distinctive character and considerable charm. The best are usually produced from the Riesling, but there are also excellent everyday wines, either produced solely from the Silvaner or by blends of Silvaner with either Müller-Thurgau or Riesling.

The region divides into two *Bereiche* – Kreuznach and Schloss Böckelheim – and these two *Bereich* names are widely used to commercialize Nahe wines. The leading *Grosslagen*, with their towns and villages, are as follows:

Bereich	*Grosslage*	*Towns/Villages*
Kreuznach	Kronenberg	Bad Kreuznach
Kreuznach	Schlosskapelle	Bingen, Burg Layen, Dorsheim
Schloss Böckelheim	Burgweg	Schlossböckelheim
Schloss Böckelheim	Paradiesgarten	
Schloss Böckelheim	Rosengarten	Rüdesheim

When selecting Nahe wines, look for the co-operative at Bad Kreuznach which offers exceptional value in the *QbA*, *Kabinett* and *Spätlese* categories. The finest wines are to be found from three important estates – Staatlichen Weinbaudomänen at Niederhausen Schlossböckelheim (a superbly positioned vineyard which has for long had the reputation of being the best run of the State domains), Von Plettenberg and August Anheuser.

Rheinpfalz

THE PALATINATE, as Rheinpfalz (or Pfalz) is known in English,[1] produces more wine than any other region of Germany, with an average annual output of some 1,700,000 hectolitres. Viticulturally it divides conveniently into two halves – the Mittelhaardt, which is incorporated in the Mittelhaardt Deutsche Weinstrasse *Bereich*, and the Oberhaardt in the Südliche Weinstrasse *Bereich*. The Mittelhaardt produces the great quality wines of the region; the Oberhaardt is the great mass production region which regularly produces the cheapest wines in Germany.

In the region as a whole 33 per cent of the plantings are Sylvaner, 23 per cent are Müller-Thurgau and 14 per cent are Riesling. 16 per cent of all Rheinpfalz wines are red and are made from the Portugieser blue grape.

Although all Pfalz wines have a certain family resemblance, the difference between the north and south of the region is strong enough to make it more practical to deal with the wines separately. The region as a whole is dominated by the Haardt mountains, a northward extension of the Vosges; whereas the predominant factor in the other three great regions are the rivers Mosel and Rhine, here it is the famous Deutsche Weinstrasse, wending its way from north to south across the undulating plateau of the Pfalz, that provides the area's outstanding characteristic. It is in the Mittelhaardt that nearly all the Riesling plantings are to be found, mostly on three famous estates – Dr Bürklin-Wolff (the largest, with vineyards in Wachenheim, Forst, Deidesheim and Ruppertsberg), von Buhl and Dr Bassermann-Jordan.

Most Palatinate wines – there are some exceptions – have great body and vinosity and a certain unctiousness (sometimes rather unfairly described as oiliness); the Rieslings develop a distinct spicy character all their own. However, many of the *Kabinett* wines produced solely from Riesling

[1] It is the longer German version, however, that appears on wine labels.

Measuring the sugar content of the must at Bad Durkheim (G)

GROSSLAGEN OF
THE RHEINPFALZ

Bereich Mittelhaardt Deutsche Weinstrasse

1 Schnepfenflug vom Zellertal
2 Grafenstück
3 Höllenpfad
4 Schwarzerde
5 Rosenbühl
6 Kobnert
7 Feuerberg
8 Saumagen
9 Honigsäckel
10 Hochmess
11 Schenkenböhl
12 Schnepfenflug an der Weinstrasse
13 Mariengarten
14 Hofstück
15 Meerspinne
16 Rebstöckel
17 Pfaffengrund

Bereich Südliche Weinstrasse

18 Mandelhöhe
19 Schloss Ludwigshöhe
20 Ordensgut
21 Trappenberg
22 Bischofskreuz
23 Königsgarten
24 Herrlich
25 Kloster Liebfrauenberg
26 Guttenberg

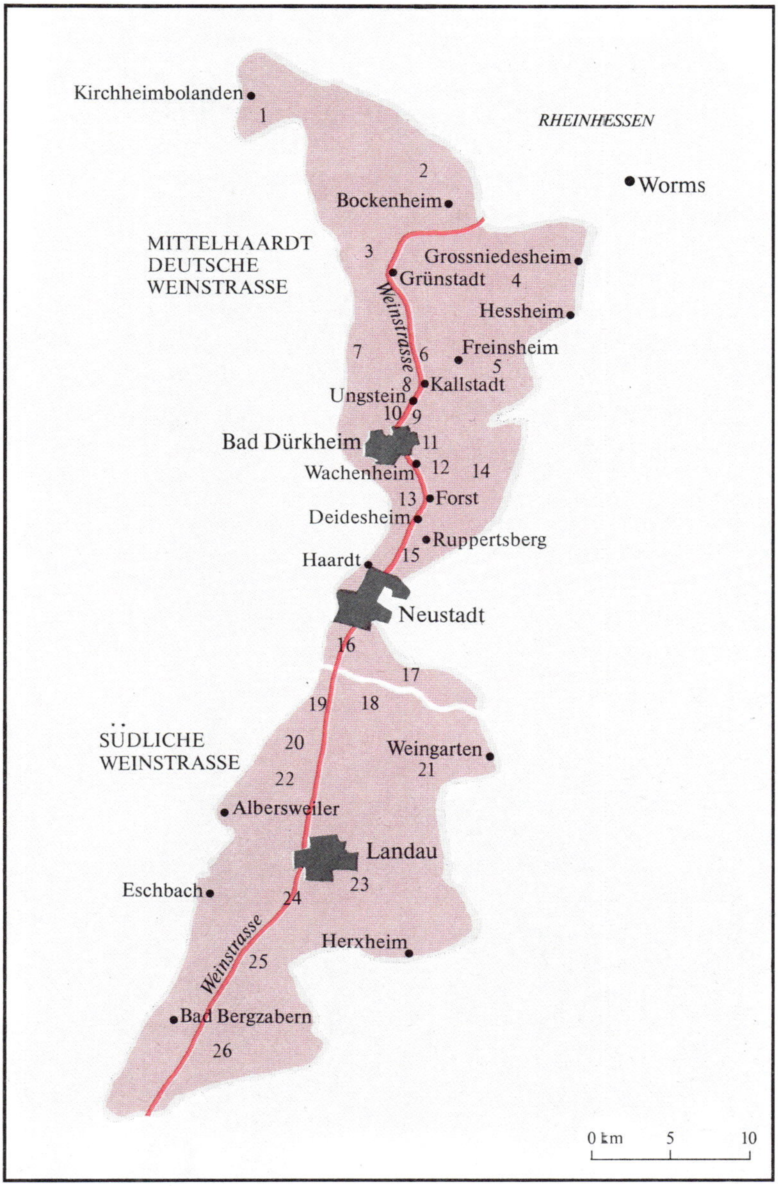

grapes in the best vineyards achieve considerable elegance combined with a marked persistence of flavour. This is also a region which produces some of the greatest *Auslesen*, *Beerenauslesen* and *Trockenbeerenauslesen*.

The wines of the Oberhaardt used to have a reputation for being coarse and ordinary, but large modern co-operatives, using the latest techniques, have achieved a marked improvement in quality. Much of this wine in the past was sold as Liebfraumilch (see note, page 102), but today more and more of it is being sold under its district origin. One of the most important co-operatives, Deutsches Weintor, sells a large part of its production under a grape variety name combined with the *Bereich* designation; with a host of unknown names to play with this may well be the best way forward for these wines. They tend to be fruity, full flavoured, a little soft but with considerable youthful charm. Other Rheinpfalz co-operatives which produce some wines of high quality include those of Bad Dürkheim, Deidesheim, Forst and Kallstadt.

Of the 26 *Grosslagen* in the Pfalz the seventeen in the Mittelhaardt have rather more significance than those in the Südliche Weinstrasse. The most important are:

Bereich	*Grosslage*	*Villages*
Mittelhaardt Deutsche Weinstrasse	Feuerberg	Bad Dürkheim, Kallstadt
Mittelhaardt D W	Hochmess	Bad Dürkheim, Ungstein
Mittelhaardt D W	Hofstück	Deidesheim, Ruppertsberg
Mittelhaardt D W	Kobnert	Kallstadt, Ungstein
Mittelhaardt D W	Mariengarten	Deidesheim, Forst, Wachenheim
Mittelhaardt D W	Saumagen	Kallstadt
Mittelhaardt D W	Schenkenböhl	Bad Dürkheim, Wachenheim
Südliche Weinstrasse	Herrlich	
Südliche Weinstrasse	Kloster Liebfrauenberg	
Südliche Weinstrasse	Königsgarten	

SAMPLE TASTING

(1) A Südliche Weinstrasse *QbA* or *Kabinett* from a co-operative
(2) A Deidesheimer or Dürkheimer *QbA* or *Kabinett* from a co-operative
(3) A Forster Riesling *Spätlese* (estate or co-operative)
(4) A Wachenheimer or Kallstadter *Auslese* (estate or co-operative)

In this tasting a wine from the southern Pfalz is used as a curtain-raiser to some examples from the best villages of the Mittelhaardt. As so many grape varieties are to be found in this region, many variations can be tried, using Müller-Thurgau, Riesling, Silvaner, Scheurebe or even some of the new, more exotic varieties.

It is a tradition in the Karst vineyard at Bad Durkheim that each apprentice should make a cask carving like this one (G)

Other German wine areas

Ahr

This small valley, north of and parallel with the Mosel, produces only 30,000 hectolitres of wine. Although the main production is red, the production of white wines is growing. It is a very traditional region, and is still fighting a rear-guard action for the production of red wines from now degenerating Spätburgunder vines.

Baden

This large region bordering the Rhine immediately opposite Alsace has grown immensely in importance in the last 30 years, largely thanks to the efforts of its co-operative movement. Now some 700,000 hectolitres of wine are produced, of which 78 per cent are white. A wide spectrum of grape varieties is planted, including the Müller-Thurgau (26 per cent), Spätburgunder (22 per cent) and Ruländer (13 per cent).

These wines are still mostly drunk in Germany itself. They are full-bodied and rather lack the flair and bouquet of wines from further north. Of the four *Bereiche* and 16 *Grosslagen* into which the region is divided the name most likely to be met with is that of the Kaiserstuhl-Tuniberg *Bereich*.

Old presses in the museum at Kloster Eberbach in the Rheingau (G)

(right) Schloss Stauffenberg at Durbach, in Baden (Zefa)

Franken

This small but charming wine-producing region of Northern Bavaria produces 120,000 hectolitres from vines growing on hills overlooking the river Main; the region is dominated by the ancient city of Würzburg. This is very much Silvaner country, although the Müller-Thurgau has gained considerably in recent years; 46 per cent of the vines are Silvaner, 41 per cent are Müller-Thurgau and Riesling accounts for only 4 per cent.

Franconian wines have gained much of their popularity in export markets from being sold in their distinctive *Bocksbeutel* – the flat, flask-shaped bottle in which all *QbA* and *QmP* wines are sold. For many years there was a tendency to call all Franconian wines *Steinwein*, but only wines coming from one famous vineyard, the Würzburger Stein, are legally entitled to bear this name.

Franconian wines have a very distinctive character, with more body than most other German wines; they are nearly always noticeably dry, even at *Spätlese* quality. They are still not widely exported, and it is therefore wise to look for examples from one or two of the best estates.

The largest and most important of these, the Bayerische Landesanstalt, belongs to the Bavarian State and was formerly the property of the Prince Bishops of Würzburg; its cellars are particularly worth visiting. This estate is closely followed in interest by Juliusspital, also in Würzburg.

Hessische Bergstrasse

The smallest of all German wine-producing regions, with only 25,000 hectolitres production, this is little more than an eastern appendage of the Rheingau. Its moderate quality wines are mostly quaffed by summer holiday-makers visiting what is a very attractive tourist region.

Mittelrhein

This area runs from north of the Rheingau to Koblenz. Only 70,000 hectolitres are produced, which is either consumed locally or used for making sparkling wine (Sekt).

Württemberg

This wine-growing region centred on the river Neckar has vines which grow even into the suburbs of Stuttgart. It produces some 460,000 hectolitres on average, of which 63 per cent are red; the most important grape variety is the red Trollinger, which makes mild, full-flavoured red wines. The demand for these wines locally is such that very little is seen outside the region itself. Württembergers are reputed to have a great thirst, and to consume four times as much wine as they produce themselves.

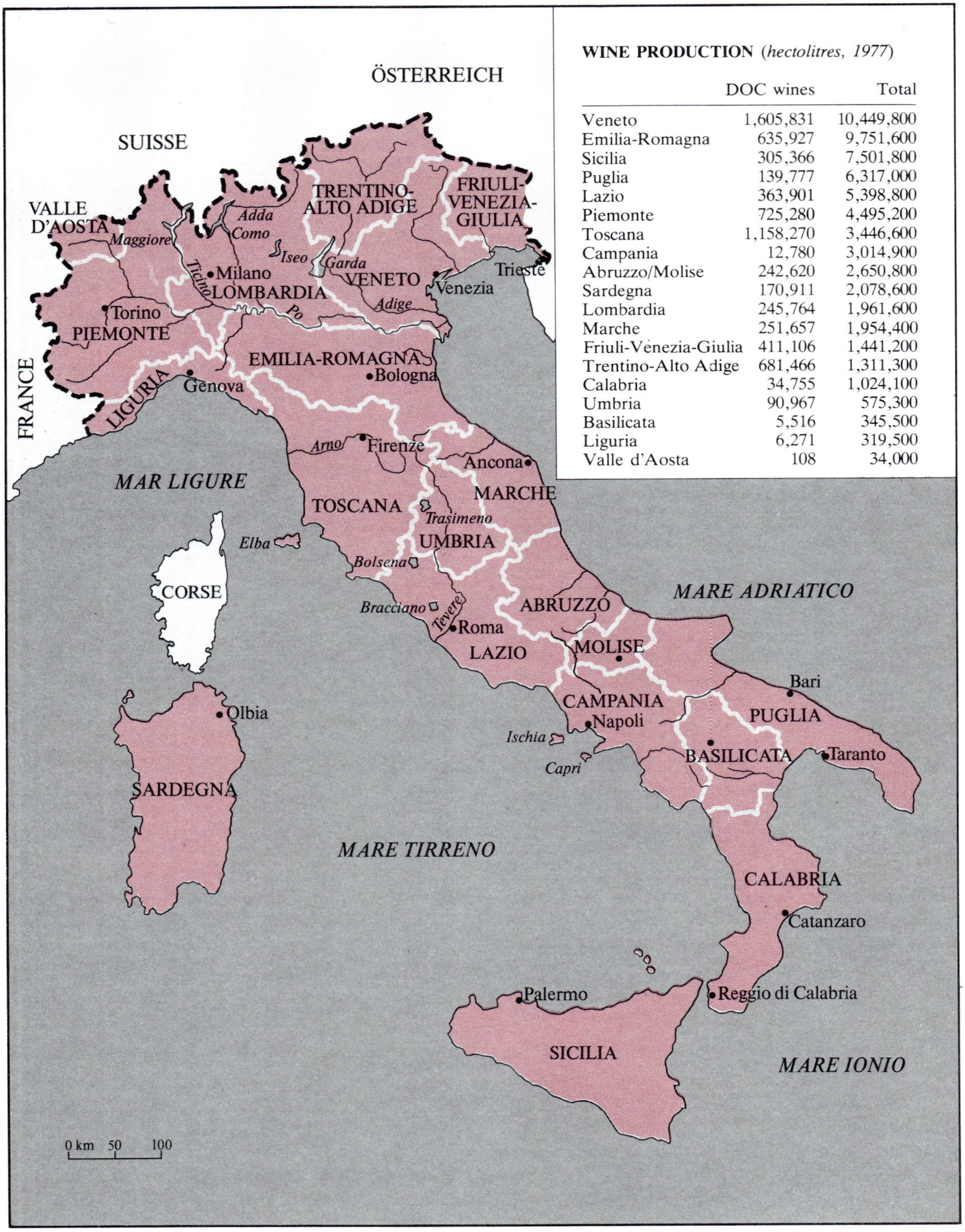

WINE PRODUCTION (*hectolitres, 1977*)

	DOC wines	Total
Veneto	1,605,831	10,449,800
Emilia-Romagna	635,927	9,751,600
Sicilia	305,366	7,501,800
Puglia	139,777	6,317,000
Lazio	363,901	5,398,800
Piemonte	725,280	4,495,200
Toscana	1,158,270	3,446,600
Campania	12,780	3,014,900
Abruzzo/Molise	242,620	2,650,800
Sardegna	170,911	2,078,600
Lombardia	245,764	1,961,600
Marche	251,657	1,954,400
Friuli-Venezia-Giulia	411,106	1,441,200
Trentino-Alto Adige	681,466	1,311,300
Calabria	34,755	1,024,100
Umbria	90,967	575,300
Basilicata	5,516	345,500
Liguria	6,271	319,500
Valle d'Aosta	108	34,000

ITALY

WITH SOME 9,000,000 acres of vineyards under cultivation, Italy produces more wine than any other country in the world. The immense variety of quality wines which it exports can hold its own against all rivals, and Italy bids well to become and to remain Europe's chief producer of sound wines in the middle price range. In 1976, out of a total output of 66,000,000 hectolitres, over 13,000,000 were drunk abroad; almost half this export total went to France.

Vines are grown and wines are produced in each one of the country's nineteen regions, and it is this enormous geographical spread – from the top to the toe of Italy is as far as from Paris to Madrid – that gives rise to the principal attraction of Italian wines: their great variety and individuality. Few individual wines, if any, can be expected to vie with a great French or German growth of a good year, but their vast range offers the enthusiast marvellous scope for discovery. Red, white and *rosé* wines are produced in abundance and in dry, sweet, sparkling and fortified forms; alcoholic strengths range from as low as 6° (e.g. Moscato d'Asti from Piedmont) to 16° or more among the sweet and heavy wines of the south, such as Primitivo di Manduria from Apulia.

Most of the notable wine regions lie in the northern half of the country. Tuscany, Veneto and Piedmont in particular offer an enchanting range of quality wines, including the finest reds in Italy – Barolo, Barbaresco, Brunello and Chianti – and a wide selection of outstanding whites. The abiding interest of Italian wines lies, however, in the fact that every single region, north and south, offers something quite individual and characteristic to tempt the palate.

At least a hundred grape varieties, indigenous and imported, are pressed into service – an astonishing fact when one thinks of the comparable range in France. The most important reds, in terms of the quality of the wine which they produce, are *Barbera, Cabernet, Merlot, Montepulciano, Nebbiolo, Pinot Nero, Sangiovese* and *Schiava*; the chief whites are *Malvasia, Moscato, Pinot Bianco, Pinot Grigio* and *Trebbiano*. From this wealth of resources, several hundred different wines are produced throughout the country. The character of each stems from the type of grape used, and the differences within the same viticultural area can be much more pronounced than those between different French wines.

The wine laws

Since 1963, almost 200 wines 'of particular reputation and quality' have achieved the DOC accolade. New wine laws of that year introduced this concept of a guaranteed name of origin (*denominazione di origine controllata*) for approved wines. Similar, both in purpose and in effect, to the *appellation contrôlée* legislation in France, these regulations have had a dramatic effect on quality control and on the appeal of Italian wines abroad. They are

EDITOR'S NOTE

For ease of recognition, all Italian place names mentioned in the text are given in their English form (e.g. Piedmont for Piemonte). On the maps they appear in their Italian form, and they are normally shown thus on wine labels. The most common variations are:

English	*Italian*
Apulia	Puglie
Florence	Firenze
Latium	Lazio
Lombardy	Lombardia
Piedmont	Piemonte
Sardinia	Sardegna
Sicily	Sicilia
The Marches	Marche
Tuscany	Toscana
Venice	Venezia

In order to distinguish grape varieties from wines called after them, the former are printed in italic: thus *Moscato* refers to the grape of that name, while Moscato d'Asti is the name of a wine.

nationally enforceable by the Ministry of Agriculture, with the aid of a three-fold army of National Committee members, government inspectors and officials of the *consorzi* or local growers' associations.

The *consorzi* came into being in the 1930s to regulate the standards of production and labelling for their own members, but their influence was only local and standards throughout the country varied widely. These days the more important ones display their own neck labels on their wines as evidence that local standards are maintained. Where, as often happens, only a strictly limited production of a wine is permitted by the association, the neck label will carry the number of bottles allocated to that particular grower.

No DOC wine can be marketed under a protected name unless it has been produced in an agreed and limited viticultural area, from the approved grapes used in the right proportions, and aged and bottled according to clearly stipulated rules. Flavour, bouquet and colour must conform to rigorous requirements; so must chemical properties and acid and alcohol content. Bottling conditions are strictly regulated, and as a result a high proportion of exported wines are bottled in the area where they are produced.

Buying DOC wines abroad, one may expect to pay a price which will depend less on the individual maker or vineyard than on the overall quantity and quality of the wines of a given year. Nevertheless, except in the case of the great wines of Piedmont and certain other reds which require ageing (such as Chianti Classico), vintages bear considerably less significance than in France and Germany, for the Italian climate is so much less capricious than on the other side of the Alps. A date on the label of a bottle indicates neither more nor less than the age of the wine it contains.

SPARKLING WINES

Italy's two best-known sparkling wines abroad are the sweet Asti Spumante and Moscato d'Asti from Piedmont. But on the home market those with most prestige are the dry sparkling wines – *spumante brut*. Asti Spumante is made, like the high quality Prosecco wines of Veneto, by the Charmat process of bulk fermentation in sealed tanks. Secondary fermentation takes place in the tank and the bottles are vacuum filled, thereby preserving the sparkle as well as the freshness and fruitiness of the wine.

Dry sparkling wines, appealing more to the taste of seasoned Champagne drinkers, have been made in Italy by the *méthode Champenoise* since the turn of the century. Fine quality *spumante brut* wines are these days made in Piedmont by Cinzano, Fontanafredda, Gancia and Riccadonna, and in Trentino by Ferrari; the latter are aged for four years in the bottle on the estate (six for a *riserva*). It is anomalous that none of these dry sparkling wines, except for Prosecco di Conegliano-Valdobbiadene, have been brought within the ambit of the DOC regulations; yet still wines can be found throughout Italy which are entitled by their DOC to a *spumante* variety.

(below left) Wagons in front of a press at Caldaro, south-west of Bolzano, in Trentino-Alto Adige (Zefa)

(below) A fine 1972 Chianti from the Colli Fiorentini, made by Fattoria Saulina. Note the number on the neck label

Vineyards near Pesaro in the Marches (G)

SAMPLE TASTINGS

The following selection of reds and whites is designed to display the taste of the leading grape varieties (indicated in italic).

Reds
(1) A Barbera – any DOC (Barbera d'Alba, for instance, or Rubina di Cantevenna) or an unclassified wine from Piedmont (*Barbera*)
(2) A Montepulciano d'Abruzzo (*Montepulciano*)
(3) A Santa Maddalena or a Lago di Caldaro (*Schiava*)
(4) A Chianti Classico Riserva from a single estate – e.g. Castello di Brolio or Badia a Coltibuono (*Sangiovese*)
(5) A Cabernet from Trentino-Alto Adige or Friuli-Venezia-Giulia (*Cabernet*)
(6) A Barolo, Barbaresco or Gattinara (*Nebbiolo*)

Whites
(1) A Pinot Bianco from Veneto or Trentino (*Pinot Bianco*)
(2) A Pinot Grigio – preferably a Collio from Friuli-Venezia-Giulia (*Pinot Grigio*)
(3) A Verdicchio dei Castelli di Jesi or a Verdicchio di Matelica (*Verdicchio*)
(4) An Orvieto (mostly *Trebbiano*)
(5) A Greco di Tufo – a taste of the south (*Greco*)
(6) A Tocai from Veneto or Friuli-Venezia-Giulia (*Tocai*)
(7) A Frascati – for preference a Superiore from the Co-operative dei Produttori di Frascati or a Fontana Candida (mostly *Malvasia*)

Additional regulations imposed in 1978 lay down that a grape variety may only be mentioned on a label in conjunction with a non-DOC place-name. Thus one finds a wine called Pinot Grigio delle Tre Venezie, combining the name of a generic variety of grape (*Pinot Grigio*) with that of an area covering three adjoining but separate DOC regions – Veneto, Friuli-Venezia-Giulia and Trentino-Alto Adige. Such wines – and there are, of course, many thousands of them, made all over Italy – are among those known as *vini da tavola* (literally, table wines). Many are exported, and some of these are as good or better than many DOC wines; notable examples include Corvo, Frecciarossa, I Piani, Lacrima Christi, Ravello, Sassicia, Torbato and Venegazzu.

The increasing care now being given to the production of finer wines, plus the inevitable fact that a number of outstanding individual growths of great quality would eventually emerge, was anticipated in 1963 by the creation of a third classification, the *denominazione di origine controllata e garantita* (DOCG). Such wines must clearly state on their label their place of origin, the name of the grower and bottler, the place of bottling, the net content of the bottle and the wine's alcoholic content; bottles for export are sealed with the red seal of the Italian Institute for Foreign Trade, and the wine may never be sold in containers exceeding five litres.

ITALY

GLOSSARY

abbaccato: slightly sweet
amabile: gently sweet
amaro: bitter
bianco: white
cantina: winery; *cantina sociale* = co-operative
casa vinicola: wine house
chiaretto: pale red, almost pink
classico: of an area which is the older, more select part of a wine-growing district, and thus of the wine made
consorzio: growers' association; they vary in effectiveness, but at their best act as a sort of super-DOC body
DOC: *denominazione di origine controllata*; the controlled place-name and delimited zone for the production of wine under regulated conditions; equivalent to the French *appellation contrôlée*
dolce: sweet
fiasco: flask
frizzante: semi-sparkling, effervescent, causing a prickling sensation on the tongue
giallo: yellow
governo: system used in Tuscany and Veneto of secondary fermentation to speed the maturing of young drinking wines
imbottigliato: bottled; *imbottigliato del produttore all'origine* = estate bottled
liquoroso: of wine in a strengthened form, usually by fortification with grape brandy; it may be sweet or dry
morbido: soft, mellow
muffa nobile: noble rot
passito: of grapes which have been left to become semi-dry before fermentation, either on the vine or spread out on racks or straw, in order to concentrate the sugar and other ingredients; also describes the stronger, sweeter wine made from them.
riserva: wine which has been matured for a specified minimum number of years
rosato: pink, *rosé*
rosso: red
sapido: sappy, lively, vigorous
secco: dry
semplice: simple; previously used to describe non-DOC wines, now in the broad category of *vino da tavola*
spumante: sparkling; of wine made by the *méthode Champenoise* or the Charmat process
stravecchio: very old
superiore: wine from selected grapes, with a higher degree of alcohol, and greater maturity
vecchio: old; of wine that has fulfilled a minimum period maturing
vendemmia: vintage, harvest
vin santo: strong, usually white, *passito* wine; a speciality in Tuscany
vino da tavola: a broad category of honest, sound wines from an identifiable but non-DOC source

Italy: where the wines come from, where the grapes are grown

REGION	BEST-KNOWN WINES (● RED ∅ ROSE ○ WHITE)	PRINCIPAL VARIETIES OF GRAPE: ● RED	○ WHITE
Abruzzo and Molise	● Montepulciano d'Abruzzo ○ Trebbiano d'Abruzzo	31, 44	23, 43
Apulia	●∅○ Castel del Monte ● Primitivo di Manduria ●∅○ San Severo	2, 4, 26, 31, 34, 36, 40, 44, 47	5, 7, 16, 22, 23, 24, 29, 43, 46
Basilicata	● Aglianico del Vulture	1	
Calabria	●∅○ Cirò	17, 20, 44	19, 23
Campania	○ Greco di Tufo ●○ Ischia ●∅○ Lacrima Christi ●∅○ Ravello ● Taurasi	1, 3, 23, 38, 44	6, 15, 20, 23, 43
Emilia Romagna	○ Albana di Romagna ● Gutturnio dei Colli Piacentini ● Lambrusco ● Sangiovese di Romagna ○ Trebbiano di Romagna	3, 5, 25, 28, 44	1, 23, 24, 32, 36, 43
Friuli-Venezia-Giulia	● Aquileia ○ Collio Goriziano ○ Colli Orientali del Friuli ●○ Grave del Friuli	7, 28, 39, 41	23, 31, 32, 33, 35, 36, 37, 38, 41, 42, 49
Latium	○ Colli Albani ○ Est! Est!! Est!!! ○ Frascati ○ Marino	2, 3, 9, 11, 28, 31, 44	3, 7, 24, 41, 43, 48
Liguria	○ Cinque Terre	43	2, 8, 50

REGION	BEST-KNOWN WINES (● RED ∅ ROSE ○ WHITE)	PRINCIPAL VARIETIES OF GRAPE: ● RED	○ WHITE
Lombardy	○ Bianco di Custoza ● Franciacorta ●∅○ Frecciarossa ● Grumello ● Inferno ○ Lugana ● Oltrepò Pavese ●∅ Riviera del Garda ● Sassella ● Valtellina	3, 5, 7, 22, 27, 28, 33, 39, 44	12, 17, 24, 36, 37, 41, 43
The Marches	● Rosso Conero ● Rosso Piceno ○ Verdicchio dei Castelli di Jesi	31, 44, 48	4, 23, 30, 32, 43, 48
Piedmont	○ Asti Spumante ● Barbaresco ● Barbera ● Barolo ● Carema ○ Cortese di Gavi ● Dolcetto ● Freisa ● Gattinara ● Ghemme ● Grignolino ○ Moscato d'Asti	3, 5, 6, 14, 16, 21, 26, 33, 49	12, 14, 24
Sardinia	● Cannonau ○ Torbato ○ Vernaccia di Oristano	10, 19, 30	23, 24, 27, 28, 43, 50, 51
Sicily	● Corvo ●∅○ Etna ○ Marsala	8, 15, 35	10, 11, 13, 21, 23, 24, 43
Trentino-Alto Adige	● Lago di Caldaro ● Marzemino ● Santa Maddalena ○ Terlano ●∅ Teroldego Rotaliano	7, 24, 25, 26, 27, 28, 32, 39, 45, 46	25, 26, 32, 33, 36, 37, 38, 40, 42, 45
Tuscany	● Brunello di Montalcino ● Chianti ● Chianti Classico ○ Montecarlo ●○ Parrina ○ Vernaccia di San Gimignano ● Vino Nobile di Montepulciano ○ Vin Santo	7, 9, 12, 31, 44	9, 19, 23, 32, 33, 38, 39, 43, 47, 51
Umbria	●○ Colli del Trasimeno ○ Orvieto ●○ Torgiano	9, 18, 44	19, 23, 43, 47, 48
Val d'Aosta	● Donnaz ● Enfer d'Arvier	33, 37	
Veneto	● Bardolino ●○ Breganze ● Cabernet di Pramaggiore ● Merlot di Pramaggiore ●○ Piave ○ Prosecco ○ Soave ○ Tocai di Lison ● Valpolicella	7, 13, 28, 29, 39, 42	18, 24, 32, 34, 38, 41, 44, 49

KEY TO
RED GRAPES

1. Aglianico
2. Aleatico
3. Barbera
4. Bombino Nero
5. Bonarda
6. Brachetto
7. Cabernet
8. Calabrese
9. Canaiolo Nero
10. Cannonau
11. Cesanese
12. Colorino
13. Corvina
14. Dolcetto
15. Frappato
16. Freisa
17. Gaglioppo
18. Gamay
19. Girò
20. Greco Nero
21. Grignolino
22. Groppello
23. Guarnaccia
24. Lagrein
25. Lambrusco
26. Malvasia
27. Marzemino
28. Merlot
29. Molinara
30. Monica
31. Montepulciano
32. Moscato Rosa
33. Nebbiolo
34. Negro Amaro
35. Nerello
36. Ottavianello
37. Petit Rouge
38. Piedirosso
39. Pinot Nero
40. Primitivo
41. Refosco
42. Rondinella
43. Rossese
44. Sangiovese
45. Schiava
46. Teroldego
47. Uva di Troia
48. Vernaccia di Serrapetrona
49. Vespolina

KEY TO
WHITE GRAPES

1. Albana
2. Albarola
3. Bellone
4. Bianchello
5. Bianco di Alessano
6. Biancolella
7. Bombino
8. Bosco
9. Canaiolo Bianco
10. Carricante
11. Catarratto
12. Cortese
13. Damaschino
14. Erbaluce
15. Forastera
16. Francavilla
17. Garganega
18. Garganega di Soave
19. Greco (Grechetto)
20. Greco di Tufo
21. Grillo
22. Impigno
23. Malvasia
24. Moscato Bianco
25. Moscato Giallo
26. Müller-Thurgau
27. Nasco
28. Nuragus
29. Pampanuto
30. Passerina
31. Picolit
32. Pinot Bianco
33. Pinot Grigio
34. Prosecco
35. Ribolla
36. Riesling Italico
37. Riesling Renano
38. Sauvignon
39. Sémillon
40. Silvaner
41. Tocai
42. Traminer Aromatico
43. Trebbiano
44. Trebbiano di Soave
45. Veltliner
46. Verdeca
47. Verdello
48. Verdicchio
49. Verduzzo
50. Vermentino
51. Vernaccia

The regions

Piedmont

Piedmont, lying in the extreme north-west of the country and bordering both France and Switzerland, produces the most distinguished of the red wines of Italy. It boasts a longer list of DOC growths than any other, and its total annual output of red and white wines, chiefly the former, runs to well over 4,000,000 hectolitres. Of the eleven regions north of Rome only two, Emilia Romagna and Veneto, produce wine in greater quantity, and neither of these offer individual growths of a comparable excellence.

The greater part of the region's output comes from an area some 60 miles long and 40 miles wide, directly south of the River Po, which can fairly claim to be one of the great wine areas of the world. The Monferrato hills, stretching across the provinces of Alessandria, Asti, Cuneo and Turin, provide from their steep slopes almost all the wines for which the region is famous. Chief among these are Barolo and Barbaresco, two great wines which for several decades have been recognized as among the finest reds in Italy. Their ascendancy was endorsed several years ago, when it was proposed that they should become the first two growths to be accorded the newly devised status of *denominazione di origine controllata e garantita* (DOCG). This proposal has yet to be implemented, and the accolade will probably be granted only to wines which have been tasted before they go on sale.

DOC WINES

- Asti Spumante ○
- Barbaresco ●
- Barbera d'Alba ●
- Barbera d'Asti ●
- Barbera del Monferrato ●
- Barolo ●
- Boca ●
- Brachetto d'Acqui ●
- Caluso Passito ○
- Carema ●
- Colli Tortonesi ● ○
- Dolcetto d'Acqui ●
- Dolcetto d'Alba ●
- Dolcetto d'Asti ●
- Dolcetto di Diano d'Alba ●
- Dolcetto di Dogliani ●
- Dolcetto delle Langhe Monregalesi ●
- Dolcetto di Ovada ●
- Erbaluce di Caluso ○
- Fara ●
- Freisa d'Asti ●
- Freisa di Chieri ●
- Gattinara ●
- Gavi/Cortese di Gavi ○
- Ghemme ●
- Grignolino d'Asti ●
- Grignolino del Monferrato Casalese ●
- Lessona ●
- Malvasia di Casorzo d'Asti ●
- Malvasia di Castelnuovo Don Bosco ●
- Moscato d'Asti/Moscato d'Asti Spumante ○
- Moscato Naturale d'Asti ○
- Nebbiolo d'Alba ●
- Rubino di Cantavenna ●
- Sizzano ●

The vineyards of Fontanafredda, in Piedmont, which produces the famous sparkling wine (G)

The region's commonest and most prolific grape is the *Barbera*, but Barolo and Barbaresco are both made chiefly from the *Nebbiolo*. The latter grape also grows in the north of Piedmont, between Turin and Lake Maggiore, where it is made into Gattinara and Ghemme – both good wines, but not quite so distinguished as the two front-runners from south of the Po.

Piedmont lies in the same latitude as the major vineyards of the Rhône valley, on the other side of the Alps, and its reds – like the Rhône wines – tend to be bigger and fuller (though not necessarily stronger) than those from elsewhere in the country. Only ten per cent of the region's total wine output is white; this is largely accounted for by the well-known sweet and sparkling Asti Spumante and Moscato d'Asti, both made from the *Moscato* grape. It is also interesting to note that Turin, the region's capital city, is the centre of the vermouth industry.

Liguria

DOC WINES

Cinque Terre ○
Cinque Terre Sciacchetrá ○
Rossese di Dolceacqua/Dolceacqua ●

Liguria's claims as a wine-producing region are slim and in proportion to its output, and although it produces slightly more quality wines than Calabria even these are of no outstanding merit. Its real fame lies outside wine drinking as the narrow coastal strip of the Italian Riviera, arched like a boomerang around the great industrial port of Genoa, and flanked by the Alps and the Apennines. This has no doubt in some part contributed to such reputation as the wines have, in particular Cinque Terre.

Valle d'Aosta

DOC WINES

Donnaz ●
Enfer d'Arvier ●

In wine terms Valle d'Aosta is often included as a part – albeit an important part – of Piedmont, although is has been an autonomous political region since 1947. The name derives from Augusta, after the Roman military town which is now the regional capital, but its chief geographical feature is the mountainous valley of the River Dora Baltea.

The *Nebbiolo*, the great wine grape of Piedmont, is grown here at a much higher altitude, producing one of the region's two DOC wines, Donnaz; the other, Enfer d'Arvier, is made from the *Petit Rouge* – perhaps a reflection of the fact that the region was once held by the kings of Burgundy, and still has a strong French influence. Another red DOC wine associated with Valle d'Aosta, Carema, is produced on the border with Piedmont, and has been included among the Piedmont wines in the gazetteer. Other Valle d'Aosta wines are made and drunk locally, but only those listed in the gazetteer are commercially viable abroad.

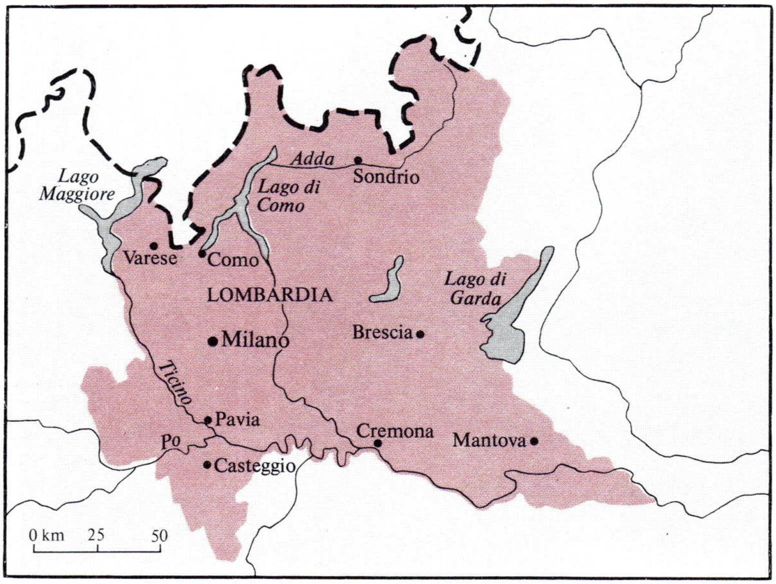

Lombardy

Lombardy, Italy's third largest region, now produces rather less wine than it has done in the past. Nevertheless, it still boasts a fine range of quality wines, though the names of its two famous cheeses, Gorgonzola and Bel Paese, are probably better known than those of its individual wines. The region's three main wine districts are widely separated. The most important, Valtellina, is a valley in the mountainous north, immediately east of Como – the lake not the town; its wines are held in great esteem, particularly at home in Italy and in Switzerland – but too often, in practice, they do not match up to their reputation.

The second area of interest is the Oltrepó Pavese, a hilly district south of Pavia, on the south bank of the River Po; it provides an interesting range of single-grape wines to DOC standards, made from native and imported grape varieties. Finally, from the western and southerly shores of Lake Garda, come pink and red wines, very similar to their counterparts on the eastern shores of the lake in neighbouring Veneto; among these are the well-known Chiaretto del Garda, now eclipsed as a name by the DOC title Riviera del Garda, and small quantities of an outstanding white wine, Lugana.

DOC WINES

Bianco di Custoza ○
Botticino ●
Cellatica ●
Colli Morenici Mantovani del Garda ● ○ ∅
Franciacorta Pinot ○
Franciacorta Rosso ●
Lugana ○
Oltrepó Pavese ● ○ ∅
Riviera del Garda ●∅
Tocai de San Martino della Battaglia ○
Valtellina ●
Valtellina Superiore ●

Trentino-Alto Adige

In any discussion of the location of a vineyard one is almost invariably talking about a river. In this case it is the River Adige (in German, the Etsch) which rises in the Austrian Alps and flows into the Adriatic just north of the Po. Its upper reaches are in the province of Alto Adige and its lower in that of Trento; both were part of Austria – Hungary until 1919, and the German language and influence still persists strongly in Alto Adige. This is reflected in the widespread use throughout the region of the German *Riesling* grape (*Renano*) alongside the Italian (*Italico*).

Trentino-Alto Adige is a wine region of growing interest. Its total output is comparatively modest – 1.3 million hectolitres a year – and only a few of its wines are widely known. However, within the last three or four years the volume of its DOC wines has become the third highest in the country (only

DOC WINES

Alto Adige ● ○
Caldaro ●
Casteller ●
Colli di Bolzano ●
Meranese/Meranese di Collina ●
Santa Maddalena ●
Terlano ●
Teroldego ●
Trentino ● ○
Valdadige/Etschtaler ● ○
Valle Isarco ○

Veneto and Tuscany produce more), and in 1977 the percentage of such wines in relation to total output was higher than in any other region. There are now eleven separately designated DOC areas.

Friuli-Venezia-Giulia

DOC WINES

Aquileia ● ○
Collio Goriziano/Collio ● ○
Colli Orientali del Friuli ● ○
Grave del Friuli ● ○
Isonzo ● ○
Latisana ● ○

The wine output of Friuli (1,400,000 hectolitres in an average year) is not great by comparison with other areas, but the region produces some of the best white wines of Italy. They are still too little known, however, since so much of the output is consumed locally. In contrast to practice elsewhere in Italy, all the region's DOC names are portmanteaus for a wide variety of single-grape wines.

The first three areas to be thus grouped were the Colli Orientali del Friuli, the Collio Goriziano (or Collio) and the Grave del Friuli. Collio wines come from a small group of villages lying near and to the west of Gorizia. The Colli Orientali cover a wider spread, mainly in the province of Udine, between the towns of Udine and Gorizia. The Grave del Friuli in the central part is of lesser importance. More recently the wines of three other neighbouring areas, spreading across the coastal strip between Gorizia and the Adriatic, have been accorded place-name status; these are centred on two small towns, Aquileia and Latisana, and the banks of the River Isonzo.

The grape varieties which these areas chiefly have in common are *Cabernet* (*Sauvignon* and *Franc*), *Merlot*, *Pinot Bianco* and *Grigio*, *Refosco*, *Riesling* and *Tocai*. There is, exceptionally, a *Traminer* in Collio and Isonzo. The use of *Riesling Renano* in Aquileia, Colli Orientali and Isonzo, and of the *Riesling Italico* in the Collio area, provides a reminder of the mixed German and Italian influences in this border region adjoining Austria.

The wines are characteristic of their grape varieties. The *Cabernets* and the *Merlots* are all ruby red, with pleasing bouquets and the dry, full flavour

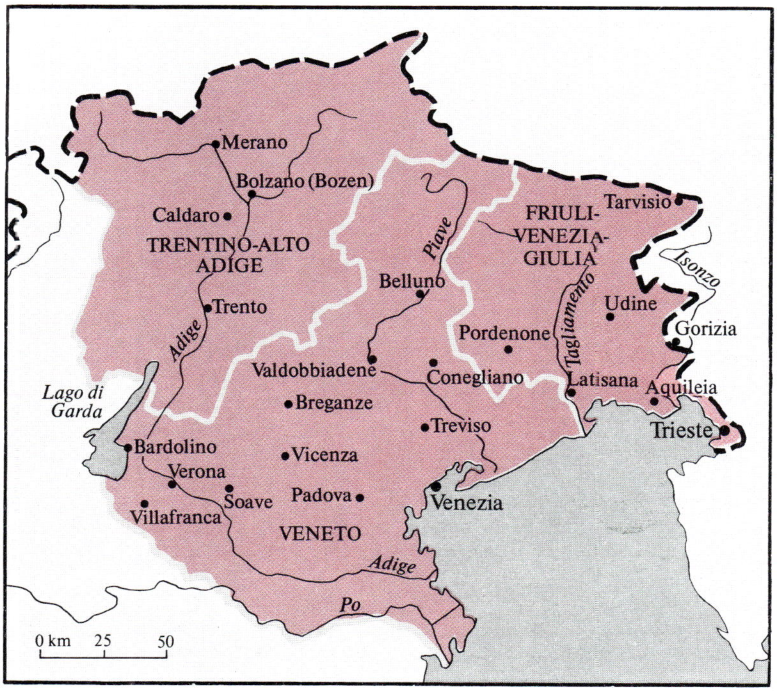

that Bruno Roncarati calls 'grassy'. *Refosco* has a more purple colour ageing to garnet; it is a heady, slightly bitter wine. The white *Pinots* are dry, delicate of bouquet but full in flavour; the *Biancos* are straw coloured and the *Grigios* are a golden yellow, sometimes with a pinkish hue. *Tocais* are pale golden, inclined to lemon; delicately scented and dry, they have an aromatic after-taste. The Rieslings are fine, pale golden wines, dry and full-bodied, and there is little to choose between the German and the Italian grape varieties. The one dessert wine from the region is Picolit from the Colli Orientali.

Veneto

Veneto's recent development as a wine-producing region has placed its significance in this respect beyond all doubt. In its total output of wine, now running at some 10 million hectolitres a year, it tends to run neck and neck with Emilia-Romagna, and in 1977 its output of quality wines surpassed even Tuscany, confirming its position at the head of the DOC league.

The three most celebrated wines of the region – Valpolicella, Bardolino and Soave – are all from the Verona area, and the principal grapes used to make them are unique to Veneto: *Garganega di Soave* for the white and *Corvina, Rondinella* and *Molinara* for the two reds. Valpolicella and Soave provide the basis for Recioto, the rich dessert wine which takes its name from the Italian for ears, *orecchie* – i.e. the ripest outer bunches on the vine.

Other notable wines of the region are the sparkling wines from the *Prosecco* grape, established in the region since the Middle Ages. These are processed by the Charmat method of bulk fermentation in sealed containers.

Reference to the Gazetteer notes on more recent additions in the attached DOC list will also reveal the extent to which French grape varieties have become established, especially *Merlot, Cabernet* (both *Sauvignon* and *Franc* where not specified) and the *Pinot*, white and black.

DOC WINES

Bardolino ●
Breganze ● ○
Cabernet di Pramaggiore ●
Colli Berici ● ○
Colli Euganei ● ○
Gambellara ○
Merlot di Pramaggiore ●
Montello e Colli Asolani ● ○
Piave/Vini del Piave ● ○
Prosecco di Conegliano-Valdobbiadene ○
Recioto di Soave ○
Recioto della Valpolicella ●
Soave ○
Tocai di Lison ○
Valpolicella ●

The hills of Chianti near Montevarchi in the Arno valley, south-east of Florence (Zefa)

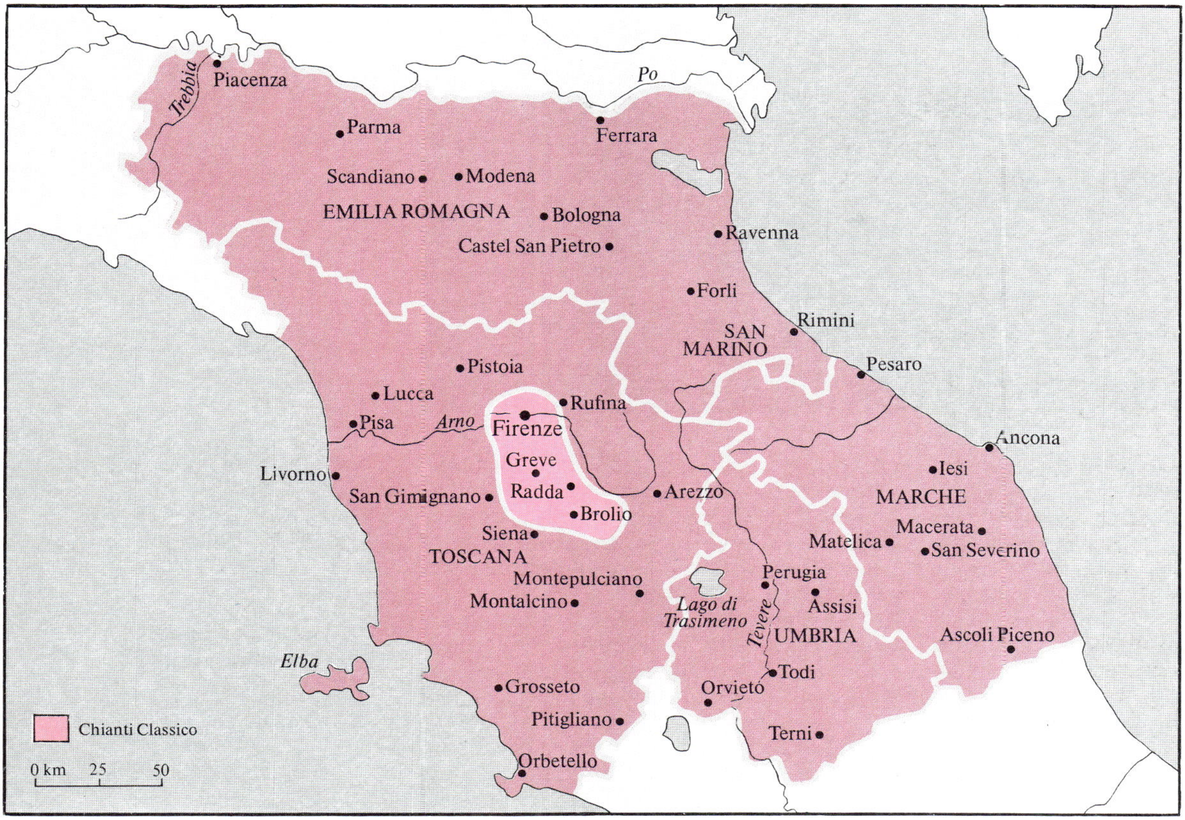

DOC WINES

Albana di Romagna ○
Bianco di Scandiano ○
Colli Bolognesi ●○
Gutturnio dei Colli Piacentini ●
Lambrusco Grasparossa di Castelvetro ●
Lambrusco Reggiano ● ∅
Lambrusco di Sorbara ●
Lambrusco Salamino di S. Croce ●
Monterosso Val d'Arda ○
Sangiovese di Romagna ●
Trebbianino Val Trebbia ○
Trebbiano di Romagna ○

Emilia-Romagna

The *autostrada* which slices across northern Italy from Rimini on the Adriatic coast to Reggio nell'Emilia and Padua runs for 150 miles across a vast agricultural plain on which wheat and maize, as well as grapes, are grown in great abundance. But despite an annual output of around 10,000,000 hectolitres, Emilia-Romagna boasts few wines of sufficient merit to complement the rich dishes served in the region's principal cities – Bologna, Modena, Ferrara and Ravenna. Among the best known, but not universally well-loved, is an unusual foaming red wine, Lambrusco, which has acquired no less than four DOC place names. Albana di Romagna and Trebbiano di Romagna are pleasing and drinkable whites.

Tuscany

For the wine lover Tuscany constitutes one of the most engaging of all the regions, with an output of DOC wines second only to Veneto. It is first and foremost the home of Chianti, the largest single DOC in the country, its 425,000 hectares staked out by Florence in the north, Arezzo in the east and Siena in the south. At its centre is a select group of Chianti Classico communes, flanked by six separately recognized Chianti districts; altogether the area produces just over one million hectolitres each year, usually about a quarter of Tuscany's total output.

Here, as elsewhere in Italy, Classico is the term that attaches to the older and better part of a wine-growing district. In the Chianti Classico zone are

In this Tuscan vineyard the modern technique of spraying is combined with the traditional method of pulling the tanker (Spectrum)

the vineyards which, due to the quality of the vines and their geographical position, are regarded as suitable for growing the very best grapes. The richness and variety of output, both inside and outside this zone, have tended to be obscured by a world-wide over-sell of cheap red wine (some of it never even Tuscan in the first place) marketed in straw-covered flasks which provide it with an instantly recognizable identity.

Chiantis kept for two years are indicated by the term *vecchio*; after a further year they become *riserva*. It is partly in order to indicate these distinctions that in both cases the bottles are of the straight-sided Bordeaux shape, either of the customary green or an attractive and individual dark brown.

Chianti not intended for ageing is fermented by a method peculiar to Italy known as the *governo*. After the first natural fermentation, a lively secondary fermentation is induced by adding the concentrated pressings of a small proportion of selected grapes put aside at the harvest and allowed to dry – to become *appassito* – thereby taking on a greater concentration of sugar and glycerin. The renewed fermentation which results hastens maturity and produces in the wine a freshness and a prickle which adds to its attraction for early drinking. Certain top estates also use the *governo* method for their *riserva* wines, believing that it increases their complexity.*

Tuscany boasts several other notable wines, of course. Brunello di Montalcino and Vin Nobile di Montepulciano stand out among the most majestic red wines in the country. Montecarlo is a unique white wine, not so well known as the Vernaccia from San Gimignano. In the non-DOC category is the excellent but as yet unsung Sassicaia, which seems to offer a quite new point of departure for Italian red wines. The other speciality of Tuscany, Vin Santo, is seldom seen abroad, though most of the bigger producers make one of their own.

DOC WINES

Bianco di Pitigliano ○
Bianco della Valdonievole ○
Bianco Vergine Valdichiana ○
Brunello di Montalcino ●
Carmignano ●
Chianti ●
Chianti Classico ●
Chianti Colli Aretini ●
Chianti Colli Fiorentini ●
Chianti Colli Senesi ●
Chianti Colline Pisane ●
Chianti Montalbano ●
Chianti Rufina ●
Elba ● ∅ ○
Montecarlo ○
Montescudaio ●
Parrina ● ○
Rosso delle Colline Lucchesi ●
Vernaccia di San Gimignano ○
Vino Nobile di Montepulciano ●

Umbria

Umbria is one of the smallest of the Italian wine-growing regions. Locked into the centre of the country, it is described by Frank Schoonmaker in his *Encyclopaedia of Wine* as 'by no means a real vineyard'. Nonetheless, its wild and mountainous terrain manages to produce well over 500,000 hectolitres of wine each year. Its two most notable wines, each called after one of the region's many picturesque little hill towns, are Orvieto and Torgiano; the third borrows its name from the famous Lake Trasimene.

DOC WINES

Colli del Trasimeno ● ○
Orvieto ○
Torgiano ● ○

*Chianti, it should be stressed, is always red wine. There is no provision in the DOC regulations for 'white Chianti', although the term is often incorrectly employed to describe one or other of the many local Tuscan whites.

The Marches

DOC WINES

Bianchello del Metauro ○
Bianco dei Colli Maceratesi ○
Falerio dei Colli Ascolani ○
Rosso Conero ●
Rosso Piceno ●
Sangiovese dei Colli Pesaresi ●
Verdicchio dei Castelli di Jesi ○
Verdicchio di Matelica ○
Vernaccia di Serrapetrona ●

With its mountainous inland character and its flat Adriatic coastline, The Marches is one of the most beautiful and spectacular of Italy's wine regions. It produces between 1,900,000 and 2,500,000 hectolitres of red and white wines annually, of which about one-tenth is of DOC quality, and depends for its better wines on one major grape variety (*Sangiovese*) and two lesser ones (*Montepulciano* and *Verdicchio*). The first two produce the reds. The third, which is white, accounts for half the region's DOC wines; while all too often unspectacular, it has lent its name to one of Italy's most famous wines.

Latium

DOC WINES

Aleatico di Gradoli ●
Bianco Capena ○
Cannellino ○
Cerveteri ● ○
Cesanese del Piglio
Cesanese di Affile ●
Cesanese di Olevano Romano ●
Colli Albani ○
Colli Lanuvini ○
Cori ● ○
Est! Est!! Est!!! ○
Frascati ○
Marino ○
Merlot di Aprilia ●
Montecompatri Colonna ○
Sangiovese di Aprilia ●
Trebbiano di Aprilia ○
Velletri ● ○
Zagarolo ○

Latium is the central Italian wine region, embracing Rome. It makes a large contribution to the country's total output, but its DOC wines do not account for much of this, and though they display great variety and interest, few if any are really distinguished. Frascati, the best and best-known of the Castelli Romani wines, is a notable exception, and other Castelli Romani wines are also attractive and agreeable – fresh white wines with plenty of body like Colonna, Montecompatri, Marino, Velletri and Zagarolo. So are Colli Albani and Colli Lanuvini, which come into the same group.

Between the Castelli Romani villages and the sea, to the west of Lake Albano, three good single-grape wines which gained early DOC recognition have been developed since the early 1940s by farmers repatriated from Tunisia. The only other wine of which special mention should be made, as much for the curiosity of its name as for any intrinsic quality, is Est! Est!! Est!!! (see gazetteer).

Latium wines are mainly white, *Trebbiano* and *Malvasia* grapes predominating; the latter, in particular, impart a characteristic aroma, especially to the sweeter wines. Such reds as there are tend to be stronger in alcohol than the whites.

Abruzzo and Molise

DOC WINES

Montepulciano d'Abruzzo ●
Trebbiano d' Abruzzo ○

Few wines of consequence come from this highly mountainous region stretching down the central Adriatic coast and inland into the heart of the Italian peninsula. Those that there are come predominantly from two grapes, the red *Montepulciano* and the white *Trebbiano*. They are grown

Working in the fields, near Cisternino in Apulia (Zefa)

mostly in the northern part of Abruzzo, within a narrow coastal strip in the provinces of Pescara and Chieti, northwards to Teramo and inland to L'Aquila.

Sardinia

Better quality Sardinian wines are only just beginning to make their impact overseas, and it may be somewhat surprising to learn that the island boasts fourteen DOC wines. Much of the output is exported for blending, and DOC wines form only a very small proportion – mostly in the form of red or white dessert wines; these are high in alcohol, strong in flavour and character, sweet as well as dry, and they are often fortified. But Sardinia also produces a few surprisingly light, dry whites, among them Vermentino and two non-DOC wines, Nuraghe and Torbato. The great wine centre is the capital, Cagliari, but grapes are grown and wines are made all over the island.

DOC WINES

- Cannonau di Sardegna ●
- Campidano di Terralba/Terralba ●
- Carignano del Sulcis ∅
- Girò di Cagliari ●
- Malvasia di Bosa ○
- Malvasia di Cagliari ○
- Monica di Cagliari ●
- Monica di Sardegna ●
- Moscato di Cagliari ○
- Moscato di Sorso-Sennori ○
- Nasco di Cagliari ○
- Nuragus di Cagliari ○
- Vermentino di Gallura ○
- Vernaccia di Oristano ○

Campania

All the wines of any note in Campania come from the northern half of the region; either from around Caserta and Benevento, to the north and east of Naples, or from the neighbourhood of Mount Vesuvius and the Sorrento peninsula. Campania is at the point where the Mezzogiorno starts, and where the wines begin to be coarser and stronger, lacking in real quality.

DOC WINES

Capri ●○
Greco di Tufo ○
Ischia ● ○
Solopaca ● ○
Taurasi ●

Five have qualified for the DOC, two of them coming from the off-shore islands of Ischia and Capri.

The wine for which the region is probably best known is the dramatically titled Lacrima Christi from the slopes of Vesuvius. Legend has it that Christ wept when He saw the fallen archangel Lucifer in possession of the beautiful Bay of Naples; where His tear dropped a vine grew.

Apulia

DOC WINES

Aleatico di Puglia ●
Cacc'emmitte di Lucera ∅
Castel del Monte ● ∅ ○
Copertino ●
Locorotondo ○
Martina/Martina Franca ○
Matino ● ∅
Moscato di Trani ○
Ostuni/Ostuni Bianco/Ostuni Ottavianello ●○
Primitivo di Manduria ●
Rosso Barletta ●
Rosso di Cerignola ●
Salice Salentino ●
San Severo ● ∅ ○
Squinzano ●

Apulia is a vast, sun-drenched plain producing wheat, wine and olives in profusion. It occupies the southern third of the Adriatic coast of Italy, forming the heel of the country, over 200 miles from the northern boundary above San Severo to its southernmost tip at Capo S. Maria di Leuca. It has traditionally produced as much wine in bulk as any region in Italy, being one of the two mass-producing areas of the south and an important supplier of high-strength wines for blending – 'cutting' wines, as they are known. No doubt in response to a growing demand for lighter, more stable wines, there has been a falling off in quantity overall, down to an annual average of around 7.5 million hectolitres. Meanwhile, however, modern plant and improved viticulture have resulted in more quality wines of DOC standing. The reds are still big, vigorous wines, but there is an increasing range of lighter, more delicate whites.

Basilicata

DOC WINE

Aglianico del Vulture ●

Wedged between Apulia and Campania, both prolific wine-producing regions, Basilicata produces very little in either volume or variety of wine. Once known as Lucania, and still referred to as such, the region is rugged, mountainous and often inaccessible. The wine of most consequence, Aglianico del Vulture, is found north of Potenza, around the extinct volcano of Monte Vulture. The soil which fosters the growth of the unusual *Aglianico* grape does not spoil the wine by imparting too much of the characteristic volcanic tang.

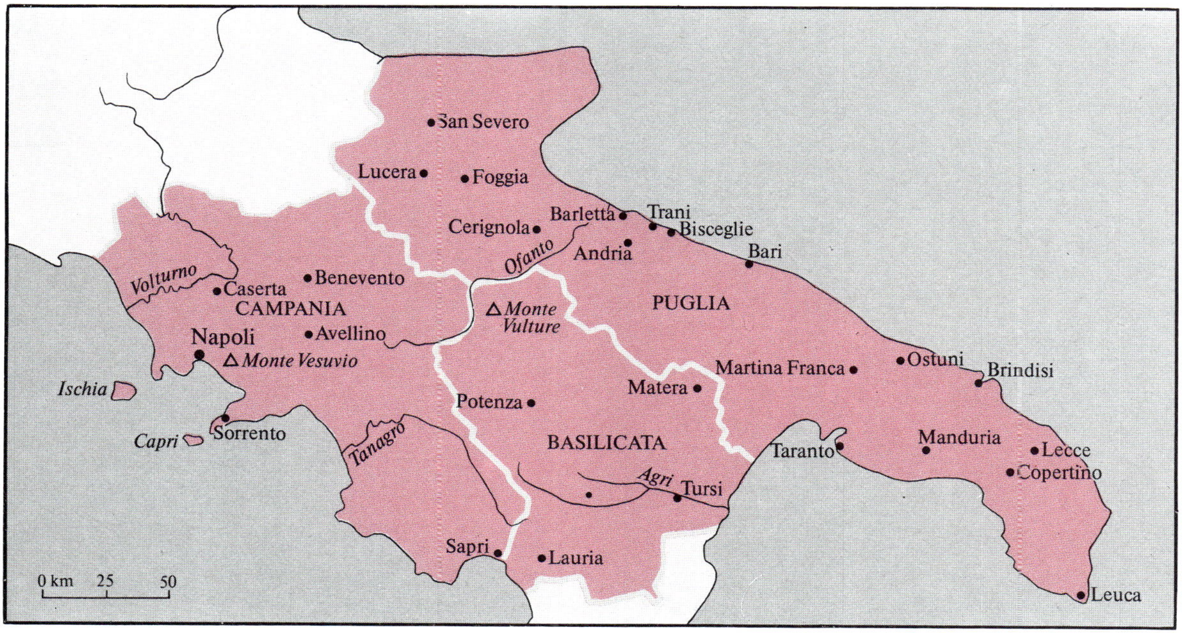

Calabria

The official catalogue of the Enoteca Italica, the wine museum in Siena, disarmingly describes Calabria as having 'a variety of sufficiently fine wines, uniting a fineness of perfume and flavour with a particular generosity'. The big mountainous toe of the country dipping into the Mediterranean offers the vine a hot volcanic soil which generally produces coarse, strong wines. One group of wines, notably the reds, grown in the eastern coastal area around Cirò has long enjoyed a reputation for excellence throughout Italy; these have deservedly achieved DOC status. The fine flowery bouquet of the white Greco di Gerace is also beginning to attract popular acclaim.

DOC WINES

Cirò ● ○ ∅
Donnici ● ∅
Pollino ●
Savuto ● ∅

Sicily

The further south one goes in the Italian peninsula the stronger – and, in the case of Sicily, the sweeter – the wines tend to become. Dessert wines (so called, although they are as likely to consumed as aperitifs) accordingly figure prominently in the list of notable Sicilian wines, led by Marsala. There are as yet few wines of note for everyday drinking, but this may well change since the island has a large output and standards and methods are constantly being improved. Wines from Etna have already joined the DOC ranks, and Corvo reds and whites are both of a high quality; two other good names still outside the DOC provisions are Partinico and Regaleali.

DOC WINES

Alcamo/Bianco Alcamo ○
Cerasuolo di Vittoria ●
Etna ● ∅ ○
Faro ●
Malvasia delle Lipari ○
Marsala ○
Moscato di Noto ○
Moscato di Pantellaria ○
Moscato Passito di Pantellaria ○
Moscato di Siracusa ○

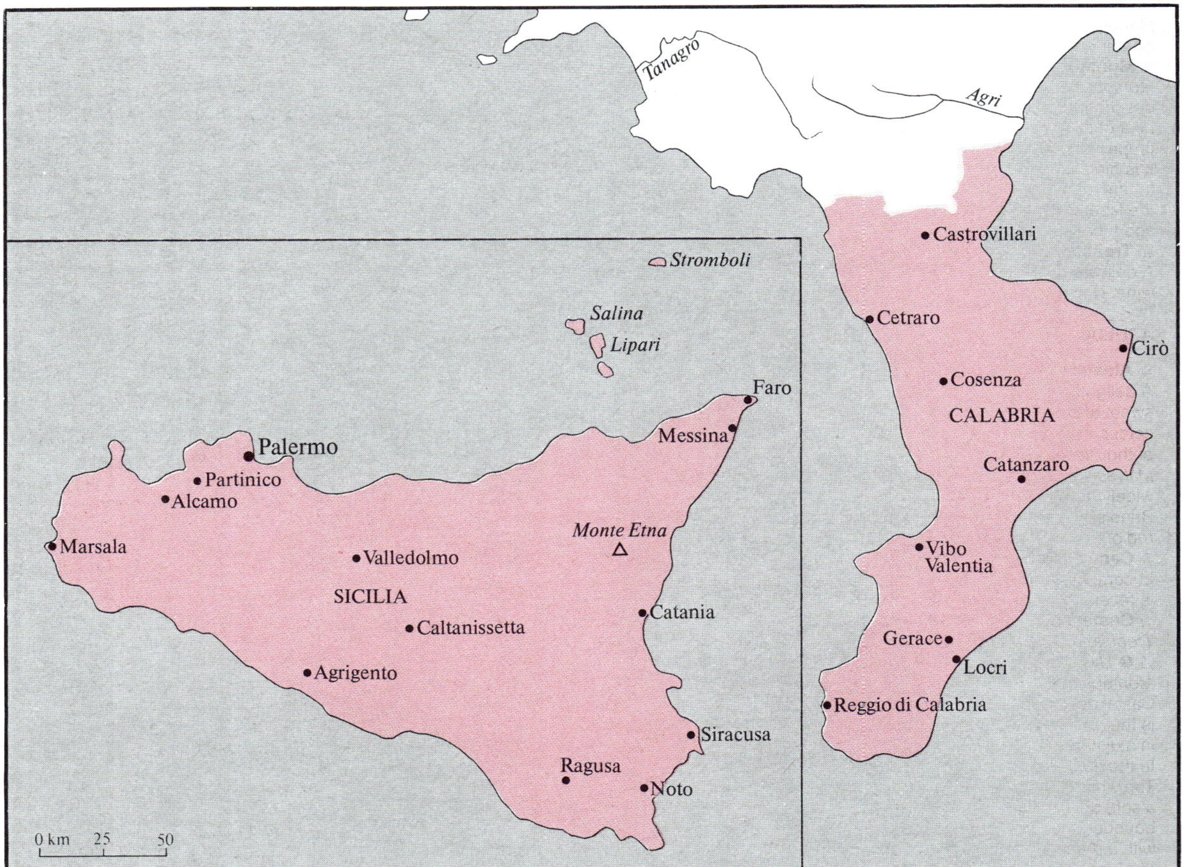

ITALY GAZETTEER

☆ DOC wine
● red grapes
○ white grapes

GRAPE VARIETIES. These are printed in italic (*Montepulciano, Trebbiano*, etc.) after the name of the wine, and are listed in the order of their predominance.

DEGREES OF ALCOHOL. These refer to the wine's total alcoholic strength. In the case of DOC wines, only the minimum content is shown; for non-DOC wines the figures indicate the usual range of degrees (e.g. 10–12°). When both natural and fortified varieties are sold under the same name (e.g. Aleatico di Puglia) the two alcoholic strengths are indicated thus: 15/18.5°.

ABRUZZO and MOLISE

Cerasuolo d'Abruzzo ● *Montepulciano* 11–13° A cherry-coloured wine (hence the name), made by well-timed fermentation on the skins of the same grape as is used for Montepulciano d'Abruzzo. Its sweet after-taste is rather more pronounced than Montepulciano's and (unlike the latter) it is intended to be drunk young.
☆ **Montepulciano d'Abruzzo** ● *Montepulciano* 12° This fine, dry DOC, described by Bruno Roncarati as among the best of the Italian reds, has a deliciously grapey aroma and a vivid, arresting flavour. It is high in alcohol and can age well for up to ten years. The term *vecchio* (old) on the label means that it has already been aged for two years or more.
☆ **Trebbiano d'Abruzzo** ○ *Trebbiano* 11.5° A delicately scented, pale yellow, dry wine. Not one to keep.

APULIA

☆ **Aleatico di Puglia** ● *Aleatico* 15/18.5° A delightful dessert wine, made in naturally sweet and fortified forms; fine garnet red in colour, with the delicate aroma characteristic of the *Aleatico* grape (some *Negro Amaro, Malvasia* and *Primitivo* can also be used); widely grown from Foggia in the north to Brindisi and Taranto in the southern half of the region.
☆ **Cacc'emmitte di Lucera** A *rosé* wine from Lucera, north-west of Foggia; its DOC status is recent.
☆ **Castel del Monte** ○ *Pampanuto, Trebbiano, Bombino Bianco, Palumbo* 11.5°. ∅ ● *Uva di Troia, Bombino Nero, Montepulciano, Sangiovese* ∅ 11.5° ● 12° Castel del Monte – the castle on a mountain – is the DOC name for a group of wines made in a district embracing Bari and three towns to the north-west, Andria, Trani and Bisceglie. The white is produced in the hilly zone and has a soft, dry flavour with a light, pleasant bouquet; the red is dry and tannic; the *rosé*, with a predominance of *Bombino* grape, is deep-coloured and dry, with a fruity perfume, and is one of the best in Italy. The fine standing of these wines has increased the reputation of the region as a whole, largely through the pioneering efforts of one producer, Rivera.
☆ **Copertino** ● The small town of Copertino lies in the middle of the heel of Italy, a few miles south-west of Lecce. It gives its name to an as yet undistinguished red wine which has recently achieved DOC status.
☆ **Locorotondo** ○ *Verdeca, Bianco d'Alessano* 11° A clear, pale green wine produced in great quantity in a number of villages near Brindisi as a basis for Vermouth; in its DOC form it has a certain dry delicacy, similar to the neighbouring wines of Martina Franca and Ostuni. A sparkling version is also permitted.
☆ **Martina/Martina Franca** ○ *Verdeca, Bianco d'Alessano* 11° Similar to Locorotondo, and from an adjacent area to the west. Also used to supply the Vermouth industry, it is pale and greenish in colour, dry with a delicacy and freshness. It can be made sparkling.
Matino ● ∅ *Negro Amaro, Sangiovese, Malvasia* 11.5° Two wines – the one a ruby red, the other a deep *rosé* – produced in the province of Lecce. Both are dry and rounded, the red rather more robust and developing an attractive bouquet with age.
☆ **Moscato di Trani** ○ *Moscato Bianco* 15°/18° *Moscato* grapes from the inland areas behind Barletta and Trani are left to dry before vinification, producing these velvety dessert wines in either a naturally sweet or fortified form; they are golden in colour and high in alcohol.
☆ **Ostuni** ○ *Impigno, Francavilla* 11° ● *Ottavianello* 11° Ostuni (or Bianco di Ostuni) is a pale, dry, balanced wine, from the area north of Brindisi which supplies so much of the white wine used for making Vermouth. The red, known as Ostuni Ottavianello, is a pale red, dry wine with a slight perfume.
☆ **Primitivo di Manduria** ● *Primitivo* 14/18° *Primitivo* grapes are widely grown in the provinces of Taranto and Brindisi, and these pleasant, balanced wines have taken the place-name of one of the 20 villages where they are made. They range from semi-sweet and fully sweet to fortified dry and sweet varieties with up to 18° of alcohol.
Rosato del Salento ∅ *Negro Amaro, Malvasia* 12–13° A dry *rosé* wine from grapes grown across the southern half of the region, between Brindisi and Lecce.
☆ **Rosso Barletta** ● *Uva di Troia* 14° Robust red wine, high in alcohol, with a vinous and characteristic bouquet reminiscent of a southern Rhône Valley wine; a late-comer to the ranks of DOC.
☆ **Rosso di Cerignola** ● *Uva di Troia, Nero Amaro* 12° Vigorous, dry red wine, with an attractive bitter after-taste, from an area between Foggia and Bari, centred on the small town of Cerignola. With two years ageing in cask and a degree more of alcohol the wine becomes a Riserva.
☆ **Salice Salentino** ● *Negro Amaro, Malvasia* 14° Dry, full-bodied, tannic wine from Salice, due south of Brindisi; a late-comer to the DOC.
San Severo ○ *Bombino Bianco, Trebbiano, Malvasia, Verdeca* 11° ● *Montepulciano, Sangiovese* 11.5° San Severo wines are produced north of Foggia around the town which provides the place name. The white is very pale, dry, fresh and drinkable; in coarser form it is transported to the north for Vermouth. The reds and *rosés* age well, and are dry and balanced. Good non-DOC wines are sold as Torre Giulia (white) and Torre Quarto (red). A sparkling white is permitted.
Santo Stephano ● *Montepulciano* 12–13° A dry red wine made in small quantities, brilliant red in colour and with a pleasant perfume.
☆ **Squinzano** ● *Negro Amaro, Malvasia* 12° Vigorous, dark red wine from the Salento near Lecce; dry and tannic, requiring time to age and mellow. Only more recently accorded DOC status.

BASILICATA

☆ **Aglianico del Vulture** ● *Aglianico* 11.5° A sturdy deep-coloured wine, fresh and full flavoured; a good balance of tannin and acidity means that it improves with ageing. Normally dry, it can also be semi-sweet. The place-name also covers a sparkling variety. The grapes are grown in the soil of the extinct volcano which gives it its name. Two similar wines, Aglianico di Matera and Aglianico dei Colli Lucani, are grown farther south around Matera, west of Potenza.
Malvasia del Vulture ○ *Malvasia* 11–11.5° A sweet, naturally sparkling, pale coloured dessert wine, with a delicate aroma from the same district as Aglianico del Vulture.
Moscato del Vulture ○ *Moscato* 11–15.5° A sweet, naturally sparkling dessert wine, straw-coloured, smooth to the tongue and varying in strength.

CALABRIA

☆ **Ciró** ○ *Greco Bianco* 12° ● ∅ *Gaglioppo* 13.5° Ciró Bianco has an intense, straw-yellow colour and is dry and fruity. The reds and *rosés* are strong wines which improve in smoothness and balance with age; both are dry, with a delicate and pleasant bouquet. The red is better than the *rosé*; with its high alcoholic content it is somewhat reminiscent of Châteauneuf du Pape.
☆ **Donnici** ● ∅ *Gaglioppo, Greco Nero* 12° Dry wine of a ruby or *rosé* colour, according to vinification; pleasant vinous bouquet and balanced flavour, recently accorded DOC status.
Greco di Gerace ○ *Greco di Gerace* 15–17° A full and harmonious dessert wine, rich and sweet, with a distinctively flowery scent like orange blossom. The wine ages to a deep amber colour. Gerace is inland from Locri, on the east coast of Calabria.
Lacrima di Castro Villari ● *Lacrima* 13–14° A dry, clear ruby red wine with a fresh, delicate aroma from Cosenza in the middle of the region (see also **Pollino**).

Melissa ∅ *Gaglioppo* 12–13° Grown in the province of Catanzaro, on the gulf of Squillace, the *Gaglioppo* grape here produces a pleasant, dry *rosé* wine with a delicate, violet-like scent (see also **Pollino**, **Savuto** and **Donnici**).
Moscato di Cosenza ○ *Moscato* 15–16° Around Cosenza the *Moscato* is used to make this smooth dessert wine, amber-yellow in colour with a delicate aroma.
Pellaro ● *Nerello* 13–16° Slightly sweet wine, red tending to *rosé* in colour, grown in a small area in the far south, below Reggio.
☆ **Pollino** ● *Gaglioppo* 12° Full-bodied, dry red wine from the Cosenza area, made mainly from *Gaglioppo* grapes (known locally, among other names, as *Lacrima*) with others added in small quantity. A wine which improves with ageing.
☆ **Savuto** ● *Gaglioppo, Greco Nero, Sangiovese* 12° A full-bodied wine, similar to Pollino, from the area south of Cosenza.

CAMPANIA

☆ **Capri Bianco** ○ *Greco, Fiano* 11–14° A pale-coloured dry wine, fresh and fragrant; an excellent accompaniment for sea food, when served cold. It is made in very small quantity and unlikely to find its way abroad; if it does so it probably comes from the same grapes grown on the Sorrento peninsula.
☆ **Capri Rosso** ● ∅ *Piede di Palumbo, San Nicola, Barbera* 11–14° Pleasantly flavoured dry table wine; like the white, it is made in small quantity and drunk locally.
Falerno ● *Aglianico* 13–13.5° ○ *Falanghina* 12–13° The red is a dry wine, stronger in alcohol than the white, and better known. The white, golden yellow in colour, is semi-dry and improves with age. Both are made from grapes grown on the coastal plain around Mondragone, to the north-west of Naples.
Fiano di Avellino ○ *Fiano* 11–12° The Avellino hills are thirty miles from Naples; a light wine is made, normally dry, but sparkling and sweet dessert forms are also produced. Luigi Veronelli, the Italian wine expert, describes it as having 'a subtle elegant bouquet, and the superb flavour of toasted nuts'.
☆ **Greco di Tufo** ○ *Greco, Coda di Volpe* 11.5° Outstanding among the three DOC wines from mainland Campania; a wine of distinction which belies its southern origins, it is dry and pale golden in colour and comes from the little hill village of Tufo, between Benevento and Avellino. It has a strong, distinctive bouquet and a slightly aromatic flavour.
☆ **Ischia** ○ *Forestera, Biancolella* 11–12° ● *Guarnaccia, Piedirosso, Barbera* 11.5° The white is a light wine with a pleasing scent, fresh, lively and well balanced. The wines of the island off Naples qualified early for DOC status. Ischia Bianco Superiore has a 12° minimum strength; it has more body and flavour, and comes from a slightly different balance of grapes. The red is not a wine of special note; but it is fresh, with a fair amount of body and tannin, and is dry.
Lacrima Christi del Vesuvio ○ *Greco, Coda di Volpe, Biancolella* 12–13° ● ∅ *Aglianico, Piedirosso* 11.5–13° The white at its best is a dry, delicately perfumed and fresh wine, well balanced and highly agreeable; but it is far outstripped by its reputation, and there is every chance that what you buy is not at all like it should be, either in character or quality. To obtain a genuine example one must look, in the absence as yet of a DOC provision, to one of the best producers such as Mastroberardino, Saviano or Scala. A sweeter dessert version is also made. The red, made from different grapes, is rounded and pleasing, with a slight flowery perfume. The *rosé* is semi-sweet, fragrant and delicate in flavour. All three wines are grown on the foothills of Vesuvius, the red around the outside of the areas for the white.
Ravello ○ *San Nicola, Coda di Volpe, Greco* 11–13° ● ∅ *Biede di Colombo, Serpentario, Aglianico* 12.5–13.5° Grapes for the Ravello wines are grown in the Sorrento peninsula around the well-known holiday resort. The white benefits with keeping and has a delicate, retentive perfume; a sweet sparkling white is made as a dessert wine. The red is dry, with a vinosity and freshness which becomes well-balanced with age. The *rosé* is stronger than the red and semi-sweet, with an aromatic bouquet; it is intended as a dessert wine. The best known *marque* is Gran Caruso Ravello, but there is also a Palumbo Ravello which is thought by some to be the better.
☆ **Solopaca** ○ *Trebbiano, Malvasia* 12° ● *Aglianico, Piedirosso* 11.5° These wines from near Benevento were recently given DOC standing. The red is ruby-coloured and sharp when young, but becomes lighter and smoother. The white is pleasant and smooth. Both are dry.
☆ **Taurasi** ● *Aglianico, Piedirosso* 12° A dry, robust and vigorous wine, strong in tannin in its early days; it develops bouquet and character with age and can disappoint if drunk too young. Taurasi is a small village, south-east of Benevento.
Vesuvio ● *Piedirosso, Soricella, Olivella* 10–12° ○ *Greco* 9–12° Local wines grown on the slopes of Vesuvius; not very distinguished. The red is dry with a lively frothiness; the white is light.

EMILIA-ROMAGNA

☆ **Albana di Romagna** ○ *Albana* 12° The *Albana* grapes are grown in the southern, more hilly part of the region, producing a golden-yellow wine which gives every appearance of a Sauternes. A clean, sweetish, raisin-like bouquet seems to confirm this. To the taste, however, it is a full, dry wine, slightly bitter and very drinkable, reminiscent of Orvieto. A semi-sweet version is also made (12.5° min.).
☆ **Bianco di Scandiano** ○ *Spergola, Malvasia, Scarsafoglia* 11–12° Scandiano is a village immediately south of Reggio nell'Emilia. The wine is produced in two types: a pale yellow, still wine, dry or semi-sweet, with a pleasing flavour, and a sparkling dessert wine, slightly stronger and of a deeper yellow. The grapes used are largely local varieties. The wine has a growers' association to protect its standards.
☆ **Colli Bolognesi Monte San Pietro** ● *Barbera, Merlot* 11.5° ○ *Sauvignon, Pinot Bianco, Riesling Italico* 12° A new DOC place name, applicable to a range of different red and white wines from the hills south-west of Bologna. As happens in Friuli with the Colli Orientali wines, the name of Colli Bolognesi is followed by that of the several varieties of grape from which the wines may be made. Colli Bolognesi Bianco is made from *Albana* and *Trebbiano* grapes (10.5°). All the wines can be dry or semi-sweet.
☆ **Gutturnio dei Colli Piacentini** ● *Barbera, Bonarda* 12° The grapes used are both Piedmontese varieties, and the wine comes from the north-west corner of Emilia-Romagna nearest to Piedmont, around Piacenza. It is a deep red with a good aroma, dry or slightly sweet, and will age with advantage for a year or two before drinking.
Lambrusco ● *Lambrusco* 10.5–12° *Lambrusco* grapes are grown widely in the north of the region, producing a number of varieties each taking the name of its growing district. Variations of strength and colour arise through the use of the different local strains of the grape. Lambrusco is a unique, naturally effervescent red wine. It forms a frothy head when poured, which immediately subsides leaving the wine bubbly on the tongue. Usually bright red in colour, tending to purple, it has a fresh, appley smell and flavour, and a relatively high acid content. It may be sweetish or dry to the taste. Not a wine to linger over, and best drunk young.
☆ **Lambrusco di Sorbara** ● *Lambrusco* 11° Sorbara is just south of Modena. Its Lambrusco is regarded as the best available, and is credited with extraordinary thirst-quenching and digestive powers.
☆ **Lambrusco Grasparossa di Castelvetro** ● *Lambrusco* 10.5° Made in a group of villages immediately south of Modena; it can be sweetish or dry, and has a good perfume.
☆ **Lambrusco Reggiano** ● *Lambrusco* 10.5° Light-bodied, with a persistent frothiness, this is a refreshing drink on a hot day. Its colour ranges from pink to ruby red.
☆ **Lambrusco Salamino di S. Croce** ● *Lambrusco* 11° Usually dry, but sometimes semi-sweet, this wine is named after the salami-like shape of the *Lambrusco* grape. It is pleasing to both the nose and the palate, fruity and fresh.
☆ **Monterosso Val d'Arda** ○ *Malvasia, Trebbiano, Moscato* 11° Despite its name this is a white not a red wine – in fact it is almost golden-yellow; dry or slightly sweet (*amabile*) with at times a sparkle, it should be drunk fresh and young. A fully sparkling variety is also made.
☆ **Sangiovese di Romagna** ● *Sangiovese* 11.5° The *Sangiovese* grape is grown and vinified in great quantity in over 50 villages from Ravenna on the Adriatic coast to Bologna. Here, the wine is full-bodied, fruity and deep red in colour, containing quite a lot of tannin; this helps it to improve with age both in character and bouquet.

☆ **Trebbianino Val Trebbia** ○ *Ortrugo, Malvasia, Trebbiano, Moscato* 11° Grown in the valley of the River Trebbia, south of Piacenza. This recently elevated DOC wine can be dry or slightly sweet, and at times a little sparkling.
☆ **Trebbiano di Romagna** ○ *Trebbiano* 11.5° A single-grape white wine produced in tremendous quantity across the same wide span of the province of Romagna as the *Sangiovese*. On the whole intended as a wine for immediate drinking; straw-coloured, fresh and lively, with a pleasant bouquet.

FRIULI-VENEZIA-GIULIA

The following list shows the region's six chief wine-producing areas together with the grape varieties with which each is linked to form the name of a DOC wine.

☆ **Aquileia** ● Cabernet 11.5°, Merlot 11°, Refosco 11° ○ Pinot Bianco 11.5°, Pinot Grigio 11°, Riesling Renano 11°, Tocai Friulano 11.5°.
☆ **Colli Orientali del Friuli** ● Cabernet 12°, Merlot 12°, Pinot Nero 12°, Refosco 12° ○ Picolit (the one dessert wine from the region) 15°, Pinot Bianco 12°, Pinot Grigio 12°, Ribolla 12°, Riesling Renano 12°, Sauvignon 12°, Tocai Friulano 12°, Verduzzo Friulano 12° (both table and dessert wine; the latter is allowed to ferment in the bottle to become *frizzante* – i.e. slightly sparkling). A Malvasia del Friuli is made, but does not qualify for the DOC.
☆ **Collio Goriziano** (or **Collio**) ● Cabernet Franc 12°, Merlot 12°, Pinot Nero 12.5° ○ Malvasia 11.5°, Pinot Bianco 12°, Pinot Grigio 12.5°, Riesling Italico 12°, Sauvignon 12.5°, Tocai 12°, Traminer 12°. There is a Riesling Renano del Collio and a Verduzzo del Collio, neither of which is a DOC; and an unexceptional dry DOC, Collio Goriziano (i.e. without the name of a grape variety), is made from a mixture of *Ribolla, Malvasia* and *Tocai* (11°).
☆ **Grave del Friuli** ● Cabernet 11.5°, Merlot 11°, Refosco 11° ○ Pinot Bianco 11.5°, Pinot Grigio 11°, Tocai 11°, Verduzzo 11°.
☆ **Isonzo** ● Cabernet 11°, Merlot 10.5° ○ Malvasia 10.5°, Pinot Bianco 11°, Pinot Grigio 11°, Riesling Renano 11°, Sauvignon 11°, Tocai 10.5°, Traminer Aromatico 11°, Verduzzo Friulano 10.5°.
☆ **Latisana** ● Cabernet 11.5°, Merlot 11°, Refosco 11° ○ Pinot Bianco 11.5°, Pinot Grigio 11°, Tocai Friulano 11°, Verduzzo Friulano 11°.

LATIUM

☆ **Affile** (see **Cesanese**).
☆ **Aleatico di Gradoli** ● *Aleatico* 12° The *Aleatico* grape usually produces a strong dessert wine, which is what this is, although not high in alcohol; purplish-garnet red, it has a soft aromatic bouquet and is smooth to the taste. A *liquoroso* variety is made by fortification with alcohol.
Aprilia (see **Merlot di Aprilia**, **Sangiovese di Aprilia** and **Trebbiano di Aprilia**).
☆ **Bianco Capena** ○ *Trebbiano, Malvasia* 11.5° A range of red and white wines of no special note are produced in the hills north of Rome. One of these whites is a dryish, straw-coloured wine which has recently emerged as a DOC.
☆ **Cannellino** ○ *Malvasia, Trebbiano, Greco* 11.5° This is the sweet version of Frascati, made from grapes which have contracted noble rot.
Cesanese, ☆ **Cesanese del Piglio** (or **Piglio**), ☆ **Cesanese di Affile** (or **Affile**), ☆ **Cesanese di Olevano Romano** (or **Olevano Romano**) ● *Cesanese* 12° DOC standards of production are required of three local wines made from the *Cesanese* grape in southern Latium, between Olevano, just to the east of Rome, and the Campanian border. Cesanese del Piglio, described by Alexis Lichine as Latium's best red wine, is produced around Frosinone. All three wines can be dry, semi-sweet or sweet, and there are also sparkling forms. The non-DOC Cesanese is a deep red wine, soft and slightly bitter to the taste.
☆ **Cerveteri** ○ *Trebbiano, Malvasia* 11.5° ● *Sangiovese, Montepulciano, Cesanese* 12° A straw-coloured white, in dry and sweet forms, and a dry, ruby red, each with a slightly bitter after-taste, are made near Cerveteri and Civitavecchia, on the coastal strip to the north of Rome.
☆ **Colli Albani Bianco** ○ *Trebbiano, Malvasia* 11.5° One of the Castelli Romani wines, pale yellow, dry or semi-sweet, delicate and fruity; for drinking young. It comes from the hills to the west of Lake Albano. A sparkling version is permissible.
Colli Albani Rosso ● *Sangiovese, Montepulciano, Ciliegiolo, Cesanese* 12–12.5° A fresh, dry red from the same area as Colli Albani Bianco, and higher in alcohol, but non-DOC.
☆ **Colli Lanuvini** ○ *Malvasia, Trebbiano* 11.5° A dry or semi-sweet Castelli Romani white, made from the same grapes and of similar character to Colli Albani; from the Lanuvio and Genzano region, south of Rome.
☆ **Cori** ○ *Malvasia, Trebbiano* 11° ● *Montepulciano, Cesanese* 11.5° The Lepini hills to the south-east of the Castelli Romani region produce both red and white wines, soft and pleasant. The red is dry and stronger; the white can range from dry to sweet.
☆ **Est! Est!! Est!!!** ○ *Trebbiano, Malvasia* 11° A wine from Montefiascone, in the north-western end of the region, immediately south of Lake Bolsena. The name, and indeed the exclamation marks which the producers persist in retaining, are said to derive from the enthusiasm shown by the clerk to a twelfth-century German bishop, sent ahead by his master on their journey to Rome to test the desirability of the inns by the quality of their wines. When he reached Montefiascone his enthusiasm knew no bounds and his standard comment of '*Est*' ('Here is a good wine') was twice reiterated. With a legend like that to live up to, it is not surprising that the wine can sometimes be disappointing. At its best it is the colour of pale straw, lighter bodied than Frascati, dry with just a hint of sweetness. Semi-sweet and sweet versions are also made.
☆ **Frascati** ○ *Malvasia, Greco, Trebbiano* 11.5° Frascati is one of the most picturesque of the hill towns skirting Rome, commanding magnificent views down into the city from the south-east. This is the area of the Castelli Romani wines, among which Frascati stands out as the most distinctive and original. It is full-bodied and fragrant, well-balanced and clear golden in colour. The flavour of good Frascati is quite distinctive, with the scent of apricots in its aroma. Despite frequent suggestions that it ages better than other Castelli Romani wines, it should in fact be drunk young. Frascati Superiore, which is required to have one more degree of alcohol, rises to real heights of quality and is worth seeking out. The sweet wine of Frascati is sold as Cannellino. A sparkling version is permitted under the DOC.
☆ **Marino** ○ *Malvasia, Trebbiano* 11.5° This Castelli Romani wine, although not yet well-known abroad, is a great favourite among knowing Romans; it is named after a village between Frascati and Lake Albano. Fruity and well-balanced, it can be dry or semi-sweet and, like most Castelli wines, it is best drunk young. The sweeter variety can also be slightly sparkling. Marino Superiore has a higher alcoholic content (12.5°).
☆ **Merlot di Aprilia** ● *Merlot* 12° A dry, garnet-red wine of a marked vinosity; it combines a fullness of tannin and acidity, with the softness characteristic of *Merlot* wines. The commune of Aprilia lies in the Latina province, south of Rome (see also Sangiovese and Trebbiano).
☆ **Montecompatri Colonna** ○ *Malvasia, Trebbiano* 11.5° A lesser-known Castelli Romani white which has more recently joined the ranks of DOC wines, taking its name from two communes 15 miles south-east of Rome. It has a slight, pleasing bouquet, and a dry or semi-sweet finish.
☆ **Olevano Romano** (see **Cesanese**).
☆ **Piglio** (see **Cesanese**).
☆ **Sangiovese di Aprilia** ● *Sangiovese* 12° The Aprilia wines (see also Merlot and Trebbiano) have been developed in the last 40 years by expatriate settlers from Tunisia; the Sangiovese is pale red, dry and high in alcohol, with a distinctive fragrance and flavour.
☆ **Trebbiano di Aprilia** ○ *Trebbiano* 12° The third of a trio of single-grape wines from the Aprilia commune (see Sangiovese and Merlot above), made from the grape most commonly used in the region; it is a clear, pale yellow wine, dry, with the delicacy and balance characteristic of the *Trebbiano* grape.
☆ **Velletri** ○ *Malvasia, Trebbiano* 11.5° ● *Cesanese, Sangiovese, Montepulciano* 12° Velletri Bianco is one of the better Castelli Romani wines, from the lower end of the district; it is straw-yellow, dry or slightly sweet, full-bodied, soft and well-balanced. Velletri Rosso is dry, velvety and tannic, with a vinous bouquet.
☆ **Zagarolo** ○ *Malvasia, Trebbiano* 11.5° Zagarolo lies to the east of Rome, just beyond Frascati, and has recently given its name to

another DOC Castelli Romani wine. A red Zagarolo, made from *Cesanese* and *Buonvino* grapes, does not appear to carry the official place name.

LIGURIA

☆ **Cinque Terre** ○ *Bosco, Albarola, Vermentino* 11° Originally the only DOC from Liguria, and the best known of its wines. It represents the output of a group of villages known as the 'five lands' – Manarola is reputed to be the finest – whose vineyards, often inaccessible by road, are strung out along the steep coastline between Levanto and La Spezia. The wine is dry, pale yellow with greenish reflections (though not usually high in acid), and has a light, flowery aroma. It should be drunk fresh and young.
☆ **Cinque Terre Sciacchetrá** ○ *Bosco, Albarola, Vermentino* 17° A strong dessert wine which can range from sweet to almost dry; golden yellow in colour, it is made with *passito* (sun-dried) grapes, in the same way as for Vin Santo in Tuscany.
Coronata ○ *Vermentino, Bosco* 11–12° A pale yellow wine from two of the grape varieties used for Cinque Terre; grown further along the coast towards Genoa, it is light and fresh in character, and normally dry.
☆ **Dolceacqua** (see **Rossese di Dolceacqua**).
Pigato di Salea ○ *Pigato* 13–15° From the western end of the region, just north of Alassio; a strong, bright yellow wine with a full, firm flavour, and a distinctive aroma (likened by one writer to damp wood). Despite its high alcohol content, it should be drunk young and cool.
Polcevera ○ *Vermentino, Bosco* 11–12° Similar to Coronata, fresh and slightly sweet.
☆ **Rossese di Dolceacqua/Dolceacqua** ● *Rossese* 12° Dolceacqua lies away from the coast, north-west of Bordighera, and produces the one red wine of note in the region. It is a soft, rounded wine, deep ruby in colour becoming garnet with age, which it does gracefully over several years. There is a slight bitterness in the flavour.
Vermentino ○ *Vermentino* 10–13° A dry, pale yellow wine, grown in the hills behind San Remo, with a delicate aroma and a fresh flavour; it is sometimes slightly sparkling.

LOMBARDY

☆ **Bianco di Custoza** ○ *Garganega, Cortese, Malvasia, Riesling Italico, Toccai Friulano, Trebbiano* 11° One of several whites from the area south of Lake Garda. A delicately flavoured, straw-yellow wine, with a slightly bitter taste; it is made from a variety of grapes, all or only some of which may be used in any one bottling.
☆ **Botticino** ● *Barbera, Schiava, Marzemino, Sangiovese* 12° A ruby red, dry, full-bodied wine, taking its tannin and robustness from the *Barbera*, its fruitiness from the *Sangiovese*, and its name from the village of Botticino on the western shores of Lake Garda.
☆ **Cellatica** ● *Schiava, Barbera, Marzemino* 11.5° Cellatica is north-west of Brescia, not far from Botticino, and the wines are similar. More *Schiava* and fewer *Barbera* grapes are used, and a dry, sappy wine with a slightly bitter after-taste is produced.
Chiaretto del Garda (see **Riviera del Garda**).
Clastidio ○ *Riesling Italico, Riesling Renano* 12° ● ∅ *Barbera, Croatina, Uva Rara* 13° White, red and *rosé* wines from Casteggio (Clastidium to the Romans) and a number of adjoining villages in the province of Pavia. The white and the *rosé* are high in acidity, and both red and *rosé* are full-bodied; all three need ageing. A sweet white dessert wine, made from *Pinot Nero* and *Pinot Grigio* grapes, is sold as Clastidium Gran Riserva.
☆ **Colli Morenici Mantovani del Garda** ○ *Garganega, Trebbiano* 11° ● *Rosinella, Rondinella, Negrara* 11° The DOC covers white, red and *rosé* wines from a group of villages north of Mantua in the south-east corner of the region. All are dry wines, the reds and *rosés* characteristically slightly bitter, the whites of higher acidity. If the *rosé* is sold as *chiaretto* (a pale pink) an 11.5° alcohol minimum is required.
Fracia ● *Nebbiolo (Chiavennasca)* 12–13° One of the lesser wines of the Valtellina; agreeable, it is thought to improve with age.
☆ **Franciacorta Pinot** ○ *Pinot Bianco* 11.5° Cortefranca, north-west of Brescia, is the centre of a production area for a pale yellow wine, with greenish reflections, made from white *Pinot* grapes in both dry and sparkling forms. The dry has a delicate aroma and is well-balanced; the *spumante* version has a higher but agreeable acidity.
☆ **Franciacorta Rosso** ● *Cabernet Franc, Barbera, Nebbiolo, Merlot* 11° A dry, medium-bodied and lively red wine from a blend of well-known grapes grown in the hills south of Lake Iseo at Cortefranca. The wine is purple when young and should be aged to a deep red with three to four years in the bottle.
Frecciarossa ○ *Pinot Nero, Riesling* ● *Barbera, Croatina, Uva Rara* 12–13° Frecciarossa is a town and a proprietary brand name, the former in the Oltrepó Pavese near Casteggio. The wines enjoy a high reputation, without yet being classified as DOC, and are the product of a single 70-acre estate where they are bottled. They sell under the trade names of La Vigne Blanche (white), Vino St George (*rosé*), Sillery (*ambrato*, or semi-dry dessert wine) and Grand Cru (a well reputed red, matured for four years in cask before bottling).
Grumello (see **Valtellina Superiore**).
Inferno (see **Valtellina Superiore**).
☆ **Lugana** ○ *Trebbiano* 11.5° Widely appreciated as an attractive, dry white wine, from a small district south of Lake Garda. Lugana is a pale wine with a fresh and delicate flavour when drunk young, as it should be; with age it takes on a golden amber colour.
Moscato di Casteggio ○ *Moscato* 8–9° Like the other Lombardy *Moscato* from Oltrepó Pavese, this is a fresh and delicately flavoured wine, with a firm and pleasing aroma, but without the other's body and alcoholic strength; it is sweet but not cloying, and is normally sparkling.
☆ **Oltrepó Pavese** ● *Barbera* 11.5°, *Bonarda* 11° ○ *Cortes* 11°, *Moscato* 10.5°, *Pinot* 11°, *Riesling* 11° In the province of Pavia, south of the River Po, a range of single-grape red and white wines (and one *rosé*) are made under the umbrella DOC of Oltrepó Pavese – the name of the grape in each case appearing on the label. Oltrepó Pavese, without such an addition, is a red wine made from a mixture of *Barbera, Croatina, Uva Rara* and *Ughetta* grapes (11.5°). The reds are deep ruby in colour, the Bonarda especially having an intense, pleasing bouquet and a soft, full flavour; the Barbera is more robust, and is drier and richer in tannin. The whites are straw-yellow, the Pinots and Rieslings having green tints; all of them are fairly high in acidity, and except for the Moscato, which is sweet, they are fresh, dry wines. There are sparkling varieties of Moscato, Pinot and Riesling.
☆ **Riviera del Garda Bresciano/Chiaretto/Rosso** ● ∅ *Groppello, Sangiovese, Barbera, Berzemino* 11–11.5° Riviera del Garda embraces a wide area of production and three separate DOC place-names. Riviera del Garda Rosso obtained DOC standing early; it has a deep, ruby-red colour, a pronounced bouquet, and while not entirely dry is more so than the *rosé*. The latter, Riviera del Garda Chiaretto, is a fine, rich wine; cherry-pink in colour, it often has a high acidity, and it also has a slightly higher alcoholic minimum than the other two. Similar wine from further afield, on the surrounds of Brescia, has now acquired its own DOC as Riviera del Garda Bresciano. The Rosso and the Chiaretto should both be drunk young.
Sassella (see **Valtellina Superiore**).
Sforzato di Spina (see **Valtellina Superiore**).
☆ **Tocai di San Martino della Battaglia** ○ *Tocai Friulano* 12° As it does in Friuli, the *Tocai* grape also produces at San Martino della Battaglia, two miles south of Lake Garda, a dry, pale golden aromatic wine, protected by its own DOC.
Valgella (see **Valtellina Superiore**).
☆ **Valtellina** ● *Nebbiolo (Chiavennasca), Pinot Noir, Merlot, Rossola, Brugnola, Pignola* 11° The valley of the River Adda, in the vicinity of Sondrio, is the home of a range of mixed red wines, all made from a minimum 70 per cent of the *Nebbiolo* grape (known here as the *Chiavennasca*). At their best the wines are dry, generous and fairly high in acidity, with a noticeable tannin content, and they display a firm, pleasing aroma; but two or three years development in the bottle are needed before they show their paces, and even then they do not always live up to their great reputation.
☆ **Valtellina Superiore** ● *Nebbiolo (Chiavennasca)* 11.5° Four wines made entirely (or almost so) from *Nebbiolo* grapes stand out sufficiently among Valtelline wines to merit their own DOC as Valtellina Superiore. They all take the names of their sub-districts – Grumello, Inferno, Sassella and Valgella – and are better known in these forms than their portmanteau DOC place-name. They are all ruby-red wines, and they share the great quality of ageing, when their colour varies to garnet and a fine, persistent perfume develops characteristic of the *Nebbiolo*; a minimum of two years in cask is required. Grumello

and Inferno, widely regarded as fine quality wines, benefit from up to six years more in bottle; Sassella, if anything better, but harder, takes still longer to mature. Valgella does not have quite the standing of the other three. A sweet wine, Sforzato di Spina, is made from semi-dried grapes to reach a minimum strength of 14.5°, and may be sold under the Superiore title.

THE MARCHES

☆ **Bianchello del Metauro** ○ *Bianchello* 11.5° *Bianchello* grapes, together with a little *Malvasia*, are grown in the lower valley of the River Metauro before it flows into the Adriatic, south of Pesaro. They provide a dry, light-coloured and fresh-tasting white wine which should be drunk young.
☆ **Bianco dei Colli Maceratesi** ○ *Trebbiano, Maceratoni* 11° A dry white wine, mainly from the inland province of Macerata; although recently established with its own DOC, it has still to make a name for itself.
Bianco Piceno ○ *Vernaccia* 11–13° A modest wine from a string of hillside villages in the southern part of the region, between Ancona and Ascoli Piceno; it is dry, or semi-dry, fresh and pleasant, with a slight bitterness attributable to the grape.
☆ **Falerio dei Colli Ascolani** ○ *Trebbiano, Verdicchio, Malvasia* 11.5° Another recently created DOC, made in the province of Ascoli. Pale and slightly green, it is a dry wine with a hint of bitterness.
Montepulciano del Conero (see **Rosso Conero**).
☆ **Rosso Conero** ● *Montepulciano, Sangiovese* 11.5° At one time known as Montepulciano del Conero, after the name of the main grape used, it achieved its DOC status as Rosso Conero; a bright, clear ruby-red, dry wine, sappy and flavoursome, with its share of tannin. It is made in half a dozen villages in the hinterland of Monte Conero, just south of Ancona. Ages well for three to five years in the bottle.
Rosso Montesanto ● *Sangiovese, Montepulciano* 11–13° A dry, ruby-red wine, made largely from *Sangiovese*; it has a grapey smell and a balanced, pleasant flavour.
☆ **Rosso Piceno** ● *Sangiovese, Montepulciano, Trebbiano* 11.5° The grapes are grown widely in the southern half of the region, from north-west of Ancona to Ascoli Piceno; they are concentrated around the latter town, where a restricted area also produces a Rosso Conero Superiore (12°). Rosso Piceno is a dry, full-bodied wine, well-balanced and fruity, with a slightly bitter flavour. It develops well with age.
☆ **Sangiovese dei Colli Pesaresi** ● *Sangiovese* 11.5° Here, in the hills around Pesaro, the *Sangiovese* is used on its own, or with the smallest addition of the very similar *Montepulciano*; it produces a pleasing wine, dry and flavoursome, with a slight touch of bitterness.
☆ **Verdicchio dei Castelli di Jesi** ○ *Verdicchio, Trebbiano, Malvasia* 12° Verdicchio, a white wine of potentially distinctive character, has suffered from an otherwise laudable desire for stability by being too often vinified depressingly neutral; much depends on the maker. A good Verdicchio is brilliant, straw-coloured with pretty green glints; the bouquet is elusive, but the taste is fresh and assertive, not fruity but a subtle blend of high acidity and a bitter base, and it is at its best drunk young. The more carefully made wines are sold as Verdicchio Classico.
☆ **Verdicchio di Matelica** ○ *Verdicchio, Trebbiano, Malvasia* 12° Similar in character to its namesake from Jesi, and produced in the hills around neighbouring Matelica, this is a wine of quality, with a fresh and pleasantly bitter flavour. It is vinified dry, to accompany fish, or sparkling as a dessert wine.
☆ **Vernaccia di Serrapetrona** ○ *Vernaccia, Sangiovese, Montepulciano* 11.5° Unexpectedly, this *Vernaccia* is a red wine grape; it comes from Serrapetrona and its neighbour San Severino, south-east of Matelica. Mixed with up to 20 per cent of the other two varieties, it produces a frothy red dessert wine, ranging from dry to sweet in flavour, underlaid with a bitter but pleasing base.
Vin Santo ○ *Trebbiano* 16–18° A sweet wine, amber gold in colour; made, as in Tuscany, from semi-dried grapes.

PIEDMONT

☆ **Asti Spumante** ○ *Moscato* 12° The *Moscato* (or muscat) grape, which gives its inimitable flavour and aroma to this famous sparkling wine, is grown in 49 villages south of the city of Asti. The well-known growers' association neck-label shows the city's patron saint, San Secondo, on horseback in blue on a gold background. The wine is produced by bulk fermentation of Moscato Naturale d'Asti, a naturally sweet still wine, and is made throughout the year to preserve its freshness and flavour. Good Astis are practically colourless. They are best served very cold as dessert wines.
☆ **Barbaresco** ● *Nebbiolo* 12.5° This is one of the great red wines of Italy, usually

Vines trained up trees near Fiastra in The Marches (G)

compared with its equally eminent stable-mate, Barolo. The softer and slightly less powerful of the two, it is nonetheless a robust, full-bodied wine, rich and fragrant, which requires at least two years' ageing (three for a Riserva and four for Riserva Speciale). The grapes are grown in the village of Barbaresco and three others adjoining, to the south-west of Asti. A single *consorzio* jealously guards the standards of both the Barbaresco and Barolo place-names.

Barbera ● *Barbera* 12–15° *Barbera* grapes, widely grown in Piedmont, make a robust, popular wine which can vary in quality. High acidity and tannin content give it an initial harshness, mellowed by time and maturity. The better examples are protected by three DOC place-names which overlap each other confusingly within the triangular area bounded by Asti, Alba and Acqui.

☆ **Barbera d'Alba** ● *Barbera* 12° A deep ruby-red wine, maturing to garnet and becoming fuller and more balanced. It must be aged for at least two years (three for a Superiore, which has a 13° minimum alcohol content).

☆ **Barbera d'Asti** ● *Barbera* 12.5° An excellent wine when aged, reputedly the best of the three DOC Barberas. It is made exclusively from the name grape in a large area stretching across the provinces of Asti and Alessandria. The wine can be dry or slightly sweet, and benefits from three to six years in bottle. There is a 13° Superiore.

☆ **Barbera del Monferrato** ● *Barbera, Freisa, Grignolino, Dolcetto* 12° Unlike the Barberas from Alba and Asti, this is a bright, ruby-red wine, with a multiple grape content. The growing area is geographically identical to that of Barbera d'Asti, but vinification can take place outside Piedmont in parts of Lombardy. Not thought to be as good as the Asti, but it too can be dry or semi-sweet, or even sometimes *frizzante*. The Superiore has a 12.5° minimum strength.

☆ **Barolo** ● *Nebbiolo* 13° Barolo is a village south-west of Alba, and the wine made in a group of villages between the two is one of the classic reds of Italy. A matured Barolo – it must be aged for at least three years before being sold – appears in the glass as a beautiful, bright, reddish brown, still retaining the slightest tints of purple. The bouquet is strong and warm, and the common ascription of a deep-seated flavour of violets mingled with tar is not misplaced. Usually it is a well-balanced, full-bodied wine, which can throw a sediment in the bottle; but sometimes, as with Barbaresco, the heavy tannin content can upset the balance. Riserva is aged for a minimum of four years, and Riserva Speciale for five.

☆ **Boca** ● *Nebbiolo, Vespolina, Bonarda* 12° One of a group of low-output wines from the Novara hills, where Fara, Ghemme and Sizzano also come from. Bright ruby-red and violet-scented from the *Nebbiolo*, Boca is dry and vigorous, capable of a lot of bottle age and singular for its strange after-taste.

Bonarda ● *Bonarda* 11.5–12° A fresh, bright red wine from the Gattinara district in the north of the region; should be drunk young.

☆ **Brachetto d'Acqui** ● *Brachetto* 11.5° This is a pinkish red, slightly sparkling, sweet dessert wine, though not strong in alcohol; soft on the tongue and persistently frothy.

☆ **Caluso Passito** ○ *Erbaluce* 13.5° Grapes for *passito* wines are part-dried in the sun after picking to concentrate the sweetness and flavour. The *Erbaluce* gives smoothness and a fragrant bouquet to this sweet, golden-yellow dessert wine. The Liquoroso is a fortified version.

☆ **Carema** ● *Nebbiolo* 12° A pale ruby wine from a part of the Valle d'Aosta which lies within the province of Turin, Carema has a distinctive aromatic bouquet; it is softer and lighter than most other *Nebbiolo* wines.

☆ **Colli Tortonesi** ○ *Cortese* 10.5° ● *Barbera* 12° White and red wines, the output of 30 villages in the Tortona hills, just east of Alessandria. Both are dry; the white is fresh and light, with a slight bitterness; reds are fresh and robust, becoming mellower with age. The Superiore (red) is aged for at least two years.

☆ **Cortese di Gavi** (see **Gavi**).

☆ **Dolcetto d'Acqui, Dolcetto d'Asti, Dolcetto di Diano d'Alba, Dolcetto di Dogliani, Dolcetto delle Langhe Monregalesi, Dolcetto di Ovada** ● *Dolcetto* Widely cultivated in the provinces of Asti, Alessandria and Cuneo, the *Dolcetto* vine produces fresh, grapey wines, ruby-red and delicately bitter; they are of medium strength and acidity, with an appeal similar to that of the *Gamay* wines of Beaujolais. In seven neighbouring areas, all in central Piedmont, separate DOC place-names have been established. They all have a minimum alcohol content of 11.5° except the delle Langhe Monregalesi (11°) and the di Diano d'Alba (12°). The Diano d'Alba is the finest.

☆ **Erbaluce di Caluso** ○ *Erbaluce* 11° The *Erbaluce* grape makes a straw-coloured dry, fresh wine with a delicate bouquet. Unexpectedly for a white wine, ageing for up to four years is recommended. Widely grown in the province of Turin, some of it finds its way abroad. See also Caluso Passito.

☆ **Fara** ● *Nebbiolo, Vespolina, Bonarda* 12° One of a group of wines from the Novara hills (see Boca), Fara possesses the general qualities of Gattinara without its eminence; it is aged for three years before sale.

☆ **Freisa d'Asti, Freisa di Chieri** ● *Freisa* 11° *Freisa* wines have a delicate scent of strawberry in their bouquet and a fruitiness of flavour which is particularly evident in the sweeter varieties. Two districts south-east of Turin, Chieri and Asti, have acquired DOC place-names. Wines from Asti are fresh and semi-sweet; the better-known Chieri wines can be either dry or semi-sweet. Sparkling versions are permitted.

☆ **Gattinara** ● *Nebbiolo* 12° Gattinara is the outstanding wine from the Novara hills and is ranked among the best in Italy. A combination of small production and great prestige makes it hard to come by. Garnet-red, ageing towards orange for at least four years before it is sold, it acquires a rich mellowness and elegance that compares favourably with the firmer, more tannic and reserved nature of Barolo.

☆ **Gavi/Cortese di Gavi** ○ *Cortese* 10.5° This little-known wine comes from a handful of villages in the south-east corner of the region. It is an excellent, fragrant wine, with its own special aroma, and is only moderately alcoholic; a clear golden yellow, fresh and dry, it should be drunk young.

☆ **Ghemme** ● *Nebbiolo, Bonarda* 12° A deep red wine of good quality from the Novara hills (see Boca). Ghemme needs four years of maturing before it begins to lose its initial harshness, taking on a smooth, harmonious character.

☆ **Grignolino d'Asti, Grignolino del Monferrato Casalese** ● *Grignolino* 11° The *Grignolino* wines from Asti are made entirely from the name grape; those from Casale Monferrato contain a small admixture of *Freisa*. Both are light-bodied wines, palish red to orange, with a balance of tannin and acidity, and a slightly bitter after-taste.

Lessona ● *Nebbiolo, Merlot* 12.5–13.5° A not so widely known wine, of small output – one of a group of *Nebbiolo* wines produced in the Novara hills. It is non-DOC, but of at least comparable standing with Boca and Fara, and capable of ageing for between five and 20 years.

☆ **Malvasia di Casorzo d'Asti** ● *Malvasia* 10.5° This dessert wine is made from the local variety of the red *Malvasia* – sweet, aromatic, but not highly alcoholic. It is made in the provinces of Asti and Alessandria, taking its name from the village of Casorzo. A sparkling variety is also permissible.

☆ **Malvasia di Castelnuovo Don Bosco** ● *Malvasia, Freisa* 10.5° Similar in character to the Asti wine above, this is a cherry-red, fragrant dessert wine, which can also be made sparkling or semi-sparkling. The commune of Castelnuovo del Bosco lies just to the north-west of Asti.

☆ **Moscato d'Asti/Moscato d'Asti Spumante** ○ *Moscato* 11.5° A sparkling wine from the same area and source as Moscato Naturale d'Asti, and made by the same process of bulk fermentation; it is slightly sweeter than Asti Spumante, and not as strong.

☆ **Moscato Naturale d'Asti** ○ *Moscato* 10.5° A sweet, non-sparkling wine, naturally fermented, which provides the base for Asti Spumante and Moscato d'Asti; it is straw-yellow, with the fragrance and character of the muscat grape, and is potentially high in acidity.

Terraced vineyards at the foot of Mount Etna (Spectrum)

☆ **Nebbiolo d'Alba** ● *Nebbiolo* 12° A deepish ruby-red wine, with the characteristic violet-like fragrance of the grape, which is perfected with age. It is not dissimilar to Barolo, whose area of production it adjoins just north of Asti, but lacks its reputation. The wine can be dry or *amabile* (semi-sweet); strangely, a sparkling version is also permissible under the DOC.

☆ **Rubino di Cantavenna** ● *Barbera, Grignolino, Freisa* 11.5° A dry, ruby-red wine, grown on the Monferrato hills; it has a light, pleasing perfume, with a full, well-balanced flavour.

☆ **Sizzano** ● *Nebbiolo* 12° One of the dry, generous, harmonious red wines from a related group in the north-east corner of the region (see Boca), of which Gattinara is the leading growth. Sizzano tends to be harder than the others at first, and it requires at least the regulatory three years' maturing before it begins to mellow satisfactorily.

Spanna ● *Nebbiolo* 12–13° *Spanna* is the northern Piedmontese name for the *Nebbiolo* grape, and the name can appear on bottles of non-DOC wine. Deep red, robust and harsh when young, Spanna has many of the outstanding qualities that belong to the Gattinara family; it is worth looking out for.

SARDINIA

☆ **Cannonau di Sardegna** ● *Cannonau* 13.5° The *Cannonau* grape grows in various parts of the island and provides a gamut of red wines from dry to sweet *liquoroso* (fortified with alcohol), and even a *rosé*. The everyday reds are dry or semi-sweet, warm and full-bodied and high in alcohol. The special nature of those from the village of Oliena is recognized by allowing the name to appear on the label. The DOC covers them all.

☆ **Campidano di Terralba/Terralba** A red wine from Terralba on the Campidano plain, north of Cagliari; a newcomer to the DOC lists.

☆ **Carignano del Sulcis** ● *Carignano* A *rosé* wine which has only recently acquired DOC status.

☆ **Girò di Cagliari** ● *Girò* 15/15.5/17.5° The *Girò* grape, which is grown widely in the southern and western parts of the island, produces a bright ruby-red wine, warm and velvety. In and around Cagliari it is vinified very strong, in dry, sweet and fortified forms; the dry is required to be of a minimum 15°.

☆ **Malvasia di Bosa** ○ *Malvasia* 15/17.5° A sherry-like dessert wine produced in a restricted area around Bosa on the west coast; it is vinified dry or sweet with a minimum of 15° of alcohol, and in sweet and dry *liquoroso* form at over 17.5°. The *Malvasia* imparts elegance and a rich fragrance to the wines, and a deep golden colour which deepens with age as does the flavour and bouquet.

☆ **Malvasia di Cagliari** ○ *Malvasia* 15/17.5° Similar to Malvasia di Bosa in style and characteristics. The grapes used must be entirely *Malvasia*, grown within the province of Cagliari, and can be part-dried before vinification.

☆ **Monica di Cagliari** ● *Monica* 15/17.5° This wine is made entirely from *Monica* grapes. Both dry and sweet (15.5°) natural and fortified wines are produced. The *liquoroso* varieties when aged in casks may be labelled Riserva. Monica is a robust wine with a delicious aroma and flavour, ruby-red fading to orange with age.

Monica di Sardegna ● *Monica* 12° Principally made from the *Monica* grape and drawn from all parts of the island (other grapes may be added in small quantity); pale ruby-red, and fragrant both to nose and palate. Its alcohol content is more modest than the Monica di Cagliari, but it is still intended as a wine for dessert. With a further degree of alcohol and ageing it can be sold as Superiore.

☆ **Moscato di Cagliari** ○ *Moscato* 16/17.5° A golden-yellow dessert wine, sweet, rounded and harmonious, with the voluptuous aroma and flavour of the muscat grape; made in natural and fortified (17.5°) forms.

☆ **Moscato di Sorso-Sennori** ○ *Moscato* 15° A sweet, full, fine, golden dessert wine from the northern end of the island, between Sassari and the sea. There is a sweet *liquoroso* variety.

Moscato di Tempio ○ *Moscato* 13° An attractive, semi-sweet *Moscato*, from Tempio in the north of the island, which has not yet been accorded a DOC rating.

☆ **Nasco di Cagliari** ○ *Nasco* 15.5/17.5° A brilliant, golden-yellow wine, notable for a delicate grape aroma which has been compared to orange blossom, and for a somewhat bitter edge to its flavour. It is made in both sweet and dry forms, together with their fortified counterparts.

☆ **Nuragus di Cagliari** ○ *Nuragus, Trebbiano* 11° A dry, fresh, full-bodied white wine, with a wide area of production in the provinces of Cagliari and Nuoro. The alcoholic minimum is 11°, but it can be several degrees stronger. Recently accorded DOC standing.

Nuraghe Majore ○ *Clairette, Vermentino, Trebbiano* 11° A fairly dry, straightforward white, light and delicately aromatic, from the hinterland of Alghero in the extreme north-west corner of the island.

I Piani ● *Carignano* 11.5/12.5° Light red, attractive, dry wine which should be drunk fairly young.

Torbato ○ *Torbato* 11.5/12° A dry, lively, wine from the Alghero area; it has a bitterish after-taste, without being harsh, and is light yellow with greenish reflections.

☆ **Vermentino di Gallura** ○ *Vermentino* 12/14° A dry, fresh, slightly bitter but elegant wine, very pale in colour, intended to accompany food or as an aperitif. The *Vermentino* grape, also found in Liguria, crops up here in the north of the island, in the province of Sassari. A Superiore will have 14° alcohol. Vermentino di Alghero is a similar wine, coming from the same part of the island, but does not carry DOC status.

☆ **Vernaccia di Oristano** ○ *Vernaccia di Oristano* 15° This has established itself, among many characteristically Sardinian wines, as a unique island product; it is made in 15 villages, including Oristano, on the west coast. Despite its high alcoholic content it is a dry dessert (or aperitif) wine, deep amber in colour, with a delicate scent similar to that of almond flowers. On the tongue it has a blend of bitterness, smoothness and generosity. It may be vinified to 15.5° as a Superiore or fortified as a *liquoroso*.

SICILY

Albanello di Siracusa ○ *Albanello, Grillo* 16/19° A golden-yellow, dry, dessert wine of note, which attains great alcoholic strength by natural fermentation and even more in its *liquoroso* form.

☆ **Alcamo/Bianco Alcamo** ○ *Catarratto, Grecanico, Damaschino, Trebbiano* 11.5° These wines have long been exported in great quantity to supply the Vermouth industry. They are made from grapes grown in the north-west of the island, not far from the famous Greek temple at Segesta. DOC regulations demand only 11.5° of alcohol, but it can in practice be considerably more. It is a dry, full-bodied, pale wine, with a slight grapey aroma.

☆ **Cerasuolo di Vittoria** ● *Frappato, Calabrese* 13° A dry, cherry-coloured newcomer to the DOC lists, with a flowery bouquet and a high alcoholic content. With age, the colour fades and the aroma intensifies. Produced in the south-east of the island.

Corvo ○ *Insolia, Catarratto, Grecanico* 12–14° ● *Nerello, Pericone, Frappatto* 12–14° The name associated with those Corvo wines which find their way abroad is that of the Duca di Salaparuta; from near Palermo, they have for long been well thought of in Italy. Corvo Bianco is a full-bodied wine, the better examples of which are sold as Prima Goccia and Colomba Platino. The red Salaparuta Corvo is an exceptionally fine wine, lively, fruity, well-balanced and fairly full-bodied, as good or better than many DOCs.

☆ **Etna** ○ *Carricante, Catarratto, Trebbiano* 11.5° ● *Nerello* 12.5° 20 villages contribute to the output of white and red wines from the eastern slopes of Mount Etna, between the mountains and the sea. The whites are dry and fragrant, straw-yellow with greenish reflections. Etna Bianco Superiore has 12° of alcohol and a more fruity quality; they are wines to drink young. The reds and *rosés* from varieties of the *Nerello* grape are robust, developing bouquet and flavour with age and becoming very good.

☆ **Faro** ● *Nerello, Gaglioppo, Mantonico* 13° A quick-maturing, dry, fresh, sappy red wine from Messina on the north-east tip of the island. Not produced in great quantity, but now recognized as of DOC standing.

☆ **Malvasia delle Lipari** ○ *Malvasia* 11.5/20° A rich, sweet, amber-coloured dessert wine with a firm, gentle perfume; highly considered, it is produced from sun-dried grapes on the islands of Lipari, Salina and Stromboli, off Sicily's north coast. The sweet *liquoroso* version attains a massive 20°.

Mamertino ○ *Catarratto, Insolia, Pedro Ximenes* 15–17° Usually, a strong, semi-sweet, golden-coloured wine, but there is also a dry variety, which is considered to be a good accompaniment to fish! Produced near Messina.

☆ **Marsala** ○ *Catarratto, Grillo* 12/19° The sea town of Marsala lies on the western tip of the island, and the grapes that make the wine are grown in the hinterland north and south. Choice Marsalas – Fine (17° minimum, and ranging from dry to sweet), Superiore (18°, also varying from dry to sweet) or Vergine (dry, with 18° or more of alcohol and a minimum of five years ageing) – derive from a dry, fragrant, golden-yellow wine of 12°, which can be sold as such. Elaborations on the Vergine are Vergine Extra and Stravecchia (very old).

The alcoholic strengths and degrees of sweetness required for these world-famous dessert wines are achieved by the additions of high-proof grape brandy and extremely sweet concentrated grape juices. The resulting mixture is matured in the barrel to emerge as a dark amber wine with a burnt caramel flavour and a delicious, characteristic bouquet. Veronelli calls it 'the wine of meditation'.

☆ **Moscato di Noto** ○ *Moscato* 11.5/13/22° Sweet dessert wines with the characteristic muscat fragrance are made all over the island, this one at its southernmost tip around Noto and several adjoining villages. It is made in *naturale, spumante* and *liquoroso* forms.

☆ **Moscato di Pantelleria, Moscato Passito di Pantelleria** ○ *Zibibbo* 12.5/14° The *Zibibbo* grape is the local variant of the *Moscato* on the island of Pantelleria, south-west of Sicily. The full, rich aroma and flavour of the wine has earned it DOC status as a *naturale* dessert wine. A separate DOC has been given to the stronger, fuller, more generous version (14°) made from part-dried (*passito*) grapes.

☆ **Moscato di Siracusa** ○ *Moscato* 16.5° This sweet dessert wine achieves its character and high alcoholic content by natural fermentation of semi-dried grapes; it has a rich golden colour and a smoothness and generosity, but is not made in great quantity.

Partinico ○ A well-considered white wine from Partinico, a few miles south-west of Palermo.

Regaleali ○ *Catarratto, Insolia* 12.5° ● ∅ *Nero d'Avala, Nerello* 13/12° High quality white, red and *rosé* wines, produced and bottled in the Valledolmo area.

TRENTINO-ALTO ADIGE

☆ **Alto Adige** ● ○ The Alto Adige wines are in a real sense mountain wines: the DOC requirements lay down that the red varieties must be from grapes grown at an altitude of over 900 metres, and the whites at over

A vineyard near Merano (Spectrum)

700 metres. They are all single-grape wines covered by the portmanteau DOC of Alto Adige.

There are nine whites: Moscato Giallo (11° minimum alcohol content), Pinot Bianco (11°), Pinot Grigio (11.5°), Riesling Italico (11°), Riesling Renano (11°), Müller-Thurgau (11°), Sauvignon (11.5°), Sylvaner (11°) and Traminer Aromatico (11.5°). The reds are Cabernet (11.5°), Lagrein Rosato (11.5°), Lagrein Scuro (11.5°), Malvasia (11.5°), Merlot (11°), Moscato Rosa (12.5°), Pinot Nero (11.5°) and Schiave (10.5°).

The Moscato and the two Pinot white wines are straw-yellow in colour; the two Rieslings and the Müller-Thurgau, Sylvaner and Sauvignon tend to be greenish, while the Traminer Aromatico is a characteristic golden-yellow. Merlot, Malvasia and Lagrein Scuro among the reds are the more usual ruby colour; but Lagrein Rosato and Moscato Rosa are both fine *rosés*. The Cabernet and the Pinot Nero are the wines for ageing, both developing from deep ruby red to a maturer garnet with orange reflections. Schiave is the lightest of the reds. Sparkling wines are made from all three of the *Pinot* grapes.

☆ **Caldaro/Lago di Caldaro** ● *Schiava, Pinot Nero, Lagrein* 10.5° Made largely from three varieties of the *Schiava* grape (*Grassa, Gentile* and *Grigia*); Caldaro is a garnet red wine with an extremely perfumed bouquet. Lighter in style than most others from the region, it has a lively vinosity; it is dry without harshness, and displays an under-lying bitter flavour. Nine out of the 19 villages making the wine produce a Classico which displays the qualities of the *Schiava* to greater effect.

☆ **Casteller** ● *Schiava, Lambrusco, Merlot* 11° Casteller is a fine, full, light, red wine from the southern half of the region – i.e. from Trentino. The *Schiava* grape is a basic but not necessarily predominant constituent; *Lambrusco* can contribute up to 40 per cent and *Merlot* 20 per cent.

☆ **Colli di Bolzano** ● *Schiava, Lagrein, Pinot Nero* 11° DOC regulations require that no less than 90 per cent *Schiava* grapes are used in this wine from the Bolzano hills; it is soft, full-bodied, well-balanced and scented.

Meranese/Meranese di Collina ● *Schiava, Tschaggele* 10.5° A light, ruby-red to garnet wine – dry, sappy and well-balanced; like Santa Maddalena it is made principally from four varieties of the *Schiava* grape, grown on hills near Merano, north of Bolzano.

☆ **Santa Maddalena** ● *Schiava, Tschaggele* 11.5° Four varieties of the *Schiava* grape and the *Tschaggele* are used to make this dry, velvety wine, one of the better wines of Italy – thought at one time to be one of its three best reds. It has a distinctive flowery bouquet characteristic of the *Schiava*, and a slight bitterness which gives it an agreeable after-taste.

Sorni ○ *Müller-Thurgau, Nosiola* 11–11.5° ● *Schiava* 11–12° Produced just north of the city of Trento. The white is a light, everyday wine; the red is full-bodied.

☆ **Terlano** ○ The small town of Terlano, a few miles north-west of Bolzano, has long been a notable producer of white wines which were certain to qualify in due course for DOC rating. They have now done so. Terlano (11.5°), the traditional wine of the area, is a dry, straw-yellow wine made from a minimum 50 per cent of *Pinot Bianco* grapes. Five other grape varieties can be added and may also attach their names after the DOC designation: Pinot Bianco (11°), Riesling Italico (10.5°), Riesling Renano (11.5°), Sauvignon (12°) and Sylvaner (11.5°). All are full-bodied wines (the Riesling Italico a little less so than the others), greenish-yellow in colour, and they retain the delicate aroma and flavour of the grape types; they are generally thought to improve in the bottle.

☆ **Teroldego Rotaliano** ● *Teroldego* 11.5° Four villages north of the city of Trento, on the Rotaliano Plain, produce this deep ruby-red wine; Bruno Roncarati rates it as the best in the province. It is dry, tannic and full-bodied, robust rather than elegant, but nonetheless it ages well and develops a harmony and a big aroma. A lighter, slightly bitter-tasting *rosé* is vinified from the same grape. The red's qualities are exemplified in the stronger (12°) Superiore.

☆ **Trentino** ●○ Four white and five red single-grape wines are sold under the generic DOC title of Trentino, each either preceded or followed by the name of the grape variety. The whites are Pinot (11°), Riesling (11°), Traminer Aromatica (12°) and Moscato (13°); the reds are Cabernet (11°), Lagrein (11°), Marzemino (11°), Merlot (11°) and Pinot Nero (11.5°).

Trentino Pinot is either a fresh, still wine or a sparkling wine of great quality, both made from the *Pinot Bianco* grape. The Riesling can be either a mixture of *Riesling Italico, Riesling Renano* and *Müller-Thurgau* grapes or it can be made from any one of them singly: so it can vary in character. The Traminer Aromatico has the same splendid nose as its Alsatian namesake, but can be more delicate. Trentino Moscato is sweet and strong.

The reds are all full-bodied, dry wines, usually a good degree higher in alcohol than the required minimum. All demand and benefit from a period of ageing, including the Lagrein, although most of it is made as *rosé*. A Trentino Vin Santo, covered by the DOC, is made from *Pinot Bianco* grapes in a natural as well as a *liquoroso* form.

☆ **Valdadige/Etschtaler** ○ *Pinot Bianco, Pinot Grigio, Riesling Italico, Müller-Thurgau* and six other grapes, together or singly ● *Schiava, Lambrusco* and five others, singly or together. As many as 73 villages stretching right through the region along the Adige (Etsch) valley produce these red and white wines in great quantity. The broad spread of grapes that may be used means that the wines can vary in quality and style, and that the reds range in colour from *rosé* to deep ruby. The whites are pleasant enough, tending (like the reds) to be slightly sweetish.

☆ **Valle Isarco** ○ The DOC Valle Isarco covers five single-grape wines from the mountainous district north-east of Bolzano; they are light, dry, fresh wines from the *Müller-Thurgau* (10.5°), *Pinot Grigio* (11°), *Sylvaner* (10.5°), *Traminer Aromatico* (11°) and *Veltliner* (10.5°) grapes (the last-named is more commonly found in Austria).

TUSCANY

Aleatico di Portoferraio ○ *Aleatico* 14–15° The *Aleatico* grape is one of the *Moscato* family and has the same characteristic taste. The wine is likely to be aged for 15 years or so, up to five of them in cask, to produce a clear, ruby dessert wine, with a big aroma and a generous flavour; from Portoferraio on the island of Elba.

☆ **Bianco di Pitigliano** ○ *Trebbiano, Greco, Malvasia, Verdello* 11.5° Pitigliano is in the very south of Tuscany, in the Grosseto district. It produces a pale white wine with greenish reflections, dry, medium-bodied, with a slight bouquet and an underlying trace of bitterness.

Bianco Val d'Arbia ○ *Trebbiano* 11–12° A familiar Tuscan white, from the southern end of the Chianti Classico zone; often incorrectly referred to as 'white Chianti', it is a local drink, pleasant, full-bodied, dryish, golden-yellow.

☆ **Bianco della Valdonievole** ○

☆ **Bianco Vergine Valdichiana** ○ *Trebbiano, Malvasia* 11° One of the better Tuscan whites, with its own DOC; firm yellow with a greenish tinge, semi-dry, with a fresh, fruity bouquet. It can have a slight prickle on the tongue, perhaps from the iron in the soil of the River Chiana valley near Arezzo where the grapes are grown. Called 'virgin' because only the grape juice is fermented.

☆ **Brunello di Montalcino** ● *Brunello* 12.5° An exquisite red wine of great character and reputation. It is produced in a picture book setting, at Montalcino in the hills south of Siena, and is made exclusively from *Brunello* grapes (a variety of *Sangiovese*); three vineyard owners – Biondi Santi, Colombini and Francheschi – compete to produce the finest. Brunello has a deep, firm, brilliant ruby-red colour, tinged with purple in youth and mellowing to a rich orange-tinted garnet; it is full-bodied, tannic, elegant, and displays a heady perfume. Above all it needs age; it is matured in wood for four years before sale, becoming a *riserva* with five years ageing, and a further ten years in bottle is recommended. It ought to be opened 24 hours before serving, and it should be decanted.

☆ **Carmignano** ● *Sangiovese, Canaiolo, Cabernet, Trebbiano, Malvasia* 12.5° This newcomer to the DOC ranks is similar in character to Chianti, and is made from mostly the same grapes, but it is a bit softer and suaver. It is produced just outside the area, a few miles to the north-west of Florence.

☆ **Chianti** ● *Sangiovese, Canaiolo, Trebbiano, Malvasia* The vines to be used for Chianti wines were laid down in the 19th century, and are a combination of two reds and two whites. A single DOC covers all the Chianti wines, and requires a minimum 11.5° from the Classico zone and 11° from the others.

☆ **Chianti Classico** The Classico zone stretches from Siena to the southern fringes of Florence, with the little hill villages of Castellina, Greve, Gaiole and Radda at the heart of the production area. The owners of the individual estates, large and small, are constantly striving to improve the standards and reputation of their wines. Some are world-famous names, like Antinori and Ricasoli; among many others are the not so well-known but excellent wines of Badia a Coltibuono, Caste lo di Uzzano, Monsanto, La Paneretta, and Vignamaggio.

Over 90 per cent of growers in the Classico zone are members of the Consorzio Vino Chianti Classico, an association of growers started in 1924 to defend the integrity and

quality of Chianti Classico. It has provided the model for many others founded since, and today it provides a kind of super DOC for the region.

The colour of Chianti Classico is a lightish, clear ruby-red, which mellows with age, as will a good Burgundy. It has a clean, fresh, fruity aroma, not too marked in a young wine, and is very dry, full of flavour, well balanced, with a firm after-taste. When aged in wood for two years it becomes a *vecchio*, and a *riserva* after three.

The Tuscan countryside around San Gimignano (Fotofass)

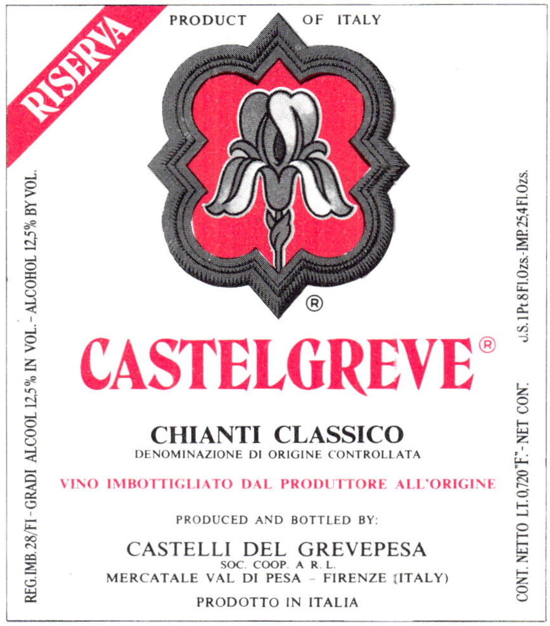

☆ **Chianti Colli Aretini** ● The wines from the hilly country north of Arezzo are not always rated among the best Chiantis; best drunk young, they are dry, lively, very tannic, and frequently have a slight sparkle.

☆ **Chianti Colli Fiorentini** ● The Colli Fiorentini are south of Florence; they produce deep-coloured, full-bodied, fresh wines which are among the better Chiantis.

☆ **Chianti Colli Senesi** ● These wines are from grapes grown in the area between Siena and San Gimignano which also provides the white Vernaccia wine; not always among the best, but they can nonetheless be soft, fruity and well-balanced, and full of flavour.

☆ **Chianti Colline Pisane** ● Moderately good dry, light, red wines, produced in small quantity for drinking young, in the hilly district south of Pisa.

☆ **Chianti Montalbano** ● Montalbano, to the north-west of Florence, produces some of the best of the Chiantis – purplish, robust and scented.

☆ **Chianti Rufina** ● Rufina lies 20 miles north-east of Florence in the valley of the River Sieve. Its wines, like those of Montalbano and the Colli Fiorentini, are protected by a local growers' association which uses a della Robbia-like cherub as the symbol on its neck label. Rufina is among the best of the non-Classico Chiantis.

☆ **Elba** ○ *Trebbiano* 11° ● ∅ *Sangiovese, Canaiolo, Trebbiano* 12° Elba Bianco is a dry, light, straw-coloured wine, which can often be stronger in alcohol than the minimum provided by the DOC rules; it comes from the island of Elba, in the province of Livorno, as does the red, Elba Rosso. The latter, normally a deep ruby-red, is dry, slightly aromatic and of good quality. A *rosé* version is also made.

☆ **Montecarlo** ○ *Trebbiano, Sémillon, Pinot Bianco, Pinot Grigio, Vermentino, Sauvignon, Roussanne* 11.5° Montecarlo is one of the finest Tuscan whites and one of the most original wines in Italy – dry and golden, with a delicate perfume. It is made in large part from *Trebbiano* grapes, but includes a sizeable proportion of the others listed (among them interlopers from the Graves district of Bordeaux – *Sauvignon, Sémillon* – and the *Roussanne* from the Rhône Valley). It hales from western Tuscany, near Lucca.

Montecarlo Rosso ● *Sangiovese, Trebbiano, Canaiolo* 12–13° A dry, ruby-red with a good bouquet, this is regarded as an excellent wine, but it has not succeeded like its white namesake in becoming a DOC.

☆ **Montescudaio** ● *Sangiovese, Canaiolo, Trebbiano, Malvasia* 12° The hills around the village of Montescudaio, in the province of Pisa, are the source for this red, Chianti-like wine, which has latterly aspired to its own DOC.

☆ **Parrina** ○ *Trebbiano, Ansonica, Malvasia* 11.5° ● *Sangiovese, Canaiolo, Montepulciano, Colorino* 12° The two Parrina wines are from Orbetello in southern Tuscany. The Rosso is a robust, dry wine with a delicate bouquet; its balance tends to improve with age. The white is also dry, pale golden in colour, and has a bitter after-taste; it is better thought of than its near neighbour at Pitigliano (see Bianco di Pitigliano).

☆ **Rosso delle Colline Lucchesi** ● *Sangiovese, Canaiolo, Colorino, Trebbiano, Malvasia* 11.5° A newcomer to DOC status from the Lucca hills in western Tuscany; made like a young Chianti, dry with a slight prickle to drink *nel annata* – in the year it is made – but it can also be aged in a good year.

Sassicaia ● *Cabernet Sauvignon* 12.5° Although non-DOC, this is a remarkable wine to be compared with some of the best New World *Cabernets*, or with a Bordeaux or an Australian, rather than with those from northern Italy. Made entirely from the *Cabernet Sauvignon*, it is capable of long ageing.

☆ **Vernaccia di San Gimignano** ○ *Vernaccia* 12° A distinguished Italian white wine. The pale yellow of a young Vernaccia deepens with age to a golden hue; it has a trace of honey in the bouquet, but on the palate it is not noticeably sweet or fruity. It is a balanced wine, dry and mellow, preserving both a freshness and the underlying bitterness which gives it its character. Labels can carry a picture of the famous seven towers of San Gimignano.

☆ **Vino Nobile di Montepulciano** ● *Sangiovese, Canaiolo, Trebbiano, Malvasia* 12° At Montepulciano, south-east of Siena, the classic combination of Chianti grapes gives rise to one of the finest Italian red wines: robust, dry and full-bodied, somewhat stern from its fair share of tannin when young, it demands ageing – like Brunello. It develops into a full, soft, generous and elegant wine.

Vin Santo ○ *Trebbiano, Malvasia* 15–18° Vin Santo is special to Tuscany, although made elsewhere as well. The grapes are first laid out or hung up to dry, in order to provide a higher sugar to liquid content; four months later they are pressed and the juice is placed in small oak barrels for a four-year period of closed fermentation. The result is a maderized wine, deep amber in colour, not all that sweet, but of great character and alcoholic strength. Usually drunk soon after bottling, but will keep another 20 years.

UMBRIA

☆ **Colli del Trasimeno** ○ *Trebbiano, Malvasia, Verdicchio, Verdello, Grechetto* 11° ● *Sangiovese, Trebbiano, Malvasia, Gamay, Cigliegiolo* 11.5° The red wine, with its predominant *Sangiovese* character, is like a simpler, more rustic Chianti; it has a direct, fruity appeal when young, but it can also age well for three or four years, emerging as full-flavoured and harmonious. The white is distinctly reminiscent of Orvieto. Before they were granted their DOC, both these wines from the hills around Lake Trasimene were bought by merchants in Tuscany for blending.
☆ **Orvieto** ○ *Trebbiano, Malvasia, Verdello, Grechetto, Drupeggio* 12° Traditionally this pale golden, well-balanced wine was made full-bodied and semi-sweet. With changes in methods of vinification it is now more likely to be encountered as a dry wine, subject to marked differences of style; some wines are bottled within six months and are very fresh, light and crisp. Others retain a fuller quality, with a characteristic seductive softness in the middle of the flavour, combined with a dry almost bitter finish. There is in practice little real difference between Orvieto Classico and Orvieto, although there are two separate *consorzi*. Quality depends largely on the individual producer.

☆ **Torgiano** ○ *Trebbiano, Grechetto, Malvasia, Verdello* 11.5° ● *Sangiovese, Canaiolo, Trebbiano* 12° Torgiano Bianco, or Torre di Giano, is a straw-yellow wine from the hills circling the little country town of Torgiano, just south of Perugia. It has a fresh, lively character, with a distinct similarity to Orvieto; although pleasant enough, however, it is not in the same class as its red stable-mate.

Torgiano Rosso, otherwise encountered as Rubesco Torgiano Rosso or Rubesco di Torgiano, is a dry wine with a firm, flowery bouquet. It is reminiscent of Chianti, but tends to be rounder and softer; nevertheless, it ages well, and a good *riserva* (three years

in the wood) can be in peak condition when over ten years old. The peculiarity of the DOC is that it is the production of one large estate, owned by Dr Lungarotti.

VALLE d'AOSTA

☆ **Donnaz** ● *Nebbiolo, Freisa* 11.5°
A medium-bodied, brilliant ruby wine, fading to garnet with age, Donnaz develops a fine bouquet and a slightly bitter flavour. It must be kept two years in cask and one in bottle before it is sold.
☆ **Enfer d'Arvier** ● *Petit Rouge* 11.5°
A mountain wine, like Donnaz, with a yield per hectare only one-third as high as many in Italy. It is deep red in colour and full of flavour, but it is a lightish wine and improves with age.

VENETO

☆ **Bardolino** ● *Corvina, Rondinella, Molinara, Negrara* 10.5° Bardolino should be enjoyed as a lively, young wine for everyday drinking. The village which gives it its name lies on the edge of Lake Garda which is the home of some well-known *chiaretto* wines on the other, Lombardy, shore. Bardolino is a fresh, pink wine, with a fragrant bouquet; its cherry-like flavour has a pleasing touch of sharpness, enhanced when *frizzante* by a prickle on the tongue. Six villages produce a more select Classico wine, and the broader area carries the plain designation Bardolino. Aged for a year it can be sold as Superiore, and it will last for another two or three years, but it is essentially a wine to drink young.
☆ **Breganze** ○ *Tocai, Pinot Bianco, Pinot Grigio, Vespaiolo* ● *Merlot, Cabernet, Pinot Nero* 11–11.5° The small town of Breganze on the mountain slopes north of Vicenza, is the centre for the production of six predominantly single-grape wines, each protected by the DOC, from 13 surrounding villages. Breganze Bianco (85 per cent *Tocai*) is a fragrant and rounded, straw-coloured, dry wine; the Rosso (85 per cent *Merlot*) is dry, robust, lively and harmonious, with a certain amount of tannin. The other four bear the names of their predominant grapes. Breganze Cabernet and Breganze Pinot Nero are both dry and robust reds, the Cabernet deeper coloured and with a firmer bouquet; Breganze Pinot Bianco is a pale white wine, rounded and smooth, with a good aroma; and Breganze Vespaiolo is golden coloured, dry and fresh, with a strong fruity bouquet and full of flavour. All four may be classified as Superiore if they reach 12°. They are wines of pleasing individuality and real quality.
☆ **Cabernet di Pramaggiore** ● *Cabernet, Merlot* 11.5° DOC areas, just north of Venice towards Treviso, have only recently been established for both Cabernet and Merlot di Pramaggiore, and each wine can have a ten per cent contribution of the other grape. The Cabernet is a dry, full-bodied red, which improves with age.
Cartizze ○ *Prosecco, Verdiso* 11° From the region north of the River Piave. The Superiore version is one of the best of the *Prosecco* wines (see **Prosecco di Conegliano-Valdobbiadene**).
☆ **Colli Berici** ● ○ A recent DOC covering seven predominantly single-grape wines from the mountainous region south of Vicenza. The reds are Cabernet, Merlot and Tocai Rosso; the whites are Garganega, Pinot Bianco, Sauvignon and Tocai Bianco. All have an 11° minimum alcoholic content except the Garganega (10.5°).
☆ **Colli Euganei Bianco** ○ *Garganega, Serprina, Tocai, Sauvignon* 10.5°
Colli Euganei Rosso ● *Merlot, Cabernet, Barbera* 11°
Colli Euganei Moscato ○ *Moscato Bianco* 10.5°
The vines covering the Colli Euganei lie to the right of the road out of Padua to Mantua. Both the Bianco and Rosso are soft attractive wines, more likely to be semi-sweet than dry; the white has an attractive aroma, and the

red a marked vinosity. The Moscato is sweet. All three may be made in a sparkling form.
☆ **Gambellara** ○ *Garganega, Trebbiano* 11/12/14° A brilliant, clear, pale-yellow, dry wine, made only five miles from Soave and often compared to it. The bouquet suggests the scent of elderflowers, and there is a bitterness reminiscent of almonds in the flavour; it is sometimes known as Garganega di Gambellara. Two dessert wines are also made: Recioto di Gambellara (12°), which can also be sparkling, and Vin Santo di Gambellara (14°) after the style of the famous Tuscan wine.
☆ **Merlot di Pramaggiore** ● *Merlot, Cabernet* 11.5° A dry red wine, full-bodied with a somewhat grassy smell and plenty of tannin (see **Cabernet di Pramaggiore**).
☆ **Montello e Colli Asolani** ● *Merlot, Cabernet* ○ *Verduzzo, Tocai, Prosecco* This wine from the Asolo area, east of Venice, has only recently acquired its DOC status.
☆ **Piave** (see **Vini del Piave**).
☆ **Prosecco di Conegliano-Valdobbiadene** ○ *Prosecco, Verdiso* 10.5/11° Conegliano and Valdobbiadene lie close together due north of Venice, on the far side of the River Piave, in an area in which the *Prosecco* grape has been widely grown over many years. The fragrant, straw-coloured wines are vinified in a bewildering number of combinations: dry, semi-sweet and sweet, each in turn in a natural, semi-sparkling or sparkling form and with its appropriate alcoholic minimum laid down by the DOC rules. The dry version is slightly more golden in colour with a pleasant bitterness; the sparkling varieties, produced in bulk by the Charmat (sealed container) process, are more delicate to the taste. The DOC specification also covers Superiore di Cartizze (see **Cartizze**).
☆ **Recioto di Soave** (see **Soave**).
☆ **Recioto della Valpolicella** (see **Valpolicella**).
☆ **Soave** ○ *Garganega, Trebbiano* 10.5/12° A delicate, medium-bodied wine, known the world over; in its comparatively rare Classico and Superiore forms it is one of the best white wines of Italy. The grapes come from around the small town of Soave some 15 miles east of Verona; they produce a very clear, pale-yellow, dry wine, which can display a greenish tint and pleasingly combines a sharpness with a bitter undertone. The best of the grapes – literally 'the ears' (*orecchie*, hence *Recioto*) or outside bunches – are allowed to become part-dried, producing a golden-yellow, sweet dessert wine, Recioto di Soave (12°).

☆ **Tocai di Lison** ○ *Tocai* 11.5° Lison lies north-east of Venice, towards Treviso and Pordenone. *Tocai* grapes, which are not grown in great quantity in this area, produce a slightly bitter, dry, pale-yellow wine, with a pleasant, delicately fruity aroma.
☆ **Valpolicella** ● *Corvina, Rondinella, Molinara* 11/14° Valpolicella, from the area immediately to the north of Verona, is vinified in two ways: like Chianti in Tuscany, fresh and ready to drink, or in a Classico/Superiore form from grapes selected for ageing. It is usually light red, not unlike Bardolino (see Tuscany section of gazetteer), and made by the *governo* process. The Superiore has a fine ruby-red colour and a delicate perfume, reminiscent of bitter almonds; there is a slight sweetness in the taste, in which the bitterness of the perfume seeks to reassert itself. A full-bodied, sweet dessert wine, Recioto della Valpolicella (14°), is the product of semi-dried, specially selected grapes from five villages in the Classico zone; Recioto Valpolicella Amarone is its dry and finer variety. Valpantena, the name of an adjoining valley, may also appear on the labels of both plain and *recioto* versions of the wine.

Venegazzu ● *Sauvignon, Malbec, Merlot* 12–13° Little known overseas, this is one of the historic red wines of Venice, eliciting great praise from those who make its acquaintance. It is high in alcohol and made from a mixture of French grape varieties. A white Venegazzu is made from *Riesling* and *Pinot* grapes.
☆ **Vini del Piave,** or **Piave** ● ○ 11/11.5° The DOC is a portmanteau for four single-grape wines from the Piave river basin, north and east of Venice. The Cabernet (11.5°) and Merlot (11°) versions are both deep red wines, ageing to garnet; they are dry, full-bodied and tannic, each developing firm, characteristic bouquets. The Tocai (11°) is a dry, fresh, slightly aromatic white wine, intended for early drinking. The Verduzzo (11°), also a wine to drink young, is a golden or greenish-yellow, with freshness and balance.

SPAIN

SPAIN HAS MORE LAND under vines than any country in the world, but this does not mean that it produces the most wine. In fact, it is only just holding on to fourth place in the world wine production stakes, behind France, Italy and the U.S.S.R. The 1978 harvest produced 25,000,000 hectolitres from a total vine-covered surface of 1,630,000 hectares. This gives a yield of sixteen hectolitres per hectare, which is extremely low. The 1978 harvest was less than the average production of the last twenty years. There are three main reasons for this decline: a climate which is becoming gradually more humid, inexperience in combatting vine diseases caused by this humidity, and the prohibition that has been imposed on new plantings.

The Spaniards would like an annual yield of 34,000,000 hecto-

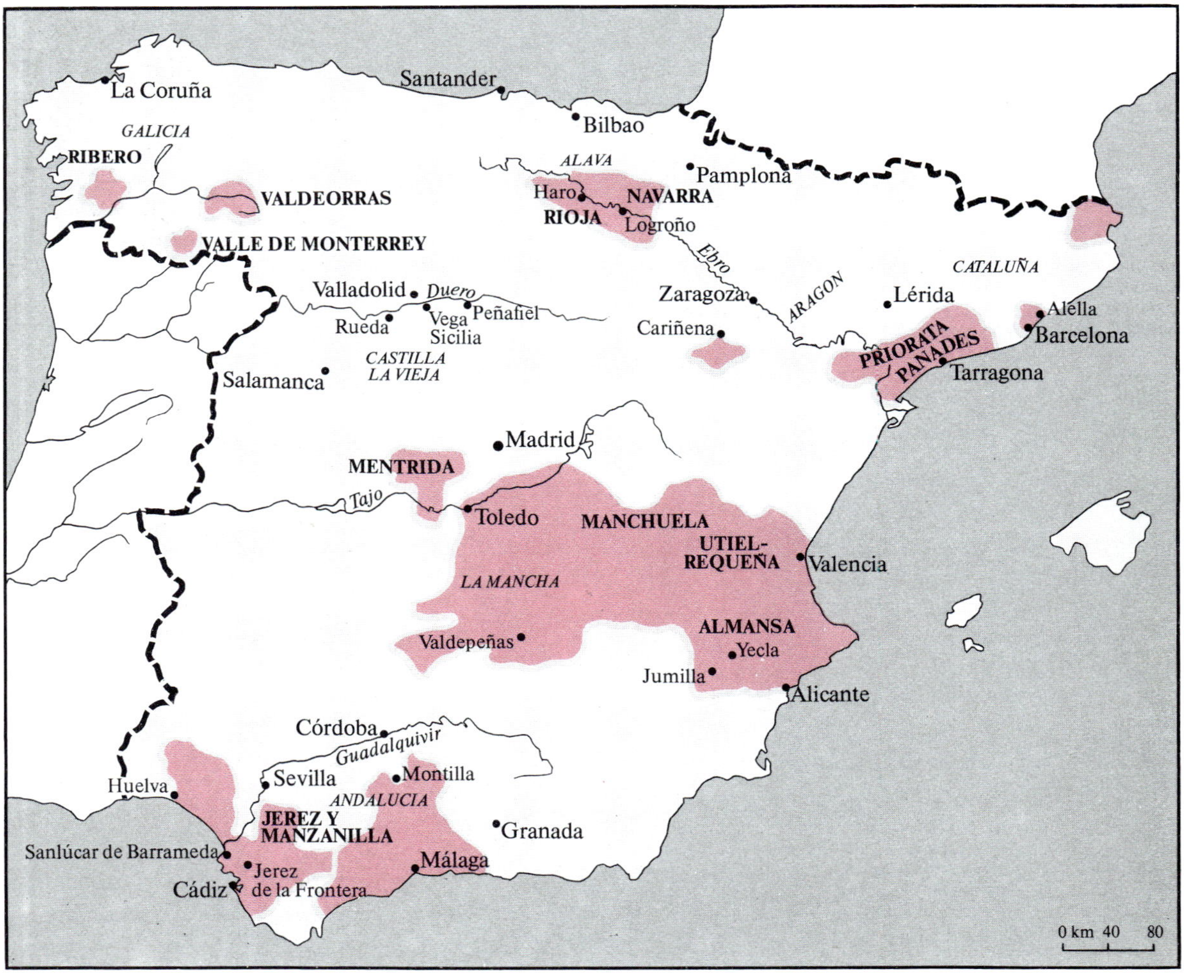

Inside a bodega *at Valdepeñas, La Mancha (Spectrum)*

(below) Showmanship in a Jerez bodega*: the* capataz *(head foreman) uses a traditional sampling cup* (venencia) *to pour Sherry into a tasting glass (Zefa)*

litres – 24,000,000 for home consumption, 4,000,000 for export and 6,000,000 for distillation and industrial use. Like other wine-producing countries, Spain wishes to increase her exports, and it is largely for this reason that she has applied to join the European Common Market. With an increased vineyard area and, above all, increased yields, she will make a formidable competitor for France and Italy.

Spain's best-known wine, Sherry, is fortified, but the country also provides table wines for all tastes – reds, whites and some very respectable sparkling wines. The great majority either goes in bulk exports, often for blending purposes, or is made for local consumption; all are controlled by a Statute of 1970 which puts wine into categories of sweetness, sets minimum alcoholic degrees, creates a top class of wine based on 'noble' grape varieties and controls the quality of fortified wine. There is a National Institute of Denominations of Origin which is administered locally by Consejos Reguladores. Standards are set and enforced for some two dozen regions of Spain, only a few of which produce individual table wines worthy of overseas attention.

Table wines

The Rioja region, in the valley of the river Ebro, produces more fine table wine than any other. The rainfall here, in northern Spain, is more conducive to quality than in the dry south, and the autumns are cooler. Bordeaux growers, fleeing phylloxera at the end of the last century, imported the idea of ageing wine in 225-litre casks, and although Bordeaux grapes did not flourish, other varieties were readily established – Tempranillo, Garnacho (Grenache), Graciano and Mazuelo for the reds, Viura and Malvasia for the whites. The region's comparatively small output (1,000,000 hectolitres from 45,000 hectares) is reflected in the weight and body of its wines, but there is no doubt that some white wine from other areas is still permitted to make its way into Rioja bottles.

The region is commonly divided into three main districts. Rioja Alta in the north-west and the adjacent Rioja Alavesa are the better; Rioja Baja, further up the Ebro, to the south and east of Logroño, produces the heavier wines for blending. As in Champagne, however, the district is less important than the style and skill of a particular house or *bodega* in blending, ageing and selecting. Vintages can be taken much more seriously than they used to be, but casks are still often topped-up – a necessary practice in a region where red wines (and to a lesser extent the whites) are kept in cask for between four and five years.

Ordinary Riojas are often sold under the names of Tinto (full-bodied red) and Clarete (light red), but the difference between the two is often slight. Reserva is the name for the best selection from good vintage years, aged separately and topped-up through the

RIOJA: SOME LEADING *BODEGAS*

Alavesas
Berberana
Bilbainas
Cuné (Compania Vinicola del Norte de España)
Franco-Españolas
Gomez Cruzadó
La Rioja Alta
Lagunilla
R. Lopez de Heredia Vina Tondonia
Marques de Cacares
Marques de Murrieta
Marques de Riscal
Martinez Lacuesta
Montecillo
Muga
Olarra
Federico Paternina
Perez de Albaniz
Riojanas
Santiago
Sociedad General de Vinas
Velazquez

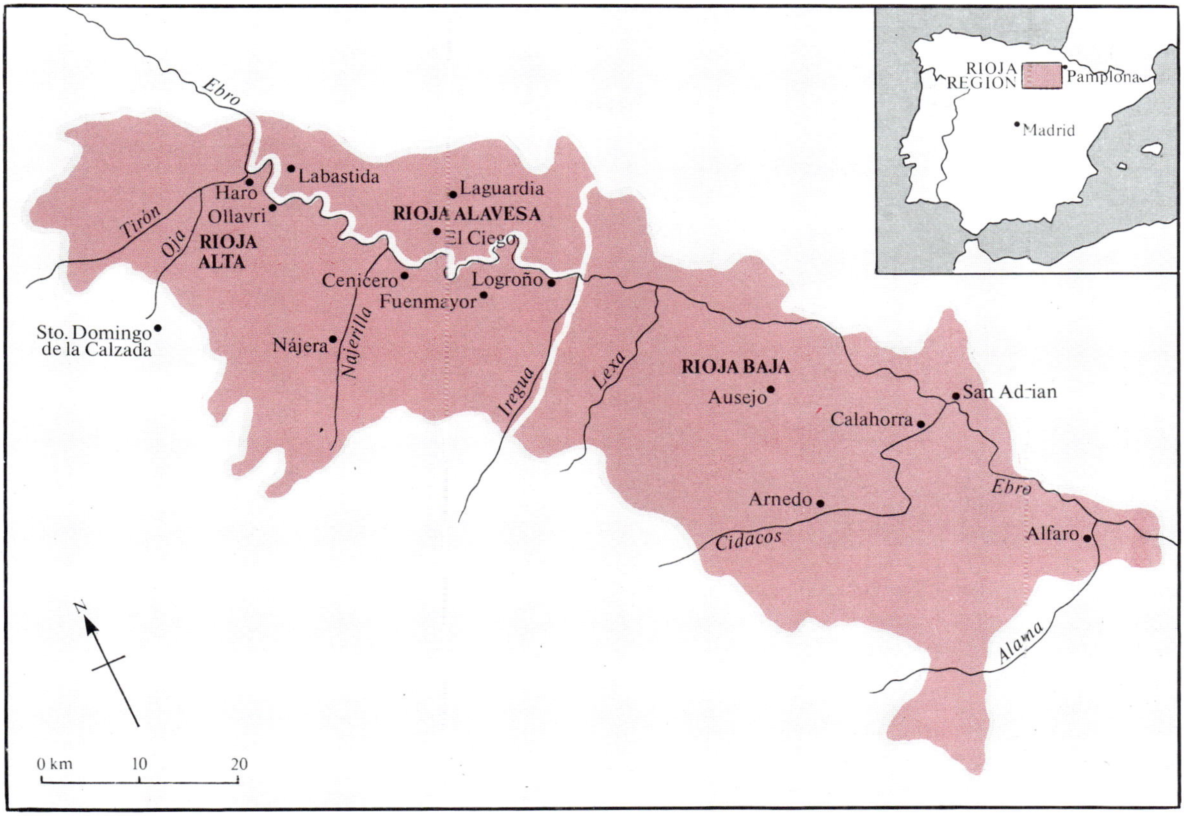

years to compensate for losses through evaporation. Good red Riojas have a wonderful depth of taste, a slight vanilla-like smell from the ageing in oak, and very good fruit and acidity. The whites today are much less oxidized than in former years, and often have a nutty richness and great flavour. Justifiably, Rioja wines are becoming increasingly appreciated overseas, and investment in the area has been considerable; many of them provide excellent drinking and good value for money.

The wines of Cataluña, Spain's next most important region in this context, are as individual as the Catalans themselves. The firm of Torres in the Panadés region, south of Barcelona, has spear-headed the export market's awareness of these wines, and there are other firms who take the same care in producing excellent red and white still wines; the reds are influenced by ageing in oak, and Torres is also experimenting with French grape varieties, with considerable success. But the region's fame rests largely on the production of sparkling wines, many of them made by the *méthode champenoise*. The best are made by Codorniú (the world's biggest producer), Conde de Caralt, Gonzales y Dubosc and Freixenet. A top Spanish *champaña* is clean and even elegant, but does not have the noble bouquet of Champagne. The cooperative at Alella, north of Barcelona, makes two good whites, Alella Marfil Blanco (sweetish) and Seco (dry). The Tarragona region, to the south of

(left) A vineyard in Tenerife in the Canaries; Mount Teide is in the background (Daily Telegraph)

(right) Ausejo: the dry, sandy soil on which the vines grow beneath the little hill-top town is characteristic of this part of the eastern Rioja (Spectrum)

Barcelona, produces ordinary, alcoholic, blending wines for exporting by the tanker-load; it includes a small enclave, known as Priorato, which makes a small amount of red wine and some sweet dessert wines.

The huge, high plateau of La Mancha in central Spain produces a vast amount of wine, of which Valdepeñas is the most famous. Reds and whites are fermented and stored in great jars of baked clay (*tinajas*), as wood is scarce in this treeless region; they have potential, but can lack acidity due to the very hot summers. If more modern vinification methods were introduced, Valdepeñas would be a bigger threat to competitors on the export markets.

Other table wines worth mentioning are Cariñena from Aragon, a powerful red, and the light, fresh, acid reds and whites from Galicia, strongly resembling the *vinhos verdes* from neighbouring Portugal. Valencia produces some good dessert wines, and Jumilla, further south in the province of Murcia, makes big, dark, alcoholic brews. The deep red Vega Sicilia, aged in wood for ten years, is something of a legend; it is produced by one *bodega*, about 25 miles south-east of Valladolid. There is also a younger wine from the same area, Valbueña de Duero, which spends considerably less time in wood. Ageing of this kind, and other methods of vinification, inevitably mean that the wines have technical faults – faults for which some people have learned to love them.

Sherry

The history of Sherry is a long one, but its fame lives on, in spite of competition from other drinks in the aperitif market. The United States has still much to learn of its merits, but northern Europe consumes it in huge quantities and of every type. In those British households where only one bottle of alcohol is kept for 'special occasions', it is almost bound to be Sherry. Its infinite variety can please most palates.

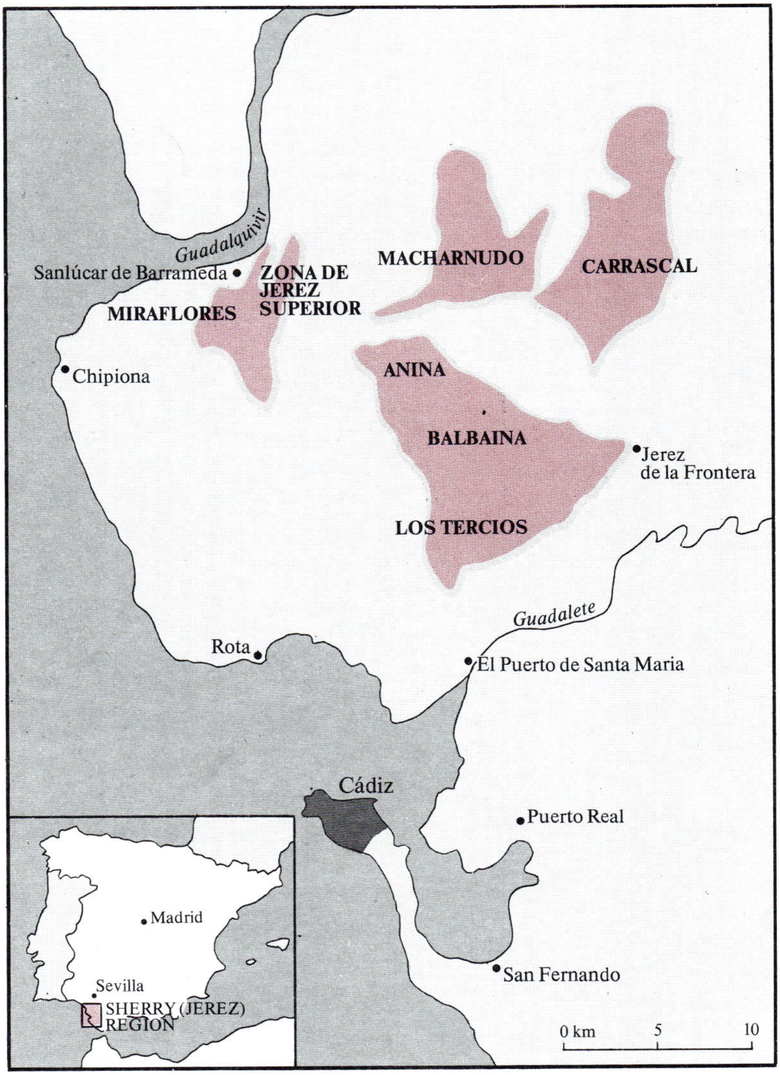

Spanish Sherry – the only true Sherry – comes from Andalusia, in the area between Cadiz and Seville, where the town of Jerez de la Frontera has given the wine its famous name. The best vineyards are on chalky soil, called *albariza*, and it is these which produce the best *finos*. The less chalky, more sandy *barro* soil gives a coarser wine; sandy soil, known as *arena*, produces high yields of low quality wine, and is not much in demand. The golden Palomino is the grape variety that gives the first quality Sherries, particularly when it is grown on *albariza*. The Pedro Ximénez is the second white grape of Jerez, and makes superb sweet wines.

The grapes are dried after harvesting (the Pedro Ximénez for much longer than the Palomino), and gypsum is added to increase the wine's tartaric acid. Mechanical presses are now the order of the day, and the must is fermented in casks that are slightly open to the

SHERRY HOUSES

Heavily advertised brands of Sherry, often household names, are not always the best. Ask your wine merchant for some less common Sherries (such as a true dry *oloroso*); most Sherry houses have a range of fine wines, some of which do not get the attention they deserve. The following is a list of leading shippers whose reputation provides a guarantee of quality.

Barbadillo (*m*)
Bertola
Agustin Blazquez
Bobadilla
Caballero
Manuel de la Calle
Cayd
Croft
Delgado & Zuleta
Diez Hermanos
Pedro Domecq
Duff Gordon
Gaspar F. Florido Cano
Garvey
Gonzalez Byass
John Harvey
Hermosilla (*m*)
La Riva
Emilio Lustau
Palomino & Vergara
Real Tesoro (*m*)
Zoilo Ruiz-Mateos
Sanchez Romate
Sandeman
José de Soto
Fernando A. de Terry
Valdespino
Varela
Williams & Humbert
Wisdom & Warter

(*m*) shippers of *manzanilla*

air. Some of the wines are affected by *flor* (a yeast 'flower') which protects the wine and gives it a special flavour; these are destined to become *finos* or genuine *amontillados* (i.e. aged *finos*). Each butt (or cask) of Sherry develops differently, so there is a real need for an efficient system of blending.

Hence the development of a system known as the *solera* (literally, a series of butts) by which Sherries are fortified with grape spirit and classified according to their types – *fino*, *oloroso*, *amontillado*, etc. New wine is kept for a time as an *añada* (wine from one year); it then goes into a *criadera* – i.e. a 'nursery' for each type of wine feeding the system – and thence into a number of other butts. The oldest wines are 'refreshed' by slightly younger ones, which in turn have received similarly small additions; at each stage the addition is sufficiently slight to ensure that the style and taste of the final blend will not be altered. Thus the shipper always has a ready stock of each type of Sherry that is matured and ready for bottling. The *solera* system provides the key to the production of fine, consistent Sherries.

Sherry falls into five main types:

Amontillado: in theory, a *fino* that has developed and aged. However, many of the commercial, cheaper *amontillados* are nothing of the sort; they tend to be coarser, and to be made medium-sweet by the addition of other wines.

Fino: the lightest and most delicate of the Sherries. They are delicious young, but some age beautifully, with a flowery bouquet of great attraction; in Spain they are sold at only 15° alcohol – usually two degrees higher for export.

Manzanilla: *finos* from Sanúcar de Barrameda, near the coast. They are light and often have a perfumed, even salty tang. *Manzanilla amontillado* is rare, but wonderful.

Oloroso: wines with little or no *flor*, darker and fuller, but completely dry by nature. However, many are made into dessert or 'cream' Sherries and sweetened, and they are usually rather high in alcohol.

Palo Cortado: tends to be dark in colour, but it has a unique crispness and fragrance, with a style somewhere between *amontillado* and *oloroso*; rather rare.

SPAIN
GLOSSARY

abocado: semi-sweet
aloque: a mixture of red and white grapes
añejado por: aged by
blanco: white
bodega: wine shop, wine company, winery, wine cellars
cepa: variety of grape
clarete: red, usually light
corriente: ordinary wine
dulce: sweet
criado por: grown by
elaborado por: made by
embotellado por: bottled by
embotellado de origen: estate bottled
espumoso: sparkling
reserva: matured red wine from Rioja
rosado: *rosé*
seco: dry
tinto: red, usually dark
viña: vineyard
vino de agujas: slightly sparkling wine from Galicia
vino de cosecha propria: wine from own harvest or estate
vino de lagrima: wine from unpressed grapes, usually sweet
vino de mesa: table wine, better than *corriente*
vino de pasto: light, everyday wine

PORTUGAL

PORTUGAL, Europe's fourth largest wine-growing country, can offer some of the best value wines on the market today. Unfortunately, as a result of the nation's political and economic troubles in recent years, its push into the export markets has not been as dynamic as might otherwise have been the case and there are still some relatively undiscovered Portuguese wines of great quality. Laws relating to the demarcation of production areas are rigorously enforced (dishonesty in other countries tends to occur only when sales grow so fast that a particular area comes under pressure to increase its production), and there exists a great variety of wines and flavours to suit all palates. Some of the demarcated wines are of less importance now, and wines as yet unrecognised in law are coming to the fore.

About half the country's wine exports are ordinary *rosés*, many of them marketed by Mateus and Lancer's. These often serve to introduce British (and other) people to Portuguese wine, and indeed to wine drinking itself, but they are industrially produced and dull, with an unbalanced extra sweetness and added carbon dioxide to give them sparkle. The serious wine drinker should look elsewhere – to the excellent table wines, red and more often white, from the Dão, Minho and Setúbal areas, and above all to the splendid, fortified wines of the Douro, famous world-wide as Port.

Vila Mateus, home of the famous rosé *sparkling wine (Fotofass)*

Table wines

The Dão area of central Portugal, around Viseu, produces the best non-fortified wines in the country. High granite slopes, small yields, and cooler weather than in the south combine to create wines of body and richness, high in glycerine and often velvety. Many of the wines have at least three years in wood, and there are good stocks of older vintages in the area. Dão reds are generally very reliable, representing excellent value; there are also a few whites – dry with a lot of earthy character. Grão Vasco is the best-known house, but names you have not heard of will still give you good wines.

Vinho verde (literally 'young wine'; it is pronounced 'veenyo vairday') is produced in the Minho region in the far north-west of Portugal, roughly between the rivers Minho and Douro. The vines are trained high over the granitic terrain, and the cooler Atlantic weather ensures that the wines are light, with a high acidity. The whites are exported, but 75 per cent of the production is red. The slight sparkle is caused by the malolactic fermentation taking place in bottle. Most of the exported *vinhos verdes* are slightly sweetened, in order to lessen the impact of their acidity. They are reasonably priced wines, very refreshing in hot weather; the best-known names are Aveleda, Casal Garcia, Lagosta and Cepa Velha, but do not be afraid to try others.

The relatively few table wines produced in the Lisbon area are only widely seen around the city itself. White Bucelas is light and dry, with a rather unusual after-taste contributed by the pre-

A typical Douro landscape (Fotofass)

A wall tile from a Douro vineyard (Fotofass)

dominant Arinto grape; people tired of rather neutral whites should look out for it. Colares red wines are being squeezed out by the area's proximity to Lisbon (the town lies on the coast road between Sintra and Estoril), but they provide a pronounced taste with a degree of tannin. The vines are planted in deep trenches, so that the roots go through a thick layer of sand before reaching clay, hence immunizing them from phylloxera.

The only demarcated wine from the Setúbal area, a short distance to the south-east of Lisbon, is Moscatel de Setúbal, one of the best sweet, fortified wines in the world. The heady aroma of the black and white Moscatel grapes enhances the wine's full, fruity flavour, and even the old vintages maintain a delicious freshness. Sweetness is obtained by adding alcohol during fermentation, which causes

Grape-pickers in the Douro valley (Fotofass)

some of the grape sugar to remain in the wine, and the resulting alcoholic strength is about that of Sherry. There is also an excellent red wine from the same region called Periquita, shipped by the firm of J. M. da Fonseca. Two table wine areas to watch for the future are Douro in the north (much better known for Port) and Bairrada, centred on the city of Coimbra, where a number of white sparkling wines are made.

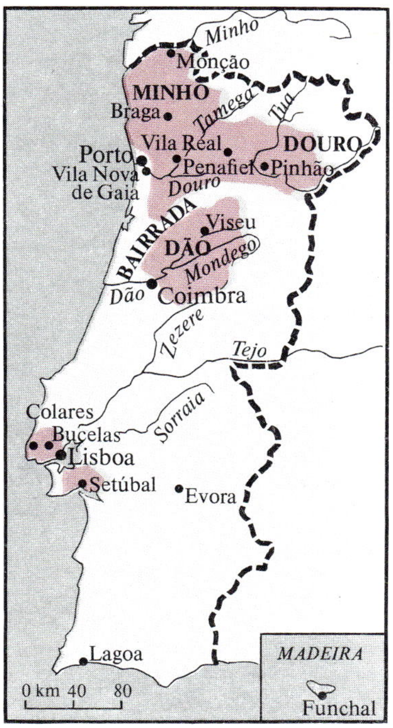

Port

Two main factors combine to ensure that Port, the treasure of Portugal and one of the world's fine wines, is complicated to make: the extremely steep and wild terrain on which the grapes are grown, in the mountainous region surrounding the river Douro, and the exceptional skill required in the blending of the wine. The fierce heat of the Douro summer sun causes the many different varieties of grape to develop thick skins, and these are left in contact with the juice to give Port its marvellously deep red. Then, at a particular stage of fermentation, the process is stopped by the addition of brandy, so conserving some residual sugar and boosting the wine's total alcoholic content. The new wines are sold to the Port shippers, and taken down to their 'lodges' at Vila Nova de Gaia, at the mouth of the Douro river opposite Oporto (Porto in Portuguese). The shippers then make their selections and blends, and the different types of Port are determined: Vintage Port does the greater part of its maturing in bottle, while old Tawny Ports mature and form their character in cask. Altogether, there are seven distinct types of Port.

Vintage: the jewel of the trade. If the shippers consider a year to be outstanding, they declare it as a 'vintage' and select their best wines to mature for two years in wood; these are then put in bottle, to mature for a much longer period – most need to be kept for between twenty and forty years to show themselves at their best.

When young, Vintage Port is deep-coloured, tannic and rough, but it matures to a smooth, subtle perfection, with a scented bouquet and a long after-taste. It should be decanted carefully off the deposit formed during its long maturation in bottle. Houses make up their blends from the best sites of different vineyards, but there are a few single-property (or *Quinta*) wines, such as Croft's Roeda or Taylor's Vargellas. Vintage Ports are now always bottled in Portugal, and each house shows a distinctive style.

Crusted: a high quality blend of different years, or of one year that was not quite good enough to be 'declared' as a vintage. It forms a

SOME LEADING PORT SHIPPERS

Calem
Cockburn Smithes
Croft
Delaforce
Dow
Ferreira
Feuerheed
Fonseca
Gonzalez Byass
Graham
Kopke
Martinez
Offley
Quarles Harris
Quinta do Noval
Ramos Pinto
Rebello Valente (*a*)
Sandeman
Smith Woodhouse
Taylor
Tuke Holdsworth (*b*)
Warre

(*a*) vintage brand of Robertsons
(*b*) vintage brand of Hunt Roope

Recent Port vintages generally declared:
1945, 1947, 1948, 1950, 1955, 1958, 1960, 1963 1966 1970 1975

(left) Picking grapes on the Noval estate at Pinhão in the Douro valley. The vineyards date from the 18th century (Fotofass)

(right) Riverside wine lodges at Oporto (Spectrum)

CROFT
CROFT
SANDEMAN
SANDEMAN

The white concrete balloons used for bulk storage of wine by the firm of Fonseca at Vila Nogueira de Azeitão, south of Lisbon (Daily Telegraph)

'crust' or a deposit in the bottle, like Vintage Port, but it has an extra year in cask before bottling, so that it is ready to drink as soon as it is sold.

Late-bottled Vintage: wine of a single year, declared to the authorities, and aged from four to six years in wood. It may then be bottled and sold, after having thrown its deposit in wood.

Tawny: cheap Tawnies are either very young (some are not even tawny in colour) or are a mixture of red and white Ports. The genuine article is aged in wood, and sometimes contains amounts of very old wines. Light Tawnies are young, but the intense, concentrated Tawnies of elegance and breed are between twenty and forty years old. They are necessarily expensive, and are highly prized by the Port shippers themselves.

Ruby: young red Ports, aged for about two years and blended to a consistent house-style.

Vintage Character (or Vintage Style): aged longer than Ruby Port, with a fuller style and greater body and depth – a lighter imitation of Vintage Port.

White: this has never become really popular outside Portugal, but it is an excellent aperitif, whether dry or sweet.

PORTUGAL GLOSSARY

adamador: sweet
adega: winery or cellar
branco: white
clarete: light red
engarrafado na origem: bottled at place of origin
espumante: sparkling
garrafeira: from a particular stock (implies that the wine comes from a private cellar, but not necessarily that it is of a special quality)
maduro: matured (white)
quinta: estate
seco: dry
tinto: dark red
velho: matured (red)
verde: young

Madeira

A FAMED FORTIFIED WINE of the past, Madeira today is entitled to an increasing claim on our palates as a multi-purpose wine of immense character. Although 400 miles off the coast of Morocco in the Atlantic, the little windy island which gives the wine its name belongs to Portugal, and its wines are subject to Portuguese controls; they are totally different from Port, however, and they merit a place all their own in a wine-drinker's library.

Madeira suffered two viticultural disasters in the last century: first oïdium (powdery mildew) and then phylloxera. The resulting hardship encouraged the development of wild American vines on the island, and today direct producer (or ungrafted) vines form the backbone of Madeiran viticulture. Of the 4,500,000 litres of Madeira wine exported in 1977, only 2,700,000 were made from grafted *vitis vinifera* vines. This is not so bad as may appear, given the fact that Madeira is a fortified wine with a unique vinification process which completely changes the character of the base wine. There are, however, considerable efforts to plant more 'noble' grape varieties, of which the most prominent are set out in the adjoining list.

The process that makes Madeira entirely different from any other wine is known as the *estufa* system. The wine is heated in large vats up to approximately 50°c, the temperature being slowly raised and reduced over a period of three months. The very best wines, those destined for special old reserves or even vintages, are very slowly heated in cask by raising the temperature of the room. The system contributes greatly to the longevity of Madeira wines.

Fortification usually takes place after the *estufa*, and the fortifying spirit is nowadays of vinous origin. The best, sweet Madeiras are fortified at a very early stage, in order to arrest fermentation and retain natural sugar; the others must rely for their sweetness on the addition of sweetening wine, largely produced on the neighbouring island of Porto Santo.

The date of a Solera Madeira denotes the year of its inception. Thereafter, the wine is 'refreshed' with younger wine in small quantities, so as to keep the original quality. Absolute proof is now required before a Vintage wine can be authenticated, and such wines are now considerably rarer than they were.

Blandy, Cossart, Rutherford & Miles, Leacock, Henriques & Henriques, Lomelino, and Barbeito produce Madeira wines of consistent quality. After their basic Sercials, Verdelhos, Buals and Malmseys (these are now more generic descriptions of relative sweetness than accurate grape variety nomenclature: Malmsey is the sweetest) there are the Old Reserves, Soleras and Vintages. Rainwater, originally no more than a trademark, is usually a blend somewhere between Sercial and Verdelho. The drier wines are ideal as an aperitif or with soup, the sweeter wines with fruit and nuts, or just on their own.

GRAPE VARIETIES

Sercial: related to the Riesling of Germany and makes the driest Madeiras; it is grown on the higher slopes and is the last to be picked.
Verdelho: once the most widely grown grape on the island, it is now mostly restricted to the south, where the soils are generally less acid, the weather is warmer and the rainfall less. The grape is related to the Pedro Ximénez of Spain.
Bual or *Boal:* mostly grown in the south; makes full, rich wines.
Malvasia: found in small quantities in the south; the grape gave its name to Malmsey.
Tinta Negra or *Negra Mole:* one of the most widespread of the grafted varieties; much used for blending.
Terrantez, Bastardo, Moscatel: rarely seen today, but there are some fine old wines made from these varieties.

U.S.A.

Despite its long history and America's enormous natural resources, the U.S. table wine industry is chiefly a product of the 1960s and 1970s. Demand for dry dinner wines has led to a swing away from the traditional concentration on dessert and aperitif wines, and the entire industry is now in the process of frantic expansion; new vineyards are being exploited, new grape varieties are being developed; wine technology receives wide-spread and serious attention.

Wine-making establishments vary from family enterprises of a few acres to huge national concerns. While smaller wineries succeed in making a name by the excellence of their products, the big corporations are faced with an upsurge of interest in better quality wines and are compelled either to buy their way into wineries with an established reputation or to divert some of their own productive resources accordingly.

The bulk wine industry, producing blended wines for everyday drinking ('jug wines') and dessert, aperitif and sparkling wines, is

(above) Picking grapes in the Masson vineyards (Paul Masson)

The Christian Brothers' winery at Mont La Salle, in the Napa valley (Christian Brothers)

The viewing gallery at the Paul Masson winery allows visitors to see the huge redwood and oak casks used for ageing the wines (Paul Masson)

dominated by a small group of big corporations: E. and J. Gallo (who are calculated to supply one out of every three or four bottles drunk), Heublein, National Distillers, Nestlé, Seagram and now Coca-Cola (Taylor). Total annual output at present averages 350 million gallons (150 million cases), but this figure is likely to increase dramatically as newly planted acreages begin to make their contribution.

Only a small proportion of the national output, under 20 per cent, consists of wine above the 'jug' level (so-called because such wines are often sold in half-gallon or gallon containers). These are the 'premium' wines – i.e. wines of good standard quality which include a very small but increasing fraction of really outstanding fine wines. There are as yet no detailed regulations governing their place of origin, of a kind comparable to those relating to the French *appellations contrôlées*; everything depends on the reputation and integrity of the winery.

In terms of the size of their production, the names of four premium wine-makers stand out: the Christian Brothers, Almadén, Paul Masson and Sebastiani. Between them, these four giants handle over 75 per cent of the American trade. Other names of note among medium-sized wineries include Beaulieu, Charles Krug, Concannon, Inglenook, Louis Martini, Mirassou and Wente Bros. – all of them in California. But it has also to be remembered that individual wines of distinction may emanate from the smallest family wineries.

The point has not yet been reached when the wine of a given geographical region is made from a particular grape variety, as has happened with the great French and German vineyards. The richness of the country's resources, especially in California, allows individual vineyards to offer a wide choice of wines from different grapes, and most wineries still feel it incumbent upon them to do so – Almadén, for instance, offers a range of over forty; in the smaller experimental wineries, however, a lead has been given towards selectivity and specialization.

WINE GRAPES: ACRES UNDER VINE

California	326,000
Michigan	17,000
New York State	43,000
Ohio	4,000
Oregon	1,200
Pennsylvania	11,000
Washington	22,500

The regions

Wine production in the United States is dominated by California, which accounts for some 85 per cent of the country's output. The grape varieties used are mostly *vitis vinifera*, that is European grape types, or American hybrids developed from them. Outside California, although grapes of the indigenous *vitis labrusca* varieties are grown in almost every State of the Union, and made commercially in some thirty of them, quality wines are only slowly being developed – principally in New York State, Maryland, Ohio and Michigan in the east, and in Oregon and Washington in the west. They are usually grown from *vitis vinifera* or its derivatives.

Bulk wines tend to be sold either generically or under proprietary names which form a trade mark for the winery. The better quality wines are usually varietals. Blended generics are allowed by U.S. regulations to be sold under 14 specified titles (see attached list) which were originally intended to resemble their geographical European namesakes. Varietals are wines made predominantly from a single grape variety, which gives its name to the wine on the label. They offer the U.S.A. its prime opportunity to develop an authentic native wine industry, whether the grape is a European derivative (such as the Cabernet Sauvignon, which at present holds pride of place) or a Ruby Cabernet, an Emerald Riesling or a Carnelian – three of the new varieties developed within the country. Outside these categories is Zinfandel, a peculiarly Californian grape of which the origins are obscure. It may come from southern Italy; certainly it is capable of producing very interesting wine.

GENERIC TITLES

Burgundy	Madeira*
Claret*	Moselle*
Chablis	Port
Champagne	Rhine wine
Chianti	Sauternes
Hock*	Sherry
Malaga*	Tokay

*These names are permitted by law, but are not used in practice: the place of origin (e.g. 'California') must always be stated.

The Charles Krug vineyards in the Napa valley (Spectrum)

PRINCIPAL GRAPE VARIETIES

EUROPEAN (*vitis vinifera*)

Barbera ●
Cabernet Sauvignon ●
Carignane ●
Chardonnay ○
Chenin Blanc ○
Gamay ●
Gewürztraminer ○
Green Hungarian ○
Grenache ●
Merlot ●
Petite Sirah ●
Pinot Noir ●
Riesling (White or Johannisberg) ○
Sauvignon Blanc ○
Sémillon ○
Sylvaner ○

CALIFORNIAN (*vitis vinifera*)

Carnelian ●
Centurion ●
Emerald Riesling ○
Ruby Cabernet ●

NATIVE AMERICAN (mainly *vitis labrusca*)

Catawba ●
Concord ●
Delaware ●
Duchess ○
Elvira ○
Ives ●
Moore's Diamond ○
Niagara ○
Scuppernong ○

FRANCO-AMERICAN HYBRIDS

Aurora Blanc ○
Baco Noir ●
Chancellor Noir ●
de Chaunac ●
Chelois ●
Maréchal Foch ●
Seyval Blanc ○

● red ○ white

The winery rather than the vineyard is the focal point of the industry; it is where the wine is fermented and probably bottled, but not necessarily where the grapes are grown. E. and J. Gallo, for instance, has its winery in Modesto, California, but draws its grapes from all over the state. The two tend to be synonymous in the case of the smaller, more distinguished wineries – but it is the winery's reputation rather than its location which is of importance to the consumer.

U.S. wine laws

Federal and state controls on the way vines are cultivated, and the methods by which wines are made, bottled and sold, are pretty minimal. Such regulations as exist are intended more to protect the consumer from misrepresentation than to regularize growing practices. Where a geographical source is shown on the label, for instance New York State Gewürztraminer or Napa Valley Chenin Blanc, federal regulations require that 75 per cent of the grapes used must come from that region.*

*Californian law is stricter, insisting on 100 per cent for wine bearing the state name, though only 75 per cent for wine from a particular district.

A Californian vineyard scene, emphasizing the gently rolling character of the terrain (Christian Brothers)

Otherwise, there is no strict requirement as to the grapes to be used in generic wines; so there need never, for instance, be any Pinot Noir grapes in American Burgundy. Even in varietals only 51 per cent of the named grape has to be used, although in practice better wineries use 75 per cent and some, especially in California, aim at 100 per cent. Recent federal regulations impose a minimum of 75 per cent, to be effective by 1 January 1983.

Vintage years may be declared, provided that 95 per cent of the grapes were grown in the year in question. Labels normally quote the alcoholic content of the wine by volume – usually 12°, although the minimum required by federal law is only 7°. California at present stipulates 10° for its whites and *rosés*, but the state law is being changed in order to allow for a lower minimum.

UNITED STATES GLOSSARY

botrytised: wine made from grapes with the noble rot (*pourriture noble*)
champagne: sparkling wine made by the Charmat process or *méthode champenoise*. The term continues to be used in the USA, despite the opposition of French Champagne growers, but by US law it must be preceded by the name of an area
estate-bottled: the term cannot always be strictly interpreted; its use is permissible if the vineyard and the winery are in the same county and the latter controls the former
foxy: term used to describe a pungency of scent and flavour common to native American grape wines; strongest in the Concord grape
generic: a blended wine which can take one of fourteen permitted names – see note on page 162.
hybrid: phylloxera-resistant cross-bred vines, matching the hardy qualities of American stocks to the elegance and subtlety of European varieties
jug wines: cheap, every-day wines below the premium level (see below); they are often sold in half-gallon and gallon containers
pop wines: fruit-flavoured wines, low in alcohol, appealing to the less tutored palate
premium: the term used for all wines intended to be of better quality, embracing both generics and varietals
varietal: a wine of premium quality, made predominantly or entirely from the grape whose name appears on the label – e.g. Napa Valley Chenin Blanc
vintage: signifies that 95 per cent of the bottle content is from the same harvest; vintage years do not have the same significance as in France and Germany
vitis labrusca: the most common of the indigenous American grape varieties, originating in its wild state on the borders of Persia
vitis vinifera: the European grape species; needing sympathetic climatic conditions, it flourishes in California, and in New York State when grafted onto hardy Canadian stocks

California

CLIMATIC REGIONS OF CALIFORNIA

I	Up to 2,500 degree-days of sunshine, presenting growers with conditions comparable to those of the Rhine, Moselle and Champagne
II	2,501 to 3,000 degree-days, similar to Bordeaux
III	3,001 to 3,500 degree-days, similar to northern Italy and the Rhône Valley
IV	3,501 to 4,000 degree-days, similar to central Spain
V	More than 4,000 degree-days, similar to North Africa

THE 326,000 acres of wine grape vineyards in California produce three out of every four bottles of wine drunk in the United States – most of it in the form of table wine. The nine districts into which the state is traditionally divided, ranged north, south and east of San Francisco Bay, fall into three main regions. For ease of comparison, the wines listed in the following gazetteer are divided into these three regions – i.e. north of San Francisco Bay, the central inland valley, between the Coast Range and the Sierra Nevada, and south of San Francisco Bay.

The cool, northern coastal region embraces the older wine-growing areas of the Napa Valley; it produces almost all the state's finest still wines and a great deal of top quality sparkling wine, as well as the customary dessert and aperitif wines. The warm, southern coastal region is comprised of Santa Cruz and Monterey, with the adjoining inland counties of Santa Clara and San Benito; it provides table wines of note and still greater promise, and it is also the traditional centre of production for Californian sparkling wine. The hot central valley – principally a source of bulk wines, dessert wines and brandies – extends from Lodi and Sacramento in the north right down to Fresno and Bakersfield at the south end of the San Joaquin Valley; it takes in the Modesto, Ripon and Escalon districts on the way, ending up in Cucamonga and the outskirts of Los Angeles.

California thus provides a variety of micro-climates comparable to those experienced in vineyards situated across the entire breadth of Europe.

A terraced Californian vineyard, high in the foothills (Wine Institute of California)

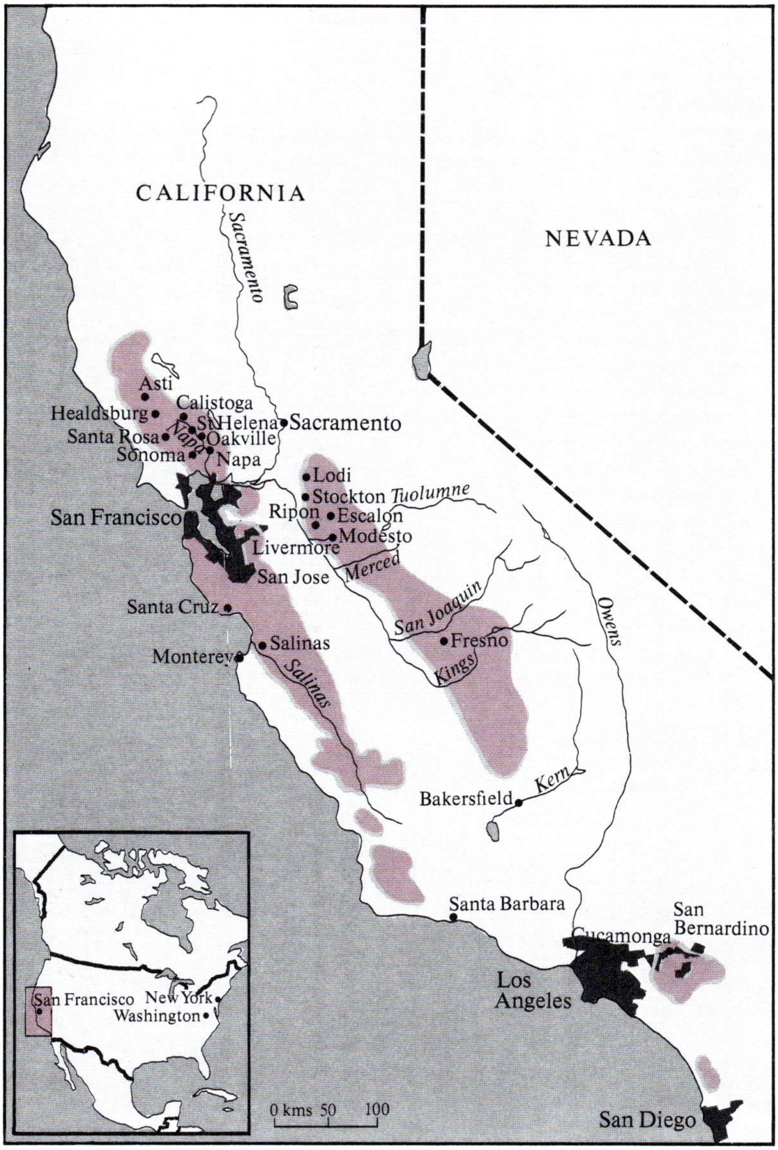

SAMPLE TASTINGS

To identify the distinctive styles which the mostly European grape varieties achieve in Californian conditions, two sample tastings (each selected, if possible, from the output of three-star wineries) are suggested:

Reds: Zinfandel
Petite Sirah
Pinot Noir
Cabernet Sauvignon

Whites: White or Johannisberg Riesling
Chenin or Fumé Blanc (dry)
Sauvignon Blanc
Chardonnay
Late Harvest White Riesling or
Chenin Blanc

The character of each is determined not so much by its latitude, or by the amount of the sunshine which is an ever-present friend to Californian wine-growers, as by the particular geographic relationship of its vineyards to the Pacific on one flank and the mountain ranges on the other. The department of oenology in the University of California at Davis has established boundaries for the state's five climatic regions, as specified in the column on page 165.

In each case the number of degree-days of sunshine is measured by the average daily temperature above 50°F enjoyed by the region during the growing season from April until September. Thus five days with an average daily temperature of 60°F would register 5 x 10° = 50 degree-days. The region in which each vineyard is located gives some indication of the nature of the wines it produces. Region II for instance, as might be expected,

Checking the fermentation at Louis Martini's winery in Napa County (Wine Institute of California)

PEPPERCORN ★ RATINGS

It is particularly difficult to assess individual ratings for Californian wineries at present, because of the speed at which the State is developing: it is as though the *Guide Michelin* was awarding rosettes in a new country. Certainly, some of the three-star wineries are likely to become four- or even five-star in the foreseeable future – but for the time being it is necessary to adopt a conservative approach.

In the case of some of the largest wineries a range of stars is shown: a single rating could be either unfair or over-generous. In no case should the ratings be taken as referring to 'jug' wines: they apply only to the so-called premium wines or varietals.

is most favourable to California's leading varietal, the Cabernet Sauvignon.

Such inferences can be misleading, however, since it must be remembered that a vineyard or winery may buy in some or all of its grapes from some quite different area. Fruit can be very swiftly harvested and transported to another district for fermenting and finishing, and provided that the place where the grapes were grown lies within the same state as the winery it is permissible to quote the name of that place on the label.

CALIFORNIA GAZETTEER

★ Peppercorn rating
● Noteworthy reds
○ Noteworthy whites
⊘ Noteworthy *rosés*
Ⓢ Noteworthy sparkling wines

North of San Francisco: Alameda (Al), Livermore (L), Mendocino (M), Napa (N), Solano (Sol), Sonoma (Son).

Alexander Valley Vineyards (*Son, Healdsburg*) ★★ A new winery, with its first crush in 1975, producing a stunning ★★★ Chardonnay, sold surprisingly cheaply. A tart, attractive, slightly sweet Johannisberg Riesling is not in the same class.

Beaulieu Vineyard (*N*) ★/★★ A large winery with over 250,000 cases output. Set up at the end of the last century by French immigrant Georges de Latour, it has been owned since 1969 by Heublein. Had an outstanding reputation especially for Cabernet Sauvignon which it still retains, but has otherwise latterly been disappointing. Red, white, rosé, sparkling, apéritif and dessert wines are all made. Georges de Latour Cabernet Sauvignon Private Reserve is 100 per cent varietal and still the flagship wine. Pinot Noir, Chardonnay and Johannisberg Riesling of lesser quality are also produced.

Beringer Vineyards (*N, St Helena*) ★★/★★★ Jacob Beringer, a native of Rheingau, founded the vineyard in 1876; bought by Nestlé in 1970, it is now owned by La Bruyère of Macon. Produces jug and premium wines, the former under the Los Hermanos label, including red, white and sparkling blends from French, German and Italian grapes on 1,800 acres. Output increasingly centred on varietals under the Beringer label, of which the following are good. ● Zinfandel, Cabernet Sauvignon ○ Fumé Blanc, Johannisberg Riesling, Chardonnay, Gewürztraminer.

Buena Vista Winery (*Son*) ★★ One of the best-known Sonoma Valley wineries. Originally the property of the legendary Col. Agoston Haraszthy, now in the ownership of the German firm of A. Racke since 1979. Premium wines are sold from a range of red, white and rosé varietals, and there are sparkling, apéritif and dessert wines. Extensive new plantings in the Carneros region already show improvement in the whites. ● Cabernet Sauvignon, Zinfandel, Pinot Noir ○ Gewürztraminer, Fumé Blanc (their best wines at present).

Burgess Cellars (*N, St Helena*) ★★★ Like many other small cellars, Burgess buys fine, specially selected grapes from independent growers. Cabernet Sauvignons are more subtle than some, especially the Vintage Selection; the Zinfandel is good and the Petite Syrah has potential. Johannisberg Riesling is promising, both regular and late-picked; and there are small lots of Chardonnay, Chenin Blanc and Pinot Noir.

Bynum Winery (*Son*) ★★ Wines are sold either as Bynum or Davis Bynum, the name of the owner, a former newspaperman, who set up the firm in 1965. A number of varietal wines, with largely bought-in grapes, are made on the Russian River near Healdsburg. ● Cabernet Sauvignon, Zinfandel, Pinot Noir ○ Gewürztraminer, Chardonnay, Fumé Blanc.

Cakebread Cellars (*N*) ★★ A small outfit offering four wines by mail order, its reputation firmly based on its own-grown Sauvignon Blanc. Good-quality Cabernet is made from Stag's Leap vineyard grapes, and Chardonnay from Trefethen. The fourth, Zinfandel, is a wine of great intensity.

Cambiaso Winery and Vineyards (*Son*) ★ Started in 1934 by an Italian family, but bought up and substantially enlarged more recently by a firm of Thai distillers, Likitprakong. Cabernet Sauvignon and Petite Sirah come from vineyards adjoining the winery; other grapes are bought in.

Carneros Creek Winery (*N*) ★★/★★★ A winery constructed in 1973 and expanded in 1978 at the southernmost end of the Napa Valley, to concentrate on Carneros-grown Pinot Noir and Chardonnay wines. Both are of fine quality, particularly the former. Highly rated Zinfandel and Cabernet Sauvignon are also produced, the Zinfandel from St Joaquin Valley (Amador) grapes, the Cabernet from Stag's Leap in Napa Valley.

Caymus Vineyards (*N*) ★★/★★★ Half the 70-acre estate, east of Rutherford, is given up to Pinot Noir grapes, from which in addition to red, a white Oeil de Perdrix is made. Charles Wagner's reputation rests equally on a top-quality, rich and well-balanced Cabernet Sauvignon, and he has a potentially great Sauvignon Blanc. Zinfandel is made from Amador grapes; there is some Chardonnay.

Chappellet Vineyard (*N, St Helena*) ★★/★★★ Capable of making 25,000 cases of wine a year, Chappellet was started in the late 1960s by an ex-industrialist who now concentrates on six varieties only: ○ Chenin Blanc, Johannisberg Riesling, Chardonnay ● Cabernet Sauvignon, Merlot, Gamay.

Château Montelena (*N, Calistoga*) ★★★ Wines are grown in the Napa and Alexander valleys; about half the company's needs are supplied by their own vineyards, planted mostly with Cabernet Sauvignon and Zinfandel. Cabernet Sauvignons are made for keeping, Zinfandels are fruity and full of flavour; there is a rich Chardonnay, resembling a fine white Côte de Beaune, and an early-bottled Johannisberg Riesling, fresh and fruity. These are wines of great balance and breed.

Château St Jean (*Son, Kenwood*) ★★★/★★★★ Brand new winery that has already made a notable impact for the remarkable (four star) quality of its Late Harvest Johannisberg Rieslings. Chardonnays, too, have great breed. The other whites, on which the winery concentrates, are Sauvignon Blanc and Gewürztraminer. There are small amounts of Cabernet Sauvignon and Zinfandel. Seventy per cent of the grapes are bought in from the Sonoma, Alexander and Napa Valleys. Wine-maker Richard Arrowood has established a fine standard and a fine reputation.

The Christian Brothers (*N*) ★★ The large vineyards of this well-known concern, a religious order of Brothers, lie eight miles to the north-east of Napa itself, alongside the Novitiate at Mont La Salle. Profits from the business support the Novitiate. They also own the Reedley vineyards in Fresno County in the hot central valley, and wineries at St Helena, where they produce dessert wines and brandies. They sell generic and varietal, red, white and sparkling wines under their label, of good, middling quality. The varietals are all blends of varying complexity, mostly non-vintage. Château La Salle is a brand name given to a light, sweet wine made mainly of Muscat grapes. There is an interesting red Pinot St George, a Napa Fumé and Pineau de la Loire, all estate-bottled.

Clos du Bois (*Son*) ★★ This Healdsburg-based company produces three estate whites and two estate reds. Gewürztraminer and Johannisberg Riesling, its best two, with Chardonnay come from Alexander Valley vineyards; the Chardonnay is rather full-blown in style. Cabernet Sauvignon, blended with some Merlot, and Pinot Noir are from Dry Creek Valley.

Clos du Val (*N, Yountville, Silverado Trail*) ★★★ Another new winery that has already acquired a considerable reputation, largely thanks to the efforts of Bernard Portet, its wine-maker – he is the son of a former *régisseur* at Lafite. Cabernet Sauvignons and Zinfandels are wines of class and concentration, though sometimes they show too much oak influence. His more recently introduced Chardonnay is increasingly good.

Concannon Vineyards (*L*) ★ Ownership of the vineyard went out of the hands of the third generation of Concannons in 1980, when it was bought by the former President of Paul Masson, Agustin Huneeus. Extensive planting of its 300 acres has made possible a range of varietal wines with an output of some 75,000 cases a year. Petite Sirah produces an attractive varietal red. ● Cabernet Sauvignon, Petite Sirah ○ Sauvignon Blanc, Sauternes, Johannisberg Riesling ⊘ Zinfandel Rosé Ⓢ Concannon Brut Extra Dry.

Conn Creek (*N*) ★★★ Small winery with new cellars near Rutherford, built in 1979, five years after its first emergence. Concentrates on three varietals, Chardonnay, Zinfandel and Cabernet Sauvignon. The Cabernet is classic Napa Valley and attracted immediate attention on its first appearance in 1974. In 1981 the Dewavrin-Woltners of La Mission Haut Brion acquired a 25 per cent stake.

Cresta Blanca Winery (*M*) ★ Once had a good reputation for quality wines, but now part of a larger group, Guild of Lodi, which markets non-vintage blended wines of a good but unremarkable standard. There are moves to produce fine wines under the Cresta Blanca label from Zinfandel, Petite Sirah and Pinot Noir among others.

Cuvaison (*N*) ★★ Purchased by a Zurich banker in 1979, it at present makes relatively small quantities of good quality Chardonnay, Cabernet Sauvignon and Zinfandel, all of them very alcoholic wines. Output of Chardonnay will increase when plantings on a newly purchased 400-acre vineyard in Carneros mature.

Domaine Chandon (*N*) ★★★ Remarkable new venture of Moët and Chandon in 1973, already making very fine wines, with more bouquet than seen before in Californian champagnes. Chandon Napa Valley Brut and Chandon Blanc de Noirs were introduced in 1976 – now labelled as *méthode champenoise*.

Dry Creek Vineyards (*Son, Healdsburg*) ★★★ A small new Californian winery started in 1972 with some 50 acres. It is already producing really good white wines with promise of being even better, and some good-quality reds. ○ Chardonnay, Chenin Blanc, Fumé Blanc ● Gamay, Zinfandel, Cabernet Sauvignon.

Edmeades Vineyards (*M*) ★★ A 35-acre vineyard and winery centred in the cool, coastal region of Anderson Valley. Cabernet Sauvignon can be good, but the growing season is unpredictable. Chardonnay, Gewürztraminer and Zinfandel are its other varietals, and a French Colombard which makes an 'ice wine'. The whites are clean with high acidity.

Fetzer Vineyards (*M*) ★★ A once small Mendocino family winery, which built up its reputation on red varietals, particularly Zinfandels. Still in the same ownership, it has enormously expanded its output and offers a wide range of reds and whites. ● Cabernet Sauvignon, Pinot Noir, Zinfandel, Petite Sirah ○ Chardonnay, Sauvignon Blanc, Gewürztraminer, Johannisberg Riesling.

Fisher Vineyards (*Son*) Small Santa Rosa 1979 venture. Has made a start with a commendable Chardonnay and a Cabernet Sauvignon.

Foppiano Wine Company (*Son, Healdsburg*) ★ The produce of 200 acres, previously used to supply bulk wine, now goes to making premium varietals. Still in family hands, the firm specializes in ● Cabernet Sauvignon, Petite Sirah and Pinot Noir ○ Chardonnay, Chenin Blanc, French Colombard, Sonoma Fumé.

Franciscan Vineyards (*N*) New German owners, Peter Eckes, In 1979, are seeking to capitalize on Justin Meyer's wine-making, with a range of table wines, both generics and varietals.

Freemark Abbey Winery (*N*) ★★★ A recently restored winery, which within a decade has established a fine reputation for high-quality varietals. The Johannisberg Riesling Edelwein, from botrytized grapes, resembles Rheingau *Beerenauslese* of the finest quality. ● Cabernet Sauvignon, Petite Sirah ○ Chardonnay, Johannisberg Riesling.

Geyser Peak Winery (*Son*) ★ In 1980 Geyser Peak celebrated its 100th anniversary, but only began to attract interest after 1972 when it was taken over by Schiltz Brewing Company of Milwaukee. Pinot Noir, Gewürztraminer and Fumé Blanc are now offered in a trend towards better varietal wines. As yet they remain pretty ordinary, but 625 acres of new planting and a 600,000-case capacity hold out promise.

Grand Cru Vineyards (*Son*) ★★ Another vineyard of promise, not from size but from experimentation. Excellent straight Gewürztraminer, as well as a botrytized version; Zinfandel straight and late-harvested; a well-made Chenin Blanc and a promising Cabernet Sauvignon. There are new plantings of Sauvignon Blanc.

Grgich Hills Cellars (*N*) ★★★ Named for the winemaker and the owner respectively, this new (1977) winery looks for highest-quality varietal flavour and aroma in its wines. Concentration is mainly on Chardonnay, and on Johannisberg Riesling, with a smaller quantity of finely made Zinfandel.

Gundlach-Bundschu Winery (*Son*) ★★/★★★ A famous 19th-century winery which began a new lease of life in 1973. Production is now 25,000–30,000 cases. The 1977 Cabernet Sauvignon showed what the winery was capable of; while good Chardonnay, Zinfandel and Merlot are also made. A curiosity is the Kleinberger, better known as the Elbling of the Upper Mosel.

Hacienda Wine Cellars (*Son*) ★★ A winery with a small, quality output in the cool foothills of the Mayacamas Mountains in Sonoma Valley. Chardonnay, Johannisberg Riesling and Cabernet Sauvignon are grown there. Zinfandel is grown in the warmest part of Sonoma at Cloverdale. Consistent, often above average, wines.

Hanzell Vineyards (*Son*) ★★★ The development of Hanzell is a saga of idealism. It has pointed the way for other wineries in California by planting its 20 acres with Pinot Noir and Chardonnay vines, on the pattern of the fine vineyards of Burgundy; it has also introduced the use of barrels made of French oak, which transmits a special characteristic to the wine. A four-acre planting of Cabernet Sauvignon wines has also been made. ● Pinot Noir ○ Chardonnay (both estate-bottled).

Heitz Wine Cellars (*N, St Helena*) ★★★/★★★★ A name associated by many with the finest Californian wines, especially Cabernet Sauvignon and Chardonnay; it is a family concern, built up over the last 15 years by a graduate of oenology from the University of California at Davis. Red and white varietals are made to exacting standards, from grapes largely bought in from leading Napa vineyards; they are sold as Heitz Cellar, often as vintages. Some are rated among the best in the state, with enormous individual character. The very best Cabernet Sauvignons, from the legendary Martha's Vineyard, have great intensity of flavour, reminiscent of wild spearmint or even eucalyptus. ● Cabernet Sauvignon, Pinot Noir (rare), Barbera, Grignolino ○ Chardonnay, Pinot Blanc (rare), Johannisberg Riesling ⊘ Grignolino Rosé.

Inglenook Vineyard (*N, Rutherford*) ★/★★ Founded by a Finnish seafarer, Inglenook is now part of the Heublein Corporation and is one of the largest premium wineries in the state. The original vineyard pioneered the introduction of quality varietal and *rosé* wines in California. On size of output and past record, half a dozen wines from a wide and variable range might, at their best, be considered among the leaders. The Cabernet Sauvignon cask wines (blended with some Merlot) have breed and elegance. ● Cabernet Sauvignon, Pinot Noir, Gamay, Charbono (a sharp, full-bodied wine from an Italian varietal) ○ White Pinot (from the Chenin Blanc), Traminer.

Iron Horse Ranch & Vineyards (*Son*) ★ One of the more recent Sonoma wineries, in the lower Russian River Valley. Concentration is on Chardonnay and Pinot Noir, with Cabernet Sauvignon (from Alexander Valley).

Italian Swiss Colony (*Son, Russian River Valley*) This winery at Asti (after the town in Piedmont) is chiefly notable for its enormous capacity (eight million gallons); it is now part of United Vintners, the main wine-producing division of the Heublein Corporation. Most of the wines put out under the ISC label are of medium quality and inexpensive.

Jordan Vineyard & Winery (*Son*) ★★★ Established in 1976 to produce a top-class Bordeaux-style Cabernet Sauvignon/Merlot blend, the wine was first released in 1980 to much acclaim and great promise. Future wines are to be aged for five years before release. A Chardonnay is also made.

Kenwood Vineyards (*Son*) ★★ Varietal wines with emphasis on reds to date; future production is aimed at more classic style, vineyard-designated wines ● Cabernet Sauvignon, Zinfandel ○ Chardonnay.

F. Korbel & Brothers (*Son, Russian River Valley*) ★★ The brothers who gave their name to the firm emigrated from Czechoslovakia in the 1860s. The winery, now in different hands, still concentrates on the production of the highest quality sparkling wines, primarily from Pinot Noir, Pinot Blanc, Chardonnay, French Colombard and Sauvignon Blanc grapes. Their Californian champagnes, made by the *méthode champenoise*, share the honours with Schramsberg and Domaine Chandon among the State's leading sparkling wines; they also produce some good estate bottled vintage varietals. Ⓢ Korbel Natural, Blanc de Noirs, Blanc de Blanc, Brut, Extra Dry, Sec, Rosé (semi-dry), Rouge.

Hanns Kornell Champagne Cellars (*N, St Helena*) ★ The emphasis in this family business, named after its founder, is on the production by the *méthode champenoise* of high quality sparkling wines; these are based on Sylvaner and Riesling, and must figure in any list of outstanding Californian generic champagnes. Ⓢ Third Generation Sehr Trocken, Brut and Extra Dry (crisp, light and fruity), Third Generation Pink Champagne, Third Generation Sparkling Burgundy.

Charles Krug Winery (*N, St Helena*) ★★ The firm retains the name of its 19th-century founder (there is no connection with the French Champagne concern); but it is now owned and operated by Peter Mondavi, and is one of the largest family-held wineries in the Napa Valley. Production is primarily of premium wines, generics and red, white and rosé varietals. ● Cabernet Sauvignon, Zinfandel, Gamay ○ Chenin Blanc, Sauvignon Blanc (sweet), Gewürztraminer, Grey Riesling ⊘ Vin Rosé (from Gamay grapes).

Lambert Bridge (*Son*) ★★ Eighty-acre vineyard in Dry Creek Valley given over since 1975 to making high-quality value-for-money Cabernet Sauvignon and Chardonnay. The red is big-bodied, the Chardonnay somewhat severe when young; both are made for ageing. Some Pinot Noir and Johannisberg Riesling is also being grown.

Mill Creek Vineyards (*Son*) ★★ Like Mark West, a small Russian River Valley concern, starting out in 1976, with wine from their own grapes; Cabernet Sauvignon, Pinot Noir, Merlot and Chardonnay, in soft, delicate styles.

Louis M. Martini (*N, St Helena*) ★★/★★★ One of the largest Californian wineries still in family hands, owning 850 acres in Napa and Sonoma. Martini's varietals, which are all vintage wines, are rated among the finest quality table wines in California and offer very good value. One of the vineyards is high in the Mayacamas Mountains, dividing Napa from Sonoma, and the best of their wines are known as 'Mountain'.

● Cabernet Sauvignon, Cabernet Sauvignon Special Reserve, Mountain Zinfandel (medium-bodied), Mountain Pinot Noir, Mountain Barbera ○ Mountain Dry Sémillon, Mountain Pinot Chardonnay, Mountain Dry Chenin Blanc, Folle Blanche (crisp, white), Mountain Johannisberg Riesling, Mountain Gewürztraminer.

Martini & Prati (*Son, Santa Rosa*) The second largest winery in Sonoma County, and one of the oldest, produces little bottled wine, although it also owns the Fountain Grove label which once had a quality reputation.

Mayacamas Vineyards (*N*) ★★★ The Mayacamas range divides Napa and Sonoma. Four outstanding Californian varietal wines, each made exclusively from the one named grape, come from this 2,000ft high vineyard. ● Cabernet Sauvignon, Zinfandel ○ Sémillon/Sauvignon (sweet, botrytized), Chardonnay, Chenin Blanc ⊘ Zinfandel Rosé.

Robert Mondavi Winery (*N, Oakville*) ★★★★ A winery with over 600 acres of vines taken up and developed as a show-place vineyard in the 1960s by Robert Mondavi. Output has rocketed towards one million cases, including a proportion of popular table wines; but a reputation for experimentation and for volume production of fine wines has also been established, in keeping with the owner's personal standing and fame. Premium wines of a quality which constantly seems to surpass itself now account for some 400,000 cases. A recent joint enterprise with Baron Philippe, owner of Château Mouton-Rothschild, has produced two Napa vintages, so far unnamed, but known unofficially as 'Mouton-Mondavi'. ● Cabernet Sauvignon, Gamay, Petite Sirah, Pinot Noir, Zinfandel (*rosé* as well as red) ○ Chardonnay (soft and delicate), Fumé Blanc (Sauvignon with some Sémillon – particularly commendable), Chenin Blanc, Johannisberg Riesling, Traminer.

Mount Veeder Winery (*N*) ★★ A very small winery 1,000ft up Mount Veeder in the Mayascamas mountains. The 4,500-case output is almost entirely Cabernet Sauvignon, which is made with a proportion of Cabernet Franc, Merlot, Malbec and Petite Verdot. The best is from the Bernstein Vineyard named after the owner. There is also some dry Chenin Blanc and late-harvest Zinfandel.

Nichelini Vineyards (*N, St Helena*) This winery, established by a Swiss immigrant in 1890, is still a family business. A range of red and white varietals is made. ● Zinfandel ○ Sauvignon Vert.

Parducci Wine Cellars (*M*) ★★★ A 350-acre family concern which has responded to a growing market for good-quality wine by concentrating on the production of dry, vintage-dated varietals; rounded reds and fresh, young, whites, backed up by a range of generic wines. ● Cabernet Sauvignon (delicious, balanced, clean-tasting), Petite Sirah, Zinfandel ○ Chenin Blanc, French Colombard, Chardonnay.

J. Pedroncelli (*Son, Russian River Valley*) ★★★ A family winery acquired in 1927. The 135-acre vineyards have been progressively replanted with classic varietals – Pinot Noir, Cabernet Sauvignon, Zinfandel, Gamay, White Riesling, Chardonnay and Gewürztraminer. The wines are made only from local grapes, two-thirds of which are bought in, and the varietals are declared vintages.

Joseph Phelps (*N*) ★★★/★★★★ A very high-quality winery indeed, making a range of red and white varietals, each in small quantity, in the main from its own 170-acre vineyard east of St Helena. The Johannisberg Riesling Late-Harvested wines (by Walter Schug, a graduate of the Geisenheim Institute) are miracles of wine-making equal to the best from Germany. Zinfandels are gutsy and alcoholic. Phelps' longer term belief is in the emergence of Sirah as an important Californian variety. ● Cabernet Sauvignon, Sirah, Zinfandel ○ Gewürztraminer, Sauvignon Blanc, Chardonnay, Johannisberg Riesling.

Raymond Vineyards (*N*) ★★ Off the mark in 1974, its early reputation rested on a fine botrytized Johannisberg Riesling. Plantings on 80 acres extend to Cabernet Sauvignon, Chardonnay, Gamay, Chenin Blanc and Zinfandel. Chardonnay and Gamay are good, the Cabernet soft and complex.

Rutherford Hill Winery (*N*) ★★/★★★ A recent venture, instead of finding a second winery for Freemark Abbey, by some of the partners. There are high hopes for its Zinfandel; a spicy Gewürztraminer and Limousin oak-aged Chardonnay are its best whites, with a dry Johannisberg Riesling. Its Cabernet has 20 per cent Merlot, and there is also an attractive straight Merlot. 1978 reds are a big improvement on previous vintages.

St Clement Vineyards (*N*) ★★ Cabernet Sauvignon and Chardonnay only are made from a small quantity of home-grown together with carefully selected local grapes. Wines made since 1975 have already established a high reputation and price, and need ageing. Sauvignon Blanc is a planned addition.

Schramsberg Vineyards (*N, Calistoga*) ★★★ A small old-established winery in the Upper Napa Valley, reorganized in 1965, and devoted to the production of sparkling wines by the *méthode champenoise*. Its wines became famous in 1972 when the former President Nixon took some on his state visit to China. The wines, sharp, crisp, dry and elegant, had already achieved a leading place among Californian champagnes. Ⓢ Blanc de Blancs (from Chardonnay and Pinot Blanc), Cuvée de Pinot (Napa Gamay and Pinot Noir), Blanc de Noir (Pinot Noir and Chardonnay), Crémant (dessert).

Sebastiani Vineyards (*Son*) ★★ One of the largest wine producers in the whole of California, with a capacity of some five million gallons, Sebastiani is still operated by the family of the man who founded it in 1904. Most of the grapes are bought from local growers to produce some 20 different types of table wine, aperitif, dessert wine and vermouth. ● Cabernet Sauvignon (well-aged), Gamay Nouveau (sold six weeks after making), Barbera.

Simi Winery (*Son*) ★★ A small winery, now expanding, originating from 1876, which makes interesting premium wines. Once owned by the British firm, Scottish and Newcastle Breweries, who have now sold their interest. ● Cabernet Sauvignon, Zinfandel ○ Gewürztraminer.

Sonoma Vineyards (*Son, Windsor*) ★★/★★★ A huge and rapidly expanding winery, owned 51 per cent by Renfield Importers, with an area of more than 1,500 acres, a three-million-gallon capacity, and a thriving business selling wines by mail order. Its output is of no more than average quality, but it could in the future make a significant contribution to the list of leading Californian wines. Johannisberg Rieslings are produced from the River West Vineyard; Cabernet and vineyard-designated Chardonnays are of improving quality.

Souverain of Alexander Valley (*N, Son, M*) ★★ Owned by an association of vineyard proprietors from Napa, Sonoma and Mendocino, said to represent 80 per cent of the growers in these three counties. ● Cabernet Sauvignon ○ Colombard.

Spring Mountain Vineyards (*N, St Helena*) ★★★ A near neighbour of Charles Krug, but a distinct contrast; a small, developing venture, started in the 1960s with a limited range of varietal wines. Great quality is being achieved, expressing the flavour of the individual grape. ● Cabernet Sauvignon, Pinot Noir ○ Sauvignon Blanc, Chardonnay.

Stag's Leap Wine Cellars (*N*) ★★★ Built in 1972, this is a perfectionist winery. It produces outstandingly good Cabernet Sauvignon (which contains some Merlot), also good Johannisberg Riesling and Gamay. Chardonnay has now been introduced.

Stag's Leap Winery (*N*) ★★ Not to be confused with Stag's Leap Wine Cellars. Owner Carl Doumani's prime interest is in Petite Sirah and Chenin Blanc.

Sterling (*N, Calistoga*) ★★★ A modern winery, owned since 1977 by Coca-Cola, which aims to achieve wines of the highest quality from grapes grown only in its own vineyards. The Reserve Cabernets are of particular note. ● Cabernet Sauvignon, Merlot ○ Chardonnay, Sauvignon Blanc, Chenin Blanc.

Stone Creek (*Son*) ★ A modern winery near Geyserville in Sonoma Valley, owned by a San Francisco-based distributor dealing in cheaper North Coast wines. Now offers premium varietals from Cabernet Sauvignon, Pinot Noir, Zinfandel, Chardonnay and an attractive light white, French Colombard.

Stony Hill Vineyard (*N, St Helena*) ★★★ An outstanding example of a small winery, making carefully vinified white wines all of great delicacy; the vines are planted on 38 ideally sited acres, high on the Napa Valley hillside. ○ Chardonnay, White Riesling, Gewürztraminer, Sémillon.

Sutter Home Winery (*N, St Helena*) ★★ A small winery which has made its specialism Zinfandels, including a white one, with grapes from Amador County in the Sierra foothills, outside the Napa Valley. Many Zinfandels in California are light wines for early drinking, but Sutter's are big and alcoholic; they have plenty of tannin and need ageing.

Joseph Swan Vineyard (*Son, Trenton*) ★★★ The enterprise of an ex-airline pilot, who found the householder's limit of 200 gallons too restrictive, this vineyard has begun to make a name for its deep-tasting, full-bodied Zinfandels and Pinot Noirs. It is personally and meticulously directed by the owner.

Trefethen Vineyards (*N*) ★★★ The second oldest wooden winery in the Napa Valley, restored to service in 1968 by the Trefethen family. Six hundred acres are mainly planted with Pinot Noir and Chardonnay, with some Cabernet Sauvignon, White Riesling, Gewürztraminer, Zinfandel and Merlot. Grapes are sold to other leading Napa wineries, and Trefethen's own output is not that large. Its first, 1976, Chardonnay attracted world-wide attention through a Paris tasting; its reds also have character and distinction. Eschol Red (the original vineyard name) is a Cabernet/Merlot/Mondeuse (Italian Refosco) blend.

Veedercrest Vineyards (*N, Emeryville*) ★★ A youthful winery, but already its Chardonnay from the Alexander Valley has shown its quality New plantings in a 100-acre vineyard on Mount Veeder.

Weibel Champagne Vineyards (*Al*) ★ The ambitions of the Swiss founder in 1939 were clearly stated in the name of his winery. Weibel, 40 miles south-east of San Francisco, is now established as a producer of Californian champagnes, and branching out into vintage dated varietals.

Wente Bros (*L*) ★★★ Wente Bros have some 1,400 acres and a reputation for producing some of the finest of American white wines. Despite a German ancestry, they concentrate on French-style wines, among them a sweet Sauternes, from Sémillon, Sauvignon and Muscadelle stocks acquired direct from Château d'Yquem in France. There are extensive new plantings of red and white grape vines in Monterey, especially Pinot Noir and Grey Riesling for which Wente is known throughout the United States.

Mark West Vineyards (*Son*) ★★ A family enterprise which produced its first wines in 1976. There are plantings of Pinot Noir, Chardonnay, Gewürztraminer and Johannisberg Riesling. The wines, made in Burgundian and Alsatian styles, have yet to achieve a consistent standard.

ZD Wines (*Son*) ★★★ A small winery started by two engineers (one the production manager at Domaine Chandon). They make an attractive Pinot Noir from the cooler Region I around Carneros in the Napa Valley, as well as Chardonnays, Rieslings and Gewürztraminers, aged in oak.

South of San Francisco Bay: The Central Coast, Monterey (Mon), Riverside (R), Santa Clara (S. Cl), Santa Barbara (S. Bar).

Almadén (*S. Cl, Los Gatos*) ★/★★ Almadén has grown since 1941 into one of the largest premium wine producers in the United States. The winery is supplied from 7,000 acres of vineyard in four Californian counties, and buys in from 8,000 more acres. A subsidiary of the National Distillers Company since 1967, it can claim a number of leading wines in a list of over 40 varieties. Mountain Red is a very well-distributed branded wine. ● Cabernet Sauvignon, Pinot Noir ○ Dry Sémillon, Pinot Chardonnay, Pinot Blanc, Johannisberg Riesling, Gewürztraminer, Sylvaner, Grey Riesling ⦶ Grenache Rosé Ⓢ Blanc de Blancs, Brut Champagne, Rose Pink Champagne, Sparkling Burgundy.

David Bruce (*S. Cl*) ★★/★★★ A small, personal venture which has created a wider than local demand for varietal wines made in an individual style. ○ Chardonnay ● Pinot Noir, Cabernet Sauvignon, Zinfandel.

Callaway Vineyard (*R, Temecula*) ★★ A new and bold experiment in producing quality wines in southern California, where fortified styles have hitherto been the norm. The vineyards have been carefully sited to profit from a beneficial micro-climate, and some most promising wines have been produced by the talented new wine-maker, Stephen O'Donnell. Two specialities are Sweet Nancy, a late-harvest Chenin Blanc of fine quality, and Noël, a Zinfandel wine produced by *maceration carbonique* and bottled in December for immediate drinking. ● Zinfandel, Petite Sirah, Cabernet Sauvignon ○ Chenin Blanc, Sauvignon Blanc, Fumé Blanc (a Sauvignon with some residual sugar), Chardonnay.

Chalone Vineyards (*Mon*) ★★★ A small winery and vineyard, 2,000ft up in the Gavilan Mountains, taken up by the present owner in 1966. The combination of difficult conditions and chalk soils, coupled with skilled attention to wine-making, resulted in a small output of high-quality white wine, Chardonnay, Pinot Blanc and Chenin Blanc, based on a Burgundian ideal. Subsequently Richard Graff has produced a fine dark Pinot Noir of great complexity.

Durney Vineyards (*Mon*) ★★/★★★ Cabernet Sauvignon is made on the steep slopes of the Carmel Valley overlooking the Pacific, in a special microclimate which produces a very fine wine. There are also small quantities of Gamay, Chenin Blanc and Johannisberg Riesling.

Firestone Vineyard (*S. Bar*) ★★★ A new vineyard started in the Santa Ynez Valley in 1972 by Leonard Firestone (then US embassador to Belgium, hence the name of its premier Ambassador Vineyard). It has acquired an enviable reputation in the short time since its first wines came onto the market in 1975; one of the best Californian Pinot Noirs, a fine Cabernet Sauvignon and Merlot, a prize-winning Chardonnay; Gewürztraminer, both regular and late-harvest, and a stunning late-harvest Johannisberg Riesling in 1976. A part interest is owned by Suntory of Japan, and the 300-acre estate is run by Brookes and Kate Firestone.

Hoffman Mountain Ranch (*San Luis Obispo*) ★ A 60-acre estate in Region III climatic conditions, concentrating on Pinot Noir and Chardonnay. Both have body and richness and are intended for ageing. Some Cabernet and Zinfandel is also made.

Jekel Vineyard (*Mon*) ★★★ Jekel emerged in 1978 with exceptionally good white wines, which included a very fine, delicate, late-harvest Johannisberg Riesling and a well-balanced Chardonnay. The 140-acre vineyard in Salinas Valley also provides quality Cabernet Sauvignon and Pinot Noir, some of which is diverted to make a light Beaujolais-style red.

Paul Masson Vineyards (*S. Cl*) ★★/★★★ Paul Masson's is a name associated in California and elsewhere with high standards in still and sparkling table wines – both generics and varietals – as well as dessert wines and brandies. The vineyards are now owned by Seagram, and the wines are exported to some 50 overseas countries. The original Paul Masson was a Burgundian; he came to California in the 19th century, applying himself to fine champagnes and table wines on a site in the Santa Cruz mountains above Saratoga, where the best wines are still cellared. The grapes for many of the Masson varietals are now grown in newer vineyards acquired in Monterey; their Pinnacles Vineyards wines are extraordinarily good, especially the spicy, floral Gewürztraminer. ● Cabernet Sauvignon, Pinot Noir, Gamay Beaujolais ○ Château Masson (a sweet Sémillon of the Sauternes type), Gewürztraminer Ⓢ Paul Masson Brut, Extra Dry, Pink Champagne, Sparkling Burgundy.

Mirassou Vineyards (*S. Cl*) ★★/★★★ A winery which previously produced grapes for the bulk wine industry but now concentrates on premium wines that are among the best in California. Varietals contain very nearly 100 per cent of the grape on the label. Mirassou mostly use their own grapes from over 1,000 acres of Santa Clara and Monterey (the labels say which) to market about 120 high-quality wines. ● Zinfandel, Cabernet Sauvignon (with a wonderfully concentrated '*cassis*' flavour) ○ White Riesling, Monterey Riesling (Sylvaner), Fleuri Blanc (sweet Gewürztraminer), Chenin Blanc, Chardonnay Ⓢ Mirassou 'Au Naturel', Brut.

The Monterey Vineyard (*Mon, Salinas Valley*) ★★ Owned by Coca-Cola, the Monterey Vineyard is fortunate in having a gifted wine-maker, Dr Richard Peterson, who is convinced that in cooler Monterey County some wines (notably Pinot Noir) can be more successful than in the Napa Valley. The Merlot is promising, but it is the December Harvest Zinfandel which is remarkable, with enormous depth of flavour and fruit; as is the botrytized Sauvignon Blanc.

Mount Eden Vineyards (*S. Cl*) ★★ Small quantities of much-sought-after wines come from this 22-acre hillside vineyard in the Santa Cruz mountains. Chardonnay, Pinot Noir and Cabernet Sauvignon are all big, rich wines which demand time to develop.

Novitiate of Los Gatos (*S. Cl*) ★ The vineyards of this Jesuit order, in the hills above Los Gatos, are not in the same commercial league as The Christian Brothers of Napa Valley, but they are becoming more competitive and are increasing their output. Of special interest for connoisseurs is their Black Muscat, an exceptionally fine red dessert wine. ● Cabernet Sauvignon, Zinfandel, Pinot Noir ○ Chenin Blanc.

Ridge Vineyards (*S. Cl*) ★★★ A group of electronics engineers from Stanford

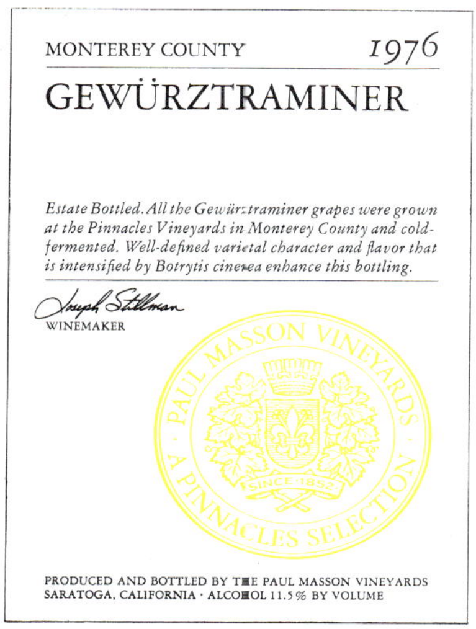

University took over and developed this old-established vineyard in the early 1960s, with the aim of producing robust, grapey varietal wines. Most of the grapes are bought in, and sources are shown on the labels. Ridge's own vineyard is on Montebello Ridge in the Santa Cruz Mountains. The Cabernet Sauvignon is incredibly dark and full-bodied, resulting from long maceration on the skins. Reds are better than whites. ● Petite Sirah, Cabernet Sauvignon, Zinfandel.

San Martin Winery (*Mon*) ★★Very clean, fresh wines. The whites show great crispness and style: the young Chenin Blancs have particular charm (unlike many in California), and are of the standard of very good Vouvray ● Soft Zinfandel and Gamay Beaujolais.

Sanford & Benedict Vineyards (*S. Bar*) ★★ A neighbour of Firestone in Santa Ynez Valley, owned by the two enthusiasts who give their names to the vineyard. They set out to make fine Pinot Noir and succeeded in doing so from their first vintage in 1976. They have accompanied this with a ripe, oak-matured Chardonnay, and some Cabernet Sauvignon and Johannisberg Riesling.

Santa Ynez Valley Winery (*S. Bar*) ★ Similar in size to Sandford & Benedict, that is 100-odd acres, and an intended 10,000-case output, the first vintage also in 1976. The partners concentrate on white wines: a notable Sauvignon Blanc, Chardonnay, Gewürztraminer, White Riesling and a white from Cabernet Sauvignon.

Turgeon & Lohr Winery (*Mon, San Jose*) ★★/★★★ Started in 1974. Plantings on 280 acres emphasize Chardonnay, Cabernet Sauvignon, White Riesling and Pinot Blanc. Excellent botrytized Johannisberg Rieslings and light, fruity Gamay *rosés*. The wines are sold as 'J. Lohr'.

Zaca Mesa Winery (*S. Bar*) ★ Yet another and even newer Santa Barbara winery, looking for an eventual output of 60,000 cases. First vintage from the winery was in 1978. Good whites from Chardonnay and Johannisberg Riesling and a full range of red varietals. Big new planting of Sauvignon Blanc, and experimental planting of Shiraz. The Pinot Noir has particular promise.

The central inland valley: San Bernardino (SB), San Joaquin (SJ), Stanislaus (St), Merced (Mer), Madera (Mad), Fresno (F).

Barengo Cellars (*SJ, Lodi*) Now a large Central Valley producer of jug wines and varietals. None of the latter is particularly outstanding, except perhaps the Ruby Cabernet (a red wine grape developed by Davis, University of California).

Brookside Vineyard (*SB*) The original vineyard was started around 1900 by a Piedmontese immigrant, Secondo Guasti, who also built and named his own town in what was then the Cucamonga desert. It came to the fore in the 1950s and 1960s and is now owned by a large Chicago food concern. The better wines are sold under the name Assumption Abbey. Holdings include a new vineyard in southern California with a micro-climatic Region III rating. ● Zinfandel, Petite Sirah.

Cucamonga Vineyard (*SB*) One of the few producers of any note in the Cucamonga area. Not large, but expanding to become so. Major concentration on sparkling wine by the Charmat process.

D'Agostini (*SJ, Lodi*) A 125-acre vineyard, specializing in robust red wines. ● Amador, Zinfandel.

Delicato Vineyards (*SJ*) An enormous concern, selling wines to other wineries in the state, but still managing to bottle approaching one million cases under its own label; still expanding. There is a wide range of generics and varietals.

East Side Winery (*SJ, Lodi*) A co-operative, and one of the largest wineries in the Lodi district. In business since 1934, it began to produce premium wines in 1962, having already established a fine reputation for brandy and dessert wines. Emerald Riesling and Ruby Cabernet are grown and bottled on the estate, the latter particularly noteworthy.

Ficklin Vineyards (*Mad*) A prestigious winery, specializing in fine port; and developing varietal wines from Emerald Riesling and Ruby Cabernet, sold only at the winery.

Joseph A. Filippi (*Mad*) A lively winery producing premium varietals and sparkling wines.

Franzia Brothers (*SJ, Escalon*) With Lamont (formerly Bear Mountain) and Gallo this is one of the three huge San Joaquin corporations. It is owned by Coca-Cola, and has a capacity of 20 million gallons. Sound, moderately priced generic wines are produced in bulk. ● Burgundy, Zinfandel.

E. & J. Gallo (*St, Modesto*) Modesto, where the two Gallo brothers started up in 1933, is in climatic Region V – but that gives no clue to the nature of their wines. They buy in selected grapes from an estimated 100,000 acres of vineyards all over California; from these, they aim to produce sound wines in bulk, tailored and blended to the American palate, marketing more than 40 different types (including bulk-fermented 'champagnes'). Among the better Gallo brands are their Hearty Burgundy, Chablis Blanc and, at the lower end of the market, their ubiquitous jug wines.

Much of the Gallo production takes place in the world's largest winery, at Livingston in Merced county; this contributes a staggering 93 million gallons to the company's total capacity of more than 200 million gallons. In response to the demand for better-made wines, a number of well-balanced varietals are also now being developed, among them Sauvignon Blanc, Ruby Cabernet and Zinfandel. Well-aged, very high quality premium wines from Chardonnay and Cabernet Sauvignon are expected to be available soon.

Giumarra Vineyards (*Kern*) A family-owned, bulk wine business with sales of one and a half million cases a year. Wines from the Region V, southern end of the San Joaquin Valley are now blended with Central Coast wines to produce low-cost drinkable generics, and a wide range of only slightly more expensive varietals. Among the latter are Cabernet Sauvignon, Zinfandel and Carnelian, and whites from Chardonnay and Johannisberg Riesling.

Guild Wine Co (*SJ, Lodi*) The third largest producer in the United States, with a capacity of nearly 60 million gallons. It has a best-selling, semi-sweet brand of red wine called Vino da Tavola, produced in bulk, as are all its still and sparkling wines.

Lamont Winery (*SJ*) Formerly known as Bear Mountain, this huge corporation was recently acquired by the Labatt Brewery of Canada. It has a storage capacity of 36 million gallons, and produces mostly bulk wines; a range of premium varietal wines is also sold, labelled as M. Lamont.

Angelo Papagni Vineyards (*Mad*) ★ A tenth of this San Joaquin Valley grower's enormous 1.25 million case output is now devoted to a range of varietal wines which are clean, fresh and attractive. These wines are building a steadily growing reputation. Zinfandel and Barbera are soft and fruity and ready for early drinking, like the unusual Alicante Bouschet. The whites include Chenin Blanc (in still and sparkling styles), Fumé Blanc and Chardonnay, and there is a delicious late-harvest Emerald Riesling.

New York State

After california, New York State, with 43,000 acres of vineyards, is the largest wine-producing state in the U.S.A. As with California, the wine industry there is in a stage of ferment and development. But there the similarities cease. The output is one-tenth that of California – about the size of one of the larger Napa wineries – and is produced by five major companies and a dozen smaller ones.

The bulk of the wine is still from native grapes, mostly Concord and Pink Catawba, but changes are coming in three ways. Franco-American hybrids are increasingly used to up-grade quality; European (*vinifera*) varieties are being introduced on a limited but spectacularly successful scale; and the larger concerns, like Taylor's, Gold Seal and Widmer's, are tending to look to vineyards of their own in California to supply *vinifera* grapes for their better quality premium varietals.

The introduction of *vinifera* wines by Dr Konstantin Frank in the early 1960s in the Finger Lakes district – first for Gold Seal Vineyards, later for his own Johannisberger Riesling – seemed to herald a new era in wine-making in the eastern states; but it was an initiative that has not been followed by others. At about the same time, in an equally significant development, Philip Wagner of Boordy Vineyard introduced the first of the Franco-American hybrid varieties. These have proved more commercially acceptable, and in their New York State vineyards the larger wineries concentrate on growing a combination of native *labrusca* grapes and hybrids, using increasing amounts of the latter.

Most of the important wineries listed in the following gazetteer are in the Finger Lakes district, south of Lake Ontario. The best are the champagnes, white table wines and dessert wines, and the Riesling, Chardonnay and Gewürztraminer wines from Dr Frank's Vinifera Wine Cellars are outstanding. Well over half the state's vineyards lie in the Chautauqua and

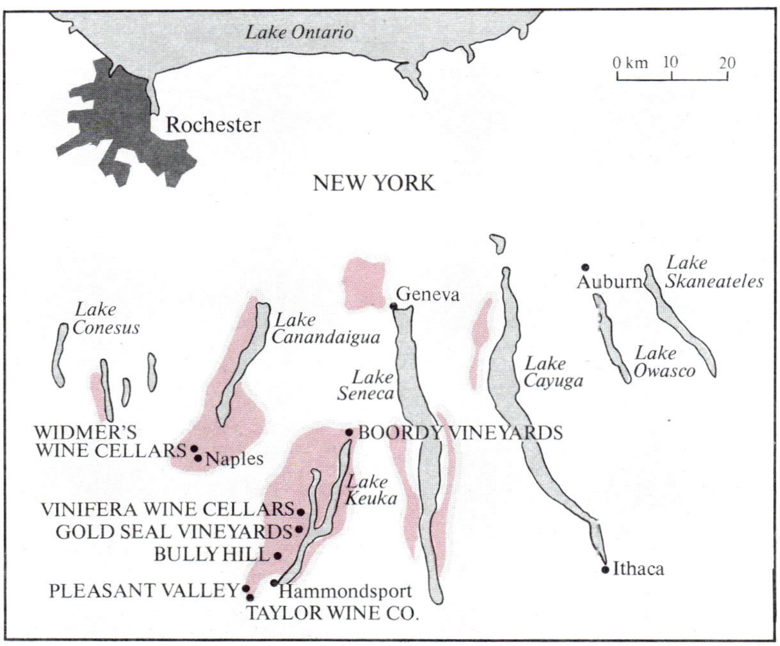

The Finger Lakes area of New York State

Niagara districts, where the broad waters of Lake Erie help to moderate the extreme cold; both districts have a big potential for developing better quality wines, as vine technologists learn to cope with cold winters and a short growing season, and the big Mogen David Wine Corporation of Chicago has its wineries in Chautauqua. The fourth district, the Hudson River Valley, is the oldest wine-growing area in the United States; however, it is dependent upon *labrusca* grapes, and only three small wineries are listed in the gazetteer – Benmarl, Brotherhood and Hudson Valley. Long Island, with no more than an embryo wine industry, is represented by Hargrave.

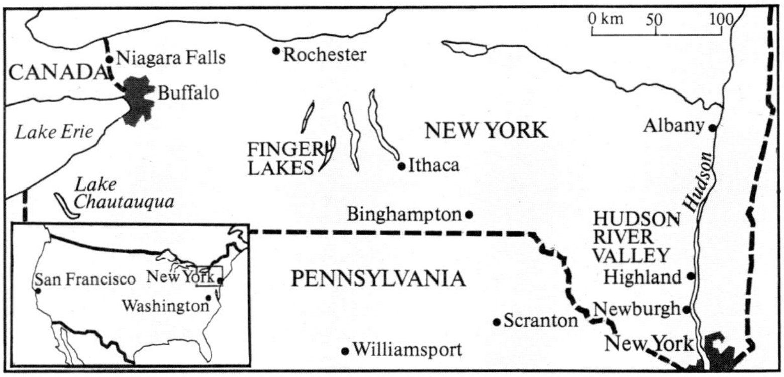

NEW YORK STATE GAZETTEER

Chautauqua (Ch), Finger Lakes (FL), Hudson River Valley (HRV), Long Island (LI).

Benmarl (*HRV*) A small winery, about 20 years old, run as a co-operative. The wines – Baco Noir, Seyval Blanc and Chardonnay – have a widespread reputation, but are only sold to members enrolled in the Société des Vignerons attached to the vineyard.

The Brotherhood Winery (*HRV*) A small concern specializing in a varietal made from the Chancellor Noir Hybrid, which produces a full-bodied red wine.

Bully Hill (*FL*) Owned since 1970 by W. S. Taylor, the controversial grandson of the founder of the giant Taylor Wine Company. Good quality estate-bottled varietal wines from hybrids (Seyval Blanc and Bully Hill Red, which is a blend of seven hybrids) and native stock (Diamond, Delaware and Ives). Seyval Blanc is made still, like a good Chardonnay, or sparkling by the *méthode Champenoise.*

Gold Seal Vineyards (*FL*) One of the biggest Finger Lakes wineries, where the first commercial *vinifera* wines were made under the direction of Dr Konstantin Frank. Gold Seal have persevered with two of these (estate-bottled Riesling and Chardonnay, both of high quality), but they have mainly concentrated on the production of champagne and *labrusca* wines from Catawba. Latterly they have looked more to their own Californian vineyards, near Modesto and in Monterey, for supplies of grapes.

Hargrave Vineyards (*LI*) A small family winery, not long established on Long Island. The first wines were harvested in 1975. Varieties grown are Cabernet Sauvignon, Pinot Noir, Chardonnay and Sauvignon Blanc.

Hudson Valley Winery (*HRV*) Has long produced *labrusca* wines, but a red Chelois varietal was introduced in 1977; since then the winery has developed estate-bottled Baco and Chancellor hybrid reds.

Johnson Estate (*Ch*) A pioneering winery seeking a future for white and red hybrid wines in the Chautauqua district. Its speciality is Liebestropfchen, a botrytised white from the Delaware grape.

Pleasant Valley (*FL*) Became a subsidiary of Taylor (now Coca-Cola) in 1961, 100 years after its foundation. Its best wine is still a *brut* champagne, sold under the Great Western brand name, but it is also introducing a range of hybrid blends and varietals.

Taylor Wine Company (*FL*) A giant in the US wine trade, and after Moët & Chandon (France) and Henkell (Germany) the largest producer of bottle-fermented sparkling wines in the world. It is now owned by Coca-Cola and is spreading its interests into California, with wineries in Napa Valley and Monterey. A range of generic wine is marketed under the title California Cellars, in addition to Lake Country, the corporation's Franco-American hybrid blended proprietary brand.

Vinifera Wine Cellars (*FL*) The name of the owner, Dr Konstantin Frank, is better known than the title of his 60-acre vineyard; the wine labels carry it in large letters – as well they might, since Dr Frank made history in the 1950s and 1960s by successfully growing *vinifera* grapes in New York State. His lead has not been widely followed, but he persists with Riesling, Chardonnay, Pinot Noir, Gewürztraminer and Gamay Beaujolais varietals among others, and his wines are among the best in the whole of the USA; his Johannisberg Riesling, introduced in 1965, is superb.

Widmer's Wine Cellars (*FL*) One of the five big Finger Lakes wineries, at the southern end of Lake Canandaigua. It has played a large part in the introduction of varietal wines in New York State, both from native grapes like Delaware and Moore's Diamond and from Franco-American hybrids. Like some other larger concerns in New York State, Widmer's has also looked towards California to provide grapes for quality *vinifera* varietals, Cabernet Sauvignon and Pinot Noir among them.

Other States of the U.S.A.

Maryland

The State of Maryland has a long wine-making history, but it has few modern wineries and little commercially made wine. Climatically it is very suitable to the cultivation of the Franco-American hybrids introduced into the eastern United States by Philip Wagner, founder of the best-known of the State's wineries, Boordy Vineyards, just north of Baltimore. European varieties, among them Chardonnay, Riesling, Pinot Noir and Muskat Ottonel, have also been planted by Montbray Wine Cellars in the Silver Run Valley, close to the Pennsylvania border.

Michigan

With some 17,000 acres of vines, mostly in the south, along the lake shores, Michigan is fifth in terms of quantity production in the United States; but as yet the State has no significant commercial wines. Concord grapes and dessert and fortified wines have been Michigan's stock in trade, and the State also lays claim to the origination of the popular red sparkling wine – a combination of 'champagne' and 'burgundy' – known as Cold Duck. But newer vineyards are beginning to plant hybrids – Baco, Chancellor, Chelois, de Chaunac and Maréchal Foch; and one of the State's better-known wineries, Tabor Hill Vineyards, includes Chardonnay and Riesling wines on its list.

The filling and packing area in one of the Taylor wineries in New York State (Zefa)

Ohio

Ohio has had its vineyards since the beginning of the 19th century, and was once the premier wine-producing state in North America. Longfellow paid tribute to its Catawba wine. It is now looking to modern technology to restore its industry, and a growing number of new vineyards are planting hybrid varieties. Meier's Wine Cellars, the largest Ohio producer, with a reputation for *labrusca* wines and champagnes, is turning its attention to the use of hybrids and European vines – among them Riesling, Chardonnay and Gewürztraminer.

Oregon

With a mere 1,200 acres under vine, growing European and native American varieties side by side, Oregon has made a belated start as a wine-growing state. Its climate and situation, at the northern, classical end of the Californian wine belt, means that it is well placed to develop wines on a commercial scale, and in the Willamette Valley it has an area ripe for expansion comparable to the Yakima Valley in Washington State to the north.

That white European grape varieties in particular can succeed in Oregon has been adequately demonstrated by the fine wines from Richard Somner's Hillcrest Vineyards; in addition to notable White Rieslings, Hillcrest offers varietals from the classic Burgundian grapes (Pinot Noir, Chardonnay, Sémillon and Sauvignon Blanc) and from the American Zinfandel and the Austrian Muskat Ottonel. Other new vineyards are springing up, and State regulations are intended to ensure the purity of the varietal wines (90 per cent of the grape named) and a correct attribution of origin.

Pennsylvania

Pennsylvania is something of an oddity among leading producers in the United States. Its 11,000 acres produce enough grapes for it to rank high in the national output table, but most of that output is not for vinification; the industry has also been held back by a state law which until 1968 forbade growers to sell direct from their vineyards – a regulation which enabled a number of Californian vintners to establish themselves in the state. Even now the output of wineries is limited to 100,000 gallons a year, vinified from fruit grown in Pennsylvania.

Washington State

Some 22,500 acres of Washington State are already under vine – only California and New York State have more – and the State's climate is sympathetic to the production of quality wines from European grape varieties. Until latterly its wines were mostly made from the widely grown native Concord grape, but its two most prominent vineyards, Boordy and Ste Michelle, have both established international reputations for quality *vinifera* wines, particularly whites. Other new wineries are constantly being opened, with widespread plantings of red Cabernet Sauvignon and Merlot vines, and white Riesling, Chardonnay, Chenin Blanc and Gewürztraminer. Parts of the new development area in the Yakima Valley have been identified as having the climatic characteristics of the Californian Regions I and II; this means that they should prove suitable for the production of varietal wines comparable to German whites and Bordeaux reds.

AUSTRALIA

AUSTRALIA is not a new wine-producing country. In the late 18th century vines from Europe were planted by settlers determined to make wine their livelihood, and the dynasties they founded remain today. Table wine, port and sherry-type dessert wines and brandy are all produced, but table wine provides the latest success story, and all Australia's best wines fall into this category. On account of the climate all the wine-growing districts are in the southern areas of the country. Even so technology, such as the cold fermentation process, has to be enlisted to cope with the Australian heat, and this together with changing taste has contributed to the development and expansion of the quality wine industry.

It is an industry which receives enormous encouragement from government and big business, resulting in a breed of highly trained winemakers who produce wines which now have an excellent reputation far beyond the shores of Australia. Annual production of wines is now over 2¼ million hectolitres, of which only 3 per cent is, as yet, exported. Home consumption is boosted by the immense output of cheaper 'bag in the box' wines, mostly from

THE WINE DISTRICTS

New South Wales

Hunter Valley
Mudgee
Murrumbidgee Irrigation Area
Corowa

South Australia

Barossa Valley
Coonawarra
Clare–Watervale
Southern Vales

Victoria

Great Western
Glenrowan–Milawa
Rutherglen
Mildura–Robinvale
Swan Hill
Drumborg
Yarra Valley
Goulburn Valley

Western Australia

Swan Valley
Margaret River
Mount Barker

A seedling nursery at Milawa in the Ovens Valley, Victoria

the irrigated areas of the Murray and the Murrumbidgee Rivers, and there is a falling proportion of fortified dessert wines. 'Bag in the box' wines, packs of three litres upwards, account for 40 per cent of sales in Australia.

The practice of calling Australian wines by French generic names is losing ground, although 'Burgundy' is still popular and can be a good quality wine and 'Riesling' has tended to become a generic term for dry white wine. The grapes used to make wines, often 100 per cent varietals, are now indicated on the labels with the vineyard and vintage. The smaller, fine wine concerns either draw on their own estates in one area or buy in from surrounding vineyards. Large firms can own land in different regions of Australia and in many cases blend the wines to produce an acceptable commercial product.

In spite of its remoteness from other wine-producing countries and the major markets of the world, Australia has not been isolationist in its policy towards wine legislation. While variations in additives are permitted, such substances as sulphur dioxide and volatile acidity are limited by law. The use of cultured yeasts is far more widespread than in Europe. There are, however, no country-wide appellation standards. Quality rests with the individual winery, the fierce pride which Australian winemakers take in the wines they produce, and their response to the widespread and well-informed interest of the Australian public.

While some 60 per cent of quality wines come from South Australia (between 3 and 4 per cent come from Western Australia and the balance more or less evenly from Victoria and New South Wales) probably the best known vineyard area in Australia is the Hunter Valley in New South Wales, about 100 miles north of Sydney. Heat in this region is concentrated in February, and rainfall can be heavy at vintage time. The Australian vintage runs from mid-February to early May. As a result, Australian wine of a given year is six months ahead of its French counterpart. Because of the heat there is a growing practice of harvesting grapes at night or in the cool early hours of the morning to obtain maximum quality. Shiraz (alias Hermitage, or Syrah), Cabernet Sauvignon and Pinot Noir are the major red varieties. Among the whites after Sémillon, White Hermitage (the Ugni Blanc or Trebbiano), Rhine Riesling and increasingly Chardonnay are important, with Clairette (known as Blanquette) also producing fine wine in the Hunter Valley.

The Hunter Valley is really one side of the Broken Back Range, and the very best soils and situations are found in the foothills around Pokolbin; there are also some good vineyards nearer Sydney, notably at Rooty Hill and Parramatta. The emerging wine areas of Muswellbrook and Mudgee lie north of the Hunter. To the south near the Murray River is Corowa, which adjoins the Rutherglen district of Victoria.

Victoria, with one or two exceptions, was badly hit by phylloxera in the 1910s. The northern Victoria districts, with some claim to be among the earliest of Australian wine-producing areas, retain their reputation for luscious dessert wines and brandies, combining with this the new opportunity presented for the replanting of vines for

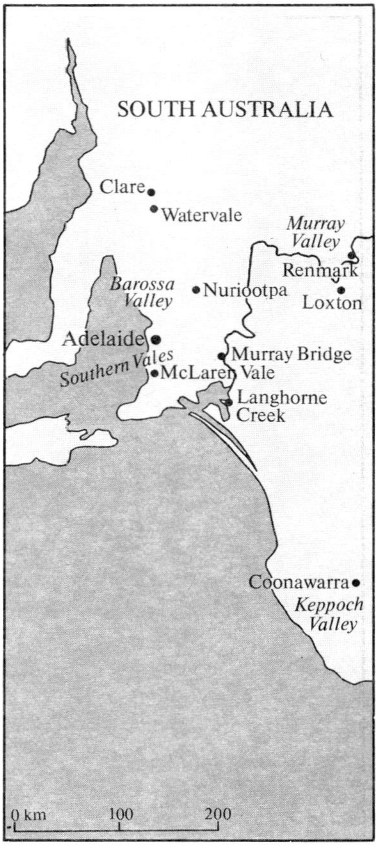

PRINCIPAL GRAPE VARIETIES

White – Chardonnay
Sémillon
Traminer
Rhine Riesling
Muscat de Frontignan
Chenin
Sauvignon
Sylvaner
Ugni Blanc

Red – Shiraz (Hermitage)
Cabernet Sauvignon
Merlot
Malbec
Grenache
Pinot Noir

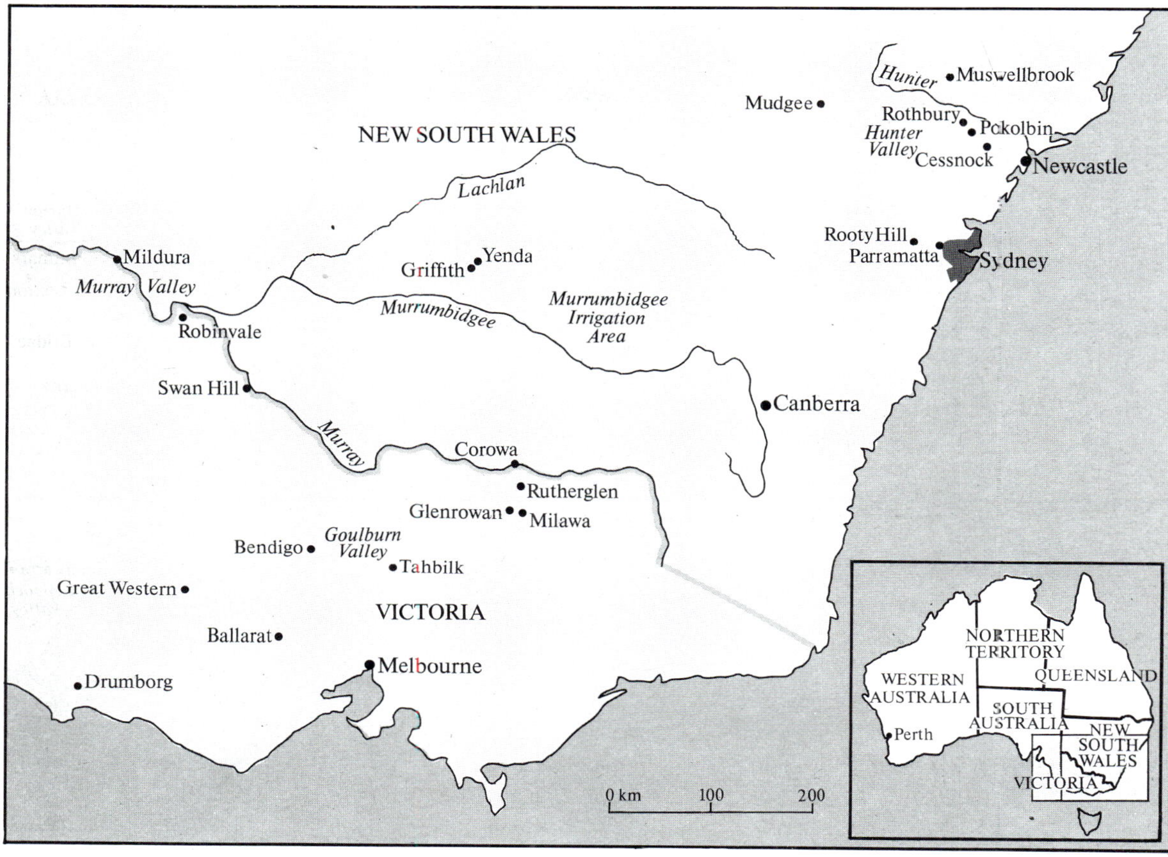

high-quality table wines. Shiraz and Cabernet predominate, as at Tabilk (which has Château Tahbilk, *sic*), with Muscat widely used for white wines, dry and sweet. Mildura, west of Swan Hill and Robinvale, and close to the border of South Australia, was untouched by phylloxera, as was Great Western at the end of the Great Dividing Range, north-west of Melbourne, a district which is now particularly famous for its sparkling wines.

South Australia contains the country's largest quality wine district, the Barossa Valley, about thirty miles due north of Adelaide. The area has historical links with Germany, and it is thus fitting that it should be most famous for its Rhine Riesling (not to be confused with the Hunter Valley 'Riesling', which is in fact a Sémillon wine); its best, high, vineyards produce Rieslings of genuine finesse, and there is also a number of worthy reds made from Cabernet grapes, blended with some Shiraz. The soil in the Barossa is gravelly, sandy loam. Clare/Watervale is a developing South Australian area north of the Barossa Valley, with a hot climate.

In the Southern Vales district of South Australia, almost in the suburbs of Adelaide, the cooling influence of the sea is evident (it is not for nothing that there is a 'Seaview' winery); grape combinations are the same as in the Barossa Valley. Coonawarra, by contrast, is somewhat isolated geographically, its position in the south-east corner of the state ensuring cooler weather and even some frosts, with corresponding variations between vintages; an outcrop of red earth over limestone gives the district's wines a special character and balance – but vinification counts for much, as it always does, and you can still find 'whopping' wines in Coonawarra's southern reaches.

The following gazetteer embraces wineries and vineyards throughout the continent. Each entry also identifies the state, because although few overseas consumers are likely at present to identify a particular Australian wine with one state rather than another, each has its own styles and character which with time will become more apparent. Such a lengthy and varied listing, although quite inadequate to cover the 5,000 or so labels available on the Australian home market, is a tribute to the quality emerging from this vast land, and to the range of its better wines beginning to be available abroad.

PEPPERCORN ★ RATINGS

Most wines in Australia are the product of the judicious blending of wines from a number of vineyards, and are sold by relatively large firms. The starring system is therefore used to indicate the general level of quality achieved by the house as a whole.

A firm awarded three stars will most probably produce at least one wine worthy of a fourth, as well as some which would be more lowly rated. Superior ratings should therefore be regarded as indicative of the standard achieved by the company's top wines, rather than of that of its basic or lower range. Few Australian wines are available in export markets, and a more detailed assessment must await a future edition of this book.

AUSTRALIA GAZETTEER

(*NSW*) New South Wales
(*SA*) South Australia
(*V*) Victoria
(*WA*) West Australia
★ Peppercorn rating

Amery (Kay Bros) Winery (*SA*) ★★ The Amery vineyards in the Southern Vales, near Seaview, are not irrigated and vary from sand to alluvial soil. The red wines are very reliable, based on McLaren Vale; the Cabernet Shiraz and the Kay's Amery Shiraz have a pleasant spiciness. There is an attractive late-picked Rhine Riesling among a range of whites.

Bailey's Bundarra Vineyards (*V*) ★★ A family business in north-east Victoria owning vineyards at Bundarra and Huceynia (near Glenrowan). The Bundarra soil is extremely rich, does not need irrigation, and produces excellent yields. The wines are very individual with enormous body, Bundarra Hermitage being especially noteworthy. Dessert wines are also made, with very good liqueur Muscat.

Balgownie (*V*) ★★/★★★ Small winery signalling the re-emergence of wine-making in the Bendigo district, to the north-east of Great Western. It emerged commercially in 1973, and produces superb red Cabernet Sauvignon and Balgownie Hermitage (Shiraz) from its own grapes. The wines are aged in small oak, and are 100 per cent varietal. A small planting of Chardonnay has been made.

Berri Co-operative Winery and Distillery (*SA*) ★★ This is a true co-operative and all grapes processed are supplied by the 500 grower-members. Lying between Renmark and Loxton in the Murray Valley, the co-operative claims to have the largest single wine-making and distilling plants in Australia, with an output greater than the whole of the Hunter Valley. It produces red and white wines, fortified wines, brandy and grape fortification spirit. Here 'Hock' is made from Clare Riesling, Pedro Ximenez and Palomino grapes. The 'Mine Host' range covers all types of wine. Berri Fruity Gordo Moselle is well known. Berri Cabernet Sauvignon and Rhine Riesling are well thought of.

Best's Wines (*V*) ★ A Great Western firm along with Seppelts. The firm began to make light-bodied table wines at its Concongella vineyards when most companies were concentrating on fortified wines. Best's Hock No. 0 comes in two versions: Rhine Riesling which is distinguished, and Golden Chasselas, which is attractive. There are also Shiraz wines and fortified wines.

Bilyara, Wolf Blass (*SA*) ★★★★ Wolfgang Blass, trained as an oenologist in Germany, was technical director of Tolley Scott and Tolley's Nuriootpa winery. He now makes his own Barossa wines at the Bilyara winery, just north of Nuriootpa, which have acquired a high reputation and won sought-after medals; his Cabernet/Shiraz blends (Dry Red Gold Medal) are great wines, with considerable fruit to match the oak, and there is a fine Rhine Riesling. Wolf Blass is one of Australia's foremost wine-makers, and his wines are not to be missed. The grapes are bought in as needed from Barossa and Eden Valleys, Langhorne Creek and Great Western. Grey labels indicate individual vineyard bottling, yellow labels the eagerly sought individual blends, black labels trophy winners.

Brokenwood (*NSW*) ★★★ Increasingly well-thought-of small winery on red clay soil in the Lower Hunter Valley. Has concentrated, since 1973, on Cabernet Sauvignon, Hermitage and Pinot Noir, with small quantities of other Bordeaux red grapes. The Cabernet is big, long-lasting; Hermitage Cabernet (60 per cent, 40 per cent) is a blend of 100 per cent Hunter grapes; Cabernet Hermitage has some Cabernet from Coonawarra, SA.

Brown Bros (*V*) ★★★ Proximity to the Victoria Alps produces a cooler micro-climate at Milawa, favouring production of wines from the classic grape varieties. Chardonnay, Pinot Noir, Merlot, Cabernet Sauvignon and Riesling are 100 per cent varietals. Muscat Blanc, Shiraz and Gewürztraminer are also grown. Reds are wood-matured for 18 months; whites are cold-fermented. Brown Bros are responsible for some very fine wines indeed, combining modern techniques and experimentation with the best of traditional methods. The reds include a big-bodied, soft, Cabernet, a Shiraz and a Cabernet/Shiraz/Mondeuse (the Italian Refosco). The Muscat à petits grains (Frontignan) is used to make an excellent dry white, and when late-picked, a rich, delicious dessert wine. The winery is among the few Australian producers regularly experiencing suitable climatic conditions for 'noble rot' for the production of sweet, late-harvest wines.

Leo Buring (*SA*) ★★★ A prominent Barossa winery, owned by Lindemans (q.v.) and famous for its Château Leonay wines. Grapes from Barossa, Watervale and Eden Valley, and Coonawarra (reds), are largely bought in; perfectionist techniques are practised, and the white wines are very good indeed. Private Bin Rhine Riesling in limited quantity makes claim to be rated among the world's best, with excellent bouquet and great length. A blended White Burgundy is remarkably good for its price, and the Moselle (Clare Riesling) has won many awards. There is a Black Label range which also gathers medals. High quality Private Bin reds are based on Cabernet Sauvignon and Shiraz.

Campbell's (*V*) ★★ Campbell's at Rutherglen (north-east Victoria) is a family farm, raising wheat and sheep as well as vines. Table wines are being developed strongly; a white wine made from Trebbiano (White Hermitage) grapes is of particular interest, and the Rutherglen Collector's Muscat and Tokay dessert wines have great character. Campbell's also make good fortified wines.

Chambers' (*V*) ★ A small family firm at Rutherglen, noted for its Sherry and dessert wines, including an excellent dessert Tokay and a Muscat Old Liqueur wine (very Australian).
Château Clare Estate (*SA*) ★★ Clare/Watervale is the most northerly of the South Australian vineyards, with a resulting hot climate. Taylor's Château Clare Estate is a young family winery (first wines in 1973) with a planting mainly of Shiraz and Cabernet Sauvignon. Grapes are also bought in. Cabernet and Hermitage, both 100 per cent varietals, are aged in French oak to produce good quality wines. There is also an attractive Rhine Riesling.
Craigmoor (*NSW*) ★/★★ The oldest vineyard in Mudgee on the central western tablelands of New South Wales. Big, soft Shiraz wines and wood-matured Sémillon are its principal output, with a smaller quantity of Chardonnay consistently good.
Château Tahbilk (*V*) ★★★ This is a show-piece property in the Goulburn Valley in north/central Victoria. Only non-fortified wines are made, and Château Tahbilk has long preferred to call them by their grape variety names, rather than by misleading generic terminology. The wines have a marked individuality. The Cabernet improves all the time in bottle, the Shiraz is somewhat faster-maturing. The Special Bin Reds of Eric Purbrick encompass some really fine wines; these are special selections released years after the normal Cabernet and Shiraz wines. Marsanne (which ages very well for a white wine), Rhine Riesling and White Hermitage (Trebbiano) are also made. In all, real flagship wines for Australia.
D'Arenberg (*SA*) ★★★ The Osborne wineries and vineyards (the wines are, however, named after the owner) are near McLaren Vale in the Southern Vales area. Some wine is also supplied to McLaren Vale Wines. D'Arenberg Burgundy, made from Shiraz and Grenache, is rich and full of flavour with great bottle age (the Special Award Burgundy 1967 was amazing); the Shiraz is also good value. The wines have substance, and take some maturing, although some seem to 'dry out'.
W. Drayton (*NSW*) ★★/★★★ A Hunter Valley firm which has survived various vicissitudes to go from strength to strength. They own the well-known Bellevue vineyard, and four other estates are either owned or connected and are identified on the labels. Drayton's Bellevue Dry Red Hermitage is a collector's piece. The Cabernet Sauvignon can still be good in poor years; the Rhine Riesling is typically Hunter and full-bodied; the Hunter Riesling (Sémillon) is outstandingly good and long-lived. Since 1978 these wines have been joined by a remarkably good Chardonnay aged in German oak.
Evans and Tate Pty Ltd (Gnangara Wines) (*WA*) ★ A small well-run winery in Swan Valley near Perth, with modern equipment and temperature-controlled fermentation. Concentrating on good quality Shiraz and Shiraz/Cabernet, aged in French oak. Developing also in Margaret River to the south.
Hamilton's (*SA*) ★★ The very old Hamilton's outside Adelaide has gradually expanded (as the town did) and has wineries at Springton and Eden Valley, hilly areas in the Barossa particularly suitable for white wines and vineyards at Swan Hill, Victoria. These wineries only make table wines, but the Hamilton stable produces wine of every type. Ewell Moselle, Hunter–Barossa Cabernet Sauvignon and Nildottie White Hermitage stand out in a long list.
Thomas Hardy & Son (*SA*) ★★★ A huge wine-producing concern, with its headquarters in Adelaide, but with branches in every state of Australia and agencies overseas. This is a very dynamic group, which is now expanding into new areas such as Keppoch, near Coonawarra. The original Hardy's Tintara is in the Southern Vales, near McLaren Vale. The firm's great skill is in blending: Hardy's Cabinet Claret, for instance, is produced from Cabernet Sauvignon and Shiraz grapes grown in several districts: McLaren Vale, the Barossa Valley and Coonawarra in South Australia and the Hunter Valley in New South Wales. This is a commercial wine at a reasonable price, but consistent.

Hardy's Cabernet Sauvignon is a great wine, a really clever blend based on McLaren Vale but with varying additions, Coonawarra predominating. These are huge wines, severe when young and built for long life – a real example of what Australia can do. Hardy's Reserve Bin Burgundy is softer and more suitable for younger drinking. The range of wines is enormous, as befits a national company, and includes a sweet dessert Sauvignon Blanc, a Grand Reserve Champagne and the Siegersdorf Rhine Riesling which comes from the Springton and Eden Valley areas in the Barossa.
Henschke (*SA*) ★★★ This is a specialist family firm, justifiably famous for its red and white wines, situated at Keyneton in the Barossa: but the land lies higher than the Valley proper, and the soil is poorer. Henschke Hermitage is made from Shiraz grapes grown in the Springton district, and is a delicate wine with good flavour that has impressed many. The Hill of Grace Vineyard wine is a worthy red, and Mount Edelstone has a long-held reputation (both are made from Shiraz grapes). The Rhine Riesling and Sémillon are also in a high category.
Houghton (*WA*) ★★ This Western Australian firm is in the Middle Swan Valley, north of Perth, and now belongs to Thomas Hardy & Son. The winery is impeccably kept and many of the wines are prized, perhaps most of all the nutty White Burgundy and the wood-matured Ports and Muscat wines. Liqueur wines are made with great attention to detail.
Hungerford Hill (*NSW*) ★★/★★★ Hungerford's main holdings are at Pokolbin in the Hunter Valley, among the largest in the area. Their interests extend elsewhere in NSW and to the Swan Valley, and they have a further large vineyard at Coonawarra. With the latest in equipment, white wines are cold fermented and early bottled, the reds more traditionally aged in oak. A range of high quality 'Collection' wines includes Pokolbin Sémillon, an attractive, perfumed Traminer, Cabernet Sauvignon in separate styles from Hunter and Coonawarra, and a Shiraz with lots of potential. Coonawarra is also the source of a fine, late-picked Rhine Riesling.
Huntingdon Estate (*NSW*) ★★/★★★ A small family business at Mudgee offering good quality, value for money, red and white wines. The first emerged in 1973. An enquiring approach is leading to the development of reds with richness, complexity and elegance, including a notable Cabernet Sauvignon. Also Sémillon and more latterly Chardonnay in whites.
George Idyll (*V*) ★★ Situated in Moorabool Valley near Geelong, and established in the mid-1960s by descendants of Swiss immigrants. Specializes in an exceptionally good Gewürztraminer, a Shiraz/Cabernet Sauvignon blend, and Idyll Blush, a Shiraz Rosé matured in stainless steel.
Kaiser Stuhl (Barossa Co-operative Winery) (*SA*) ★★/★★★ A progressive co-operative, marketing wines from individual vineyards as well as a full range which includes aperitifs and dessert wines. The late-picked Rhine Rieslings should not be compared with German models, but possess a fine range of flavours and have great interest, without enormous sugar. These wines, and an individual vineyard Shiraz, are sold under various 'Ribbon' colours.
Krondorf Winery (*SA*) ★/★★ Owned since 1972 by Dalgety Wine Estates and more recently modernized, Krondorf, at Rowland Flat in the Barossa Valley, has a range of quality wines. Rhine Riesling is its chief white, made from Barossa and Eden Valley grapes in Bin 1 and Bin 2 styles. There is also a sparkling dry Chenin Blanc and a White Sauvignon. Reds are based on Shiraz, and some Cabernet Sauvignon is made.
Laira Winery (Eric Brand) (*SA*) ★★ A small winery that attracts attention for its red wines, all from Coonawarra. The Shiraz can be exceptionally good, and the Cabernet Sauvignon demands bottle age. A well-balanced rosé is made from Grenache.
Dr Max Lake ('Lake's Folly') (*NSW*) ★★★★ One of Australia's wine jewels, and it took a surgeon to do it! Dr Lake writes on wine and is a fine taster; when he decided to become a grower, he did much for the Hunter Valley as well as the entire country. The vineyard is small, but is being gradually expanded, and the wine-making is very personal. Lake's Folly wine is grown on a basalt outcrop, near Pokolbin, and the grape variety is predominantly Cabernet Sauvignon, with a small amount of Hermitage. New oak for maturation is used, and the results are red wines of infinite quality and a balance not seen before in Australian reds.

The wines have great style and clean fruit, and age beautifully. At the moment there is a Cabernet Sauvignon which shows real complexity, difficult to achieve in such climates. The 1968 and 1969 wines were both amazingly good, the latter in top world class. Lake's Folly Dry Red contains Cabernet Sauvignon, Shiraz, Merlot and Malbec. This man is a master wine-maker, who has now added a distinguished Chardonnay to his range. Anyone who tastes his wines for the first time will look at Australia in a new light.

Lindemans *(NSW)* ★★★★ One of the very biggest Australian wine concerns; it is now owned by Phillip Morris, but it has not suffered the fate of many less fortunate take-overs; continues to make and distribute fine wine with probably the greatest reputation in the Hunter Valley for classic whites and reds. Originally a Hunter Valley firm, with its Ben Ean vineyard on volcanic soil, the company now also owns extensive vineyards in Coonawarra, South Australia (they bought Redman, with the Rouge Homme label), Corowa (on the border between New South Wales and Victoria) and in the developing Keppoch area, about 40 miles north of Coonawarra.

With two successive German wine-makers, Lindemans have been at the forefront in developing new styles of wine. They produce some of the best sparkling wine in Australia, notably the much-lauded Dry Imperator Brut Champagne. The white wines are clean and fresh (a Lindeman trademark), in particular the vintage-dated Bin 23 Riesling, made from Riesling grapes grown in the Hunter, Barossa and Clare Valleys. The Bin 77 White Burgundy (also vintage-dated) is a highly successful blend of grapes and areas, it is pleasant and fresh when young, but gains immensely in flavour in bottle. There is also a very good value sweet white wine, Bin 36 Porphyry.

Lindemans Hunter River wines enjoy a high reputation, most notably the Hunter River Riesling (Sémillon) and the White Burgundy, sold under bin numbers. The latter is astonishing; although made entirely from Sémillon grapes grown in the Pokolbin area, with bottle age it develops a quite remarkable similarity to its French namesake. Reserve Hunter River Burgundy, made from Shiraz and Pinot Noir from the Ben Ean vineyard, is a consistently fine red.

The list goes on and on; fine Sherries, wines from Rouge Homme in Coonawarra and from Watervale in South Australia, even a fine Reserve 'Madeira' Solera, made chiefly from Verdelho grapes grown in the Hunter. There is now also a Hunter River Chardonnay in the list. Lindemans proves that big can be beautiful.

McWilliams *(NSW)* ★★★ Another giant, McWilliams encompasses Hunter Valley vineyards (the Mount Pleasant label), three huge wineries at Hanwood, Yenda and Beelbangera in the Murrumbidgee Irrigation Area of New South Wales, and a large winery at Robinvale on the Victoria side of the Murray River. Quality production is dominated by the Mount Pleasant wines, including Anne, and Elizabeth, Riesling (not another type of Riesling, but just a top selection of Sémillon), Mount Pleasant Philip Hermitage, Pinot Hermitage (Pinot Noir and Shiraz) and many special bottlings showing the versatile nature of the Hunter Valley. There is the Private Bin series (note particularly the Cabernet Sauvignon: a 1974 sampled recently had great varietal flavour and nice body) and a full range of wines for every taste. McWilliams Mount Pleasant Old Paddock Hermitage is a winner.

Mildara Wines *(SA)* ★★★ Situated confusingly at Mildura, the business and commercial centre of the Victorian Murray irrigation settlements, Mildara Wines have always made fine Sherries and Brandies. They believe in the value of blending from different areas, and have bought vineyards in Coonawarra. They are now making very good red wine indeed.

Different bins of Mildara Cabernet Shiraz Reserve were introduced in the early fifties, producing some magnificent blended wines from the Hunter Valley, Southern Vales and Coonawarra. Other wines of note are Mildara Coonawarra Cabernet Sauvignon, a Cabernet/Shiraz/Malbec blend from Coonawarra, and an impressive Rhine Riesling from the same area. The company's George Dry Sherry is excellent – absolutely dry, with strong *flor* character.

Miramar Vineyards *(NSW)* ★★★ Although its first wines were not made until 1977, this small Mudgee winery has quickly made its mark. Its wines, which combine quality and value, are partly from its own grapes, largely bought in. Eurunderee Rosé and its half and half Sémillon/Chardonnay are both notable, as is the Rhine Riesling for quality and for Mudgee. Shiraz is the winery's top red.

Mitchell Cellars *(SA)* A husband and wife family winery, its first wines marketed in 1977. A promising Rhine Riesling and a red Cabernet Sauvignon, both 100 per cent varietal. Clare/Watervale.

Morris Wines *(V)* ★★/★★★ Recently taken over by Reckitt and Colman, Morris's of Rutherglen in north-eastern Victora should do well from the new injection of capital. In addition to its own vineyards, the company also buys in quite large quantities of grapes from the Murray Irrigation Area. Morris Liqueur Muscat is its most famous wine, made from Rutherglen Brown Muscat grapes (Frontignac) and fortified; the wine is matured in wood and vintages are blended, adding many old wines. The lovely aroma of Muscat is maintained, while the influence of oak gives the wine body and character and prevents it from being cloying; it is equal in calibre to any dessert or *digestif* wine from the Iberian peninsula. There is a dry red, excellent Port-style wines, and a magnificent dessert Tokay, probably made from the Harslevelu grape from Hungary – big, luscious wines, with a lovely fruit aroma.

Orlando (G. Gramp & Sons) *(SA)* ★★★ Orlando is another giant which has led the field in quality wines, now under the Reckitt and Colman hat – and judged on recent drinking experience, the takeover has proved beneficial. The firm's headquarters is at Rowland Flat in the Barossa Valley, where there are extensive vineyards, and they own more land under vine in Eden Valley and on the Murray River, near Waikerie. Nevertheless, Orlando has to buy in an enormous amount of grapes to satisfy their production.

Gramp's were always a forward-thinking company. In 1953 they adopted the cold and pressure-controlled fermentation system; this resulted in white wines with bouquet and flavour which have enormously contributed to the current big demand for white wine. Modern equipment enabled them to produce the huge-selling Barossa Pearl, a naturally sweet sparkling wine which has had great success in Australia; they also pioneered such machinery as centrifuges and gravity separators.

The tiny, six-acre Steingarten vineyard, 1,600ft up on the mountain behind Rowland Flat, is as stony as the name suggests and is a brave experiment in Rhine Riesling growing if yield can be achieved, the result could well be a wine of real class, with that great steely finesse found in the best German Rieslings. Their straight Barossa Rhine Riesling is remarkable, with great elegance and fruit, combined with a *goût de terroir* that is almost Rheinpfalz in character. Orlando Barossa Cabernet (Cabernet Sauvignon/Shiraz, basically all from Rowland Flat) is a consistentl fine wine, with an attractive fruity flavour, available on a commercial level and excellent value. There are dessert wines and various 'sparklers'; throughout the range Orlando means more than reliability – it means pleasant drinking.

Penfold Wines *(SA)* ★★★★ Any serious drinker of Australian wines has a thick file of Penfold tasting notes and long ago ran out of superlatives. Penfold's is now multi-State, with its headquarters in Sydney, but Magill, on the outskirts of Adelaide, is the heart of the company; it is the centre of blending operations in South Australia, and it is also where Dr Christopher Rawson Penfold from Sussex planted his first vineyard in the 1840s. Later, Penfold's started 'collecting', taking over cellars in McLaren Vale, establishing a winery at Griffith in the Murrumbidgee Irrigation Area, expanding hugely in the Hunter Valley. They are also strongly established in the Barossa Valley, with wineries and vineyards at Kalimna, Nuriootpa and Eden Valley. The company is now owned by Tooth's, the New South Wales brewery.

Many of the company's Kalimna grapes go into private bin dry reds, such as Penfold's Bin Red – Cabernet Sauvignon Bin 707. Their Cabernet Shiraz Bin 389 is often surprisingly good, maturing to great depths. Coonawarra Claret Bin 128 is made entirely from Shiraz grown at Coonawarra; the 1966 and 1968 vintages are outstanding.

There are two gems: Penfold's Grange Hermitage (named after the cottage of the original Dr Penfold) and Penfold's St Henri Claret: people discuss vintages of both as they would a Latour or a Mouton. Grange was established in the early 1950s and bought in Bordeaux-size (225 litres) new French or American oak barrels for maturation. The wines which resulted are of great richness and complexity, fetching very high prices and sweeping the board at competitions; they are made for keeping, and often have a great sweet, ripe flavour, matched with the oak. A marvellous 'Grange' is the Bin 60A Kalimna/Coonawarra Dry Red 1962; still showing great depth of colour and an intense, deep bouquet, it is exceptional.

St Henri Clarets are basically lighter wines, originally made by John Davoren, the wine-maker at Auldana near Magill. They are elegant and fruity, with a degree of stalkiness integral to the wine. Europeans may ponder the art of blending in all these wines, for they are not single vineyard products, and often not even single-state. St Henri Shiraz is a bigger wine with a real kick in it.

Grange and St Henri should not eclipse the rest of the Penfold output. There is the reliable Dalwood range of table wines (named after the original Hunter Valley vineyards) and Sherries, Ports and sparkling wines. There are two excellent whites: Hunter Valley Pinot Riesling Bin 365 (Chardonnay and Sémillon); and Penfold's Traminer Riesling Bin 202 – a blend of Traminer with some Rhine Riesling, gloriously aromatic when young.

Petulama (*SA*) ★★ The Petulama Rhine Riesling vineyard is at Clare producing wine of great flavour and longevity. Established in the 70s, with Brian Croser as wine-maker. He also makes Chardonnay and Cabernet Sauvignon, from Coonawarra, in limited quantities. Undoubtedly a name to follow.

Pipers Brook (*Tasmania*) There is very little Tasmanian wine. Pipers Brook with 8½ hectares of vineyard is the largest of a small group of Tasmanian vineyards. Its whites include Chardonnay, Traminer, a marvellous Rhine Riesling and there is a small planting of Cabernet Sauvignon.

Quelltaler (H. Buring & Sobels) (*SA*) ★★/★★★ This quality firm, with vineyards and winery at Watervale, about eight miles north of Adelaide, is now wholly owned by a large holding company, Vignerons Distillers and Vintners. There are over 500 acres under vine, with more expansion to come. Quelltaler Brut Champagne is excellent value, clean and crisp, and the Hock Bin 65 has found real popularity in Australia, with its full flavour and oak influence. Quelltaler Granfiesta is an outstanding dry sherry, strong with *flor* and oak tastes, but with the clean delicacy of a top Jerez *fino*. A full range of wines is made.

Reynella (Walter Reynell) (*SA*) ★★★ This long-established Southern Vales producer was bought up by Hungerford Hill in 1970, but now belongs to a subsidiary of Rothmans. The extensive vineyards at Reynella and McLaren Flat are not irrigated and benefit from the cooling influence of the sea. The winery and old cellar are well worth visiting. The company buys almost two-thirds of the grapes it needs from other growers, but there are also newly planted vineyards in Hunter Valley and Coonawarra. Reynella is particularly known for its red wines – Claret and Burgundy – and for its Alicante Flor Sherry with its marked flavour and beautiful finish. The Vintage Reserve Claret (Cabernet Sauvignon and Shiraz) is very slow-maturing, being tannic and firm when young. Coonawarra Cabernet Sauvignon, Shiraz and Rhine Riesling have now been added to the list.

The Shiraz is impressive, and the same grape is blended with Grenache to produce a leading vintage Port full of character. The sweeter late-picked styles of Rhine Riesling grown on the Terra Rossa (red clay loam) of Coonawarra hold out great promise.

Richmond Estate (*NSW*) ★★/★★★ A newly enlarged vineyard near Sydney specializing in premium quality dry Cabernet and Shiraz reds, the latter being particularly impressive. Malbec is blended with the other two to make a red wine typical of the vineyard.

Richmond Grove (*NSW*) ★★★ A specialist in white wine varieties in the Upper Hunter Valley with a 100-hectare vineyard, which has made its presence felt very quickly. Chardonnay, Traminer, Rhine Riesling, Sauvignon Blanc and Sémillon are grown and produced as high-quality varietals. The Chardonnay is ripe and full-flavoured and will take some bottle age, but in general the wines mature quickly and should be drunk young.

Robson Vineyard (*NSW*) ★★★ Meticulous care goes into producing the wines from this very small, but leading, Hunter Valley winery; the first of them appeared in 1974. Beautifully made Cabernet Sauvignon and Shiraz vie with each other for the top honours, alongside an impressive Chardonnay. There is also a Cabernet/Merlot/Shiraz blend and a white Semillon; all are oak-matured.

The Rothbury Estate (*NSW*) ★★★/★★★★ A relative newcomer to the scene, this perfectionist Hunter Valley winery has already made a great impact on all who have been lucky enough to try its wines. The dynamic Len Evans, whose book on the wines of Australia and New Zealand is acknowledged as the prime authority on the subject, is behind the syndicate that owns the estate; the wine-maker is Gerry Sissingh, who must take great credit for the result. The first plantings at Rothbury, near Pokolbin, were made in 1968, and the estate now owns some 700 acres; a further 1,000 acres of vineyard properties are associated with it, of which about 900 are already under vine. Vineyards are necessary, as the estate does not buy in.

The Rothbury winery combines modern machinery with top architecture (its design won the Blacket Award in 1970), and it has been created by people who know what they want – i.e. to make very good wine. Hermitage and Sémillon grapes predominate, but Cabernet Sauvignon and Chardonnay are also important, and experiments are made with several other varieties. However, none of this appears on the front label, which is remarkable (in Australia) for its simplicity.

White Rothbury wines are amazingly full and flavoury. Some are pure Sémillon, others have some Chardonnay in them or can be 100 per cent Chardonnay; their richness, depth and sheer class show what Sémillon can do; they need bottle age to show their full weight and interest. The 1971 is delicate and fine, improving all the time; the straight Sémillon 1972 has a very classy nose, and is distinguished, clean and balanced – with perfect balance, wines like this go on and on. The 1974 (with a small proportion of Chardonnay) was gloriously rich and lanolin-smooth, with a great intensity of taste; the 1976 pure Sémillon was an elegant wine but it has not yet opened out fully.

The reds are beginning to show their quality, but with young vines this takes time. In 1971 no red was thought good enough for the Rothbury Estate label, but the wines chosen for the 1972 vintage are maturing well. The 1973, made from Hermitage with a small proportion of Cabernet Sauvignon, has a lovely clean taste of pure fruit – a very healthy wine, heading for a graceful future. These are not overpowering, blockbuster wines, but they are designed to show breed. Individual Paddock whites and reds represent the top end of the range each year.

St Hubert's Wines (*V*) ★ Promising small vineyard from the Yarra Valley area of Victoria, offering a well-balanced white, Rhine Riesling, and a readily drinkable Shiraz.

Saltram (*SA*) ★★★ Taken over by Dalgety, which has in turn recently handed over its wine interests to Seagram, Saltram is an old Barossa wine concern, near Angaston; today only about ten per cent of the grapes they use come from their own properties. Saltram's wines have always had a good reputation, and some are remarkable value. The Mamre Brook Cabernet, predominantly Cabernet Sauvignon with about 25 per cent Shiraz, is perhaps their prestige wine, and has many medals to its credit; its wonderful smokey/fruity flavour has been mistaken for top quality Graves.

Saltram's Selected Vintage Claret represents one of the best buys in Australia. Apart from the usual Cabernet Sauvignon/Shiraz combination, up to 20 per cent of white Tokay is added; this undoubtedly adds to the perfume of the wine. Saltram's White Burgundy is another excellent buy; it is made from Sémillon from Eden Valley and Angaston, Clare Riesling from Angaston and Tokay from Wilton. There are also good Ports and Sherries and a fresh Rhine Riesling.

Sandalford Wines (*WA*) ★★ Sandalford has vineyards in Swan Valley (warm climate) and Margaret River (cooler climate). The hot sunshine of Swan Valley, 30 metres above sea level, produces flavourful wines with low acidity which characterizes its Zinfandel. Cabernet Sauvignon grapes from both areas are vinified in Swan Valley to produce different wine styles. There are plans to use Rhine Riesling from Margaret River for sweeter late-harvest wines to supplement the already attractive dry style.

Seaview (*SA*) ★★★ Now in the same group as Wynns of Coonawarra (owned by Tooheys, the Sydney brewery) the Seaview vineyards near McLaren Vale in the Southern Vales are over 120 years old. They are five miles inland from St Vincent's Gulf and the climate is temperate, with a long cool ripening period – relatively rare in Australia. The gravelly soils are rather poor and give low yields.

Seaview Cabernet Sauvignon can be elegant, undoubtedly aided by the site's proximity to the ocean. Seaview Moselle is made from an interesting blend of Pedro Ximénez, Sémillon amd Sauvignon Blanc, and somehow manages to taste very like good Mosel. Sauvignon Blanc is an unusual grape for dry wines in Australia, and wine made exclusively from it could perhaps do with a bit more ripeness and sweetness. There is also very good sparkling wine.

Seppelt (*V*) ★★★ One of the great names in Australian wine. An impressive inventory of vineyards and wineries starts with Great Western in Victoria, famous for sparkling wine and the centre for making the company's prestige table wines; then there are wineries at Seppeltsfield and Château Tanunda in the Barossa, South Australia, and extensive vineyards at Keppoch near Coonawarra and at Drumborg in Victoria, 100 miles to the south-west of Great Western; there is another big holding at Rutherglen, north-east Victoria; and there is a research and viticultural station at Barooga, New South Wales, just down the Murray River from Rutherglen. All this adds up to a lot of wine.

Seppelt's Great Western Imperial Reserve Champagne springs readiest to mind; perhaps the vast quantity sold has had an effect on quality, but it is still a good 'sparkler'. Great Western Vintage Brut Champagne is quite a different thing – very delicate and fine. Older vintages can mature gracefully like fine Champagne. Seppelt's Moyston Claret is justifiably well reputed, but has become lighter to keep the price reasonable: it is a Cabernet Sauvignon/ Shiraz wine from Great Western, Rutherglen and the Barossa Valley.

Stanley Wine Company (*SA*) ★★★ Now owned by Heinz, Stanley have wineries and vineyards at Clare, Leasingham and Watervale, about ninety miles north of Adelaide; over half the grapes which they process are bought from other growers. Their Leasingham white wines have been making an increasing mark on the quality wine scene: Bin 5 and Bin 7 Rhine Rieslings are consistently very good indeed, and there is a remarkable Bin 9 Spätlese Riesling. Among the reds, Bin 49 Cabernet stands out; it is a Cabernet Sauvignon/Malbec blend built for long life, like many Clare red wines. There is a marvellous Bin 56 Cabernet Malbec 1972, with fruit, a velvety texture and an oaky 'vanilla' nose. A Bin 17 Dry Rosé 1977 is quite excellent of its kind, but only popular apparently with professional wine people. All these wines have immense potential. Stanley is experimenting with a *primeur* wine, Shiraz Nouveau, remarkably like a young Beaujolais.

Stonyfell (*SA*) ★★ This was another member of the Dalgety camp, until it too fell to Seagrams. The Saltram winery works closely with Stonyfell, with the latter now concentrating on maturing and bottling. Stonyfell Metala Cabernet/Shiraz is made at Saltram with grapes from the Metala vineyard at Langhorne Creek. Stonyfell itself is just to the east of Adelaide. A diverse range of table and fortified wines is put out under the Stonyfell label.

Tolley, Scott, and Tolley Ltd (*SA*) ★/★★ The company were originally brandy distillers and are in fact now part of Distillers Company Ltd. Since 1966 there has been extensive vineyard planting near Adelaide and elsewhere in South Australia at Nuriootpa and Qualco. A wide range of red and white, sparkling and dessert wines are marketed under the Tollana label (Tolley wines come separately from Douglas Tolley Ltd). Up-to-date equipment is employed and grapes are mechanically harvested. Shiraz, Shiraz/ Cabernet and late-picked Rhine Riesling show well.

Tulloch (*NSW*) ★★★ Taken over by Reed Consolidated Industries in 1969, Tulloch is now owned by Gilbeys and continues to make fine wines. The Tullochs began with a vineyard of 50 acres at Glen Elgin near Pokolbin in the Hunter Valley, later expanding at Fordwich, in the adjacent Broke district; a new winery has been built since the takeover. Pride of place must go to the Pokolbin Dry Red Private Bin: it is a big, classic Hunter Shiraz wine, with great keeping potential (the 1954 is still going strong).

Some people refer to the 'sweaty saddle' character of Pokolbin Hunter River Reds, but it is certain that they are aromatic and rich, and that they clearly show the differences between the vintages; a lighter version is to be found in the Pokolbin Dry Red. Glen Elgin Bin 22 Dry White and Tulloch Pokolbin Riesling Private Bin are very worthy whites. Pokolbin Sémillon is an attractive wine. The Selected Vintage Sémillon Chardonnay is outstandingly good.

Tyrrell's Vineyards (*NSW*) ★★★★ The land that became known as Ashmans Vineyard – for the foothills of the Broken Back Range are of volcanic soil – was bought by Edward Tyrrell in 1858; it was acquired by his great nephew Murray almost one century later. His white wines, which are fresh and crisp, are headed by the relatively new Hunter Valley Pinot Chardonnay. The 1971 vintage, the first made exclusively of that variety, was fine and delicate; the 1972, a great year for whites, is naturally richer and fuller; while the 1979 Vat 47 is crisp and well-balanced. There is also the Pinot Riesling blend (actually Chardonnay Sémillon) and the Hunter Valley Riesling (Sémillon). The white Blanquette Shiraz (Clairette Trebbiano) is rather unusual – unsubtle with plenty of straightforward flavour.

Tyrrell's Hunter Valley Dry Reds are made from Hermitage grapes. Another relative newcomer, Tyrrell's Pinot Noir, has established a world-beating reputation for itself in Paris against some of the finest red Burgundy – and now has a price to match.

Vasse Felix (*WA*) A longer-established, but much smaller, neighbour of Sandalford in the Margaret River area of Western Australia. Cool climatic conditions promise well for good-quality wines, and Vasse Felix has already produced consistently good Cabernet Sauvignon and Rhine Riesling from its minute 9-hectare holding.

Virgin Hills (*V*) ★/★★ A small early 70s vineyard at Kyneton near Great Western which has come to the fore through the excellence of its Shiraz, sold as Virgin Hills Dry Red. Cabernet Sauvignon is also grown, and small quantities of Gewürztraminer and Rhine Riesling.

Wyndham Estate (*NSW*) ★★ Reputed to be Australia's oldest vineyard, replanted in the 1970s. Now jointly owned by Australian and Anglo-Thai corporations. Wyndham's has a big output of commercially popular wines which include some individual wines of distinction and quality. Its big, full-flavoured Hunter Valley reds include a good Cabernet Sauvignon and Cabernet Shiraz. From a range of whites Traminer Riesling has shown consistently well.

Wynns (*SA*) ★★★ Now part of Tooheys, the Sydney brewery, Wynns is a widespread enterprise making important wines. They spearheaded the emergence of Coonawarra as a fine table-wine area, and now have about 350 acres under vine there; over 120 acres comprise Cabernet Sauvignon, and Shiraz accounts for about the same. There are also about 50 acres of Rhine Riesling – not all the soil of the vineyards is the *terra rossa* type for which Coonawarra is famous.

Wynns Modbury Estate vineyards were extensive in the Adelaide foothills, but have been lost to urban development. Instead the 1,000-acre High Eden Estate has been established high up on the range between the Barossa and Eden Valleys, with new plantings of Pinot Noir, Chardonnay and Rhine Riesling.

Romalo (now Seaview Champagne Cellars), known for sparkling and *méthode champenoise* wines, is Wynns. The company is also established at Yenda in the Murrumbidgee Irrigation Area of New South Wales.

The wine for which Wynns is justifiably famous is the Coonawarra Estate Cabernet Sauvignon. The wines vary a great deal and are somewhat difficult to assess, as they seem to need years in bottle. The 1973 has great fruit, even opulence, as well as tannin and depth, and more recent vintages are showing well. The Hermitage (sometimes called Claret) can vary too, but the best have great character. The other important wine from Coonawarra Estate is the Rhine Riesling; it is still too early to say exactly how these wines will turn out, but early examples display finesse, good Riesling style, fruit and character.

The company has pioneered developments in the marketing of 'bag in the box' wines.

Yalumba (S. Smith & Son) (*SA*) ★★★ Yalumba is an important Barossa wine firm, with its winery and vineyards at Angaston. It owns over 400 acres in the Barossa and there is about the same amount of acreage under vine on the Murray River; even so, 75 per cent of the grapes needed in both areas are bought from outside sources. The company makes very good Ports and Sherries; amongst the latter is a remarkable 1970 Fino Champion Show Sherry – a wine from Barossa with a lovely flowery nose, light in style and very true.

Yalumba Pewsey Vale Rhine Rieslings from high in the Barossa hills have been much acclaimed. They are full of flavour in the mouth and pack in all the concentration of a fine Rhine Riesling which has had a long ripening period. There is also a Sémillon from Pewsey Vale, sold as Hock. Yalumba Carte d'Or Riesling made in the Eden Valley represents very good value for money.

Among Yalumba reds, Wyndhams Blend Galway Vintage Claret 1973 has a spicy, interesting, fruity nose; it displays a great intensity and concentration on the palate, with an almost iron-like grip and a real oaky flavour – the result of maturing in new Yugoslav casks for 18 months before bottling. This is a Yalumba special bottling; for more everyday drinking, there is Galway Vintage Claret *tout court* – and very good it is, too.

SECTION 2

Other countries

Austria

Mostly whites, ranging from pleasing, well-made *vins ordinaires* to a few fine quality wines. The pride of Austrian viticulture are the *Trockenbeerenauslesen*, produced in relatively commercial quantities at reasonable prices.

THE LAND: Wines of commercial interest are made in the four eastern provinces of Austria, the most productive being the northern province (confusingly known as Lower Austria or Nieder-Österreich) which straddles the River Danube and encircles Vienna. The others, in order of output, are Burgenland, Styria (or Steiermark) and Vienna itself. Most Austrian wines encountered abroad will have come from Lower Austria or Burgenland, their landscapes ranging from the steep river banks of Wachau and the rocky slopes of the Vienna woods to the broad plains bordering the Neusiedlersee, the great lake of Burgenland.

The names of the wine districts within these two provinces are likely to appear on the label. In Lower Austria they are Retz, Falkenstein, Wachau, Krems, Langenlois, Klosterneuburg, Gumpoldskirchen and Vöslav. The two Burgenland districts are Rust-Neusiedlersee and Eisenberg.

PRINCIPAL GRAPE VARIETIES: ○ Grüner Veltliner, Müller-Thurgau, Welschriesling, Neuberger, Weisser Burgunder, Muskat Ottonel, Rheinriesling, Traminer, Zierfandler, Rotgipfler. ● Blaufrankischer, Blau Portugieser, Blau Burgunder, Blau Wildbacher, St Laurent.

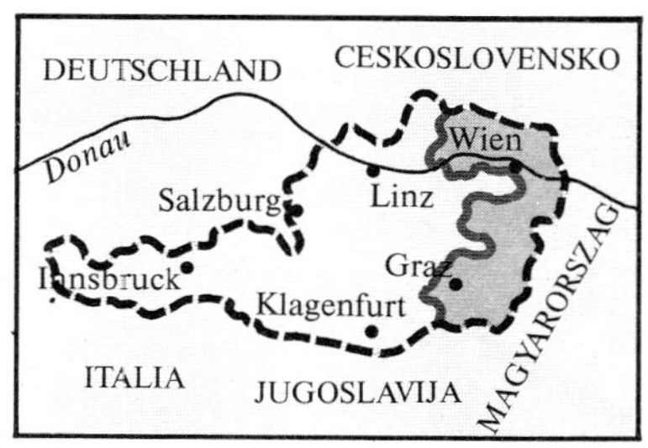

WINE-GROWING DISTRICTS

1 Retz
2 Falkenstein
3 Langenlois
4 Krems
5 Wachau
6 Traismauer-Carnuntum
7 Baden
8 Vöslau
9 Rust-Neusiedlersee
10 Eisenberg
11 Weststeiermark
12 Klöch-Oststeiermark
13 Sudsteiermark

NAMES TO LOOK OUT FOR: The better wines are all white, notably Kremser and Wachauer Rheinrieslings (a grape which does particularly well in these districts) and Grüner Veltliners (the typical grape of Austria). Steiner Hund is an outstanding Rheinriesling wine from a single estate at Stein near Krems. Gumpoldskirchen – properly within the wine district of Baden – is well known for the individual wines it makes from the lesser known Neuberger, Zierfandler and Rotgipfler grapes.

Auslese quality wines are to be encountered in Lower Austria, especially from Rust in the Neusiedlersee district of Burgenland. This area benefits sufficiently from the moderating influence of the lake to produce sumptuous and delicately perfumed *Beeren-* and *Trockenbeerenauslesen* – late-vintaged wines made from Welschriesling, Muskat-Ottonel, Traminer, Müller-Thurgau, Neuberger or Weisser Burgunder grapes.

REGULATIONS: Quality wine of exclusively Austrian origin, from registered grapes grown in a legally defined wine-growing area (*Weinbaugebiet*), is permitted to carry the Government's seal of approval – the *Weingutsiegel Österreich* – as a neck label. A minimum sugar content (75° Oechsle) is required for such a quality wine (*Qualitätswein*). Higher sugar contents are necessary for the still finer *Prädikat* wines.

AVAILABILITY OVERSEAS: Most of the relatively small amount of Austrian wine which is exported goes to West Germany; some is also sold in Belgium, Canada, Denmark, Holland, Sweden, Switzerland, the United Kingdom and the United States.

WORDS ON THE LABEL: Austrian wine labels usually carry the name of the province (e.g. Burgenland), the district (e.g. Falkenstein) and the town or village name (e.g. Klosterneuburg) in one combination or another, together with the grape variety used, the alcoholic strength and the bottle capacity. Many of the terms used are the same as those appearing on German labels (see pages 96–7). Two common words that may not be immediately familiar to non-German speakers are Wien (Vienna) and Österreich (Austria).

THE TRADE: There are some 70,000 vineyard owners, but only a few big estates. The largest private proprietor is Lenz Moser.

England

English wines* are clean, honest and intended for presentation as fine wines, for there is little prospect of quantity production. To the smell they are reminiscent of German wines, but their depth of flavour and their ability to last on the palate often leave much to be desired. The industry is young, made up almost entirely of single vineyard owners who are struggling against an unhelpful, erratic climate and a tax system which they regard as particularly unfair.

THE LAND: The weather determines the concentration of English vineyards in the southern half of the country – and, even there, the normally regarded minimum of 1,000 degree-days of sunshine is rarely experienced. Despite this handicap, wine grapes are grown as far north as Sheffield, and wines are successfully made in Norfolk on a latitude of 52.5N – marginally further north than the great German vineyards of the Rhine and Moselle. Planting has taken place most extensively in the East Anglian counties of Essex and Suffolk and the southern counties of Somerset, Hampshire, Sussex and Kent.

PRINCIPAL GRAPE VARIETIES: Müller-Thurgau, the famous German hybrid, has come to be known as the English grape. Other varieties include Seyval Blanc (used successfully with Chardonnay by one of the better vineyards), Reichensteiner and Ortega (quality hybrids, used to improve Müller-Thurgau wines) and Schönburger (a cross between Pinot Noir and an Italian hybrid). A range of other hybrids and cultivars is being tried experimentally, as well as Pinot varieties, Riesling and Gewürztraminer.

NAMES TO LOOK OUT FOR: As with wines in the United States, there is much to be said for seeking out a good varietal (i.e. a wine made from a single

*Not to be confused with 'British Wine' – a beverage manufactured from imported grape juice.

Vineyards at Beaulieu in Hampshire (G)

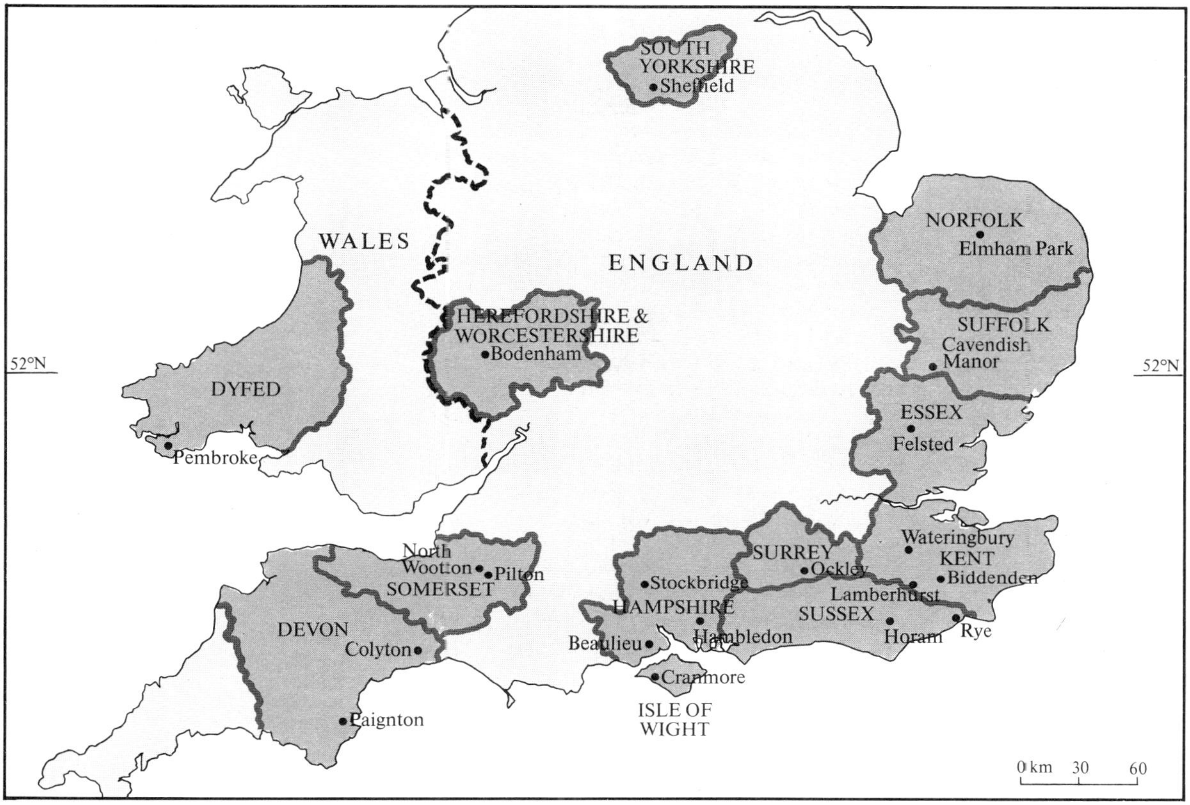

grape) rather than a more or less anonymous blend, although there are as many of these on the market as anything else. Among the more distinctive Müller-Thurgau varietals are those from Biddenden (Kent), Cranmore (Isle of Wight), Cavendish Manor (Suffolk), Elmham Park (Norfolk), Lamberhurst (Kent), Pilton Manor (Somerset, named as Riesling Sylvaner) and North Wootton (Somerset). Magdalen Rivaner (Norfolk) is indeed a Müller-Thurgau, and one of some distinction.

A notable combination of Seyval Blanc and Chardonnay grapes from vineyards at Felsted in Essex is vinified as Felstar. The products of a German hybrid called Reichensteiner, used at Biddenden and at Bodenham in Herefordshire, bear favourable comparison with these other English wines. Wootton Schönburger is a distinctive varietal, based on an equally little-known Riesling cross-breed.

REGULATIONS: E.E.C. regulations govern varieties grown, minimum standards of quality and the information shown on the label. As a preliminary to achieving full Community acceptance of English wines, the English Vineyards Association, formed in 1967, has issued its own seal of approval in the manner of an Italian *consorzio*. Wines which pass a careful analytical scrutiny, intended to be at least as searching as the conditions imposed in France and Germany, are entitled to use the Certification Trade Mark of the Association.

AVAILABILITY OVERSEAS: The products of a number of better-known vineyards are beginning to find their way abroad in small quantities, notably to the United States, France, Germany, Italy, the Netherlands and Norway.

Greece

Wine is often incomparably better drunk on the spot, but even the magic of Greece cannot, as yet at any rate, achieve for its wines (reds, whites; sweet, dry and sparkling) any great depth or delicacy. Retsina, the tipple of the ancient world, survives vigorously into the present.

THE LAND: Greece offers a wide variety of climatic conditions – and soils, usually rocky. The most important wine-growing area is the Peloponnese, whose vineyards account for 55 per cent of the country's total. Macedonia and Thrace in the far north, Crete to the south, the region of Attica immediately to the north of Athens (with the biggest wine output), and the islands of the Aegean (Lemnos and Samos especially) are all distinctive districts, each with its own characteristic products.

PRINCIPAL GRAPE VARIETIES: Peloponnese: ● Aghiorghitico, Mavrodaphne, Mavroudia ○ Roditis, Robola. Crete: ● Liatiko, Romeiko. Attica: ○ Savatiano. Epirus: ○ Debina. Aegean Islands: ○ Muscat.

NAMES TO LOOK OUT FOR: Among the best-known Greek wines are branded names like Demestica, Santa Helena and Antika. Retsina (which is normally white but can be pink) is a wine type, unique to Greece, made from the Savatiano grape. It acquires its name and character from the pine resin which is used during fermentation, giving it a distinctive 'gluey' flavour

Handcarved wine casks at the Achaïa-Clauss winery, Patras

to be loved or hated but never disregarded. The best Retsina comes from Attica. Mavrodaphne, from the Peloponnese, and the Muscat wines from the Aegean islands, are luscious sweet dessert wines, high in alcohol – the one red and the others golden yellow.

Twenty-three regional wines have been identified by the Greek Government to qualify under E.E.C. regulations in the VQPRD category (i.e. quality wines produced within a defined district). It is interesting to note that while most Greek wines are still white the more important include a number of dry reds – notably Amydeon, Archanes, Heraklion, Naoussa, Nemea, Pezon of Heraklion, and Sitia. Among the better whites are Mandinia, Robola from Cephalonia and Zitsa (dry and sparkling); the sweet Mavrodaphne and the Muscats of Samos and Patras are also designated.

REGULATIONS: The designation of 23 VQPRD wines sees the beginning of the application of wider European standards of wine-making. The viticultural output of Greece can thus be seen to fall under three groupings: the blended trademark wines (Demestica Red is a mix of Mavroudia and Aghiorghitico grapes, the white is from the Roditis grape); the now recognized regional wines which account for about 12 per cent of the total; and the rich variety of minor *vins de pays*.

AVAILABILITY OVERSEAS: About a fifth of total output is exported, well over half going to E.E.C. countries, especially West Germany. Much of the rest finds its way to North America, with small quantities to the United Kingdom and Italy.

THE TRADE: Wines are produced by both co-operatives and private companies, as well as individual growers. Achaïa-Clauss, Cambas and the Société Hellénique des Vins et Spiritueux are among the leading concerns.

Hungary

A wide variety of both red and white wines are produced, their quality ranging from ordinary to good; whites tend to be the more distinctive and interesting. The great speciality, Tokay, is unfortunately still made as of old and hence is oxidized.

THE LAND: Hungary is a country of mountains, valleys and plains, with differing soil conditions and an ideal climate (good rainfall and abundant sunshine – 2,000 hours a year on average). Its northerly mountainous regions produce two of its best known wines (Bull's Blood of Eger, and Tokay), but the finer dry whites come from the west – Transdanubia. The bulk of the output, again mostly white, comes from the Great Plain.

PRINCIPAL GRAPE VARIETIES: Four varieties predominate: Furmint – the main grape of the blended Tokay wines, used with Hárslevelü and Sárgamuskotály (a form of Muscat); Kékfrankos (Gamay); Kadarka – the principal constituent of Bull's Blood, blended with Médoc Noir (Merlot) and Kékfrankos; and Olaszrizling – a Riesling that makes dry, crisp wines on the Great Plain and medium dry ones around Lake Balaton (Transdanubia). Other whites include Cirfandli, Ezerjó, Leányka, Muscat Ottonel, Rizlingszilváni, Sauvignon, Sémillon, Sylvaner, Traminer and Veltliner. For some reds Cabernet and a form of Pinot Gris called Szürkebarát are used.

NAMES TO LOOK OUT FOR: Tokaji (Tokay) Aszu, Tokaji Aszu Eszencia, Tokaji Szamorodni and Tokaji Furmint all appear on the labels. Aszu is made from over-ripe grapes with 'noble rot', and is in consequence sweet and rich; the finest – and rarest – of these juices can be fermented to a mild degree of alcohol, producing Aszu Eszencia. Szamorodni is a less exotic combination of Aszu and normally ripened grapes, and can be sweet or dry. Tokaji Furmint is made from the single Furmint grape, yielding a medium sweet, everyday wine. Bull's Blood from the Eger district (Egri Bikavér) is

A cellarmaster tests the wine at Eger (Zefa)

among the better of the reds, as are the Kékfrankos grape wines from Sopron, Szekszárd and Villány. Notable white Olaszrizling wines come from Lake Balaton and Pécs in Transdanubia, and Kecskemét on the Great Plain.

REGULATIONS: Hungary has its own version of *appellations contrôlées*, denoted by the phrase *minöségi bor* on the label. These wines are recognized by the E.E.C. as *vins de qualité produits dans les régions délimitées* (VQPRD). The seal of the State wine cellars, *Magyar Allami Export Pincegazdaság*, at Budafok near Budapest, is used as a mark of authenticity. 80 per cent of the vineyards in the country belong to the State, and exports are handled by a national agency, Monimpex.

AVAILABILITY OVERSEAS: Eastern Europe provides Hungary with its largest market, but sales are increasingly strong in western countries.

WORDS ON THE LABEL: *Agker:* the organization controlling the 125 State farms. *Aszu:* sweet wine from over-ripe grapes, applied to Tokay. *Edes:* sweet. *Fehér:* white. *Hungarovin:* the State-owned wine trust, controlling cellarage and bottling. *Monimpex:* the State import/export agency. *Puttonyos:* measures of sweetening must added to Tokay while it is fermenting; the number which follows provides an indication of the wine's sweetness. *Száraz:* dry. *Vörös:* red.

Jugoslavia

Lots of pleasant if mostly ordinary wine. Whites are more varied and attractive than the reds.

THE LAND: Of the country's six original states – Serbia, Croatia, Slovenia, Bosnia-Herzegovina, Macedonia and Montenegro – the first two provide by far the largest output. Most wines likely to be drunk abroad, however, come from the northern, terraced hillsides of Slovenia, third largest in output.

PRINCIPAL GRAPE VARIETIES: ○ Pinot Blanc (*Bijeli Pinot* or *Burgundac*); Riesling – mostly the Italian variety (*Laski Rizling* or *Graševina*) but some German (*Rajnski* or *Renski Rizling*); Furmint (*Šipon*); Sauvignon – makes the best wines; Sylvaner (*Silvanac*); Traminer (*Traminac*). ● Prokupac – widely-grown indigenous vine, giving a heavy rich wine; Merlot; Pinot Noir (*Modri Burgundac*). A torrent of other grape and wine names are used, including, as varietals, Cabernet, Gamay and Sémillon from France; Refosco and Barbera from Italy; Ezerjo, Kadarka and Muscat Ottonel from Hungary; and a host of native varieties.

Labels will often quote the grape used, and in the case of the better

ones the village or district name precedes it – e.g., Lutomer Riesling (*Ljutomeri Rizling*). Jugoslavia's oldest wine-growing traditions are linked with the small Slovenian market town of Lutomer and its neighbour Ormož, and the best of the exported white wines come from that area. Sauvignon is the predominant grape, but Lutomer Rieslings and Traminers are equally popular. Jerusalem and Svetinje are two notable single estates. Just to the north is Gorna Radgona, home of the sweet, fruity white Tiger's Milk (*Tigrovo Mleko*). Cviček is a light red Slovenian wine.

AVAILABILITY OVERSEAS: The Comecon countries are the main importers of Jugoslav wines, the U.S.S.R. taking the largest quantities of bottled wine; it is also exported to West Germany, Britain, Switzerland, Scandinavia, the U.S.A. and Canada.

WORDS ON THE LABEL: *Bijelo:* white. *Biser:* sparkling. *Crno:* red. *Čuveno vino:* selected wine. *Kvalitetno vino:* quality wine. *Modri:* black. *Ružica:* rosé. *Slatko:* sweet. *Stolno vino:* table wine. *Suho:* dry. *Vrhunsko:* highest quality wine.

Luxembourg

White wines (no reds) grown on the slopes of the Moselle tend to a rather austere acidity, and are of modest quality.

THE LAND: The vineyards spread across south-east facing slopes along the left bank of the Moselle, on Luxembourg's south-eastern border with West Germany. They lie on a latitude approximately 49½° north, just south of most of the great German vineyards and just north of Champagne.

PRINCIPAL GRAPE VARIETIES: The most widely grown, and first of the quality wine grapes, is the Rivaner (Riesling × Sylvaner, or Müller-Thurgau). Others in order of importance are Riesling, Auxerrois, Pinot Blanc, Pinot Gris and Traminer. Sylvaner and Muscat are grown in very small quantities. Everyday white wine is produced – less now than previously – from the native Elbling grape.

REGULATIONS: Quality is controlled by the Government through the State Wine Institute, which is also responsible for consumer protection and conformity to E.E.C. regulations. A *marque nationale* is awarded, displayed as a neck label, for three superior levels of quality: *vin classé* (selected wine), *premier cru* (high quality) and *grand permier cru* (very high quality). This accolade is restricted to wines made from Riesling, Traminer, Muscat, Pinot, Auxerrois, Rivaner and Sylvaner grapes.

AVAILABILITY ABROAD: Belgium takes the lion's share of the few wines exported (72,000 hectolitres in 1977). Some goes to the Netherlands and West Germany.

THE TRADE: Vineyards are in the main small family holdings but 70 per cent of them are grouped into six co-operatives. Vinsmoselle is the name for an association of five of them – Greiveldange, Grenenmacher, Remerschen, Stadtbredimus and Wellenstein. The sixth is called Wormeldange.

A wine press at Schwebsange (Spectrum)

Switzerland

Most Swiss wines are drunk on the home market – nobody else can afford them. They are pleasant and well-made – the reds soft and fruity, the whites attractively fresh.

THE LAND: The French-speaking south-west corner of Switzerland is the country's most productive wine region, accounting for 90 per cent of its total output – by far the greater part of it white. The varied landscape to the north and east of Lake Geneva (Lac Léman) provides a striking backdrop to a progression of wine varieties: from the steep terraces of the Valais, in the mountainous valley of the Rhône, to the gentler slopes of Vaud and the lakeside vineyards of Geneva, Neuchâtel, Bienne and Morat. The Italian-speaking Ticino in the south-east is a predominantly red wine region, and there are numerous vineyards in the German-speaking north-east, producing both red and white wines.

PRINCIPAL GRAPE VARIETIES: The vine producing the majority of Swiss white wines is the Chasselas, known as Fendant in the Valais, Dorin in Vaud and Perlan in the lakeside areas of Geneva and Neuchâtel. Dôle (Valais) and Salvagnin (Vaud) are both blends of Gamay and Pinot Noir, and the latter is also used to produce the delicate Neuchâtel *rosé*, Oeil de Perdrix, and the red wines of the north-east (where it is known as the Klevner). French Merlot is planted in Ticino; Riesling and Sylvaner are employed in the Geneva area and the north-east.

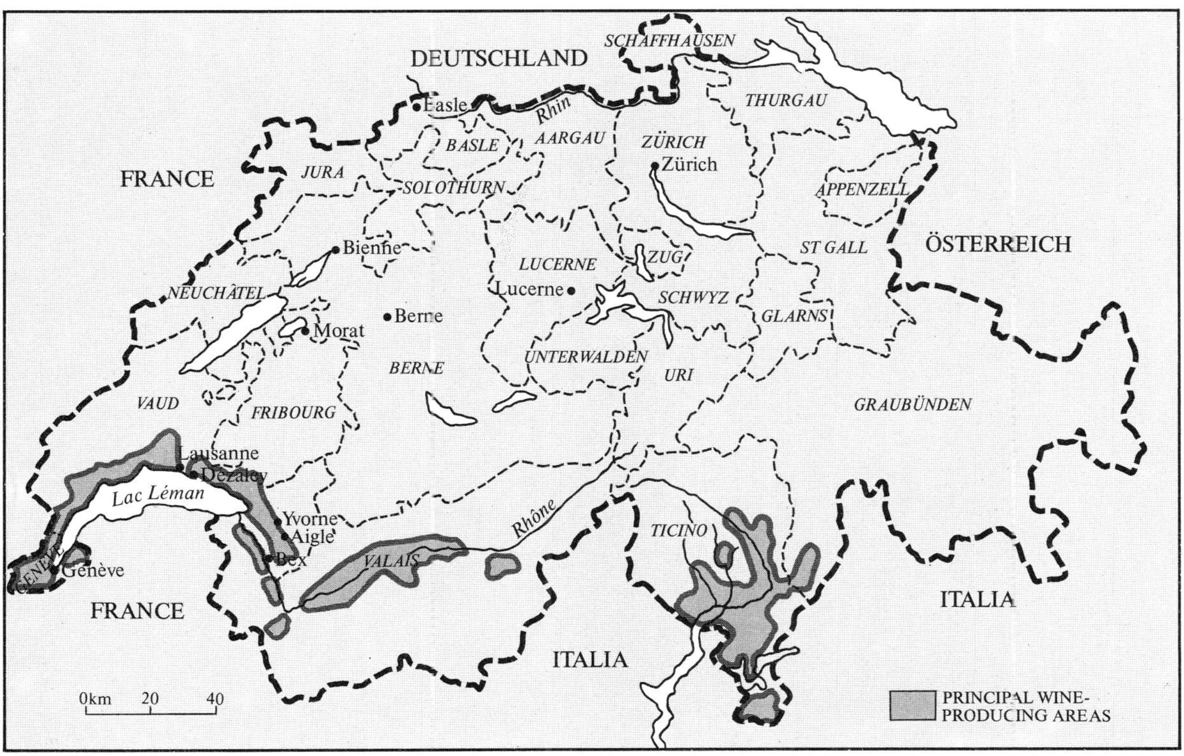

NAMES TO LOOK OUT FOR: Within Switzerland, the wines of the Valais – notably the white Fendant (dry and fruity) and the red Dôle (soft, full-bodied, perfumed) – are among the most popular. The better Vaud white wines use the generic name Dorin, attaching to it the name of the particular village of origin: Dézaley is an outstanding example. The small towns of Aigle, Bex and Yvorne, in an area between Vaud and the Valais known as Chablais, produce strong, dry whites. The Oeil de Perdrix and Gamay *rosés* are well thought of; Johannisberg is a speciality wine from the Valais, made from Sylvaner grapes, and a sweet white Malvoisie is made from Pinot Gris. Better Merlot wines from Ticino are distinguished by the use of the name Viti.

REGULATIONS: The strict laws applied by the Swiss to food production also govern wine-making. There is an official wine-tasting committee which judges wines for export, and a Swiss Wine Growers Association.

AVAILABILITY OVERSEAS: The small quantity of Swiss wines exported goes mainly to Germany, the United States, Canada, Belgium and Holland.

Aigle, in the Chablais area of Switzerland (Daily Telegraph)

Cyprus

The Cypriot wine industry has long been dominated by cheap imitation sherries. Table wines are ordinary, but a speciality dessert wine, Commandaria, is noteworthy.

THE ISLAND: The majority of the vineyards are in the south-west of the island on the sunny, south-facing slopes of the Troodos mountains, where the rainfall is sufficiently high. The administrative districts of Limassol and Paphos embrace this area and the two towns are the main centres of production – Paphos predominantly for white wines. Vineyards on a smaller scale can be found in the neighbourhood of Nicosia, Larnaca and Famagusta.

PRINCIPAL GRAPE VARIETIES: The two main grapes native to Cyprus are the black Mavron and the white Xynisteri, the former more widely grown than the latter; both are used to make the fabled sweet red Commandaria. A small quantity of Muscat of Alexandria is also grown. Because Cyprus has remained free of phylloxera there has been a natural reluctance to introduce new vines. However, under pressure to improve range and quality, some sixteen European varieties have been imported, including Cabernet Franc,

Grape harvest in the hills behind Limassol (G)

Carignan Blanc, Grenache, Sauvignon and Shiraz. Palomino and Pedro Ximénes have been brought in to improve the sherries.

NAMES TO LOOK OUT FOR: 'Cyprus sherry' was developed for the British market, which still takes half the output. It can be sold at full strength (17°–18°), or at low strength (when it is normally sweet) or in a form blended from the two by the importer; styles range from pale dry to cream. Commandaria, which takes its name from the Grande Commanderie of the crusading Knights of St John, is traditional Cypriot wine; luscious and sweet, like a red liqueur, it is made in relatively small quantities. Better everyday white wines include Aphrodite (medium dry) and Arsinoe (dry); Afames, Domaine d'Ahera and Othello are among the reds.

REGULATIONS: The Vine Products Commission was set up in 1968 to maintain standards and quality. Wine-growing is restricted to hilly regions between 1,000 and 2,500 feet above sea level, and the size of the production area is controlled. Cyprus has associate membership of the E.E.C.

AVAILABILITY OVERSEAS: The way is now open for Cyprus sherries to be exported to E.E.C. countries other than Britain; they can already be found in North America and Poland. Red and white wines find their way to Scandinavia, Switzerland and the east European countries.

THE TRADE: Five main companies handle the production and export of Cyprus wines – Sodap, Keo, Etko-Haggipavlu, Loel and Christophorou. All are based around Limassol, which has a modern port to handle the trade. Sodap (the Vine Products Marketing Union) is a large co-operative, with modern wineries in both Limassol and Paphos; together with Keo and Etko it handles the bulk of exports.

Israel

Despite their biblical fame, Israeli wines are the despair of Jewish wine-lovers in Europe and the U.S.A. Somehow, in spite of their undoubted talents, the nation's vintners produce very mediocre wines; they are mostly exported only for Kosher purposes.

THE LAND: Israel has Mediterranean sunshine and excellent soil conditions. While additional vineyards are continually being established, the notable areas at present lie in the Judaean hills, on the slopes of Mount Carmel, around Galilee and on the coastal plain, and in the dry Negev, just to the north-east of the Sinai peninsula.

PRINCIPAL GRAPE VARIETIES: These include Carignan and Alicante Grenache, Sémillon, Bourboulenc and Dabuki. Others used in smaller quantities are Cabernet Sauvignon, Chenin Blanc, Concord, French Colombard, Muscat of Alexandria and Ugni Blanc.

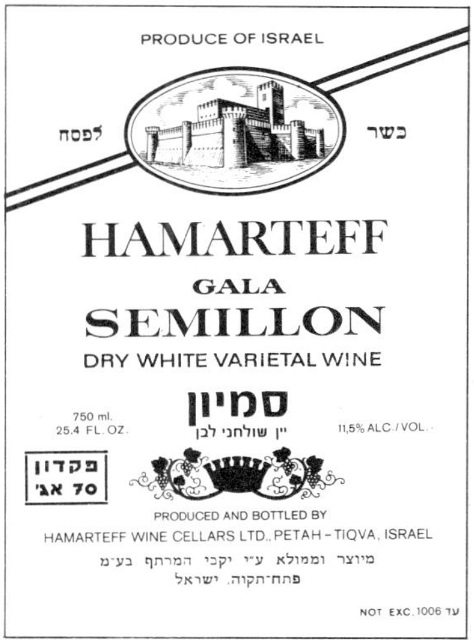

NAMES TO LOOK OUT FOR: Israeli wines are normally marketed under brand names. The label will mention the grape in the case of varietal wines, but not its provenance. Among the leading companies are Askalon, Aviva, Carmel, Eliaz, Israeli Distillers, National Distillers, Societé Co-opérative Vigneronne, Richon-le-Zion and Zicron-Jacob.

REGULATIONS: The Israel Wine Institute, established in 1957, controls quality and gives a seal of approval. Wines are in many cases produced and bottled under the supervision of the Chief Rabbinate.

AVAILABILITY OVERSEAS: Exported mainly to the U.S.A. and western Europe, but in smaller quantity to as many as 40 other countries.

Turkey

It comes as a surprise to discover that Turkey is the largest producer of grapes in the world, although its wine industry is small. In recent years some surprisingly good red wines have been exported in small quantities – certainly of a higher quality, for instance, than most Greek wines.

THE LAND: Under the influence of the Turkish State Monopolies, a body set up in 1927 to improve exports, efforts are being made to produce quality wines from three main areas: Trakya (Thrace) and Marmara in the north-west, the central region of Anatolia (embracing Ankara, and stretching south to Konya and Urgup) and the eastern and south-eastern parts of Anatolia, from Elazig south towards the Syrian border at Gaziantep and Urfa. The latter produces over half the total output. White wines from the Sultaniye and Muscat grapes come from the western, Aegean, district (Izmir and Manisa are the main centres), but the largest part of the crop is used for sultanas and table grapes. Tokat in north-eastern Anatolia is a centre for two good quality wines, Narbag (white) and Bogazkarasi (red).

NAMES TO LOOK OUT FOR: Seven brand names for classified quality wines are approved by the Turkish State Monopolies: Hosbag (● ○), Guzbag (∅) and Trakya (● ○) from Trakya; Kalebag (● ○) from Ankara; Buzbag (●) from Elazig; Narbag (○) from Tokat; and Urgup (○) from Urgup. Trakya red is fairly light, Buzbag somewhat heavier. The white Trakya is made from a Sémillon grape derivative (Yapincak), but the better whites tend to come from the central and eastern regions.

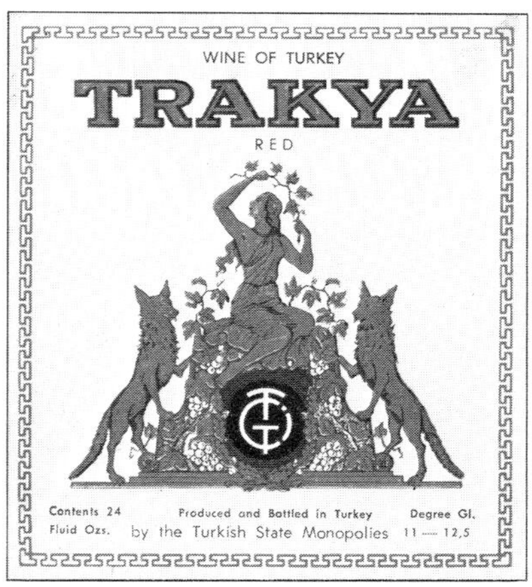

REGULATIONS: Quality control is in the hands of the State Monopolies, whose wines carry the word *Tekel* on the neck label as a guarantee of quality. A number of private firms produce and export Turkish wines, based mainly either in Istanbul or Ankara.

AVAILABILITY OVERSEAS: Exports are small but have recently shown an increase. West Germany, followed by Sweden, Norway, Britain and Italy, are the principal importers.

Algeria

Algeria owes its vines to the Phoenicians and its extensive knowledge of viticulture to the French. Quality and output have both declined in the recent past – partly owing to political developments – but production is still by far the highest in north-west Africa.

THE LAND: The vineyards planted by the French a century ago within the departments of Alger, Constantine and Oran were spread out in great profusion across the coastal plains as well as higher up on the slopes of the Atlas mountains. Independence for Algeria in 1962 brought a recession in demand from its principal market, mainland France, with a consequent decline in the industry. In the pursuit of higher quality, seven principal wine-growing areas have been defined on the better hill sites: three are in Alger – Ain Bessem-Bouira, Coteaux du Zaccar and Medea; and four in Oran – Coteaux du Mascara, Coteaux de Tlemcen, Dahra and Monts du Tessalah.

PRINCIPAL GRAPE VARIETIES: Red wines are vinified chiefly from Carignan, Cinsault and Grenache, with additions of Cabernet Sauvignon, Alicante Bouschet, Mourvèdre, Pinot Noir and Syrah permitted. These same grapes produce *rosé* wines. The whites, which tend to be rarer, are made from Clairette, to which may variously be added Chardonnay, Ferrana, Furmint, Grenache Blanc, Macabeo and specified local varieties.

REGULATIONS: Since 1968 there has been a sole agency, the Office National de Commercialisation des Produits Viti-Vinicoles (ONCV), dealing with the

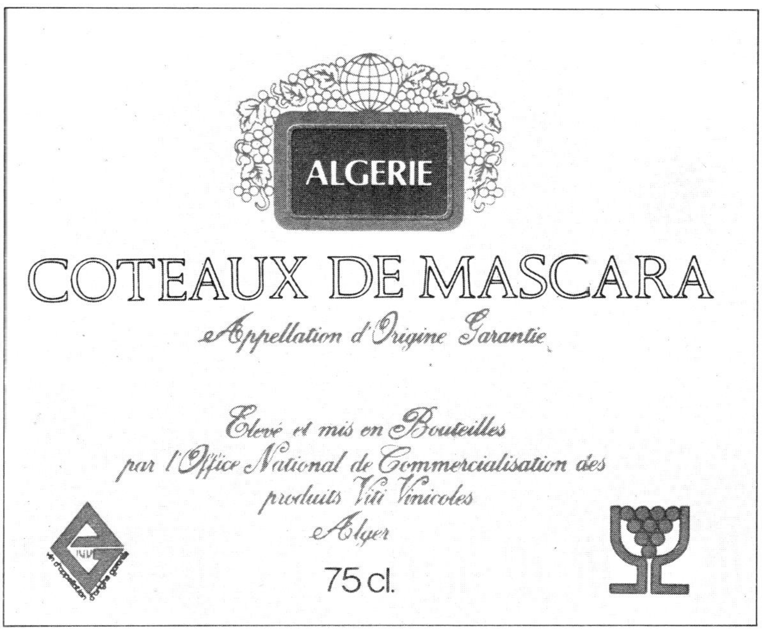

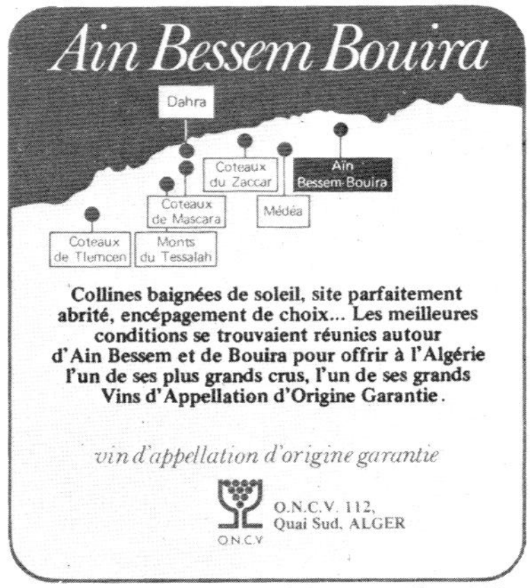

production and distribution of Algerian wines, and supervising quality. The seven growing areas were defined two years later, and are covered by French-style regulations, the resulting wines being recognized as *vins d'appellation d'origine garantie.*

NAMES TO LOOK OUT FOR: Reds and *rosés* come from each of the seven areas. Among the reds, Coteaux du Mascara is robust, highly coloured and strong (as high as 14°); Dahra reds vary slightly between the better-known villages, Taoughrite (previously Paul Robert), Ain Merane (Rabelais), Mazounn (Renault) and Khadra Achaacha (Picard); Medea and Coteaux du Zaccar reds are considered to have a measure of delicacy. The whites – there are less of them – are from Medea, Coteaux du Mascara and Coteaux de Tlemcen. La Trappe and Cuvée du Président are two non-*appellation* wines.

THE TRADE: Being no longer part of and protected by the French market, Algerian wines now have to compete on their own merits. Overall output has dropped by nearly two-thirds since the middle 1960s. There is no real home market, and there is thus every incentive to produce sound, inexpensive wines for sale abroad – a role which the country's natural resources readily permit.

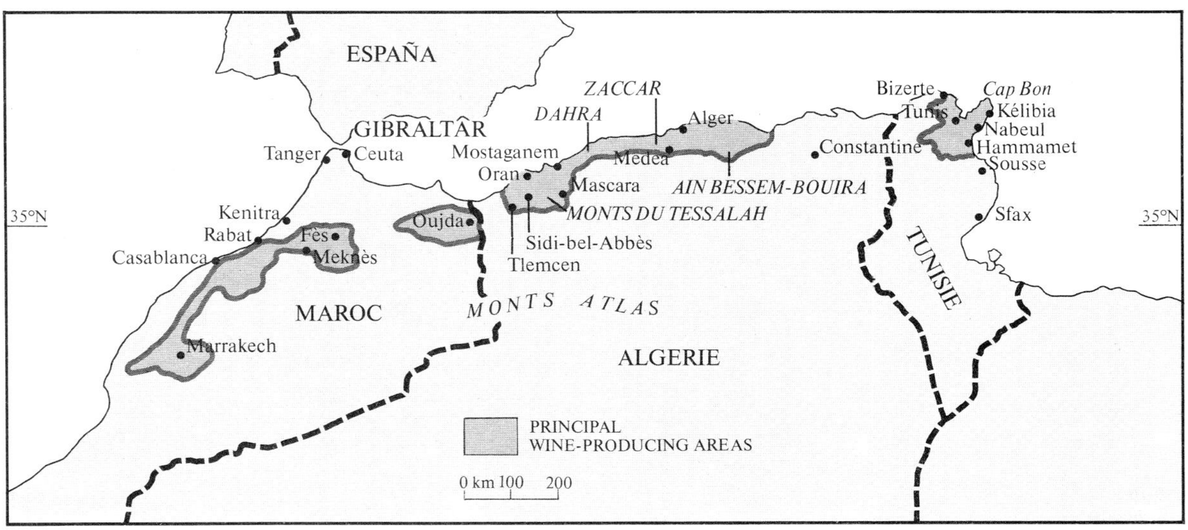

Tunisia

Tunisia – Carthage to the ancient world – has a long history of viticulture. Strabon, the Greek historian of the 1st century BC, declared that the region led all of Africa in its output of wheat, fruit and wine; a Carthaginian agronomist, Mago, was one of the earliest codifiers of the vine. The industry's past is more distinguished than its present: nevertheless, strong efforts are being made to raise quality and to increase exports.

THE LAND: The vineyards of Tunisia are concentrated along 400km of Mediterranean coastline, from the Gulf of Hammamet round Cap Bon and the Gulf of Tunis to the Bay of Bizerta. The Cap Bon peninsula, centred on Nabeul, is the most prolific region, with an output nearly twice as large as those of Tunis and Bizerta combined.

PRINCIPAL GRAPE VARIETIES: ● Alicante Bouschet, Cabernet, Carignan, Mourvèdre, Pinot Noir, Alicante Grenache, Cinsault; ○ Clairette, Muscat of Alexandria, Pedro Ximénes, Beldi de Tunis.

Berber women at work in the vineyard in spring (Zefa)

NAMES TO LOOK OUT FOR: The dry and sweet white Muscat de Keliba, and the wines of Sidi Salem, Coteaux de Tebourba, Mornag and Sidi Saad have protected place-names. A national committee scrutinizes quality. Haut Mornag and Coteaux de Carthage are better-known reds, and Sidi Rais is a notable *rosé* from Takelsa. Nahli and Schuigui are popular brands from two of the leading co-operatives in the Union des Caves Co-opératives Vinicoles de Tunisie (UCCVT) – an organization controlling 70 per cent of the country's output.

REGULATIONS: The control of price and quality is entrusted to the Office du Vin in Tunis. Traditional grape varieties must be used, hybrids are forbidden. To improve quality Tunisia has turned its face against irrigation, chaptalization (adding of sugar) and *mouillage* (watering the wine).

THE TRADE: Like Algeria, Tunisia has suffered from the falling-off in demand from the French market, although a large part of her output still goes to France. The search for other markets has been accompanied by efforts to improve quality. A lot goes to other African countries, but wine is also now imported by West Germany, Poland, Czechoslovakia, Switzerland, Austria, Malta, Hungary and Britain – in that order of quantity.

Morocco

The modern wine industry of Morocco is little more than fifty years old, and some of its vineyards much younger than that. It has the lowest yield of the North African wine-producing countries, each with a large, though falling, output; like them, it is a major supplier of blending wines to the Common Market.

THE LAND: Vines are grown in the still, flat inland regions at the foot of the Atlas mountains around Meknès (20,000 of Morocco's 55,000 hectares of vineyard), Oujda on the border with Algeria and Marrakech to the south-west; also, to a lesser extent, in the coastal districts of Kenitra, Rabat and Casablanca. Much of the Moroccan coast is not Mediterranean but North Atlantic, and Casablanca lies on latitude 33°N.

PRINCIPAL GRAPE VARIETIES: ● Alicante Bouschet, Carignan, Cinsault, Grenache. ○ Clairette, Grenache, Macabeo, Pedro Ximénes.

Argentina

Outside Europe, Argentina is the world's biggest wine producer. Its wines are mostly ordinary – red, white, sparkling and fortified – but there are a few of higher quality. The reds are much better than the whites.

THE LAND: The vine is not native to Argentina, but climatic conditions are highly compatible to its cultivation. The principal wine-growing region is centred on the provinces of Mendoza and San Juan, just to the north. The Mendoza vineyards, which account for 70 per cent of the country's output, are in a high flat region, 3,500ft above sea level, along the foothills of the Andes. Water for the vines has to be provided by irrigation, linked to the rivers which carry melted snow down from the mountains, or by boring wells. A mere five per cent of Argentina's wine comes from six other provinces: Rio Negro, Córdoba, Entre Rios, Litoral, Norte and Occidente.

PRINCIPAL GRAPE VARIETIES: Argentina has taken a pride in eschewing hybrids, and only selected European vinestocks are planted. Cabernet, Malbec, Merlot, Pinot Noir and Syrah have been borrowed from France for red wines, and Chardonnay, Chenin Blanc, Sauvignon, Sémillon and Pinot Blanc for whites. Italian Barbera, Bonarda, Lambrusco and Riesling, and the Spanish Pedro Ximénes are also used. The latter is the next main white

A vineyard near Cafayate in Salta province, in the foothills of the Andes (Michael Frenchman)

A Cafayate bodega *(Michael Frenchman)*

wine grape, after the Criollas (a near native imported by the Jesuits in the 16th century). Malbec is the most widely grown of the reds.

NAMES TO LOOK OUT FOR: Too much Argentinian wine is still sold under a brand name, the greatest part of it being exported in bulk and bottled abroad. Some finer varietal wines are exported in bottle, mostly to the north and south Americas. Andean Cabernet Sauvignon from the giant wine concern Penaflor is intentionally blended like a Médoc with smaller quantities of Malbec and Merlot. Others labelled as varietals – Chardonnay, Chenin Blanc, Malbec, Merlot and Riesling – are likely to be more nearly 100 per cent single grape.

REGULATIONS: Strict laws govern labelling and bottling, and will continue to contribute to improving standards. A national body, the Instituto Nacional de Vitivinicultura (INV), was set up in 1959 to control production methods and commercial practices. Grape and wine samples are analysed, wineries, bottling plants and retail outlets are subject to scrutiny. Wine cannot be offered for sale without authorization by the INV.

AVAILABILITY OVERSEAS: Wine in bulk and bottle is exported all over the world – principally to the U.S.S.R., the Americas, East and West Germany, Jugoslavia, Japan, Britain, Belgium and Czechoslovakia.

THE TRADE: The largest part of the industry is of vineyards under ten hectares in size. Exports are handled by a small group of companies – pre-eminently Penaflor, which is thought to be the third largest producer and distributor in the world. Others include Angel Furlotti, Greco Hermanos, José Orfila and Pascual Toso.

Chile

A much smaller producer than Argentina, but some of its Cabernets have real quality. The industry is still recovering from the dislocation of the Allende era. Whites are much less interesting than reds.

THE LAND: Chile runs north to south for 3,000 miles, and commercial cultivation takes place over two-thirds of its length, between latitudes 27.5° and 38°S. It splits into three regions, the northern central, the central valley and the southern. Finer red wines come from the central region around Santiago, particularly from two districts ideally suited to the vine, the Aconcagua and Maipo river valleys. Strong and fortified wines are made in the north, and everyday reds in the south, but the south has some better whites. Protected by the Pacific and the Andes, and the Atacama desert in the north, Chile has remained phylloxera-free; this, coupled with a sympathetic climate, has enabled the finer varieties of European grape to flourish.

PRINCIPAL GRAPE VARIETIES: Cabernet for finer wines and País for others are the two principal grape varieties. The latter (a long-established near-native, imported by the Spaniards) is found mostly in the south. Cot Rouge, Carignan, Merlot, Petit Verdot, Pinot Noir and Romano are grown in smaller quantities. Whites are chiefly from Sémillon and Sauvignon, with lesser, more local, names like Italia, Cristal, Torontel, and Moscatel, as well as a minimum of Pinot Blanc and Riesling.

NAMES TO LOOK OUT FOR: Chilean wines are more usually encountered in North and South America. Wagner Stein, however, is a leading exporter to Belgium, Germany, Spain and Switzerland, and to New Zealand. Other exporters, based in Santiago, are Concha y Toro, Fuenzalida Eyzaguirre, José Rabat, Viña Undurraga and Vinos de Chile, Vinex. More red wine is made than white, and the most likely red is a Cabernet under one name or another. Riesling is reputed to be one of the best whites, but there is little of it.

REGULATIONS: French influence remains strong – it was French planters who started many of the Chilean vineyards – but as yet there is no equivalent to the *appellations contrôlées* system. The Government takes a keen interest, however, and there is a National Council which supervises exports. Wines must be at least a year old and are tested for clarity and quality. Whites are expected to have a minimum strength of 12°, and reds 11.5°.

AVAILABILITY OVERSEAS: Mainly in the Americas, but efforts are also made to market further afield. Venezuela is the largest single importer.

WORDS ON THE LABEL: *Blanco:* white wine (if used without a grape name it is likely to be made from Sémillon, with a possible addition of Sauvignon). *Courant:* one-year-old wine. *Gran Vino:* wine at least six years old (whites are aged as well as reds). *Reservado:* wine aged two years in oak casks. *Reserve:* Four-year-old wine. *Special:* two-year-old wine. *Tinto:* red wine (usually made from Cabernet grapes, sometimes blended with Merlot).

Vineyards near Santiago (Spectrum)

New Zealand

Viticulture in New Zealand is still something of a pioneering activity; but considerable advances have been made in the last decade and some good wines, red and white, are produced on both islands, particularly in the north.

THE LAND: New Zealand's vineyards are mostly in North Island, above latitude 40°S, with the majority concentrated in three districts: around Auckland (the largest) and around Hawke's Bay (centred on Napier) and Poverty Bay (centred on Gisborne). Auckland in particular has a plentiful rainfall, and the climate generally is suited to the production of light table wines.

PRINCIPAL GRAPE VARIETIES: There are some 50 varieties in all, but most of the dry white wines are made from Riesling Sylvaner; this has supplanted the white hybrid Baco 22A and the Palomino in popularity, in keeping with a general change from high yielding low quality hybrids to higher quality European vines. Chasselas provides the sweeter white wines, and Chardonnay and Gewürztraminer make the finer quality whites. The better reds are invariably Cabernet Sauvignon, though much wine is made from Pinotage, a prolific high yielder, and from Baco 1 and Seibel hybrids.

NAMES TO LOOK OUT FOR: Cabernet Sauvignon varietals hold the field in red wines, and the choice lies between one or other of a very few firms – McWilliams, Mission Vineyards and Western Vineyards among them. McWilliams also make notable white Pinot Chardonnay, Traminer and Riesling Sylvaner wines. Corban Wines is another name to be associated with Pinot Chardonnay; like McWilliams again, and like Penfold's, they also make sparkling wines by the Charmat process. A *méthode champenoise* wine called Sparkling Fontanella is made by Mission Vineyards.

REGULATIONS: Since 1975 a New Zealand Wine Institute has co-ordinated the activities of a number of bodies concerned with the development of the wine industry. Licences to make wine are only granted to members of the Institute.

AVAILABILITY OVERSEAS: A limited quantity of New Zealand wines is exported to Canada, Japan, Australia, the U.S.A., Britain and Hong Kong.

THE TRADE: The move has been away from small family-owned vineyards, and two-thirds of all wine produced comes from six large firms: Cook's Wine Company (Waikato); Corban Wines (Auckland); Glenvale (Hawke's Bay), a private family concern with nonetheless the country's fourth largest output; McWilliams (Hawke's Bay); Penfold's Wines (Auckland); and Montana (Auckland), linked with Seagrams. An increase in vineyards planted with *vinifera* grapes can be expected.

South Africa

More famous for its imitation sherries than anything else, and indeed the standard of these wines is impeccable. White wines are well made, but lack flair and character. The reds have recently made strides, but still tend to be tannic and tough.

THE LAND: South Africa's important vineyards are restricted to the south-western districts of Cape Province, where vines were first planted on the slopes of the Table Mountain by Dutch settlers in 1655. The three chief districts are firstly the coastal belt (Constantia, Durbanville, Paarl, Stellenbosch, Tulbagh and Malmesbury); the hotter, drier area of Klein Karoo to the east and the Breede River Valley; and the more northerly area of Picquetberg and Olifants River, where lighter everyday wines are being developed as well as the traditional distilling wines.

Vineyards below the Jenker Shoek Mountains in Cape Province (Spectrum)

DEMARCATED DISTRICTS FOR PRODUCTION OF 'WINES OF ORIGIN'

1 Olifantsrivier
2 Piquetberg
3 Malmesbury
4 Tulbagh
5 Constantia and Durbanville
6 Stellenbosch
7 Paarl
8 Worcester
9 Robertson
10 Klein Karoo
11 Swellendam

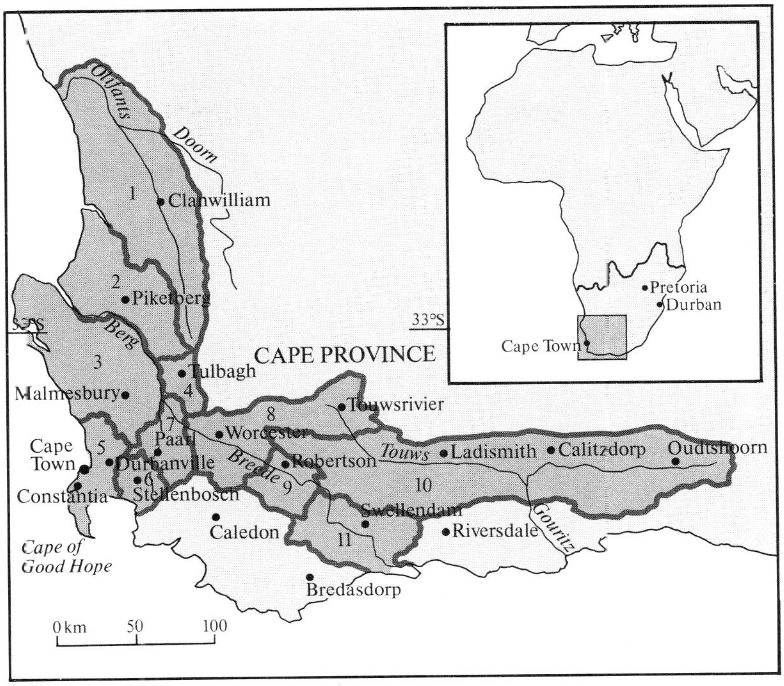

PRINCIPAL GRAPE VARIETIES: Cabernet Sauvignon, Cinsaut and Shiraz for light-bodied (12°) red wines from Constantia Valley and coastal Stellenbosch; Cinsaut, Shiraz, Pinotage and Tinto Barocca for the fuller-bodied (13.2°) reds from Durbanville, Paarl, Stellenbosch and Malmesbury; Clairette Blanche, Colombard, Riesling and Steen for dry and semi-sweet whites (11°–12°) from Paarl, Stellenbosch, Robertson and Worcester; and Riesling and Clairette Blanche for sparkling wines (10°–12°). Palomino and Chenin Blanc (or Steen) are the principal sherry grapes.

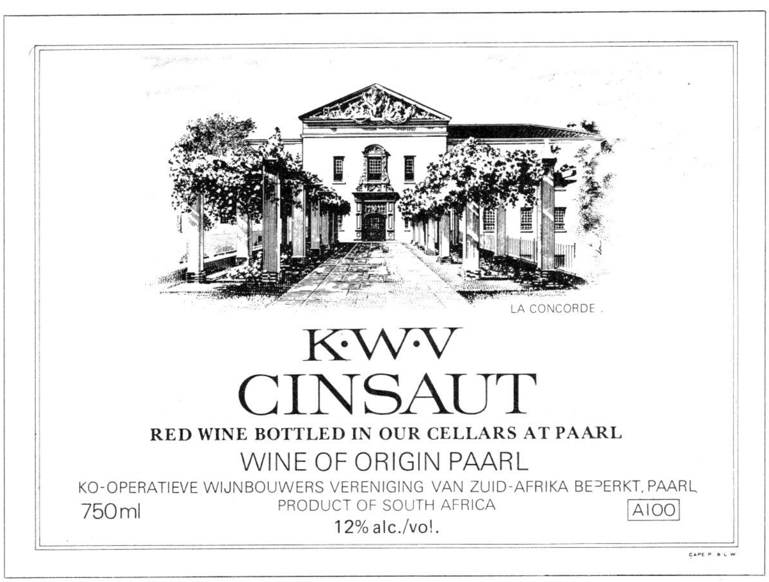

The late 17th-century wine cellar at Groot Constantia (South Africa Wine Farmers Assn.)

NAMES TO LOOK OUT FOR: Over 40 estates have been accorded individual place-names, including Groot Constantia and Meerendal (in the Cape division); Alto, Middelvlei, Muratie, Neethlingshof, Overgaauw, Simonsig, Uiterwyk, Verdun, Koopmanskloop, Spier, Uitkyk, Vergenoegd and Devon Valley (Stellenbosch); Backsberg, Fairview, Landskroon and Villiera (Paarl); Montpellier, Theuniskraal and Twee Jongegezellen (Tulbagh); and de Wetshof (Robertson). The lighter South African sherries come from the coastal region districts, particularly Paarl and Stellenbosch.

REGULATIONS: Since 1972 a national Wine and Spirit Board has controlled the use of place names. 15 districts, Paarl and Stellenbosch being the most prominent, have been designated for the production of 'Wines of Origin', and that phrase appears on the label of approved wines from those districts. Similarly, as mentioned above, a number of individual estates have been nominated. A wine of approved origin, vintage and grape variety carries a blue, red and green banded seal as a neck label, certifying the Board's approval.

AVAILABILITY OVERSEAS: The production and marketing interests of the Cape wine farmer are looked after by the national association of wine co-operatives, known as the KWV (Ko-operatieve Wijnbouwers Vereniging). Wines are exported to 26 countries, chiefly Britain and Canada.

CERTIFICATION SEALS

Each bottle of wine complying with the South African Wine and Spirit Board's requirements bears a pale blue neck seal authenticating the information printed on the main label. This seal, which carries the Republic's coat of arms, indicates that the wine conforms with some or all of the Board's regulations, as follows:

BLUE BAND – *area of origin*

RED BAND – *vintage year*

GREEN BAND – *variety of grape*

IDENTIFICATION NUMBER – *traces the wine from vineyard through cellar to point of distribution*

'Estate' – signifies that the wine was produced within a demarcated area
'Superior' – signifies that the wine conforms to this quality, as defined by the Board.

The purchaser should carefully note which of these guarantees appear on the seal if he wishes to ensure the accuracy of the main label.

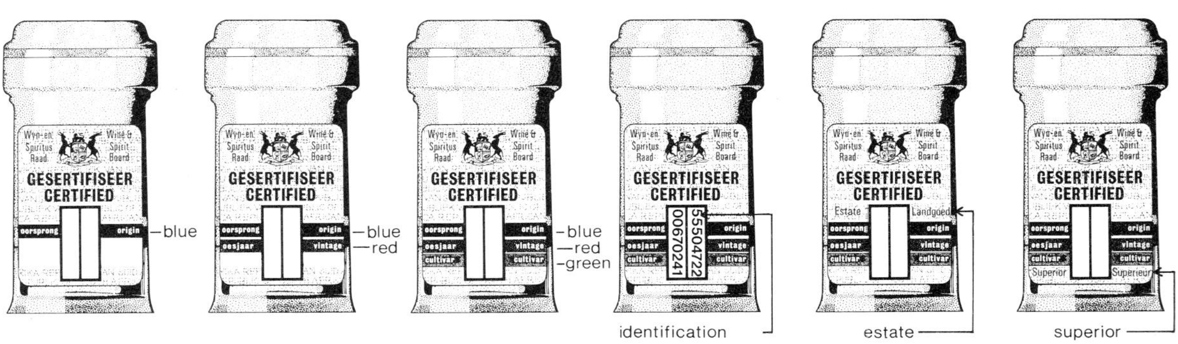

SECTION 3

The rules of the game

The rules of the game

UNDERSTANDING WHAT WINES ARE made of and where they come from occupies the longest part of the journey towards mastering the arts and pleasures of wine: it takes most people a life-time, and some experts would say that it can never be completed. But there is no point in embarking on the course unless you have also learned how to choose wine for yourself, and how to treat it.

I Tasting

Sometimes science and the language of the expert can be a help rather than a hindrance. Wine tasting is a case in point. Professionals talk about the 'sensory evaluation' of wine, a phrase which tells us a good deal more about what we should be doing than the simple word 'tasting'. It immediately implies that all the relevant senses should be used to evaluate or judge a wine.

This means the use of eye, nose and taste. With the eye we can judge the limpidity of a wine as well as its colour. Bubbles around the rim of the glass can denote the presence of carbon dioxide in the wine (*spritzig* in German, *pétillant* in French), cloudiness shows either the presence of a fine deposit, indicating that the wine needs decanting, or that it is out of condition. On the other hand, a brilliant and beautiful colour is usually the sign of a fine and healthy wine.

The more experienced you become in judging wine, the more importance will you attach to its bouquet, 'nose' or smell. These factors will indicate whether the wine is clean or unclean, whether it is young, mature or too old, and whether its quality is ordinary or fine. They may even tell you from where the wine comes. But the basic indications they give as to condition and quality are far more important than any guessing games.

To obtain the best from the 'nose' of a wine it is important that the glass is so shaped that it will trap the aromas or esters which the wine releases. The ideal shape is that of a tulip, filled no more than one

third full. The wine should then be agitated in the glass: the mixture of oxygen causes it to release the maximum quantity of esters.

Last of all, the wine is tasted. A small amount is taken into the mouth, and then gently agitated by sucking in air. This again releases esters and extracts the maximum taste from the wine. If a number of wines are to be evaluated concurrently it is a good idea to spit out the wine after you have formulated your impression, in order to preserve a clearer sense of judgement. It is important that the wine, once it has been sipped, should be spread around the mouth, because various taste buds are located in different parts of the mouth. Sweetness is best appreciated at the tip of the tongue, acidity on its upper edges, bitterness at the back and saltiness at the sides. The act of swallowing the wine adds nothing to its evaluation; that is why professional tasters will usually spit out rather than swallow.

A book can give you an idea of what to look for when tasting but nothing can replace the experience of tasting with a knowledgeable companion. Only someone on the spot can answer those vital questions as to the identity of this or that sensation which you experience through the nose or on the palate. You can often recognize a particular smell or taste as being unpleasant, and therefore probably faulty; but it is hard to identify such a sensation at all accurately without someone at your elbow to consult. This is the value of wine groups or circles, where wine lovers of varying experience taste together.

This brings us to the question of the best way to organize a tasting. Much the same rules apply, whether it is to be a small informal gathering of a few friends, or a large formal affair.

Order of tasting

No matter how large or small the tasting, it is important to arrange the wines in an order which will enhance and not detract from any one wine in particular. A few general rules apply:

1. Young wines should be tasted before old ones: if a number of different vintages are to be compared, always taste in chronological order, from youngest to oldest.
2. When reds of different areas are being shown, taste St Emilions and Pomerols after Médocs and Graves (they have more alcohol and body, and less tannin), Burgundies after Bordeaux or Beaujolais, Barolos after Chiantis. In general, lighter, more delicate wines should be tasted before fuller, heavier ones. When arranging a tasting of Italian wines the alcoholic strength will be shown on the bottle; this will help you arrange them in a logical order, even if you know nothing about them in advance.
3. If red and white wines are shown at the same tasting, taste reds before whites.
4. When arranging the order of white wines, place aromatic wines (Gewürztraminers, strong Sauvignons like Sancerre and Pouilly Blanc Fumé) and sweet or semi-sweet wines at the end of the tasting; otherwise the latter will impair your judgement of dry and more delicate wines.

Preparing the room

The ideals, not always attainable, are: good natural light, a white background and surface for observing colour, absence of extraneous smells (cooking odours, tobacco, etc), a moderate temperature (65°–68°F), spittoons (boxes filled with saw-dust are traditional but not essential; any bowl or bucket or similar receptacle will do) and, of course, good glasses (see above and below). It should go without saying that cigarettes, let alone pipes, ought never to be allowed during a tasting; the smoker may claim that he is not affected, but any non-smoker certainly will be.

Keeping a record

It helps to set out your impressions on a form prepared in advance. Some points to be noted are:

a. colour: clarity, depth, hue.

b. bouquet: projection, intensity, grape or regional characteristics (if any), cleanness/dirtiness, development in glass.

c. taste: dryness/sweetness, intensity, persistence of flavour, body, tannin, acidity, balance – i.e. the harmony of all the elements.

d. quality: this is determined by complexity, persistence of flavour (finish) and finesse, as well as the wine's overall harmony.

II Buying

Precise advice about the selection of wines is difficult, for the range of choice depends so greatly on where you live. In Britain there are few shops outside London where you can still find the range of wines which was common enough ten years ago. On the other hand, the number of mail-order firms offering specialist selections has greatly increased. There is nothing quite like being able to see the actual bottles at the time of purchase, but you may well have to make do with perusing catalogues instead.

If you do not know where to start, try buying a specialist magazine (e.g. *Decanter*) in which you will find a number of interesting firms advertising and making offers. Once you have discovered a firm that stocks the sort of wines that interest you – and you may well find it advantageous to deal with several firms – try to make contact with an individual, even by telephone, in order to obtain personal advice.

Supermarkets can provide useful wines for everyday drinking, if not for laying down. Remember that they only carry a very limited range, and goods have to move rapidly to justify their place on the shelves, so prices are often keen. Quality varies greatly from firm to firm: often a shop which aims for quality in its foods will apply similar standards to its wines.

The auction rooms can prove useful, provided that you observe one or two basic rules. Do not buy without tasting, unless you both know the wine and know that it has been well kept. Before bidding, obtain a very clear idea as to the price that the wine would command if bought through a shop or by mail-order: people often get carried away at auctions, paying more than the price which might be asked for the same wine in the shop around the corner. Remember, also, that you may be bidding against a buyer from Zürich, Hamburg or Texas who is prepared to pay over the odds because that shop around the corner is not so easily accessible to him. Be very cautious about paying a lot of money for old wines, especially those over thirty years old: so much depends on how such wines have been kept – and even if they have been well cellared, they may still be past their best.

For buyers in the United States the situation is slightly different. If you are lucky enough to live in a State where there are good wine stores, the range you can view on the shelf is far better than in Britain. A good way to obtain information about what is available in your State is to join your local chapter of Les Amis du Vin. Apart from running conducted tastings, they also have affiliated stores operating in 36 States.

III Starting a cellar

What sort of cellar you keep will naturally depend on your personal tastes, on what you can afford and on how much storage space you have available. Do not forget that many firms offer storage facilities which can be rented; but, if you take advantage of this, be sure that your own stock is clearly identified as such. In several recent cases of wine merchants going bankrupt, the Receiver has refused to release stock to its owners because it was not specifically identified.

The most logical way to start a cellar is to concentrate on buying wines which you like, and particularly those which are likely to rise in cost and to become hard to find as they reach maturity. This applies particularly to fine red Bordeaux, Sauternes, red and white Burgundies, the best German wines, and Vintage Port. When planning your purchases, try to achieve a balance so that you always have some fine wines which are ready to drink, as well as some which need keeping.

IV Storage

The essential requirements of a good cellar are an even temperature and the absence of light. 55°F for red wines and 50°F for whites is usually about right, but the stability of the temperature is much more important than its level, always provided that the latter is not too extreme. The author has known cellars with an even temperature of 60°–65°F, in which wines have aged magnificently. Equally, lower temperatures are not harmful, but they may cause a greater precipitation of tartrates.

Damp is often a cause for concern. If excessive, it destroys labels: this does not matter, provided that your cellar is carefully catalogued and the bins marked, but it could prove a disadvantage should you ever wish to sell your wine. A certain level of humidity is essential to keep corks in good condition.

Most people know that bottles should always be kept lying down, so that the wine remains in contact with the cork. This preserves the cork from shrinking and prevents oxidation. What is not always realized is that this also applies to fortified wines, such as Port, Madeira and Sherry. Spirits, on the other hand, should always be stored standing up, for spirit attacks cork; old cognacs, for instance, can acquire a corky taste if stored lying down for any length of time.

V Serving

Too much mystique, accompanied by too many prohibitions, has grown up over the years around the serving of wine. What should always be stressed is that the *raison d'être* of all such rules is to enhance the enjoyment of the wine. If anything you have been told before, or are told below, does not work for you, don't do it. Very few rules are absolute.

Temperature

More people today are inclined to serve red wines too warm than too cold: our houses, flats and drinking-rooms tend to be kept warmer than they used to be. 70°F is quite warm enough for any red Bordeaux, and if you know that your dining-room is 75°F, bring the wine in at a cooler temperature. The big Rhônes (Côtes du Rhône, Hermitage and Châteauneuf du Pape) and Italians (Barolo, Chianti Classico Riserva, etc) should also be served at this temperature.

Ideally, red Burgundy should be served at a lower temperature: 65°–67°F. The Pinot Noir has less tannin, and a touch more freshness helps it. Beaujolais when young (in its first year) is nearly always better at cellar temperature (55°F), which often means half an hour in the refrigerator. If red wines are served too warm the bouquet and taste become flat and blurred. Remember that wine will easily warm up in a room, but once it is too warm there is little you can do about it.

If red wines are often served too warm today, whites tend to be served indiscriminately too cold. Only very ordinary dry white wines deserve to be frozen. Generally speaking, the older or finer the wine, the more gently it should be chilled. Wines to be so treated (i.e. to about 55°F) are white Burgundies and old Sauternes: otherwise, the complex layers of their flavour are hidden. Much the same goes for the great *Auslesen* and *Beerenauslesen* from the Rhine and Moselle. Champagne and completely dry wines from elsewhere need slightly more chilling (45°–50°F).

Glasses

Many different types of glass have been produced over the years for particular wines. Those for still wines have one common denominator: they curve in to a greater or lesser extent towards the top, to ensure that the bouquet is concentrated. But while it is fun to have special Hock, Bordeaux or Burgundy glasses, they are not essential: good all-purpose glasses – such as the ISO tasting glass (see illustration), or any other tulip-shaped glass with a stem – will do equally well. The Champagne 'flute' is ideal for sparkling wines. The notorious 'saucer' should be avoided: bubbles need height to keep the wine lively.

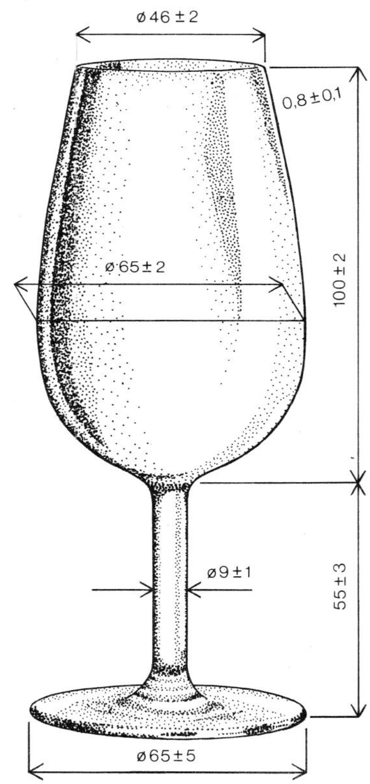

THE ISO GLASS

Diagram of an all-purpose tasting glass, based on specifications adopted by the International Organization for Standardization (ISO) in 1977. Total capacity is 215±10ml.; the recommended tasting quantity is 50ml., to allow two samplings. Dimensions shown are in millimetres; ∅ diameter.

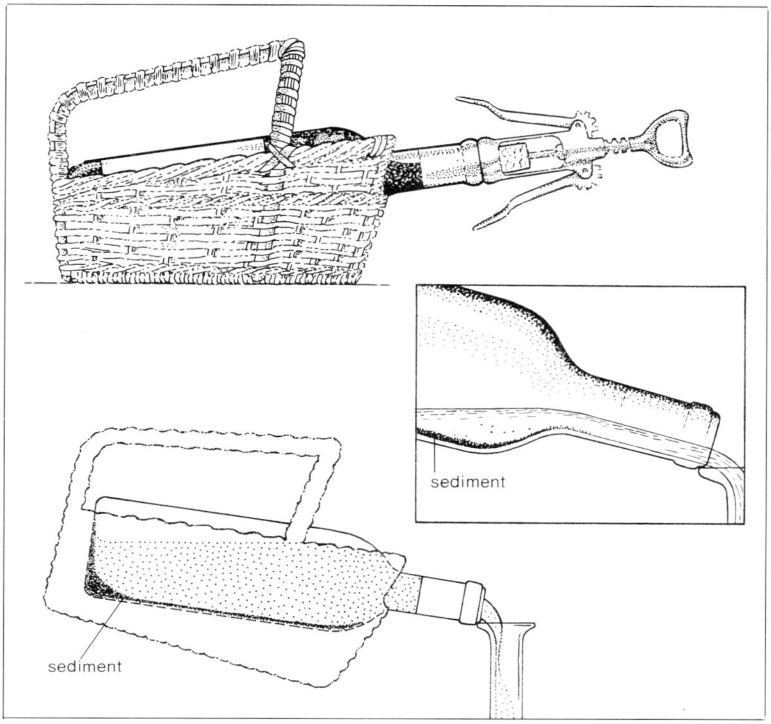

Decanting

The enjoyment of good quality red wine is enhanced by decanting it in advance. There are two reasons for this: to remove sediment, so that the wine may be served bright and clean (sediment, even if very light, can spoil the taste) and to aerate the wine, thus developing its bouquet and flavour.

How long in advance should one decant? For wines under fifteen years old, two hours before drinking is reasonable. However, the author vividly recalls drinking a wonderful bottle of Lafite 1953 at a lunch in Bordeaux in the late 1960s and being told that it had been decanted at seven o'clock that morning. The best rule is to experiment and to find out what suits your taste. Vintage Port, unless really old (pre-1945), should be decanted ten to twelve hours before drinking.

There is no mystery about the actual act of decanting. The bottle should be gently taken from its place in your cellar and laid in a wine basket or cradle of the type used in restaurants. This will enable you to uncork it without disturbing the sediment. Use one of the many forms of cork-screw which makes physical effort superfluous, so that again the wine will not be disturbed when it is opened.

Then, using a clear light (candle, bulb or daylight), pour the wine steadily into the decanter – checking first to see that it is absolutely clean – until you can see the sediment approaching the neck of the bottle. Even with quite heavy deposit the amount of wine lost by using this method should be very small. Some people believe in bringing out their wine a day or two before drinking and standing the bottle upright – but why disturb the sediment? Even if it has formed along the length of the bottle, it will adhere to the surface quite successfully while the wine is being decanted.

VI Matching wine with food

Probably more nonsense has been written on this subject than on almost any other connected with wine. Most lists of what goes with what are so lengthy and complex as to be self-defeating, and merely go to prove that most people are incurably conservative in their eating and drinking habits. The only sensible rule is to do whatever you find enjoyable, and not to hesitate to kick over the traces.

There is, for instance, no inherent reason why you should not enjoy red wine with fish. Delicate Burgundies go very well with some fish dishes, and red Bordeaux or Californian Cabernets can be enjoyed with salmon, swordfish and other firm-fleshed fish. The Marquis de Lur-Saluces (of Yquem fame) and some of his neighbours have proved – at least to their own satisfaction – that their great sweet wines can accompany almost any dish. The Germans frequently drink their white wines with meat and even game. Gewürztraminer can successfully accompany many Chinese and Indian dishes.

People's tastes in both wine and food vary so widely that it is hardly surprising that the combinations which they enjoy should also vary greatly. So have fun finding out what you enjoy, and do not be put off by the stick-in-the-mud and the conventional.

Bordeaux, Côte d'Or, Moselle, Rhine: vintages 1961–78

WHEN TASTING CLASSIFIED GROWTHS it is sensible to assemble wines of the same year, for it should always be remembered that the finer the vintage the more accentuated are the wine's regional characteristics. In Médoc, for instance, outstanding years (1961, 1966, 1970) show the characteristics of their communes very strongly, but need waiting for; the 1966 vintages have taken until the late 1970s to become really rewarding to drink. On the other hand, faster developing, less aristocratic vintages may be easier to come by, although they will not necessarily show such pronounced tendencies. The following chart matches the intrinsic quality of each vintage with its maturing characteristics.

	FRENCH RED WINES			FRENCH WHITE WINES			GERMAN WINES	
	Médoc Graves	Pomerol, St Emilion	Côte d'Or	Graves	Sauternes	Côte d'Or	Moselle	Rhine
1978	4A	4A	5A	4Q	3Q	4Q	2Q	2Q
1977	2Q	2Q	3Q	3Q	1Q	4Q	2Q	2Q
1976	3Q	4Q	5A	4Q	2Q	4Q	5A	5A
1975	5S	5A	1Q	5Q	5A	3Q	4A	4A
1974	2Q	2Q	2Q	3Q	1Q	3Q	2Q	2Q
1973	3Q	2Q	3Q	3Q	1Q	4Q	3Q	3Q
1972	1Q	2Q	4A	2Q	2Q	3Q	1Q	2Q
1971	3Q	4Q	4A	4Q	4Q	5A	5A	5A
1970	5S	5A	3Q	5Q	4A	3Q	2Q	3Q
1969	2A	2Q	5S	3Q	3Q	4A	4Q	3Q
1968	2Q	1Q	1Q	1Q	1Q	2A	1Q	2Q
1967	3A	3Q	2Q	4Q	5A	4Q	3Q	3Q
1966	4S	4A	4A	4Q	3Q	4A	4A	4Q
1965	1Q	1Q	1Q	1Q	1Q	2Q	1Q	2Q
1964	3A	4A	3A	4Q	1Q	4A	4Q	3Q
1963	1Q	1Q	1Q	2Q	1Q	2Q	—	—
1962	4A	4A	4A	4A	4A	5A	—	—
1961	5S	4A	4A	4Q	4A	4A	—	—

QUALITY

5 An outstanding vintage, generally successful in all districts and among *petits châteaux* as well as the great growths.
4 First class, without quite the all-round qualities of the top category.
3 A good all-round vintage; some growths will produce a wine bordering on the excellent, while others will produce only average quality.
2 A year when there are rather more wines below par than above it; nothing really exciting, taking the region as a whole, but some of the wines are worthwhile.
1 A year when a lot of really poor wine was made and even the great growths de-classified much of their production.

MATURING CHARACTERISTICS

Q Quick to mature: these wines will be drinkable and enjoyable within four years, even if not at their best.
A Average length to maturity: great growths should begin to be drinkable after seven years, lesser wines will generally be ready a year or two earlier.
S Slow to mature: these require at least ten years before they are drunk; some of the best growths may take even longer, but lesser wines may be drunk with pleasure two or three years earlier.

About the vine

Important as are environment and the intervention of man, the grape is the starting point for all wines, and from it all else flows. The differences between grape varieties, the different types of wine which these varieties produce in different places, the particular characteristics which each is responsible for implanting in the wine – all these provide a fascinating field for study; they are dealt with separately, grape by grape, at the end of this book. Here we shall touch only on those aspects of the grape which bear directly on the general picture of wine production.

The greatest single influence in the selection of grape varieties was, curiously enough, the great scourge of the phylloxera which devastated European vineyards at the end of the 19th century. Because vineyards had to be replanted on American root-stocks, European growers were given a chance to re-select the grape varieties they used. This led to a significant reduction in the number of varieties planted. It also concentrated attention on the production of improved varieties of the types which were being re-selected.

One of the most fundamental factors in selecting a particular grape variety is to find one which will ripen at the right time. This task, which is clearly of special importance in northern wine-growing areas, has been a principal subject of research in Germany; many new experimental grape varieties have been produced there in the last few years, and the results have proved very relevant to the problems of those brave spirits dedicated to producing wine in England. The reverse side of this particular coin is the task of finding varieties which will ripen in hot climates but retain a sufficient acidity to produce a balanced wine; certain of the traditional varieties which for a century have been cultivated in southern Italy have proved the most satisfactory in this context, while attempts to grow some of the more famous French varieties in extreme climatic conditions, such as are found in South Africa, have been less successful. Often, in fact, the solution has lain in the treatment of the grapes and in the time of harvesting rather than in the selection of grape varieties. Thus it is common practice in parts of California and Australia to pick white grapes before they are fully ripe – even, in Australia, picking them at night – and to control the temperature of vinification.

In the beginning: the grape

The most interesting influence of the grape on the wine is, of course, in terms of its effects on the flavour. One common classification differentiates between those varieties that produce an aromatic wine and those which do not: the most obvious examples of the former are those produced from the Muscat family, of which there are many variations. In red grapes the differences are more subtle but nonetheless important. Sometimes a very strong character-

Mechanical grape harvester in a California vineyard: the grapes are crushed on board, then the juice is pumped into a tanker moving alongside (Wine Institute of California)

istic can be produced by a single grape variety, such as the Gamay in Beaujolais or the Syrah in the northern Rhône. On the other hand, the greatest wines are also often made by a subtle blend of different grape varieties which have proved over the years to be mutually complementary; the great wines of Bordeaux are the most obvious example of this.

In most regions, the phenomenon of the single grape variety is relatively recent; some of the most famous Italian wines – Valpolicella, for instance, and Chianti – are the product of a blend of varieties. In America, however, there has been a great emphasis on single varieties – at least in name, although the practice is often different. Some of the most successful Australian reds are not those produced from the straight Cabernet Sauvignon but a blend of Cabernet Sauvignon and Shiraz (an Australian version of the French Syrah). Such blends produce wines which are often more similar to the great Clarets than to wines produced from the Cabernet Sauvignon alone.

In countries like Germany and France, climatic conditions can often mean that the harvested grapes do not have a sufficiently high sugar content to produce enough alcohol to give the finished wine its normal and true attributes. In indifferent summers, this can even happen in parts of Italy. Such a deficiency is normally corrected by the process known as chaptalization – i.e. the addition of sugar during fermentation; it is a process strictly controlled by law, for it is most important that the amount of added alcohol should not affect the overall balance of the wine. The addition of 2° is usually regarded as the maximum desirable if the wine is not to be unduly altered in character. There is also an expensive alternative to chaptalization, widely used in Italy, which has many convinced advocates. Concentrated must is added during the fermentation instead of sugar; as this contains all the elements contained in grape juice, of which it is itself merely a concentrated form, the alcoholic strength of the wine can be increased without altering the balance of acidity, in the same way as happens with chaptalization. The only serious drawback of this method is its expense.

To gauge what exactly is meant by micro-climate, it is relevant to quote the experience of an English wine-grower in Essex who found that Müller-Thurgau vines in an exposed place by the gateway of his property flowered and ripened two weeks after the same vines grown on the other side of the property but sheltered with wind-breaks; the two were separated by only a few hundred yards. Altitude is another important influence on climate: many southern Italian vineyards successfully produce good quality wines because their height above sea level results in relatively late flowering and correspondingly late harvesting.

It has, on the other hand, been clearly established that certain grape varieties do much better on one type of soil rather than another. The most interesting example is the Gamay which produces a splendid wine in Beaujolais but a very common, ordinary wine whenever it has been planted elsewhere. On the steep slatey vineyards of the Moselle, and on the high rolling vineyards of Châteauneuf with their enormous stones, the soil has another property; the slate and the large fat stones both reflect heat, and thus assist in the ripening of the grapes.

Stones in the soil at Château Lafite-Rothschild help to reflect heat and to ripen the grapes (G)

Bolla's vineyard at Soave, near Verona

In cold climates, the rows of vines are often planted in such a way that the sun shines down them at its noonday peak, thus warming the soil; planted at a different angle, the vines would effectively shade the soil and keep it cool. Methods of pruning the vine can also be important. In parts of northern Italy, for instance, the vines are grown on pergolas so that the bunches of grapes hang down and are shaded by their leaves from direct sunlight. This helps to protect them from the mountain storms; the prevailing wind coming up the mountain valleys helps to dry them after rain, while the leaves prevent them becoming scorched in the extreme heat of mid-summer.

Fermentation: the dangers of over-kill

Nothing has been more important over the past thirty years than the realization that the control of temperature during fermentation can have a fundamental effect on the quality of the wine. Previously it had been recognized that if the temperature went too high – much above 34°c – there was a serious danger that yeasts would be killed off and wild yeasts take over, causing the wine to turn acetic and ultimately to vinegar. This has always been a serious danger in hot years, and not only in the distant past. In 1945, for instance, part of the crop of one of the first growths in Bordeaux had to be pasteurized

Chalk carving in the cellar of a Champagne house at Reims

because of volatile acidity caused by excessive heat during the fermentation; two years later, 40 per cent of the crop on the Côte d'Or was spoiled for the same reason, as were some of the Loire wines as recently as 1976.

It is now fairly well established that white wines give of their best if the temperature is kept below 18°c, and there are certain areas where producers like to bring it down to as low as 14°c. The most immediate effect of such long and slow fermentations is that the bouquet is enormously enhanced. For red wine, the case is rather different. If the temperature is too low the colour extraction is not so good: most people now believe that somewhere between 26°c and 30°c is about right. However, such enlightened practice is by no means universal; as recently as 1975, at a co-operative in the south of Italy, no action at all was taken to control the temperature of either the red or the white wines until it rose as high as 34°c!

One of the most important factors in improving the quality of wine by controlled fermentation, particularly in Italy, has been the growth of co-operatives and large-scale private companies to which grapes are brought in from neighbouring farms. In such large enterprises the right machinery can be introduced and maintained, and qualified oenologists can be employed to supervise their use. After the wine has been successfully made, its continuing development, either in vat or in cask, plays another vital part in its eventual quality. There is a tendency to use wood less and less, largely because of the expense involved in the making, maintenance and

Sampling at the Karst vineyards, Bad Durkheim, in Rheinpfalz (G)

Coopering at St Romain in the Côte de Beaune, Burgundy (G)

handling of the casks. It is also much easier to keep vats clean and sterile, whether made of stainless steel or metal or concrete, so long as they have been treated with a suitable resin or are glass-lined. Whether wine aged in wooden casks or vats is superior to that aged in concrete or stainless steel has long been a matter of controversy, and still is.

In California where so many experiments have been made, there has been a tendency to try small oak barrels on a considerable scale, but many people feel that such treatment can impart an excessively woody character to the wine. On the other hand, there is no doubt that some of the greatest red wines in France do owe a good deal to their ageing in small casks.

The same cannot be said of white wines, nearly all of which have been shown to benefit considerably by being kept in vat for a comparatively short time before bottling; only in the case of certain whites produced from the Pinot Chardonnay does aging in oak casks seem to have been beneficial. One of the great revolutions in the handling of wine in the past few years has been in the ability to bottle white wines much earlier; the techniques necessary to condition them into remaining stable in bottle have only recently been perfected.

The weather, the soil or the planting?

Vital, of course, to the success of a vine and its grapes is the environment in which they are grown – the climate, the soil and the methods of cultivation. In northerly climes, such as Germany or, indeed, the U.K., the climate becomes virtually all-important, and even in California, where there are problems of too much sunshine and damp, the micro-climate is studied with more attention than the soil. By contrast, in the more temperate climates of France and Italy, viticulturists normally contend that soil is the most important element.

Young grapes on the vine at Romanée St Vivant in Burgundy (G)

About grapes

WE CAN ALL THINK OF certain grape varieties which typify the wines of a particular country. The Riesling in Germany, the Pinot Noir in France, the Sangiovese in Italy are obvious examples. But there are a small number of varieties that have acquired a world-wide importance, thanks to their ability to adapt to widely varying conditions. A country such as Italy, with a tradition of viticulture that runs throughout the land and stretches back to Roman times and beyond, can boast over a hundred major grape varieties. Only a handful of these can be found beyond Italy's frontiers; but this is the exception rather than the rule.

Two points need stressing, however. The fact that varieties bearing the same name can be found in France, Italy, eastern Europe, California, and Australia does not imply that the wines which they produce will be the same or even similar. Usually, the longer the vines have grown in a particular environment, the more they will have adapted to it; in consequence, the grape may well have changed, the differences being often as great as the similarities, and sometimes even more pronounced.

The other point that needs to be taken into account is that the name of a variety can change from country to country, and even from region to region. It takes a considerable effort of memory to recall that, for instance, Ugni Blanc, White Shiraz, Hermitage and Trebbiano are all the same grape, trading under different names; and it takes many years of serious wine-tasting to appreciate all the practical implications of such facts.

The following gazetteer covers most of the major varieties grown in Europe and the New World. It should be used in conjunction with the notes on grape varieties contained in the sections of this book on individual countries.

GRAPE VARIETIES GAZETTEER

● red ○ white

● ***Barbera:*** one of the most important Italian grape varieties, especially in Piedmont, and it is also found in California. When young, it has a very simple colour and is often high in acidity; if allowed to mature it produces wines of considerable body and fruit. Tends to be high in alcohol, at around 13° to 13.5°.

○ ***Blanc Fumé:*** see ***Sauvignon.***

● ***Blauburgunder:*** see ***Pinot Noir.***

● ***Cabernet Franc:*** widely used in all regions of Bordeaux, and for the red wines of the Loire. Produces softer more spicey wines than the Cabernet Sauvignon, and ripens earlier. Also found in northern Italy and eastern Europe, where it is usually simply referred to as Cabernet.

● ***Cabernet Sauvignon:*** the classic variety in the Bordeaux districts of Médoc and Graves. Tends to moderate yields and late ripening but is very hardy. Produces wines with a fine substantial colour, tannic at first, but developing a complex fruitiness on the nose and palate, often typified as black-currant. In France it is at its greatest when blended with Merlot. In Italy, eastern Europe, California, Australia, Chile and South Africa it is either used alone or with Cabernet Franc. Blends with Hermitage have produced good results in Australia. When used alone the bouquet remains most characteristic, but the wines often lack the complexity and subtlety found in the great Bordeaux.

● ***Carignan*** or ***Corignane:*** common in the Languedoc-Roussillon and Provence regions of southern France, and to a lesser extent in the Rhône valley. Also found in north Africa and in California, where they add an 'e' on the end. A strongly perfumed wine is produced with moderate alcohol. At its best as a component of a wine rather than on its own.

○ ***Chardonnay:*** the classic variety for white Burgundy, and also one of the constituents of Champagne. A relatively high yielder, it produces wines with a very distinct personality, but varying in body, perfume and acidity, depending on soil and climate: hence the differences between Chablis, Meursault and Montrachet. Outside France the most successful results have been obtained in California, where the wines are very perfumed, high in alcohol, with a pronounced character. Could have a great future in many parts of the world, especially in chalky soil. (Also known as Pinot Chardonnay, it should be distinguished from Pinot Blanc.)

○ ***Chenin Blanc:*** also known as Pineau de la Loire, this is the classic variety of the middle Loire (Anjou and Touraine). Both dry and sweet wines are made as well as sparkling; they have a marked acidity and fruit and age remarkably, especially if there is residual sugar, as with Coteaux du Layon and Vouvray *demi-sec*. The grape, which can be advantageously attacked by *botrytis cinerea* (noble rot), has also been successful in

California and South Africa, where it is called Steen.

● ***Dolcetto:*** one of the most widely planted varieties in Piedmont. Produces wines with a vivid colour and a very grapey flavour.

● ***Gamay:*** famous as the vine of Beaujolais, where it produces a wine with a light but peculiarly intense colour when young. It is high in acidity but low in tannin, so its wines can be drunk younger than other reds. Its peculiarity is that nowhere outside the Beaujolais district does it produce wines of the same class, though some pleasing wines are made in Touraine and in the Ardèche. Also planted in California, with moderate success.

○ ***Gewürztraminer*** or ***Traminer:*** one of the greatest aromatic varieties. It is at its most celebrated in Alsace, but is also successful in Baden, Rheinpfalz and Jugoslavia, as well as in the Alto Adige in northern Italy – indeed, the small village of Tramin near Bologna claims to be its original home. The variety has also done well in California and some parts of Australia. The intensely aromatic bouquet and flavour of its wines are unmistakable and very penetrating; they are normally vinified dry.

● ***Grenache:*** one of the mainstays of the southern Rhône, now being introduced to improve quality in the Midi. Produces wine deep in colour and high in alcohol (13–14°). Also found in the Rioja and Catalonian regions of northern Spain.

○ ***Hermitage:*** see ***Trebbiano.***

○ ***Johannisberg:*** see ***Riesling.***

● ***Merlot:*** the main grape variety of St Emilion and Pomerol in Bordeaux. Producing wines with a full colour and relatively rich in alcohol (12–13°), it is an essential ingredient of the Médocs and Graves. It also produces particularly successful wines in northern Italy, but has not enjoyed the same popularity as the Cabernet in the vineyards of the New World. Top-quality Californian Merlots are beginning to appear, however.

○ ***Müller-Thurgau:*** the earliest and most famous of the German early-ripening crossings. For long it was thought to be Riesling × Sylvaner, but it is now established as being Riesling × Riesling. Ripening earlier and producing more prolifically than the Riesling, it has an obvious and scented nose, but less acidity and breed than Riesling; it is at its best when blended with other varieties. Widely planted in the new English vineyards.

● ***Nebbiolo:*** the classic grape variety of north-west Italy, where it is used in Barolo, Barbaresco, Gattinara, Carema, Ghemme, Fara, Sizzano and the Valtellina wines of northern Piedmont, where it is known as Spanna. Produces wines with colour and tannin, high in alcohol (13–14°), which take time to develop and soften.

○ ***Palomino:*** the classic Spanish variety for making Sherry. Now successfully planted in California, Australia, Cyprus and South Africa.

○ ***Pedro Ximénez:*** a common Spanish variety, cultivated particularly in the Jerez area. It makes superb sweet wines.

Pineau de la Loire: see ***Chenin Blanc.***

Pinot Blanc: found in Alsace and extensively in northern Italy (Pinot Bianco), where it produces a wine of delicacy and some distinction – but very different from the more illustrious Chardonnay.

○ ***Pinot Gris*** or ***Pinot Grigio:*** sometimes known as Tokay d'Alsace, and in Germany and Austria as Rülander. The wine has a distinctly spicey bouquet and flavour, further enhanced if the fermentation is allowed to begin in the presence of the skins, when the wines have a pinkish hue. It is grown in the Collio region of north-east Italy.

● ***Pinot Noir:*** the classic grape variety for the Côte d'Or Burgundies, and also a constituent of Champagne. When fully ripened the colour is vivid and deep, the bouquet opulent and perfumed, the wine complex and rich but delicate in texture. However, this variety is very adversely affected by over-production, and a lack of sun can mean that the wines become pale in colour and very light in texture. Also used to make red and *rosé* Sancerre, and some German red wines, notably from Assmannshausen. In Germany, it is called Spätburgunder, in Austria and the Alto Adige region of northern Italy Blauburgunder. Although many good wines are made from this variety in both northern Italy and California, they are different in character, tending to lack finesse and acidity compared with Côte d'Or wines.

○ ***Riesling*** or ***Rhein Riesling*** (Austria) or ***Riesling Renano*** (Italy) or ***Johannisberg*** or ***White Riesling*** (California): this classic German variety, which ripens late but is amazingly hardy, has also proved extremely adaptable, making the greatest Rhine and Mosel wines – sometimes with *Edelfaule* (noble rot). Fine dry wines, and now Late Harvest dessert wines are made in California; it is becoming increasingly popular for quality wines in Australia, and small quantities of fine wines are also produced from it in north-east Italy and Austria.

○ ***Rülander:*** see ***Pinot Gris.***

● ***Sangiovese:*** one of the classic varieties of Italy. Although famed as the producer of Brunello, and the major constituent of Chianti, it also appears, either on its own or with other varieties, from one end of Italy to the other. It produces wines of brilliant colour which deepens with age, a rather spicey, herby bouquet, and some astringency when young which mellows with ageing.

○ ***Sauvignon:*** a distinctly aromatic variety, especially on certain soils. It is known as the Blanc Fumé on the Loire – a name often used in California, where it makes some very successful wines – it provides acidity and breed when blended with the Sémillon to make the dry Graves or sweet Sauternes of Bordeaux; it is also extensively planted in the Dordogne. Unless the conditions are right, the wine on its own can prove excessively acid and rapidly loses its character; when it ripens fully, as in California, more full-bodied, spicey wines result.

○ ***Sémillon:*** while not as fashionable today as Sauvignon, this is nevertheless an extremely important variety, especially in Bordeaux. Here it provides both the extra body and complexity for the dry wines, and the perfumed richness for the great sweet wines. It is the most important quality white grape in Australia, and is also found in South America. Given the right conditions, it becomes affected with noble rot.

● ***Shiraz:*** see ***Syrah.***

● ***Spanna:*** see ***Nebbiolo.***

● ***Spätburgunder:*** see ***Pinot Noir.***

○ ***Steen:*** see ***Chenin Blanc.***

○ ***Sylvaner*** or ***Silvaner:*** one of the most important German varieties (Franconia, Rheinhessen and Rheinpfalz) and also found in Alsace, north-east Italy and Jugoslavia. The quality varies considerably, but at its best it produces a full-bodied spicey wine and a bouquet of some complexity.

● ***Syrah*** or ***Sirah:*** the classic variety of the northern Rhône, giving Côte Rôtie and Hermitage their distinctive character. The wines which it makes have considerable depth of colour and a very pronounced perfume; they are inclined to be tannic at first, but a spicey fruitiness soon predominates. The variety is being introduced into some Languedoc-Roussillon and Provençal vineyards to improve quality.

Versions of the Syrah are grown in South Africa (Shiraz) and in Australia (Hermitage). The Australian version has made the best wines, especially when blended with Cabernet Sauvignon. The Petite Syrah of California is not a derivative, and in fact Syrah has only been introduced into California in the last decade; the first pure Syrah was a 1976 vintage from Joseph Phelps, which was highly characteristic.

○ ***Tokay d'Alsace:*** see ***Pinot Gris.***

○ ***Traminer:*** see ***Gewürztraminer.***

○ ***Trebbiano:*** the classic and versatile Italian variety, widely planted throughout the country. Its character is elusive and varies according to soil and climate. In France it is known as Ugni Blanc, producing rather ordinary neutral wines in the south, and light acid wines in St Emilion, for distillation in Cognac. Also planted widely in Australia, where it is also known as White Shiraz or Hermitage.

○ ***Ugni Blanc:*** see ***Trebbiano.***

○ ***Welschriesling*** or ***Riesling Italico*** or ***Laski Riesling:*** a completely different variety from Rhine Riesling, this grape is widely planted in north-east Italy and throughout eastern Europe. It produces pleasing, dry and fruity wines, but they lack the distinctive fruit-acidity of the authentic Rhine Riesling.

○ ***White Shiraz:*** see ***Trebbiano.***

● ***Zinfandel:*** the distinctive California grape variety. Its origins are unknown (thought by some to be in southern Italy), and in any case it has now developed a completely distinctive character entirely its own. It is made in two different styles, one light and extremely fruity (Monterey and Ridge), the other very alcoholic and aggressively tannic (Sutter Home and Clos du Val).

A wine-drinker's glossary

acidity: a characteristic of wine, arising from the acids in it; imparts freshness, sharpness, and keeping quality
aroma: characteristic fragrance of the grape
big: powerful, full of flavour, alcohol, tannin and acidity
body: the weightiness of wine in the mouth; a combination of its alcoholic content and all its other properties
bouquet: the smell of the wine – its 'nose'; a combination of the grape aroma and the subsequent effects of fermentation and development in the bottle
breed: a quality of distinction in wine which derives from its place of origin and makes it a good example of its kind
chaptalization: the addition of sugar to the fermenting grapes to bring the alcoholic content of the wine up to the permissible level
delicacy: the subtle balance and charm in a light wine of great quality
finesse: a French tasting term taken into English: suggestive of delicacy, subtlety and grace
fragrance: the attractive, natural scent of the grape; the term is also applied descriptively to the bouquet of a wine (Fr., *parfum*)
fruity: describes the distinctive taste and smell, usually in young wine, of fully ripened grapes (Fr., *fruité*)
generous: a wine that is rich in alcohol and is warming and full of vitality; imparts a sense of well-being
growth: strictly, the locality in which vines are grown; transferred to mean the wines produced there (Fr., *cru*)
maderised: descriptive of white wine which, through a gradual process of oxidation, has acquired a deep colour and a special flavour recalling Madeira; appreciated by some connoisseurs
noble rot: *botrytis cinerea,* a fungus which attacks certain white grapes and improves their quality (Fr., *pourriture noble*; Ger., *Edelfaule*)
oenology: the knowledge, study or science of making wine
phylloxera: a vine louse which attacks the roots of indigenous European vines; it devastated French vineyards between the 1860s and the end of the century. The remedy is grafting on U.S. root-stocks
piquancy: a sharpness of flavour induced by high acidity
soft: mellow, lacking any roughness
tannin: a chemical constituent of red and (to some extent) *rosé* wines, derived from the pips and the skin of the grape, which dries the mouth. It causes young wines to be 'hard' or 'firm' and less pleasant to drink; added to acidity and given time, however, it preserves them and develops their finer qualities
vinification: the technical process of fermenting wine
vinosity: the alcoholic character of wine, expressed through smell and taste
viticulture: the cultivation of the vine

Tasting the wine at Kloster Eberbach in the Rheingau (G)

Bibliography

General

AMERINE, MAYNARD *and* ROESSLER, EDWARD: *Wines: Their Sensory Evaluation*, San Francisco, Freeman & Co., 1976

AMERINE, MAYNARD *and* CRUESS, W.: *The Technology of Winemaking*, Connecticut, Avi Publishing, 1960

AMERINE, MAYNARD *and* SINGLETON, VERNON: *Wine, an Introduction*, London/Los Angeles, University of California Press, 1976, 2nd ed.

BESPALOFF, ALEXIS: *Wine*, New York, The New American Library, 1971

BROADBENT, MICHAEL: *Wine Tasting*, London, Christie Wine Publications, 1975

BORROUGHS, DAVID *and* BEZZANT, NORMAN: *The Wine Trade Student's Companion*, London, Collins, 1975

DON, ROBIN: *Teach Yourself Wine*, London, EUP, 1968

DUMAY, RAYMOND: *Guide du Vin*, Paris, Stock, 1967

HYAMS, EDWARD: *Dionysus, A Social History of the Wine Vine*, London, Thames & Hudson, 1965

JOHNSON, HUGH: *Pocket Wine Book*, rev. ed. 1978;

JOHNSON, HUGH: *Wine*, rev. ed. 1978;

JOHNSON, HUGH: *A World Atlas of Wine*, rev. ed. 1977; London, Mitchell Beazley

LAROUSSE (Gérard Dubuigne, ed.): *Dictionnaire des Vins*, Paris, 1969

LICHINE, ALEXIS: *Encyclopaedia of Wines and Spirits*, London, Cassell, 1975, 3rd ed.

MASSEL, A.: *Applied Wine Chemistry*, London, Heidelberg Publishers, 1969

PUISAIS, JACQUES *and* CHABANON, R. L.: *Initiation into the Art of Winetasting*, Wisconsin Interpublish Inc., 1974

QUITTANSON, CHARLES: *Connaissance et Gloire du Vin*, Paris, Editions Brès, 1979 (also in English)

SCHNEIDER, STEVEN J.: *The International Album of Wine*, New York, Holt Rinehart and Winston, 1977

SCHOONMAKER, FRANK: *Encyclopaedia of Wine*, London, Black, 1977, 2nd ed.

SICHEL, ALLAN (revised by Peter Sichel): *The Penguin Book of Wines*, London, 1971

VANDYKE PRICE, PAMELA: *A Directory of Wines and Spirits*, London, Northwood, 1974

VEDEL, A., *et al.*: *Essai sur la Dégustation des Vins*, Mâcon, S.E.I.V., 1972

WINKLER, A. J.: *General Viticulture*, Los Angeles, University of California Press, 1962

France

ARLOTT, JOHN *and* FIELDEN, CHRISTOPHER: *Burgundy Vines and Wines*, London, Davis-Poynter, 1976

BREJOUX, PIERRE: *Les Vins de Bourgogne*, Paris, Société Française d'Editions Vinicoles, 1969

BREJOUX, PIERRE: *Les Vins de Loire*, Paris, Compagnie Parisienne d'Editions Technologiques et Commerciales

DUIJKER, HUBRECHT: *The Great Wine Châteaux of Bordeaux*, London, Times Books, 1975

FAITH, NICHOLAS: *The Winemasters*, London, Hamish Hamilton, 1978 (the story of the great Bordeaux wine scandal)

FORBES, PATRICK: *Champagne, the Wine, the Land and the People*, London, Gollancz, 1967

HALLGARTEN, PETER: *Côtes du Rhône*, London, Hallgarten

LICHINE, ALEXIS: *Wines of France*, London, Cassell (complete rewritten and published in the US, 1979)

LIVINGSTONE-LEARMONTH, JOHN *and* MELVYN, MASTER: *The Wines of the Rhône*, London, Faber, 1978

MORTON SHAND, R.: *A Book of French Wines*, London, Cape, rev. ed. Penguin, 1974

PENNING-ROWSELL, EDMUND: *The Wines of Bordeaux*, London, Wine and Food Society, 1971

POUPON, PIERRE *and* FOUGEOT, PIERRE: *The Wines of Burgundy*, Paris, Presses Universitaires de France, 1974

RAY, CYRIL: *Lafite*, 1968;

RAY, CYRIL: *Bollinger*, 1971;

RAY, CYRIL: *Cognac*, 1973, London, Peter Davies;

RAY, CYRIL: *Mouton*, London, Christie Wine Publications, 1974;

RAY, CYRIL: *The Wines of France*, London, Allen Lane, 1976

VANDYKE PRICE, PAMELA: *Eating and Drinking in France Today*, London, Tom Stacey, 1972

YOXALL, H. W.: *Wines of Burgundy*, London, Pitman, 1978, 2nd ed.

Germany

AMBROSI, HANS: *Germany: Wine Atlas and Dictionary*, Bielefeld, Ceres-Verlag, 1976

AMBROSI, HANS: *Where the Great German Wines Grow*, New York, Hastings House, 1976

HALLGARTEN, S. F.: *German Wines*, London, Faber, 1975

HALLGARTEN, S. F.: *A Guide to the Vineyards, Estates and Wines of Germany*, Texas, Publivin, 1974

RAY, CYRIL: *The Wines of Germany*, London, Allen Lane, 1977

Italy

DALLAS, PHILIP: *Italian Wines*, London, Faber, 1974

ENOTICA ITALICA PERMANENTE: *Carta dei Vini*, Siena

FLOWER, RAYMOND: *Chianti, the Land, the People and the Wine*, London, Croom Helm, 1978

RAY, CYRIL: *The Wines of Italy*, London and New York, McGraw Hill/Penguin

RONCARATTI, BRUNO: *Viva Vino: DOC Wines of Italy*, London, Wine and Spirit Pub., 1976

VERONELLI, LUIGI: *Catalogo Bolaffi dei Vini d'Italia*, Turin, Giulio Bolaffi Editore

Spain and Portugal

GONZALEZ GORDON, MANUEL: *Sherry*, London, The Cookery Book Club/Cassell, 1972

JEFFS, JULIAN: *Sherry*, London, Faber, 1970, 2nd ed.

READ, JAN: *Wines of Spain and Portugal*, London, Faber, 1973

BRADFORD, SARAH: *The Englishman's Wine*, London, Macmillan/Los Angeles, St Martin's Press, 1969

FLETCHER, WYNDHAM: *Port: An Introduction to its History and Delights*, London, Sotheby Parke Bernet, 1978

ROBERTSON, GEORGE: *Port*, London, Faber, 1978

United States

ADAMS, LEON D.: *The Wines of America*, New York, McGraw Hill, 1978, 2nd ed., rev.

BALZER, ROBERT L.: *Wines of California*, New York, Abrams, 1978

CHROMAN, N.: *The Treasury of American Wines*, New York, Rutledge/Crown, 1973

MELVILLE, JOHN (rev. by Morgan Jefferson): *Guide to Californian Wines*, New York, Dutton, 1968

QUIMME, PETER: *American Wine*, New York, New American Library, 1975

THOMPSON, ROBERT *and* HUGH, JOHNSON: *The Californian Wine Book*, New York, Morrow, 1976

England and Wales

BARTY-KING, HUGH: *A Tradition of English Wine*, Oxford Illustrated Press, 1977

ORDISH, GEORGE: *Vineyards of England and Wales*, London, Faber, 1977

Others

KNOX, GRAHAM: *Estate Wines of South Africa*, Cape Town, David Philip, 1976

GUNYON, R. E. H.: *The Wines of Central and South-Eastern Europe*, London, Duckworth, 1971

EVANS, LEN: *Australia and New Zealand. Complete Book of Wine*, Dee Why West, New South Wales, Paul Hamlyn, 1973

LAKE, MAX: *Cabernet: Notes of an Australian Wineman*, Adelaide, Rigby, 1977

APPENDIX 1

Leading Bordeaux négociants

Barton & Guestier
La Bergerie
Beyerman
Beylot
Borie-Manoux
Calvet
Cordier
Cruse
Danglade
Delor
Dourthe
Dubos
Dubroca
Dulong
Eschenauer
Gilbey
Ginestet
Hanappier-Peyrelongue
W. & N. Johnston
Kressman
A. Lalande
Lebegue
Lichine
de Luze
Mahler-Besse
Mestrezat
J. P. Moueix
A. Moueix
Quancard
Schroder & Schyler
Sichel

APPENDIX 2

Leading Burgundy shippers

Aujoux, *St Georges de Reneins*
Albert Bichot, *Beaune*
Jean Claude Boisset, *Nuits St Georges*
Bouchard Ainé, *Beaune*
Bouchard Père et Fils, *Au Château, Beaune*
Lionel Bruck, *Nuits St Georges*
Champy Père, *Beaune*
Chanson Père et Fils, *Beaune*
F. Chauvenet, *Nuits St Georges*
Raoul Clerget, *St Aubin*
Doudet-Naudin, *Savigny-lès-Beaune*
Joseph Drouhin, *Beaune*
Georges Duboeuf, *Romanèche-Thorins*
Joseph Faiveley, *Nuits St Georges*
Geisweiler & Fils, *Nuits St Georges*
Jaboulet-Vercherre, *Beaune*
Louis Jadot, *Beaune*
Jaffelin, *Beaune*
Laboure-Roi, *Nuits St Georges*
Louis Latour, *Beaune*
Leroy, *Auxey-Duresses*
Loron et Fils, *La Chapelle de Guinchay*
Lupe-Cholet, *Nuits St Georges*
P. de Marcilly Frères, *Beaune*
Prosper Maufoux, *Santenay*
Moillard, *Nuits St Georges*
Mommessin, *Mâcon*
André Morey, *Beaune*
Pasquier-Desvignes, *St Lager*
Patriarche Père et Fils, *Beaune*
Piat Père et Fils, *Mâcon*
Poulet Père et Fils, *Beaune*
Les Fils de Marcel Quancard, *Beaune*
La Reine Pedauque, *Aloxe-Corton*
Remoissenet Père et Fils, *Beaune*
Antonin Rodet, *Mercurey*
Ropiteau Frères, *Meursault*
Thorin, *La Chapelle Pontaneveaux*
Charles Vienot, *Prémeaux par Nuits St Georges*
Henri de Villamont, *Savigny-lès-Beaune*

Classifications of Médoc, Sauternes, Graves and St Emilion

1855: red Médocs

	CHATEAU	COMMUNE
1st growths	Lafite	*Pauillac*
	Latour	*Pauillac*
	Margaux	*Margaux*
	Haut Brion	*Pessac, Graves*
2nd growths	Mouton Rothschild	*Pauillac*
	Rausan Ségla	*Margaux*
	Rauzan Gassies	*Margaux*
	Léoville Las Cases	*St Julien*
	Léoville Poyferré	*St Julien*
	Léoville Barton	*St Julien*
	Durfort Vivens	*Margaux*
	Lascombes	*Margaux*
	Gruaud Larose	*St Julien*
	Brane Cantenac	*Cantenac Margaux*
	Pichon Longueville Baron	*Pauillac*
	Pichon Lalande	*Pauillac*
	Ducru Beaucaillou	*St Julien*
	Cos d'Estournel	*St Estèphe*
	Montrose	*St Estèphe*
3rd growths	Giscours	*Labarde Margaux*
	Kirwan	*Cantenac Margaux*
	d'Issan	*Cantenac Margaux*
	Lagrange	*St Julien*
	Langoa Barton	*St Julien*
	Malescot Saint Exupéry	*Margaux*
	Cantenac Brown	*Cantenac Margaux*
	Palmer	*Cantenac Margaux*
	La Lagune	*Ludon*
	Desmirail	*Margaux*
	Calon Ségur	*St Estèphe*
	Ferrière	*Margaux*
	Marquis d'Alesme	*Margaux*
	Boyd Cantenac	*Margaux*
4th growths	Saint Pierre	*St Julien*
	Branaire	*St Julien*
	Talbot	*St Julien*
	Duhart Milon Rothschild	*Pauillac*
	Pouget	*Cantenac Margaux*
	La Tour Carnet	*St Laurent*
	Lafon Rochet	*St Estèphe*
	Beychevelle	*St Julien*
	Prieuré Lichine	*Cantenac Margaux*
	Marquis de Terme	*Margaux*

	CHATEAU	COMMUNE
5th growths	Pontet Canet	*Pauillac*
	Batailley	*Pauillac*
	Grand Puy Lacoste	*Pauillac*
	Grand Puy Ducasse	*Pauillac*
	Haut Batailley	*Pauillac*
	Lynch Bages	*Pauillac*
	Lynch Moussas	*Pauillac*
	Dauzac Lynch	*Labarde Margaux*
	Mouton Baron Phillippe (formerly known as au Mouton d'Armailhacq)	*Pauillac*
	du Tertre	*Arsac Margaux*
	Haut Bages Libéral	*Pauillac*
	Pédesclaux	*Pauillac*
	Belgrave	*St Laurent*
	Camensac	*St Laurent*
	Cos Labory	*St Estèphe*
	Clerc Milon	*Pauillac*
	Croizet Bages	*Pauillac*
	Cantemerle	*Macau*

1855: Sauternes and Barsac

1st great growth	d'Yquem	*Sauternes*
1st growths	Guiraud	*Sauternes*
	La Tour Blanche	*Bommes*
	Lafaurie Peyraguey	*Bommes*
	de Rayne Vigneau	*Bommes*
	Sigalas Rabaud	*Bommes*
	Rabaud Promis	*Bommes*
	Clos Haut Peyraguey	*Bommes*
	Coutet	*Barsac*
	Climens	*Barsac*
	Suduiraut	*Preignac*
	Rieussec	*Fargues*
2nd growths	d'Arche	*Sauternes*
	Filhot	*Sauternes*
	Lamothe	*Sauternes*
	Myrat	*Barsac*
	Doisy Védrines	*Barsac*
	Doisy Daëne	*Barsac*
	Suau	*Barsac*
	Broustet	*Sauternes*
	Caillou	*Sauternes*
	Nairac	*Barsac*
	de Malle	*Preignac*
	Romer	*Fargues*

A proposal to up-date the 1855 classification of red wines, put forward by the INAO in 1961, has not yet been adopted. Meanwhile an interesting personal classification, embracing all the present-day leading red wines of Bordeaux, has been proposed by Alexis Lichine in his *Encyclopaedia of Wines and Spirits*.

1953: red Graves†

Haut Brion*	*Pessac*	La Tour Haut Brion	*Talence*
Bouscaut	*Cadaujac*	La Tour Martillac (Kressmann La Tour)	*Martillac*
Carbonnieux	*Léognan*	Malartic Lagravière	*Léognan*
Domaine de Chevalier	*Léognan*	Olivier	*Léognan*
Fieuzal	*Léognan*	Pape Clément	*Pessac*
Haut Bailly	*Léognan*	Smith Haut Lafitte	*Martillac*
La Mission Haut Brion	*Pessac*		

*also classified as a 1st growth in 1855 †confirmed in 1959

1955: St Emilion

1st great growths

Ausone
Cheval Blanc
Beauséjour Bécot
Beauséjour Duffau Lagarrosse
Bel Air
Canon
Clos Fourtet
Figeac
La Gaffelière
La Magdelaine
Pavie
Trottevieille

Great growths

l'Angélus
l'Arrosée
Baleau
Balestard la Tonnelle
Bellevue
Bergat
Cadet Bon
Cadet Piola
Canon la Gaffelière
Cap de Mourlin
Chapelle Madeleine
Chauvin
Clos des Jacobins
Clos la Madeleine
Clos St Martin
Coutet
Couvent des Jacobins
Croque Michotte
Curé Bon
Dassault
Faurie de Souchard
Fonplégade
Fonroque
Franc Mayne
Grand Barrail Lamarzelle Figeac
Grand Corbin
Grand Corbin Despagne
Grand Mayne
Grand Pontet
Grandes Murailles
Guadet St Julien
Haut Corbin
Jean Faure
La Carte
La Clotte
La Cluzière
La Couspaude
La Dominique
La Marzelle
La Tour Figeac
La Tour du Pin Figeac
Laniotte, Château Chapelle de la Trinité
Larcis Ducasse
Larmande
Laroze
Lasserre
Le Chatelet
Le Couvent
Le Prieuré
Matras
Mauvezin
Moulin du Cadet
l'Oratoire
Pavie Decesse
Pavie Macquin
Pavillon Cadet
Petit Faurie de Souchard
Ripeau
St Georges Côte Pavie
Sansonnet
Soutard
Tertre Daugay
Trimoulet
Trois Moulins
Troplong Mondot
Villemaurine
Yon Figeac

1959: white Graves

Bouscaut	*Cadaujac*	Laville Haut Brion	*Talence*
Carbonnieux	*Léognan*	Malartic Lagravière	*Léognan*
Domaine de Chevalier	*Léognan*	Olivier	*Léognan*
Couhins	*Villenave d'Ornon*	Haut Brion*	*Pessac*
La Tour Martillac	*Martillac*		

*added in 1960

Table of maps

Acknowledgements

The authors and John Calmann and Cooper Ltd wish to record their grateful thanks to the following:

MISS CAROLYN EARDLEY, for her painstaking research on the countries included in section 2

MR LEN EVANS, for permission to use material from his classic book on the wines of Australia and New Zealand (see bibliography) and for advice on the rating of Australian wines.

MR GUY GRAVETT, wine photographer extraordinary, for supplying many of the pictures used in the book.

MR BRIAN ST PIERRE, of the Wine Institute of California, for his generous cooperation in compiling and checking the US chapters.

MISS SERENA SUTCLIFFE, MW, for her invaluable collaboration with the authors, while they were struggling with deadlines, and for her work on four chapters in particular.

Assistance was also given by the following individuals, companies and government and trade organizations:

Anglo-Swiss, Devizes, Wiltshire
The Argentine Embassy, London
The Austrian Embassy, London
The Cape Wine Centre, London
Signor Gianni Castagno, Italvini, Wembley, Middlesex
The Chilean Embassy, London
Matthew Clark & Sons, London
Count Giovanni Colombini and Signora Francesca Cinelli, Fattoria dei Barbi, Montalcino, Tuscany
The Cyprus Trade Centre, London
Daily Telegraph Colour Library, London
Davis & Co (Wines), London
The English Vineyards Association, Felsted, Essex
Fotofass, London
The French National Tourist Office, London
L. Frumkin & Co, London
Giordano, London
The Greek Embassy, London
Hughes-Gilbey, Sturminster Newton, Dorset
The Hungarian Embassy, London
The Israeli Embassy, London
Klosterneuburger Wines (UK), Aylesbury, Buckinghamshire
Monsieur R. Lambert, Dourthe Frères, Bordeaux
Jim Lucas, The Christian Brothers, San Francisco
The Luxembourg Embassy, London
Mr Hugh Mackay, Italian Institute for Foreign Trade, London
Paul Masson, California
Merrydown Wine Co, Horam, Sussex
The Moroccan Embassy, London
Navip, Belgrade
Oddbins UK, London, and Mr Tim Jackson
Office International du Vin, Paris
Office National de Commercialisation des Produits Viti-Vinicoles, Algiers
The Portuguese Government Trade Office, London
R & C Vintners, Norwich, Norfolk
The Rioja Wine Information Centre, London
Société des Exportateurs de Vins Suisses, Lausanne
Spectrum Colour Library, London
Teltscher Brothers, London
The Tunisian Ministry of Agriculture, Tunis
The Turkish Embassy, London
The Wine Development Board, London
Wines of Greece, London
The Yugoslav Economic Chamber, London
Zefa Picture Library, London

The drawing by Edward Ardizzone on page 216 is reproduced by kind permission of the Senior Common Room of the Royal College of Art; the print illustrated on page 9 was loaned by The Rt Hon Sir Eric Sachs; (*G*) indicates photographs supplied by Guy Gravett.

INDEX

Names of wines are followed by the country of their origin, abbreviated thus: (Al) Algeria, (Arg) Argentina, (Aus) Australia, (Ch) Chile, (Cy) Cyprus, (Fr) France, (Ger) Germany, (Gr) Greece, (Hun) Hungary, (Is) Israel, (It) Italy, (Jug) Jugoslavia, (Lux) Luxembourg, (Mad) Madeira, (Mor) Morocco, (NZ) New Zealand, (Oes) Austria, (Por) Portugal, (SA) South Africa, (Sp) Spain, (Sw) Switzerland, (Tun) Tunisia, (Tur) Turkey, (UK) England and Wales, (US) United States.

* Grape varieties are indicated by an asterisk (e.g. *Aghiokghitico) and are followed by the country to which the page entry refers. An asterisk on the left of a page number indicates that the reference is to a grape variety rather than to a place or wine of the same name.

(*m*) on the right of a page number indicates a map.

When the name occurs twice (e.g. Alto Adige), the first reference relates to a geographical location (area, town, river, etc) and the second to a wine bearing the same name.

Prefixes (du, de la, des, de l', le, la, les, l') are ignored in the alphabetical order of the main index, but are observed in the subsidiary listings – i.e. under 'Clos', 'Colli', 'Coteaux', 'Côte', 'Côtes' and 'Domaine'. 'Château' is omitted from the names of individual wines.

Page numbers in italic indicate main references.

INDEX

INDEX

INDEX